SELFISHNESS AND SELFLESSNESS

Wyse Series in Social Anthropology

Editors:
James Laidlaw, William Wyse Professor of Social Anthropology, University of Cambridge, and Fellow of King's College, Cambridge
Joel Robbins, Sigrid Rausing Professor of Social Anthropology, University of Cambridge, and Fellow of Trinity College, Cambridge

Social Anthropology is a vibrant discipline of relevance to many areas – economics, politics, religion, science, business, humanities, health and public policy. This series, published in association with the Cambridge Department of Social Anthropology but open to all scholars, focuses on key interventions in Social Anthropology, based on innovative theory and research of relevance to contemporary social issues and debates.

Volume 10
Selfishness and Selflessness: New Approaches to Understanding Morality
Edited by Linda L. Layne

Volume 9
Becoming Vaishnava in an Ideal Vedic City
John Fahy

Volume 8
It Happens Among People: Resonances and Extensions of the Work of Fredrik Barth
Edited by Keping Wu and Robert P. Weller

Volume 7
Indeterminacy: Waste, Value, and the Imaginations
Edited by Catherine Alexander and Andrew Sanchez

Volume 6
After Difference: Queer Activism in Italy and Anthropological Theory
Paolo Heywood

Volume 5
Moral Engines: Exploring the Ethical Drives in Human Life
Edited by Cheryl Mattingly, Rasmus Dyring, Maria Louw, and Thomas Schwarz Wentzer

Volume 4
The Patient Multiple: An Ethnography of Healthcare and Decision-Making in Bhutan
Jonathan Taee

Volume 3
The State We're In: Reflecting on Democracy's Troubles
Edited by Joanna Cook, Nicholas J. Long and Henrietta L. Moore

Volume 2
The Social Life of Achievement
Edited by Nicholas J. Long and Henrietta L. Moore

Volume 1
Sociality: New Directions
Edited by Nicholas J. Long and Henrietta L. Moore

Selfishness and Selflessness

New Approaches to Understanding Morality

Edited by
Linda L. Layne

berghahn
NEW YORK · OXFORD
www.berghahnbooks.com

First published in 2020 by
Berghahn Books
www.berghahnbooks.com

© 2020, 2025 Linda L. Layne
First paperback edition published in 2025

All rights reserved. Except for the quotation of short passages for the purposes of criticism and review, no part of this book may be reproduced in any form or by any means, electronic or mechanical, including photocopying, recording, or any information storage and retrieval system now known or to be invented, without written permission of the publisher.

Library of Congress Cataloging-in-Publication Data
Names: Layne, Linda L., editor.
Title: Selfishness and selflessness : new approaches to understanding morality / edited by Linda L. Layne.
Description: New York : Berghahn, 2020. | Series: Wyse series in social anthropology; volume 10 | Includes bibliographical references and index.
Identifiers: LCCN 2020002013 (print) | LCCN 2020002014 (ebook) | ISBN 9781789205497 (hardback) | ISBN 9781789205503 (ebook)
Subjects: LCSH: Selfishness. | Altruism.
Classification: LCC BJ1535.S4 S35 2020 (print) | LCC BJ1535.S4 (ebook) | DDC 179/.8--dc23
LC record available at https://lccn.loc.gov/2020002013
LC ebook record available at https://lccn.loc.gov/2020002014

British Library Cataloguing in Publication Data
A catalogue record for this book is available from the British Library

ISBN 978-1-78920-549-7 hardback
ISBN 978-1-80539-722-9 paperback
ISBN 978-1-80539-908-7 epub
ISBN 978-1-78920-550-3 web pdf

https://doi.org/10.3167/9781789205497

To my parents, with gratitude

Elizabeth Odell Layne: 14 June (Flag Day) 1924–16 January 2017

Howard Francis Layne: 4 May 1923–6 December 2017

Contents

List of Illustrations, Figures and Tables   ix
Acknowledgements   x

Introduction. Self, Selfish, Selfless   1
LINDA L. LAYNE

1. **Taking the Measure of 'Selfishness' and 'Selflessness' in the Early Twenty-First-Century US and UK**   22
LINDA L. LAYNE

2. **'Sentiment Has Struggled with Selfishness': Selfishness, Sensibility and Gender in the Late Eighteenth-Century British Antislavery Campaign**   79
G.J. BARKER-BENFIELD

3. **Selfless Advocacy? Profeminist Men's Movements in Late Twentieth-Century Britain**   105
LUCY DELAP

4. **'Doing the Right Thing for My Child': Self Work and Selflessness in Accounts of British 'Full-Term' Breastfeeding Mothers**   123
CHARLOTTE FAIRCLOTH

5. **Sexism, Separatism and the Rhetoric of Selfishness: Single Mothers by Choice in the US and UK**   141
SUSANNA GRAHAM AND LINDA L. LAYNE

6. **Selfish Masturbators? The Experience of Danish Sperm Donors and Alternatives to the Selfish/Selfless Divide**   166
SEBASTIAN MOHR

7. Inroads into Altruism 182
   MARILYN STRATHERN

8. On Being Selfish – Or Not: Explorations of an Idea from the
   Mountains of Oaxaca and the Alaskan Tundra 199
   BARBARA BODENHORN

Conclusion. Starting Points: Modest Contributions to the History
and Anthropology of Moralities and Ethics 217
   LINDA L. LAYNE

Index 229

Illustrations, Figures and Tables

Illustrations
1.1	Mother definition.	31
1.2	'Adoption is Selfless' poster from slideshare.net.	31
1.3	Cover of the book *Selfish Pigs*. Andy Riley (2009).	33
1.4	'Jesus Producing Loaves and Fishes'. Andy Riley (2009).	33
1.5	'Selfish Bitches' placard.	34
1.6	Unselfishness depicted by a diverse group of people joining together.	45
4.1	Picture accompanying *Daily Mail* article.	127

Figures
0.1	Graph of trends in usage of 'selfish', 1708–2008.	10
0.2	Graph of trends in usage of 'selfless', 1708–2008.	13
1.1	The moral landscape of the Occupy movement: 'We Are the 99'.	36
1.2	Christian moral hierarchy: 'Selfless in a Selfish World'.	36
1.3	Christian moral hierarchy: 'The Upside-Down World of Selfless Faith'.	36
1.4	Narcissism and altruism, the ends of a moral continuum.	38
1.5	Selfishness and selflessness of men and women distributed on bell curves (adapted from Baron-Cohen 2003: 85).	41

Tables
0.1	Vices and virtues.	7
0.2	Introduction of terms into the English language.	11
1.1	Result of Amazon search for the terms 'selfish' and 'selfless'.	23
1.2	Synonyms for 'selfish' and 'selfless'.	24
1.3	Dichotomy versus hierarchy.	32

Acknowledgements

Thanks are due to all those who participated in this extended exploration, especially Susanna Graham and Irenee Daily who co-organized the first set of meetings in 2012 and CRASSH for their sponsorship, Lucy Delap who organized the second meeting and St. Catherine's College and Cambridge Gender Studies for their sponsorship. The book benefited from the constructive feedback and guidance offered by Lucy Delap, James Laidlaw, Marilyn Strathern Fennella Cannell, an anonymous reviewer who gave meticulous, constructive feedback, and the editorial staff at Berghahn, especially Charlotte Mosedale and Dr Caroline Kuhtz. Thanks also go to Michael Banner for trying to keep me on the straight and narrow with regards to Christian ethics, and Barbara Bodenhorn, whose generous disposition and scholarly expertise on generosity have enhanced this volume in countless ways. G.J. Barker-Benfield has given me the benefit of his wide-ranging knowledge and unlimited, loving support.

Introduction
Self, Selfish, Selfless

Linda L. Layne

I became interested in selfishness soon after I began studying single mothers by choice (SMCs). When I told my father that a close friend was planning to have a child on her own, using sperm she bought from a sperm bank, he replied, 'That's selfish'. How odd that of all the responses he might have had – 'Oh boy, she's got her work cut out for her!', or 'I wish her well', or 'She'll make a great parent', this is what he thought.

I came to discover that his was not an idiosyncratic view, but that 'selfish' was the most frequent criticism of women in the US and UK who choose to make families without a male partner. Why was this slur applied to women who were prepared to devote themselves to the raising of children under any circumstances, let alone without the help of a co-parent? Why 'selfish', and not some other label, 'foolish' perhaps, or 'naïve', or even 'irresponsible'?

Thus began our 'problematization' of selfishness, a 'stepping back' and presenting it 'to oneself as an object of thought . . . to question it as to its meaning, its conditions, and its goals' (Foucault 2000: 117). This initial puzzle led to a multi-year exploration among anthropologists and historians.[1] Together we asked: What work do these moral judgements do, and for whom? Do selfish and selfless always have a negative or positive moral charge? What does the rhetoric of selfishness and selflessness tell us about the nature of 'selfhood' at given moments in history? What role do these concepts play in social and cultural change? How does gender enter in? In addition to addressing these empirical questions, we forge a fresh, multi-disciplinary approach, something I discuss in the Conclusions.

Some of us focused on selfishness: What does it mean to be called selfish? How can one tell if one is, in fact, selfish? What are the criteria by which such judgements are made? When, where, about whom and by whom is the label applied? How do those so-labelled respond? What is the difference between 'selfishness', 'greediness', 'narcissism', 'self-absorption', 'self-indulgence', 'egoism', 'self-centredness' or simply 'individualism' and 'autonomy'? Are some cultures or eras more selfish than others?

Some of us explored 'selflessness': Is this the opposite of 'selfish'? Does it mean eradicating the self or simply doing things for others? Is altruism the same as, or an outcome of, selflessness? How does it compare with 'other-directedness', 'empathy' or 'consideration of others'? Are certain types of people more likely to be expected to be selfless? Do certain cultures or historical periods value or encourage selflessness more than others? What circumstances are needed to get people to do things for others that may not be in their own self-interest?

Some contributors address both notions; others reject the constraints of pitting selfishness against selflessness and propose alternative, more expansive lenses. Together, though, we all endeavour, as Nietzsche did in his *Genealogy of Morals*, to 'critically . . . assess the value of the values we think of as morality' (quoted in Laidlaw 2002: 316).

Though sharing the same starting point, the chapters provide an array of views and methods, focusing as they do on specific social worlds where people grapple with selflessness and selfishness and some of the moral challenges of selfhood. We have mothers deciding how long to breastfeed (Faircloth, this volume). Breastfeeding is recognized as a 'good', but how much is too much of a good thing? How and by whom is this to be determined? The volume also affords the opportunity to compare organ and sperm donation (Strathern, Mohr, this volume). Both enterprises involve large organizations, government regulations and marketing campaigns aimed at encouraging donations; both raise moral questions about the 'proper' relationship between donor and recipient, or even whether 'donor' is an appropriate label. But organ donors are considered virtuous, held up as prime examples of altruists; sperm donors are morally suspect.

Delap also addresses moral judgements specific to men. The anti-sexist British men she studied grappled with the question of whether one can be a moral self in a society where one is automatically, inevitably the recipient of unearned privilege that comes merely from having been born with male genitalia. Even if one has not consciously taken more than one's fair share, how can one justify having been the recipient of it?

Other chapters take us further afield – to the worlds of eighteenth-century British abolitionists (Barker-Benfield, this volume), and twenty-first-century Inuit and Oaxacans (Bodenhorn, this volume). These cases, fascinating in their own right, offer useful points of comparison that bring into relief elemental aspects of moral life in contemporary Britain and mainland US.

Theoretical Approach

Each of the chapters contributes to 'the empirical study of moralities' (Howell 1997: 5). Together, the volume might be seen as in the tradition of Mauss

(1967, [1938] 1985), Douglas (1966), MacCormack and Strathern (1980) and Asad (2003), in its inquiry into cultural categories, whether they be 'the gift', 'nature' and 'culture', 'purity' and 'danger', or 'the secular', all of which, it might be noted, are ethically charged. Our joint efforts provide the beginnings of a 'social history' (Mauss [1935] 1985: 1) of the categories 'selfishness' and 'selflessness'.

Anthropologist James Laidlaw, drawing on the moral philosopher Bernard Williams ([1985] 2011), who in turn draws on philosopher Friedrich Nietzsche ([1887] 1956), makes a distinction between 'ethics' and 'morality' (Laidlaw 2002: 316), suggesting that 'morality' is a 'peculiar institution' and should be understood as just one version of 'the ethical' (Williams [1985] 2011: 7), acknowledging that 'there have been in the past and could be in the future systems of values other than "morality"' (Laidlaw 2002: 316).

I find this distinction of heuristic value and would argue that the concepts 'selfish' and 'selfless' form the bedrock of 'morality'. 'Morality' for these three thinkers is intimately linked to Christian traditions and, as I will show, so too is the history of selfishness and selflessness in the US and the UK (though in both countries, counter-cultural versions of selflessness are informed by Eastern religions). Explicit Christian rhetoric is much more prevalent in the US than in the UK (Chapter 1). Nonetheless, Christian premises inform notions of selfishness and selflessness on both sides of the Atlantic, even if not always acknowledged as such. Laidlaw reminds us that 'Nietzsche was powerfully aware that the morality he railed against was not dependent on Christian belief. God is dead, and still Europeans go on reaffirming Christian morality' (Laidlaw 2002: 318). Historian of Christian ethics Michael Banner writes: 'the story of ethics in the West has been, at its core, the story of Christian ethics. This is not ... a claim about the present authority of Christianity or about its hold on contemporary intellectual and moral allegiances, but rather about the part it has had in shaping the practices, attitudes, and values of everyday life' (Banner 2009: 5; see also Roy 2019). In Mauss's social history of the categories 'person' and 'self', he credits Christians with having made 'a metaphysical entity of the "moral person"' and, writing in 1938 France, maintained that 'our own notion of the human person is still basically the Christian one' ([1938] 1985: 1, 19).

Despite the fact that Christianity is 'the world's largest religion', representing nearly a third of the world's 6.9 billion people (Chappell 2015), anthropologists have shown something of an 'aversion to Christianity' (Robbins 2004: 29; see also Cannell 2005, 2006, n.d.; Fernandez 1982; Huber 1988; Layne 1999: 5–9). 'Ethnographic accounts were under-developed, and theoretically speaking, it was assumed that it was obvious what kind of an object Christianity might be' (Cannell n.d.). When they have studied Christianity, anthropologists have tended to do so in colonial or postcolonial settings, or focused on denominations that were, in comparison with mainline Protestant churches, considered to be on the cultic fringe (Harding 2000; Klassen 2011). If one is to understand 'selfishness' and 'selflessness', Christianity must be taken into account.

My survey of contemporary usage in Britain and America (Chapter 1) points to the importance of certain teachings of the Bible (esp. 'Love your neighbour as yourself'; 'Do unto others as you would have others do unto you'; 'It is more blessed to give than receive'; the parable of the Good Samaritan; and 'Greater love has not man than to lay down his life . . .') for making moral judgements about how one ought to treat others, or as importantly and perhaps more commonly, for judging whether others are treating us as they 'ought'.

According to Laidlaw, a salient feature of 'morality' is its focus on 'self-denying values' (Laidlaw 2002: 318). 'Ascetic ideals', according to Nietzsche, is the defining characteristic of Judeo-Christian 'slave morality', in contrast to the 'noble morality' of Greek aristocrats that was based on 'triumphant self-affirmation' (Nietzsche [1887] 1956: 170). Nietzsche did not believe that 'the ascetic "moral" values' were exclusive to Christianity, but that they dominated it. Laidlaw introduces Jainism as another religious tradition that prizes self-renunciation. But the British evangelical reformers of the late eighteenth and early nineteenth centuries do exemplify such dispositions.[2] According to the historian Ian Bradley, both Anglican and non-conformist evangelicals were 'determined to impose on others the rigorous regime of self-denial and abstinence from pleasure to which they subjected themselves'. Their efforts, though unpopular, 'produced effects in terms of social habits and legislation', which, writing in the mid 1970s, Bradley claims continued to be 'still felt in Britain' (1976: 94).

Several of the historical and ethnographic examples presented in this volume illustrate elements of asceticism, but they also reveal other aspects of Judeo-Christian morality that cannot be reduced to this. In fact, I would say, to borrow a phrase, that Nietzsche's is a rather 'peculiar' reading of Christianity. If one begins with the three dictates – to love God, to love one's neighbour, and to treat others as you would wish others to treat you – an anthropologist might be inclined to characterize Christianity as a system more focused on giving, as a means of forging and maintaining social relationships, than on 'negative' self-denial.

The other characteristic of 'morality' singled out by Nietzsche ([1887] 1956: 194–98), Williams ([1985] 2011: 193–218) and Laidlaw (2002, 2014), also germane to our subject, is the role that 'obligations' play.[3] According to Nietzsche ([1887] 1956: 197), the origin of 'the moral universe of guilt, conscience and duty' was 'the sphere of contracts and legal obligations'. Moral judgement is made in terms 'of moral obligations. . . . All ethical considerations tend therefore to be phrased in moralized forms of judicial language – rules, rights, duties, commands, and blame' (Williams, parsed in Laidlaw 2002: 316).

In the twenty-first century, a focus on obligation may strike readers as anachronistic, something more readily associated with Victorian or Edwardian morality. Indeed, during the cultural revolution of 'the sixties', some American Christian theologians endeavoured to distance themselves from the confines of obligation-centred morality. For example, the Reformed theologian Smedes explained in *Love within Limits: Realizing Selfless Love in a Selfish World* (1978: x) that 'love is a power . . . that . . . enables us before it obligates'. Recent work in the anthropology of moralities, too, has shifted emphasis from the constraints of social norms, to focus on the opportunities for freedom.

Nonetheless, obligation and duty are still present in moral discourse today. English speakers often draw on the tropes of economic obligation in accounting for their own or others' motivations. Nietzsche ([1887] 1956: 202) attributed the origins of 'feelings . . . of personal obligation' to what he maintained was 'the oldest and most primitive relationship between human beings, that of buyer and seller, creditor and debtor'. Indeed, the metaphor of debt is commonly used today to explain motivations for giving. For example, one of the mothers studied by Faircloth (this volume) explained her choice to breastfeed long past the period of time considered normal thus: 'I owe it to my child'. These types of moral obligation derive from 'a role, position or relationship' (Williams [1985] 2011: 8), and it is precisely this type of obligation that undergirds notions of selfishness and selflessness.

A moral obligation 'applies to someone with respect to an action – it is an obligation to do something – and the action must be in the agent's power. *Ought* implies *can*' (Williams [1985] 2011: 194, emphasis in original). But the fact that someone ought to do something that is within her/his power to do does not mean that s/he will do so. It is precisely when someone fails to do what s/he 'ought' that s/he is likely to engage in 'self-blame or remorse' and/or be 'blamed' by others (Williams [1985] 2011: 197); it is in these instances that one might judge oneself or others to have behaved selfishly.

As moral subjects, we evaluate our actions and adjust our behaviour based on such evaluations routinely, automatically, countless times a day. In addition, we judge other people, their actions or inactions. They may be known to us personally, for example family members, friends, guests; or those we encounter casually in the course of our lives, such as people working in a shop, riding a bus or speeding past us in their car; or they may be people who are remote to us but that we learn of in the news or through fiction. When we encounter people whom we deem to be selfish, they are not behaving as we believe they ought; they are breaking moral obligations that derive from their 'roles, positions or relationships'. The kinds of actions that are subject to such evaluations are often mundane, not the 'hard cases' of professional ethical deliberation, but 'the ethics of everyday life – the practice of appraising ourselves and others against notions of the good, or the right, or the fitting' (Banner 2014: 7). In fact, attention to selfishness inevitably leads us, as Fassin (2015: 201) would have us do, to engage not only in 'the anthropology of the good' (Robbins 2013) or 'the anthropology of evil' (Parkin 1985), but to include 'trivial negative expressions' which engender not only the Smithian 'moral sentiments' of 'sympathy' and 'gratitude' but also 'resentment'.[4]

As Williams notes, 'obligation works to secure reliability, a state of affairs in which people can reasonably expect others to behave in some ways and not in others' ([1985] 2011: 208). Why, then, do we so often encounter people who do not behave as we think they ought? There are several possible explanations for this, but the one that does the best job of accounting for the empirical cases assembled in this volume is cultural change. In the next two sections, I discuss historical moments when Britain and the US have evidenced heightened concern with selfishness, and include the present, moments during which shared expectations about who owes what to whom are changing.

A structuralist theory of cultural change proves helpful. Robbins defines culture as 'a set of values and categories ... and the relations between values and values, categories and categories, and values and categories' (2004: 6). Cultural change occurs when existing categories are stretched to encompass new referents, or when the relations between categories change, or when the values associated with cultural categories change (Robbins 2004; Sahlins 1985). In this volume, we see the categories 'humanity' and 'Christian' being expanded to include 'Africans', and new categories, such as 'freed', coming into being. We also have many cases where the values associated with the cultural categories and the relationships between the categories 'woman' and 'man', 'father' and 'mother', 'wife' and 'husband' have changed or are changing. When such change takes place, people 'are able to maintain a sense that their familiar categories are still in play. But on a very fundamental level, their culture has changed by virtue of the fact that the relations between its elements have been reorganized' (Robbins 2004: 8–9). This, I suggest, is why we feel a sense of disbelief and outrage when people do not behave as we think they should; why we so often encounter people we deem to be selfish. Many of the cases presented in the volume involve instances where norms about when, to whom and what one should give are in flux. Whenever this happens, accusations of selfishness ensue. It is not too far afield to draw a comparison with outbreaks of accusations of witchcraft, which peaked in England during the same years that the term 'selfish' entered the English language. The British historian Keith Thomas noted that 'accusations of witchcraft are normally levelled against those persons whose traits are condemned as anti-social, and a belief in witches thus becomes a sanction against undesirable social activity'. He proposes that 'the peak of the witch-scare in England ... occurred at the end of the Civil War when the consequent political and social instability bred unusual tensions and when the normal means of social control' no longer had the power that they had previously (Thomas 1963: 9).

In Chapter 1, I use this structural approach to get some purchase on a slippery topic. Barker-Benfield and Delap show that cultural changes don't just happen to people but emerge from sustained individual and collective effort. Their chapters contribute to the 'social history of ethical reform' (Keane 2016: 5). Faircloth, Graham and Layne, and Mohr focus on women and men who are innovating, and challenging social categories and the values associated with them. Strathern and Bodenhorn offer the possibility of radical cultural change enabled by shifting perspective.

The Introduction of 'Selfish' and Related Terms into the English Language

Selfishness is an entirely familiar concept, part and parcel of everyday life, but when one tries to define it, one discovers that it is impossible to pin down. A simple starting point should be the dictionary, but one encounters problems from the get-go. Dictionary.com, the largest online dictionary, defines 'selfish' as being 'devoted to or caring *only* for oneself; concerned *primarily* with one's own interests, benefits, welfare, etc.' (emphasis added). But 'only for oneself' and 'primarily for oneself' are quite different things. Which is it? This ambiguity is reproduced in *Collins English Dictionary*, the largest online dictionary devoted to British words and definitions, which defines 'selfish' as '*chiefly* concerned with one's own interest, advantage, etc., esp. to the *total exclusion* of the interests of others' (emphasis added). As shown in Chapter 1, selfishness is sometimes understood in terms of a continuum with gradations of severity, ranging from 'a little bit selfish', 'really selfish', 'excessively or pathologically selfish' to, presumably, some hypothetical endpoint of totality. Placing an act or person on that continuum requires moral judgement. The range of synonyms – egocentric, egotistic, egotistical, egomaniacal, self-centred, self-absorbed, self-obsessed, self-seeking, self-serving, wrapped up in oneself, inconsiderate, thoughtless, unthinking, uncaring, uncharitable, mean, miserly, grasping, greedy, mercenary, acquisitive, opportunistic (Dictionary.com) – also point to its lability. To be 'unthinking' is different to being 'greedy'; to be 'uncaring' is not at all the same thing as being 'opportunistic'. Selfishness, one might say, covers a multitude of sins, despite the fact that 'selfishness' is not one of the seven deadly sins, nor is 'selflessness' considered one of the 'virtues' (Tucker 2015; see Table 0.1).

According to the *Oxford English Dictionary (OED)*, the word 'selfness', defined as 'self-centredness, egoism, selfishness', was first recorded in 1586, that is, during the Elizabethan era (1558–1603), at the height of the English Renaissance and Reformation. It was also during this period that 'self' is first used as a prefix in compound words, many of which relate to selfishness, for example self-flattery (1586), self-seeking (1586), self-conceited (1595),

Table 0.1. Vices and virtues.

Vice	Virtue
Lust	Chastity
Gluttony	Temperance
Greed	Charity
Sloth	Diligence
Wrath	Patience
Envy	Kindness
Pride	Humility

Source: After Pope Gregory's list, https://en.wikipedia.org/wiki/Seven_virtues.

self-boasting (1599). Several of these new terms are attributed to Shakespeare, who was inventing words at an unprecedented rate (Shapiro 2005: 286–87). As Henrietta Moore, following Foucault (2000), notes, 'the ethical imagination is one of the primary sites of cultural invention' (2011: 16). It 'deals with the self in its relations with others, and . . . is brought into play by the advent of new . . . ideas, new ways of being and acting' (16).

During this era, understandings of moral selfhood were manifestly changing. In the theatre, medieval Catholic morality plays had been allegorical, with the hero being 'a symbol of humanity' who 'proceeds on the highway of life usually accompanied by certain abstract domestic virtues' until 'met by the figures of various abstract vices or sins who represent temptation'. The hero succumbs to temptation readily and predictably, without any 'struggle of conscience or weighing of reasons' (Craig 1950: 64), typically moving back and forth between salvation and various temptations and vices during the course of the play/life.

By contrast, Shakespeare found a 'way to internalize contesting forces' within a single individual (Shapiro 2005: 300). Influenced by Montaigne's personal essays, also a historical invention of that period, Shakespeare introduced essay-like soliloquies in *Hamlet* (1599), which include the iconic question, 'To be or not to be?' We can see Hamlet's 'inner life' as he 'wrestle[s] with a series of ethical problems' which speak to 'unresolved post-Reformation social, religious and political conflicts' (Shapiro 2005: 301). In this way, the self could be dramatically depicted as the site of recurrent moral choices, ongoing ethical struggles with unpredictable outcomes.

Self-portraiture and the glass mirror with which to regard oneself were also developed during this period. The self-portrait 'is both externally self-contemplating, as if the artist were "someone else" and at the same time typified by self-staging, self-scrutiny and masquerade'. It can express, 'This is how I see myself' and/or 'This is how I want other people to see me' (Crenzien 2012: 6). This aspect of self-portraiture is in line with the Renaissance 'self-fashioning' described by Greenblatt: middle-class and aristocratic men began to feel they possessed the ability to fashion their characters, but given the duplicity required of those who participated in court life or wanted to stay alive during vicissitudes of the religious wars and unchecked monarchs, there was a keen awareness of self-presentation as a fiction. The capacity of the self for duplicity contributed to the 'grave spiritual anxiety, an intense feeling of being in a false or sinful relationship to God', that motivated Luther and those attracted to Protestantism (Greenblatt 1980: 13, 52).

Judging by innovations in the English language, the next period of moral tumult and new questions about how a moral self should live was the seventeenth century, especially during the religious and political upheavals of the English Civil Wars and Restoration (1642–1660). The term 'selfish' (also spelled selfeish and selvish) was first recorded in 1640. The word 'selfist' (also spelled 'selfeist'), meaning a person who is selfish, was introduced in 1649, the same year that the English monarch, King Charles I, was beheaded by order of a Puritan-controlled parliament. Not coincidentally, that is also when the word 'selfhood' (1649), 'the quality by virtue of which one is oneself; that which constitutes one's own self or individuality', entered the language (*OED* 1971: 2717).

The word 'selfish' is attributed to 'the Presbyterians' "own new mint"' (*OED* 1971: 2717). The first two recorded entries in the *OED* illustrate the entities before which selves should subordinate their own desires, or put another way, entities to which one had moral obligations – God and the Publique: 'A carnal selfeish spirit is very loathsome to what is spirituall' (1640) and 'When you are so selfish in your designs and undertakings, and so far prefer your self-ends before the Publique' (1645).

Just two years after the introduction of a term to describe a person who is selfish (1649), Hobbes published *Leviathan* ([1651] 1968), where he made the case for man's essential selfishness – his passions, appetites and desires, every man's natural 'right to every thing', and the conditions needed to regulate these desires, and to entice men to lay down this right so as to live 'in Society, not in Solitude' ([1651] 1968: 118–30, 190, 189).

From the middle of the seventeenth century, compound words joining 'self' with a qualifier that describes a person's relationship with her or himself increased, often introduced 'in theological and philosophic writings' (*OED* 1971: 2717). Many of these are opprobrious; they describe improper or immoral attitudes and behaviours: self-concerned (1644), self-ended (1645), self-liking (1651), self-applauding (1654), selffull (1654), self-interested (1656), self-admiration (1661), self-glorification (1672), self-exaltation (1677), self-pleasing (1681), self-weening (1683), self-regarding (1695), self-congratulation (1712); self-important (1775).

The 'reformation of manners' to which William Wilberforce and other late eighteenth-century evangelicals devoted themselves continued into the Victorian era, a period known for its preoccupation with behaving in a manner that was 'fit and right', as the young Victoria privately pledged to do on the day she ascended to the throne in 1837 (Bradley 1976: 94, 13). The evangelical emphasis on piety and self-denial is evidenced by the introduction of the terms self-idolater (1844), self-indulged (1846), self-aggrandizing (1856), self-partiality (1865), self-love (1875) and self-advertising (1891). During this period, as both the US and the UK underwent evangelical revivals (Bebbington 2012; Bradley 1976), there was also a steep rise in the use of the word 'selfish' in the British written word (see Figure 0.1).

The nineteenth-century evangelical revivals were populist movements associated with the democratization of Christianity, that is, based on the premise of equality before God and emphasizing a personal relationship with Christ. During Tocqueville's 1831 visit to the US, he recorded his concerns that the democratic experiment taking place in this new nation might result in unprecedented levels of selfishness. He distinguished between 'individualism', which was at the time a 'novel idea' stemming from democracy, and 'selfishness', 'a vice as old as the world which does not belong to one form of society more than to another'. He defined selfishness as 'passionate and exaggerated love

Figure 0.1 Graph of trends in usage of 'selfish', 1708–2008. *Source*: Google Books Ngram Viewer, http://books.google.com/ngrams.

of self, which leads a man to connect everything with himself and to prefer himself above everything in the world'. 'Individualism', he believed, 'disposes each member of the community to sever himself off from the mass of his fellows and to draw apart with his family and friends so that he . . . willingly abandons society at large to itself' ([1840] 1990: 98).

Tocqueville thought individualism would have a corrosive effect on morals: it begins by 'sap[ping] the virtues of public life' but then 'attacks and destroys all other' virtues ([1840] 1990: 98). He concluded this chapter with the bleak view that:

> Not only does democracy make each man forget his ancestors, but it hides his descendants from him, and separates his contemporaries from him; it throws him back forever upon himself alone, and threatens, in the end to confine him entirely within the solitude of his own heart. (Tocqueville [1840] 1990: 99)

Historian Christine Levecq (2008: 3) describes this as the liberal worldview that coexisted in 'complex, always evolving ways' along with republicanism on both sides of the Atlantic in the eighteenth and nineteenth centuries. The liberal tradition (though it was not called this at the time) 'denotes a Lockean philosophy grounded in the individual, freedom, and natural rights; "Republicanism" . . . emphasizes civic responsibility and a devotion to common good'.

Today, as in the 1830s, cultural critics see an alarming trend towards increasing individualism and selfishness. One of the contributions of this book is to show that such concerns have a long history, and to remind us that so too does a commitment to the common good and to intermediate-scale social relations such as the family or community.

The Introduction of 'Selfless' and Related Terms into the English Language

'Selfless' is defined as the opposite of 'selfish' – 'having *little* or *no* concern for oneself, especially with regard to fame, position, money, etc' (Dictionary.com, emphasis added); *Collins English Dictionary* defines selfless as 'concerned *more* with the needs and wishes of others than with one's own; unselfish' (emphasis added). The 'less' of selfless seems to point to a matter of degree (less, not more), rather than to the absence of a self. In usage, however, selfless is often used to describe the annihilation of a self through death or nirvana.

Many synonyms exist: unselfish, altruistic, self-sacrificing, self-denying, considerate, compassionate, kind, noble, generous, magnanimous, ungrudging, charitable, benevolent, open-handed, though notably fewer than for 'selfish' (Dictionary.com).

In contrast with the flowering of terms related to 'selfishness' during the Elizabethan period (see Table 0.2), there was nothing comparable in terms of 'selflessness'. It would not be until the Victorian era that the term 'selflessness' was introduced, even though the concept, as a goal to be striven towards, is apparent in Christian theology much earlier. For example, *The Imitation of*

Table 0.2. Introduction of terms into the English language.

Selfish	Selfless
selfness (1586)	
self-flattery (1586)	
self-seeking (1586)	
self-conceited (1595)	
self-boasting (1599)	
selfish (1640)	self-denial (1642)
self-concerned (1644)	
	self-annihilation (1647)
self-ended (1645)	self-nothingness (1647)
selfist (1649)	
self-liking (1651)	
self-applauding (1654)	
selffull (1654)	
self-interested (1656)	self-abasement (1656)
self-admiration (1661)	self-abnegation (1657)
self-glorification (1672)	
self-exaltation (1677)	
self-pleasing (1681)	
self-weening (1683)	
self-regarding (1695)	self-abdication (1690)
self-congratulation (1712)	
self-important (1775)	self-renunciation (1791)
self-idolater (1844)	self-sacrificing (1805)
self-indulged (1846)	selfless (1825)
self-aggrandizing (1856)	self-giving (1850)
self-partiality (1865)	
self-love (1875)	
self-advertising (1891)	

Source: Oxford English Dictionary.

Christ (1418–1427) (Book III, Chap. 25) counsels 'offering oneself to the divine will and not seeking oneself in "anything either small or great, in time or in eternity" . . . The sooner one resigns wholeheartedly to God and no longer seeks anything according to one's own will or pleasure', the sooner one will find happiness and peace.[5]

One also finds an exposition on the concept of selflessness in the work of the English Protestant reformer William Tyndale (1494–1536). His book *The Obedience of a Christian Man* (1528), published two years after his English translation of *The New Testament*, illustrates how identification with Christ problematizes any simple notion of self: 'In Christ there is neither father nor son, neither master nor servant, neither husband nor wife, neither king nor subject; but the father is the son's self and the son the father's own self' (Tyndale, quoted in Greenblatt 1980: 110).

Greenblatt observes that from this perspective:

> Human actions . . . must constantly be referred to an inner state that must, nonetheless, be indeed alien to the self. The man of faith is seized, destroyed, and made new by God's Word. He gives up his resistance, his irony, his sense of his own shaping powers, and experiences instead the absolute certainty of a total commitment, a binding, irrevocable covenant. (1980: 111)

The Christian model of 'simultaneous affirmation and effacement of personal identity' (Greenblatt 1980: 77) continues today and complicates the popularly accepted, secular notion of 'the modern Western sense of self' – 'as a bounded, unique, more or less integrated motivational and cognitive universe, a dynamic centre of awareness, emotion, judgement, and action, organized into a distinctive whole and set contrastively against other such wholes' (Geertz 1984: 59).

As was the case with words relating to selfishness, many new words relating to selflessness were introduced during the religious conflicts of seventeenth-century England.[6] These include self-denial (1642), self-annihilation (1647), self-nothingness (1647), self-abasement (1656), self-abnegation (1657) and self-abdication (1690). The term 'self-renunciation' (1791) was introduced at the end of the eighteenth century; 'self-sacrificing' was introduced in 1805.

It was not until 1825, nearly two centuries later than the word 'selfish', that the word 'selfless' finally entered the English language. It did so in a clearly gendered fashion. The first recorded use is by the English poet Coleridge (1825): 'Holy instincts of maternal love detached and in selfless purity'. The term 'self-giving' was introduced in 1850, and shortly thereafter 'selfless' appears again in the work of an English poet – Tennyson (1859): 'They never mount as high as a woman in her selfless mood'. The third entry in the *OED* refers to exemplary men. Lord Wolseley used 'the noble, selfless word, "duty"' (1894) to describe three patriotic servants and military heroes: Marlborough, Nelson and Wellington. The association of selflessness with military service, particularly when the result is death, is apparent in the upsurge in usage during World War II (Figure 0.2) and is still prominent in the twenty-first century (Chapter 1).

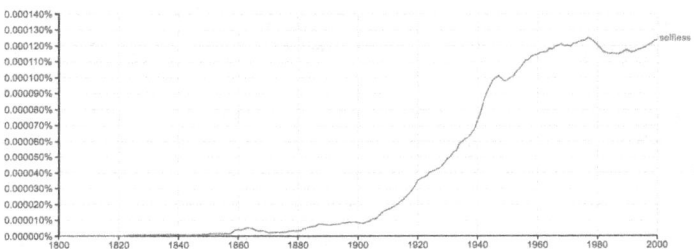

Figure 0.2 Graph of trends in usage of 'selfless', 1708–2008. *Source*: Google Books Ngram Viewer, http://books.google.com/ngrams.

The Chapters

In the opening chapter, Layne maps the place of selfishness and selflessness in the moral landscape of late twentieth-/early twenty-first-century, English-speaking residents of the US and UK, illustrating the social worlds these terms inhabit. The sheer amount of ink spilled and products sold relating to these subjects since the turn of the new century suggests that both countries are going through a period when the taken-for-granted norms about the 'proper' relationship between self and other are undergoing conscious re-evaluation and exploration. Layne argues that these are foundational cultural categories, as important as those of 'nature' and 'culture', and that they deserve the same degree of anthropological and historical attention, especially in these morally challenging times.

Self-denial is central to the efforts of British antislavery reformers that Barker-Benfield presents in Chapter 2. Members of the British public enjoyed the fruits of slave labour, not just the wealthy bourgeoise families or sailors and shipbuilders who were directly involved in the slave trade, or the settlers who returned from stints in the Caribbean with new wealth, but 'common folk' who enjoyed slave-produced goods. Abolishing the slave trade and slavery meant willingness to refrain for the sake of others.[7] Boycotts were staged against slave-grown sugar, rum and cotton. The word 'abstention' was used by British Baptist, Methodist and Quaker reformers to emphasize 'the self-denial involved in the refusal to eat slave-grown sugar' or wear 'slave-grown cotton' (Midgley 1992: 35–36, 137). In addition, there were lobbying efforts, printed pamphlets, letters to the press and to the queen, and petitions to parliament signed by thousands of British citizens, eventually including women, who were themselves struggling for greater freedom, which ultimately led to momentous changes in British law. This case, then, draws our attention not just to the moral problem of the individual will (Banner 2009: 36), but also to the public, political stage on which moral struggles take place – the problem of collective will.

The pleasure derived from doing good was one of the major arguments used by antislavery reformers to convince the British public to be good. The challenge was to convince people to be 'willing to sacrifice ... amusements or

... pleasures to obey the cause of humanity'. Reformist clerics preached: 'No sensual Pleasure in the world ... is comparable to doing good' (Ramsay, quoted in Barker-Benfield, this volume).

The association of men with selfishness and women with selflessness is also a theme in Delap's historical study of anti-sexist men in Britain circa 1971 to 1991. The thirty-eight activists she interviewed tried to combat and compensate for their perceived selfishness vis-à-vis women by actively renouncing patriarchal privilege, engaging in acts of self-denial by giving up their name, their money and their labour.

These anti-sexist men, like the selfless strivers to whom we were introduced in the chapter by Barker-Benfield, grappled with the thorny, seemingly inevitable issue of motives. Like the antislavery reformers, their selfless efforts were labelled as selfish by some. In the end, most anti-sexist men adopted a strategy like those of eighteenth-century antislavery reformers, who felt the most promising route for overcoming injustice was to convince others that doing good was in their own self-interest.

A point of comparison is who is the subject of reform. Whereas antislavery reformers trained their sights on others – slave traders, owners and overseers, as well as members of parliament – profeminist men attempted to reform themselves. Delap's fascinating study highlights some of the pitfalls of self-effacement as a political strategy. The reaction of those who were on the receiving end of these men's charitable acts also differs. The sacrifices and offerings made by these anti-sexist men were 'greeted with hostility and seen as inadequate' by the revolutionary feminists they so admired. This is very unlike what the abolitionists would have encountered from the slaves on whose behalf they worked.

'Self work' is the focus of Faircloth's study of British La Leche League members, 2006–2007, who 'breastfeed to full term', typically until their children were three or four but sometimes until they were eight. Much as we see in the counter-cultural, quasi-movement studied by Delap, Faircloth's study shows 'identity' to be 'a political project in which individuals and groups engage' (Giddens, quoted in Faircloth, this volume). Both chapters illustrate 'the active process by which selfhood is constructed, as well as the inherently social nature of this enterprise' (Faircloth, this volume). Anti-sexist men and 'militant lactivists' are acutely aware of the negative judgements of others, and they asseverate the morality of their actions in this light.

When profeminist men are accused of being selfish, they respond: '*Mea culpa*'; long-term breastfeeders counter: 'I'm not selfish. You are!' It is mothers who care more about going out drinking, or having careers, or getting their bodies back, than doing what is best for their child who are the selfish ones. Turning the tables like this, with a counter-accusation, is a rhetorical move also deployed by the slave owners and the single mothers by choice described in this volume.

Breastfeeding entails self-denial, and long-term breastfeeding represents a commitment to protracted self-denial – less sleep, less sex, less freedom. It is striking that both anti-sexist men and long-term breastfeeders sometimes describe their 'selves' as 'shattered'. But Faircloth's informants are wary of embracing the trope of self-sacrifice.

Her chapter also provides ethnographic evidence for the ongoing currency of 'obligation' in contemporary moral discourse. Faircloth quotes Beck and Beck-Gernsheim's view that 'having children is no longer primarily understood as a service, a kind of devotion of social obligation . . . [but] a way of life in which one pursues one's own interests' (this volume), but the language of obligation appears in the narratives of her informants. Alice, for example, is a 47-year-old mother who explained that she nursed her three children until the age of five because she felt she 'owed it' to them not to 'withhold the best'.[8]

Long-term breastfeeders can enjoy the satisfactions of self-righteousness and moral superiority, as well as the intimate, sensual, not to say sexual pleasures, and gratification of being needed and wanted that breastfeeding affords. These enjoyments make them vulnerable to accusations of selfishness. We are back, once again, to pleasure as a moral disqualifier.

Motivations, needs, desires and rights all play a role in the moral judgements of and about the single mothers by choice studied by Graham and Layne. The fact that these women 'want' to have children, 'desire' them, and that their children bring them pleasure, sets these women up for charges of selfishness. To defend themselves, SMCs point out that all 'good' parents want their children and enjoy them.

SMCs also invoke the rhetoric of biological drive marshalled by long-term breastfeeders. In some ways, biology takes the issue out of the realm of morality; instinctual drives are different to individual choices. A person cannot be faulted for being human. Furthermore, for some, God is immanent in nature; for others, goodness is. Either way, the trope of nature casts the wish to have children as morally sound, with or without a man.

Sources of pleasure are also ranked morally. The pre-parent pleasures of single career women – travel, holidays, dining out, luxury purchases, the ability to sleep in – are deemed selfish in comparison with the pleasures of child-raising.

Single mothers by choice provide one of the clearest cases of the ongoing importance of the trope of moral obligation. SMCs are much more likely to be deemed selfish than are gay parents or heterosexuals who become single mothers through bereavement or even divorce. Graham and Layne suggest that this is because of heterosexual men's sense of entitlement to heterosexual women. Such women, they believe, are duty-bound, morally obliged, to offer themselves to men for impregnation and parenting. To withhold themselves is selfish.[9]

The final three chapters of the volume offer alternatives to the recurrent rhetorical tug of war over whether certain actors or acts are selfish or selfless. The first of these is by anthropologist Sebastian Mohr on Danish sperm donors, who are looked at askance because of the polluting effects of both masturbation and money. This holds even though the reason Christianity condemns masturbation is because it is nonprocreative, and procreation is the *raison d'être* of sperm donation. Rather than spilling one's seed upon the ground, one must take care to collect it in a sterile cup. Money has been an issue since the beginning, but whereas Onan[10] (Genesis 38:8–10) stood to gain financially by withholding his procreative powers, these men profit by sharing/selling theirs. The apparently morally problematic nature of paid masturbation leads sperm banks to mobilize the rhetoric of 'the gift of life' to make it more attractive to both 'donors' and 'recipient/patients'.

Ironically, given the association of masturbation with illicit pleasure, self-denial looms large in the experience of sperm donors. To maximize semen samples, that is, to maximize efficiency/profits for the company, men are required to abstain from ejaculation for forty-eight hours before each donation. Mohr's interlocutors found this curtailed their freedom to engage in any other sexual activity, whether it be to masturbate simply for pleasure, or to enjoy sex with another. Mohr's ethnographic account shows how much is missed by the either/or of the selfish/selfless lens. What is missed is 'selfhood' or, more particularly, how these individuals go about being men, itself a moral matter. This case, along with those of Barker-Benfield and Delap, provides intriguing comparative material for thinking about morality and manhood.

Strathern, too, chafes at the limitations of thinking that opposes self-interest to other-interest, selfishness to selflessness. Whereas Mohr frees himself from these constraints by way of ethnography, Strathern's contribution is theoretical. She brings the notion of 'the commons' to bear on the case of organ donation as a means to side-step the persistent logic of supply and demand in which scarcity is always assumed. What if instead of conceptualizing organs as the property of the individual, even after death, one thought of them as belonging to the commons: individuals would have usufruct rights to them while alive, and at death they returned to the community, as a national resource? With this question in mind, Strathern draws attention to a particular strand of existing public policy, using the example of the Welsh system, in which everyone is automatically assumed to be an organ donor unless they make the effort to explicitly opt out. A consequence of such a system is that motivations and pleasures, which loomed so large in the other chapters of this volume, are removed from the equation. If organs automatically return to the realm of natural resources, 'motivations . . . are irrelevant'. Strathern confounds the antithesis between selfish and selfless in another way too, by noting that in the realms of kinship and friendship, 'thinking of others and thinking of oneself run together'. Where the relations between relatives or friends 'are perceived as being intrinsic to the person' (Carsten, quoted in Strathern, this volume), the antithesis between other-interest and self-interest is untenable.

Bodenhorn, too, shifts the discussion away from a selfish/selfless antithesis. She does not simply substitute 'civic' or 'generous' for 'selfless', but shows how an 'either/or' model does not reflect lived reality. To open up our thinking, she draws on extended ethnographic field research among two communities that have communal ownership and shared management of key resources, and concludes with brief reflections on volunteerism in upstate New York. She proposes that we should not reject 'rational choice theory', but that we expand it by entertaining the idea of an 'expanded self'. Among the indigenous foresters of Ixtlán and the whale-hunting Inuit of Barrow, 'to be "selfish" does not suggest an excess of self, but rather implies an incomplete one'. Nor is Bodenhorn suggesting that these 'exotic', communally oriented societies are conceptually opposed to the self-oriented US or UK. In small-town, upstate New York, as in the Alaskan Arctic, two places that prize individual autonomy, people have a 'capacity for realizing a strong sense of self', not only through autonomous action, but through collective action as well. Selves can be both 'expansive' and 'concentrated'.

The expanded selves that Bodenhorn presents from Alaska and Mexico include not just other people, but other species. In both communities, 'the universe of social membership and social responsibility is explicitly understood to extend beyond the realm of the human'. Taking nature into account not only reflects Bodenhorn's ethnography, but is a strategic effort to counter 'the relentless pressure to naturalize the selfish individual as the main driver of social life'.

With Strathern and Bodenhorn, the volume ends with some concrete suggestions, not to say prescriptions. Their cases help 'keep not just the idea, but the existence, of . . . alternatives [to brutal competition or heroic altruism] in view'. Doing so does not simply improve our scholarly understanding of selfishness and its various counterparts, but may have effects in our wider worlds. They also show how national policies and group activities can help foster a sense of '"us", not "I"' (Bodenhorn, this volume).[11]

Strathern's case demonstrates the power of 'enabling infrastructures', using the example of a policy that makes helping each other the default position. Another example might be the derelict telephone booth on the main road through the village where I live that has been repurposed as an informal lending library. Not only do the many people who deposit and borrow books relish this amenity, but this type of sharing does more. I often find myself wondering as I read a book from the booth, how many other villagers have also enjoyed it, or when I see someone selecting a book, whether it is one I have left for them there.

Bodenhorn reflects her Ixtleco interlocutors when she suggests that we can 'learn the value of expanded selves' through practice. Two of the examples she was given from Ixtlán are joining one of the bands or dance groups that perform at fiestas, weddings and funerals, both of which require practising as an ensemble. Dancing and making music together are a far cry from the morality of self-denial. Enjoy.

Linda L. Layne is a Bye-Fellow and Director of Studies for Social Anthropology, Girton College, and a Visiting Professor in the Reproductive Sociology group at the University of Cambridge (LL427@cam.ac.uk). While at the US National Science Foundation, she launched 'Cultivating Cultures for Ethical STEM'. She is currently working on *All the Credit, All the Blame: An Intimate History of One American Single Mother by Choice* and on *Uncanny Kinship: Absent Presences in Contemporary EuroAmerican Families*, a comparative study of SMC families, two-mom families, two-dad families, and families that have suffered a pregnancy loss.

Notes

1. These questions prompted two interdisciplinary workshops held at Cambridge. Three of the original nine participants are included in the volume, as are an additional three from the second workshop. One contributor was subsequently recruited.
2. One example being the son of a member of the Clapham Sect who 'once smoked a cigar and found it so delicious that he never smoked again' (Bradley 1976: 28).
3. See Sykes (2009) on the importance given to obligation by Durkheim and Mauss in terms of a state's obligation to its citizenry.
4. This is similar to the approach Collier (1989, 1997) has taken in her focus on disagreements.
5. https://en.wikipedia.org/wiki/The_Imitation_of_Christ (accessed 13 November 2019).
6. Strenski (2002) shows how the issue of sacrifice became a matter of heightened religious and political concern during the same period (early seventeenth century), in response to Protestant attacks on the sacrificial nature of the Eucharist. Self-immolation was the goal, modelled on Christ's sacrifice (2002: 18).
7. See also Keane (2016: 185–87).
8. Another mother uses the metaphor of investment to make a utilitarian argument: 'People don't see that investing now will save time later'. Bryan Caplan (2011) provides another example of this logic in his book, *Selfish Reasons to Have More Kids*, in which he encourages people to enjoy the economies of scale by having many children.
9. Compare with the accounts of the decision not to have children of the sixteen writers presented in *Selfish, Shallow, and Self-Absorbed* (Daum 2015).
10. Onan would inherit twice as much if his elder brother's widow remained childless. Onan, the source of Christian dogma against masturbation, was, we are told in Genesis, 'evil in the sight of the Lord' because he 'spilled his seed upon the ground' (https://en.wikipedia.org/wiki/Onan, accessed 13 November 2019). The fact that he did so via coitus interruptus, rather than masturbation, did not stop this story from being used as a rationale for condemning masturbation, the use of birth control and homosexuality as sins.
11. Tallbear's and Benjamin's pieces in the volume *Make Kin Not Populations* (2018) also provide helpful perspectives. See also Mattingly's focus on first-person virtue ethics, which foregrounds 'an "I" not as an autonomous actor but in relationship to a prior intersubjective "we"', that is 'an "I" connected to significant others' (2014: 204–5).

References

Asad, T. 2003. *Formations of the Secular: Christianity, Islam, Modernity.* Stanford, CA: Stanford University Press.
Banner, M. 2009. *Christian Ethics: A Brief History.* London: Blackwells.
———. 2014. *The Ethics of Everyday Life: Moral Theology, Social Anthropology, and the Imagination of the Human.* Oxford: Oxford University Press.
Bebbington, D. 2012. *Victorian Religious Revivals: Culture and Piety in Local and Global Contexts.* Oxford: Oxford University Press.
Benjamin, R. 2018. 'Black AfterLives Matter: Cultivating Kinfulness as Reproductive Justice', in A. Clarke and D. Haraway (eds), *Making Kin Not Population.* Chicago: Prickly Paradigm Press, pp. 41–65.
Bradley, I.C. 1976. *The Call to Seriousness: The Evangelical Impact on the Victorians.* New York: Macmillan.
Cannell, F. 2005. 'The Christianity of Anthropology', *Journal of the Royal Anthropological Institute* 1: 335–56.
———. 2006. 'Introduction: The Anthropology of Christianity', in F. Cannell (ed.), *The Anthropology of Christianity.* Durham, NC: Duke University Press, pp. 1–50.
———. n.d. *A Book of Life; Mormon Sacred Kinship in Modern America.*
Caplan, B. 2011. *Selfish Reasons to Have More Kids: Why Being a Great Parent is Less Work and More Fun than You Think.* New York: Basic Books.
Chappell, B. 2015. 'World's Muslim Population Will Surpass Christians This Century, Pew Says', National Public Radio, 2 April.
Collier, J.F. 1989. 'Whodunits and Whydunits: Contrasts between American and Zinacanteco Stories of Conflict', *Ethnographic Encounters in Southern Mesoamerica: Essays in Honor of Evon Zartman Vogt, Jr.* 3: 143–57.
———. 1997. *From Duty to Desire: Remaking Families in a Spanish Village.* Princeton, NJ: Princeton University Press.
Craig, H. 1950. 'Morality Plays and Elizabethan Drama', *Shakespeare Quarterly* 1(2): 64–72.
Crenzien, H. 2012. 'Self-Portrait: Introduction to the Exhibition', in *Self-Portrait.* Denmark: Rosendahls, pp. 6–15.
Daum, M. 2015. *Selfish, Shallow, and Self-Absorbed: Sixteen Writers on the Decision Not to Have Kids.* New York: Picador.
Douglas, M. 1966. *Purity and Danger.* London: Routledge.
Fassin, D. 2015. 'Troubled Waters: At the Confluence of Ethics and Politics', in *Four Lectures on Ethics: Anthropological Perspectives.* Chicago: Hau Books, pp. 175–210.
Fernandez, J. 1982. *Bwiti: An Ethnography of the Religious Imagination in Africa.* Princeton, NJ: Princeton University Press.
Foucault, M. 2000. *Essential Works of Foucault 1954–1984, Ethics, Volume 1*, ed. P. Rabinow. London: Penguin.
Geertz, C. 1984. '"From the Native's Point of View": On the Nature of Anthropological Understanding', in *Local Knowledge: Further Essays in Interpretive Anthropology.* New York: Basic Books, pp. 55–70.
Greenblatt, S. 1980. *Renaissance Self-Fashioning: From More to Shakespeare.* Chicago: University of Chicago Press.
Harding, S.F. 2000. *The Book of Jerry Falwell: Fundamentalist Language and Politics.* Princeton, NJ: Princeton University Press.
Hobbes, T. [1651] 1968. *Leviathan.* New York: Penguin.

Howell, S. 1997. 'Introduction', in S. Howell (ed.), *The Ethnography of Moralities*. London: Routledge, pp. 1–25.

Huber, M. 1988. *The Bishop's Progress*. Washington, DC: Smithsonian Institution Press.

Keane, W. 2016. *Ethical Life: Its Natural and Social Histories*. Princeton, NJ: Princeton University Press.

Klassen, P. 2011. *Spirits of Protestantism: Medicine, Healing, and Liberal Christianity*. Berkeley: University of California Press.

Kramer, J. 2017. 'The Plot Thickens: On Bernie Gunther, Third Reich Detective', *The New Yorker*, 10 July, 78–81.

Laidlaw, J. 2002. 'For an Anthropology of Ethics and Freedom', *The Journal of the Royal Anthropological Institute* 8(2): 311–32.

———. 2014. *The Subject of Virtue: An Anthropology of Ethics and Freedom*. Cambridge: Cambridge University Press.

Layne, L. 1999. 'Introduction: The Child as Gift: New Directions in the Study of Euro-American Gift Exchange', in L. Layne (ed.), *Transformative Motherhood: On Giving and Getting in a Consumer Culture*. New York: New York University Press, pp. 1–28.

Levecq, C. 2008. *Slavery and Sentiment: The Politics of Feeling in Black Atlantic Antislavery Writing, 1770–1850*. Durham, NH: University of New Hampshire Press.

MacCormack, C., and M. Strathern (eds). 1980. *Nature, Culture and Gender*. Cambridge: Cambridge University Press.

Mattingly, C. 2014. *Moral Laboratories: Family Peril and the Struggle for a Good Life*. Berkeley: University of California Press.

Mauss, M. 1967. *The Gift: Forms and Functions of Exchange in Archaic Societies*. New York: Norton.

———. [1938] 1985. 'A Category of the Human Mind: The Notion of Person; The Notion of Self', in M. Carrithers, S. Collins and S. Lukes (eds), *The Category of the Person: Anthropology, Philosophy, History*, trans. W.D. Halls. Cambridge: Cambridge University Press, pp. 1–25.

Midgley, C. 1992. *Women against Slavery: The British Campaigns 1780–1870*. London: Routledge.

Moore, H. 2011. *Still Life: Hopes, Desires and Satisfactions*. Cambridge: Polity Press.

Nietzsche, F. [1887] 1956. *Birth of Tragedy & the Genealogy of Morals*. New York: Anchor Books.

Oxford English Dictionary, Compact Edition. 1971. Oxford: Oxford University Press.

Parkin, D. (ed.). 1985. *The Anthropology of Evil*. Oxford. Blackwell.

Robbins, J. 2004. *Becoming Sinners: Christianity and Moral Torment in Papua New Guinea Society*. Berkeley: University of California Press.

———. 2013. 'Beyond the Suffering Subject: Toward an Anthropology of the Good', *Journal of the Royal Anthropological Institute* 19: 447–62.

Roodhouse, M. 2013. *Black Market Britain: 1939–1959*. Oxford: Oxford University Press.

Roy, O. 2019. 'Is Europe Christian?' Sociology Seminar, University of Cambridge, 12 February.

Sahlins, M. 1985. *Islands of History*. Chicago: University of Chicago Press.

Shapiro, J. 2005. *1599: A Year in the Life of William Shakespeare*. London: Faber and Faber.

Smedes, L.B. 1978. *Love within Limits: Realizing Selfless Love in a Selfish World*. Grand Rapids, MI: William B. Eerdmans Publishing Company.

Strenski, I. 2002. *Contesting Sacrifice: Religion, Nationalism, and Social Thought in France*. Chicago: Chicago University Press.

Sykes, K. 2009. 'Adopting an Obligation: Moral Reasoning about Bougainvillean Children's Access to Social Services in New Ireland', in M. Heintz (ed.), *The Anthropology of Moralities*. Oxford: Berghahn Books, pp. 161–81.

Tallbear, K. 2018. 'Making Love and Relations beyond Settler Sex and Family', in A. Clarke and D. Haraway (eds), *Making Kin Not Population*. Chicago: Prickly Paradigm Press, pp. 145–66.

Thomas, K. 1963. 'History and Anthropology', *Past & Present* 24: 3–24.

Tocqueville, A. de [1840] 1990. *Democracy in America*. New York: Penguin.

Tucker, T.R. 2015. *The Virtues and Vices in the Arts: A Sourcebook*. Eugene, OR: Cascade Books.

Williams, B. [1985] 2011. *Ethics and the Limits of Philosophy*. London: Routledge.

1

Taking the Measure of Selfishness and Selflessness in the Early Twenty-First-Century US and UK

Linda L. Layne

Introduction

Not quite as ubiquitous as 'I' and 'my', 'us' and 'ours', but certainly related to them, 'selfishness' is a profoundly familiar concept, against which readers were likely admonished as children. Although we may monitor our own behaviour and desires, selfishness always seems more easily recognizable in others. We are apt to find ourselves exclaiming, 'How selfish!' more often than we would like. We wish we did not have to encounter people who shout into their mobile phones on trains, bring an infant to a concert, arrive late for important events, or chat with a co-worker instead of serving us, but inevitably we do.

Such instances of selfish behaviour are much like 'the wrongs' encountered by the students of Jane Collier (1989) at Stanford in the 1970s: 'My roommate used my toothbrush again'; 'My mother said something embarrassing in front of my friends'; 'Someone pushed ahead of me in line' and so on. Such offences are relatively inconsequential, yet they often generate strong feelings, even moral outrage. 'Can you believe it?' or 'How dare s/he?' Collier was struck by how filled with emotion the 'conflict narratives' that she collected from her students were, in contrast to those she had collected in Chiapas, Mexico. The students reported feeling 'angry, upset, frustrated, mad, hurt . . . at what they perceived as others' wrongdoing' (1989: 144), even though, in sharp contrast to the Mexican victim narrators, the Stanford students 'did not posit deliberate malice on the part of those who harmed them', nor did they think that the wrongdoer had singled them out. The students' explanations tended to be that the other person had failed to follow the 'Golden Rule'; they had not 'put themselves in others' shoes to think about how they would feel if they were the recipients of their own acts' (1989: 146). Almost invariably, they understood these transgressions to be the result of 'mere thoughtlessness', which they used interchangeably with selfishness – 'to be selfish is to think only of oneself, and so, by definition, not to think about others. To be thoughtless of others, is again, by definition, to think only of oneself' (1989: 146).

Forty years on, is this still how 'selfishness' is understood and responded to in the US? Does it have the same meanings and attendant practices in the UK? To try to get a handle on how 'selfishness' is used today, and to do the same for what I initially assumed to be its opposite, 'selflessness', I turned to what, for anthropologists, may be unconventional sources. In so doing, I contribute to the emerging methodological tool kit for engaging in the 'ethnography of moralities' (Howell 1997), or as Lambek (2010) might put it, 'ordinary ethics'. My sources include dictionaries, Wikipedia, newspaper articles, blogs and popular books. They are likely to be among the sources 'my natives' – twenty-first-century, literate, English-speaking residents of the US and UK – would consult if they were interested in, troubled by, and/or aspiring to embody these moral qualities.

Starting in 2014, I was electronically alerted each time *The New York Times* (*NYT*), the newspaper of record in the US, published an article that mentioned 'selfish' or 'selfless'. For the UK, I drew mostly on theguardian.com. Although not as popular as the UK's best-selling *Daily Mail*, its readership is more similar to that of the *NYT*. (Both papers have US and UK editions and are available online to readers in the other country.) Articles addressing selfishness outnumbered those on selflessness, usually with a ratio of at least 2:1, and on one occasion 9:1.

In June 2015, I searched for the terms 'selfish', 'selfishness', 'selfless' and 'selflessness' on amazon.com, Amazon's US site, and amazon.co.uk, its British site and the company's third-largest market. I searched under the category 'books' but once inadvertently searched under 'all', thereby stumbling upon a trove of consumer goods touting these moral qualities. Together with the books, these items provide a disturbing picture of what Fassin describes as 'the banalization of moral discourse and moral sentiments in the public sphere' (2014: 433). The US site produced significantly more results than the UK site, reflecting the larger market size, and on both sites, 'selfish' produced significantly more results than did 'selfless'.

Thanks to online shopping sites like Amazon, digital newspapers, music and video streaming, Britons and Americans have easy access to many of the same sources. Thus, it should be no surprise how much overlap there is in the ways selfishness and selflessness are used in the public sphere. Some

Table 1.1. Result of Amazon search for the terms 'selfish' and 'selfless'.

17 June 2015	amazon.com	amazon.co.uk
Selfish	100 pp	67 pp
Selfless	42 pp	23 pp

Table 1.2. Synonyms for 'selfish' and 'selfless'.

Selfish	Selfless
egocentric	unselfish
egotistic	altruistic
egotistical	self-sacrificing
egomaniacal	self-denying
self-centred	considerate
self-absorbed	compassionate
self-obsessed	kind
self-seeking	noble
self-serving	generous
wrapped up in oneself	magnanimous
inconsiderate	ungrudging
thoughtless	charitable
unthinking	benevolent
uncaring	openhanded
uncharitable	
mean	
miserly	
grasping	
greedy	
mercenary	
acquisitive	
opportunistic	

of the continuities in use can be traced to the moral struggles in Britain and its American colonies during the eighteenth century in the wake of the consumer revolution taking place on both shores (Barker-Benfield, this volume, 1992, 2010, 2018). Differences in contemporary usage are noticeable too, such as the prominence of Christian sources in the US and the more frequent application of these moral judgements to 'society' in the UK. Other anthropological methods or foci would likely reveal greater differences between the two countries.

I found the terms were being applied to a remarkably wide range of objects and subjects: societies, religions, eras, politicians, financiers, husbands, bosses, mothers, children, single people, firefighters, soldiers, athletes, missionaries and humanitarian aid workers. Moral judgements get mobilized on a personal level – 'my selfish husband', 'my boss, the narcissist' – but also at the level of social categories: 'Generation X'ers are too self-absorbed'. The modes and occasions for judging oneself or others according to these moral criteria include opinion pieces, advice manuals, children's literature, bodice rippers, spiritual guides, music, movies, phone cases, coffee mugs and bibs. The tone registers (Lambek 2015: 11; Rapport 1997: 74) range from earnest and preachy to seductive and ironic.

Moral evaluations of selfishness and selflessness are fluid and wide-ranging. Neither concept is persistently 'good' or 'bad' and accusations of selfishness are sometimes embraced, the epithet co-opted as a sign of power and defiance. This 'rich semantic ambiguity' (Strathern 1980: 179) is contingent on context – who is doing the evaluating, what or who is being evaluated, and with whom the evaluation will be shared.

Selfish and Selfless: Core Symbolic Categories in Contemporary US and UK Cultures

Clearly 'selfishness' and 'selflessness' are multivalent and polysemic, and at least in some instances they work as part of what Needham (1973) would call a 'dual symbolic classification' system. Addressing as they do the 'proper' and 'improper' relationship between self and others, these classifications are as basic as 'nature' and 'culture'. Yet, whereas nature and culture have received significant and sustained anthropological and historical analysis,[1] the same cannot be said for selfishness and selflessness. How is this possible? How could we have missed this?

For my inquiry into these incredibly slippery concepts, I found structuralist approaches helpful. The anthropological debate concerning the relationship between nature/culture and female/male (MacCormack 1980; Ortner 1972; Strathern 1980), that started with, then challenged, Levi-Strauss's structuralism, provides a particularly useful model for how to make sense of the many and varied ways in which selfishness and selflessness are deployed and their gendered associations. There are striking similarities in the types of relationships Strathern (1980) observed between 'nature' and 'culture' in the twentieth-century UK, and what I have found for 'selfishness' and 'selflessness', and not merely because of the extent to which they are attributed to 'human nature'.

My survey of contemporary usage in American and British public spheres indicates that, as with nature/culture, selfish/selfless are understood alternatively, and even simultaneously, to operate as a dichotomy, be in a hierarchical relationship to one another, occur on a continuum, and/or have the ability to transform one another (Strathern 1980: 182). In the first part of the chapter, which I call 'Selfish Is to Selfless as Nature Is to Culture', I do not suggest any simple analogy, but rather use this trope to highlight the complexity and dynamism of these categories in use. I provide ethnographic detail about where, by whom, and how successfully these different types of relationships are marshalled in contemporary usage.

I discuss the frequent use of dichotomies and multiple sources of tension that undermine them. Rather than thinking of hierarchical relations as distinct from dichotomous ones, I show how the two are linked in popular usage, drawing on insults, spiritual guides, cartoons and children's books. Next, I address continua and transformations and show how, here again, two types of relationships are linked in practice. Moral transformations, whether it be of individuals or societies, are routinely conceptualized in terms of placement on a continuum. The rhetoric of health and illness informs much current thinking about the 'right amount' of these moral inclinations. In the US, the $9.9 billion self-help book industry (Groskop 2013; Kachka 2013; LaRos 2018) includes numerous titles aimed at the transformation of selves and others – to become a more caring, generous, selfless person or help others to do so, and barring that, to become better able to cope with selfish people. Self-help books are also growing in popularity in the UK (Rigby 2013), where '"intellectually credible" self-improvement books [were expected] to outsell celebrity biographies in 2014' (Groskop 2013). Most of the books that address the moral transformation of society from community-minded to selfishly preoccupied – that is, moving in the 'wrong' direction along the continuum – are British.

I suggest that these types of relationships (dichotomy, hierarchy, continuum and transformation) can be understood as folk theories about the moral universe. Cognitive anthropologist Willett Kempton used the notion of 'folk theories' to describe the mental models that upper-middle-class residents of Princeton, NJ had about how their home thermostats worked. By 'folk', he signified that the theories were shared and that they were acquired 'from everyday experience or social interaction', and by 'theory', he highlighted the use 'of abstractions, which apply to many analogous situations, enable predictions, and guide behavior' (Kempton 1986: 75).

In the second part of the chapter, I build on my analysis of four types of relationships and the relationships between them by turning my focus to values/categories relationships as modelled by Sahlins (1985) and Robbins (2004). Their attention to 'the relationships between values and values, categories and categories, and values and categories' (Robbins 2004: 6) is a helpful guide for thinking about variations and sets of combinations of the ways these categories are being used, and the values assigned them in the US and UK in the early decades of the twenty-first century. I present six variations in the meanings of the categories selfish, selfless and unselfish and/or the values attributed to them: selfishness is good if it protects private property, or because it is natural, or because it is really selflessness in disguise; selfishness is bad, but bad is good (and sexy); selflessness is bad because it is really selfishness in disguise, and the alternative – it is good, because it is really selfishness.

Part I. Selfish Is to Selfless as Nature Is to Culture: Dichotomies and Hierarchies, Continua and Transformations

Dichotomy/ies

Dichotomies have been rejected by post-structuralist scholars because they present an overly simplistic and static representation of complex and dynamic cultural symbols and practices (Kopnina 2016; Nygren 1999). If one is to understand how selfishness and selflessness are actually used, however, one cannot ignore their frequent use as a dichotomy, that is, as two halves of a whole, or as Shumaker pictures it, 'like a biscuit' broken 'clean in two . . . so that any part that is not in one half will necessarily be in the other' (1952: 34). For example, ethnographers report that in the rhetoric surrounding ova donation, 'altruistic and selfish motivations cannot exist at the same time', it is either one or the other (Curtis 2010: 83; see also Mohr, this volume).

Much as we find with nature/culture, selfishness/selflessness are often metaphorically associated with other dichotomies, such as black/white, left/right. Take, for example, the self-published e-book *Selfish or Selfless: Which One Are You?* (Watterson 2010). The dichotomy, expressed in the title, is represented on the cover by opposing chess figures – the black knight on the left under the word 'selfish', the white knight on the right under the word 'selfless'.[2] Ayn Rand (1964), a philosopher whose ideas are influential in twenty-first-century American libertarian politics, also linked selfish/selfless with black and white, but because she believed 'egoism' and 'self-interest' were good, and 'self-sacrifice' and 'altruism' were bad, she reversed the colours.

Numerous other book titles play on the dichotomy, for example *A Selfish Person's Guide to Being Selfless* (Smith 2014), *Realizing Selfless Love in a Selfish World* (Smedes 1978), and a pop-psychology quiz allows people to determine whether they are 'Selfish or Selfless, Egotistical or Altruistic' (https://psychologia.co/egoism-and-altruism/). But as Strathern found for nature and culture, selfishness and selflessness cannot be resolved into a stable dichotomy but are always in a relationship that 'involves tension of a kind' (1980: 180).

Weak Ontological Status of Selflessness Makes for an Unstable Dichotomy

This instability, I argue, derives from the relative weakness of 'selflessness' as an ontological category. Recall the asymmetry noted at the beginning of this chapter in terms of the relatively small place selflessness seems to occupy compared with selfishness in our moral imaginations. Unlike selfishness, whose existence is never doubted, the very possibility of 'true', 'pure', 'real' selflessness is routinely questioned. Recent examples include 'Is Pure Altruism Possible?' (Lichtenberg 2010), *Does Altruism Exist?* (Wilson 2015) and *The Altruism Question* which asks, 'Are our efforts to help others ever driven solely by altruistic motivation, or is our ultimate goal always some form of self-benefit?' (Batson 2016: cover). It is not just in high-brow publications that one finds this question. In 2017, upon learning that I was editing a book on selfishness and selflessness, an American working-class service provider immediately asked, 'But do you think that true selflessness can ever exist?'

Whereas 'selfishness' is routinely encountered in everyday life, selflessness seems extraordinary. No wonder, then, that one of the places selflessness inhabits is the other-worldly realm of science fiction and fantasy. In the opening decades of the twenty-first century, selflessness appeared in the titles of numerous popular fantasy novels, feature films and television shows.[3] One of the factions that makes up the fantasy world of Veronica Roth's 'Divergent Trilogy', three novels followed by three eponymous feature films (2011–2016), is 'abnegation/ selflessness', which has as its symbol 'the helping hand'. Fans who identify themselves with this faction can buy clothing or other products bearing this symbol. Selflessness also appears in several major, male-dominated,[4] online fantasy worlds, in roles (e.g. 'Selfless Spirit', 'Selfless Cathar', 'Selfless Squire', 'Selfless Exorcist') and as rewards (e.g. 'Band of Selfless Acts', 'Selfless Leadership' jewel).

Another indication or source of instability is the fact that the category that opposes 'selfishness' changes. Sometimes it is 'selflessness', but other times 'unselfishness', that completes the dichotomy. Furthermore, what counts as 'selfless' varies widely. D.S. Wilson notes that the definition of selflessness is so expansive that it is used to describe a range of things 'from simple courtesies' like 'opening a door for someone' to, 'at the opposite extreme, heroic self-sacrifice' (2015: 3). It is worth noting that the two examples he provides are behaviours most closely associated with men.

Since the advent of citizen armies, selflessness has been attributed to those who engage in military service, even though members of the armed forces are paid. When armies were manned with mercenaries or draftees, this moral credit would not have been forthcoming (Paola Filippucci, personal communication, July 2018). An early American example comes from the Revolutionary War (1775–1783) with the famous last words of 21-year-old Nathan Hale who was hung by the British for spying: 'I only regret that I have but one life to give for my country'. The notion of military sacrifice has been heavily inflected by Christian meanings (Faust 2008: 6). An example of this is the Victorian hymn, 'Onward Christian Soldiers', chosen by Churchill for a joint US/UK church service held on a battleship in 1941.[5]

In this last decade, British and American war dead have been honoured for their 'selflessness' on anniversaries of key moments of the two World Wars, and commemorations of those who have died in more recent conflicts (Houen 2016; Javid 2014). 'Selfless commitment' is the first topic addressed in *Values and Standards of the British Army* (Great Britain, British Army 2008). Soldiers must serve whenever and wherever they are needed, and this imposes 'limitations on individual freedom, and requires a degree of self-sacrifice. Ultimately it may require soldiers to lay down their lives'. This document instructs that it is the 'duty' of soldiers to 'put the needs of the mission and of the team before personal interests . . . [and] be ready to uphold the rights of others before claiming their own'. In the US, the rhetorical association between the military and selflessness is also made on products, for example an infant undershirt printed with 'US Navy – Not for self but country', or a silver bracelet engraved with 'Army – selfless, brave, courage – This we will defend'.

'Selflessness' is also found in hagiographic accounts of individual soldiers (Zembiec 2014) and in anthropomorphized accounts of animals, for example the 'selfless service' of military dogs (Bacon 2015), and ants depicted as 'selfless and heroic in battle . . . [they] rescue their injured buddies, carrying them back to the nest where they can recover to fight again' (Bakalar 2017).

In the twenty-first century, newspapers in both countries frequently use 'selfless' to honour those who risk their lives/selves for others, at least in cases when those others were deemed to be worthy of such sacrifice. As Houen shows in his rhetorical analysis of the 'war on terror', there are two versions of 'sacrificial militancy': the virtuous self-sacrifice of allied service men and women, and the morally corrupt, selfish sacrifice of Iraqi soldiers and al Qaeda militants who are blindly serving the self-interests of their leaders (2016: 574). Likewise, as shown in the documentary on Japanese Kamikaze pilots that premiered in New York City in 2007, such pilots (two of whom attended the event, as did an American survivor of one of their attacks) 'are revered for their selfless sacrifice' in Japan, but internationally, 'Kamikaze remain a potent metaphor of fanaticism' (Japan Society 2008).

Even the attribution of selflessness to American veterans is a mixed bag. As Alex Horton (2019), a former US army infantryman in Iraq, turned war correspondent for the *Washington Post*, observes, 'America's collective idea of a war veteran is split . . . One is honorable, courageous and selfless. The other is broken, violent, unstable, and a threat to society'.

Humanitarianism is 'symbolically embedded in a landscape of altruism and giving'; aid workers are often cast as 'figure[s] of virtuous self-denial engaged in good works' (Redfield 2013: 165; see also Krasno 2016). But because some humanitarian organizations, like Doctors without Borders, care for the victims of 'the sacrificial international order', they resist 'the vision of redemption through self-sacrifice' (Redfield 2013: 163–67; and Fassin 2012).

Those who fill the mostly male, socially valued roles of firemen, policemen and other rescue workers are unambiguously granted this title, especially if they have made 'the ultimate sacrifice'. (Those who perform other hazardous jobs in mining, factories, commercial fishing and on oil rigs, for example, are not granted this honour.) Following a terrorist attack in London, the queen offered thanks to the police and 'all who work so selflessly to help and protect others' (HM Queen Elizabeth II 2017), and although the voluntary crews who 'man' the British lifeboats are now praised for selflessness, in the nineteenth century it was their 'gallantry' that was noted.[6]

In the US, the attribution of selflessness to firefighters has been prominent since the World Trade Center attack of 9/11, when 343 firefighters perished. In addition to the firefighters who died or were injured at the time, many of those who survived developed a type of blood cancer that can be treated using stem cell transplants. Large numbers of firefighters in the US and UK have registered to be bone marrow donors. Regardless of whether they are ever actually called upon to give, they are praised for their selflessness (Jent 2017).

Consumer goods also give voice to this association. For example, a sentimental painting done on the tenth anniversary of the attack of a soot-covered firefighter striding back to his truck entitled 'Selfless Service' adorns a throw blanket. In describing this work, the artist begins with a verse from the Bible that is frequently invoked in contemporary discussions of selfless sacrifice:

> 'There is no greater love than to lay down one's life for one's friends',[7] a divine truism emblematic of the foundational bonds that undergird and inextricably link our nation. Nowhere has that love been more vividly expressed than in the selfless sacrifice of our beloved first responders ... and especially in the nobility of our firefighters ... their character is truly revealed as they selflessly put others above self ...

The symbolic association between selflessness and firefighting was also made in France when a Malian immigrant, after scaling a Parisian apartment building to rescue a four-year-old child dangling from a balcony, was lauded by Macron for his selfless actions, granted French citizenship, and offered an internship in the French fire brigade (Chrisafis 2018).

The other reliable location for selflessness in the news is the sports section. In this context, apparently, doing *anything* that is not entirely for oneself, especially if one is male, may be deemed 'selfless'. Players who pass the ball are 'selfless' and contrasted with those who 'hog' it (Cacciola 2016). Stephan Bannon, one of the many morally challenged members of the Trump administration, was nicknamed 'Coast-to-Coast' while in the navy because of his habit of 'running the length of the court [from one side of the ship to the other] without passing' (Shane 2016; cf Obama 2018: 131). Players are lauded as 'selfless guys' because they are 'committed to playing a real team game' (Pinchevsky 2016), and/or praised for 'unselfishly' setting up a teammate to score (Branch 2016; Morales 2016).

Sports not only illustrates the range of acts deemed to be selfless, from giving one's life to passing a ball, but also, as we saw with the allied versus enemy troops comparison, how the same acts are judged differently depending on who is doing them. When women cooperate with teammates, they are conforming to gendered expectations and the outcome is deemed 'boring' rather than selfless (D'Arcangelo 2016; Evans 2013). But female athletes can earn this commendation by different means (Sandberg and Grant 2016). Mentoring younger competitors is considered a moral 'feat'. For example, when an American woman won the New York City Marathon in 2017, the first to do so in forty years, the *NYT* reported: 'perhaps Flanagan's bigger accomplishment lies in nurturing and promoting the rising talent around her' – a 'new brand of "team mom"' (Crouse 2017).

Another example of gendered differences in the assignment of 'selflessness' is found in the roles of mother and father. Selflessness is considered to be a characteristic of mothers. Examples from the web include a popular quote website where selfless is given as a synonym for mother, and on gifts advertised for Mother's Day decorated with adjectives that spell out 'MOTHER', available from online stores (Etsy, Amazon, Barnes and Noble, etc.) on coffee mugs, t-shirts and home décor.[8] Women who do not have children may feel subject to an '"us versus them" narrative that pitches mothers (strong, selfless, valiant) against their childless peers (cold, selfish, detached)' (Abdullah 2017; see also Bindel 2016; Daum 2015). The assumption of a correspondence of selflessness and motherhood is interesting because there are so many caveats, providing an unachievable ideal against which mothers can be judged. Women who have abortions, whether or not they are mothers, are frequently attacked for their selfishness (Mcdonough 2017; Millar 2014). As Emma Brockes, a British single mother by choice living in New York observes, 'Moral superiority is quick and easy and it's kind of fun, too'. She helpfully provides a list of mothers we can judge as selfish: those who have an abortion; have only one child; have their child on their own; have children then work full time; those who wait until forty to have a child or have a child while still a teen; and those who use biotechnology to create a "designer baby"' (adapted from Brockes 2018: 53–54; see also Daly 2012; Graham and Layne, this volume; Faircloth, this volume).

In contrast, fathers are not automatically assumed to be selfless. When a father devotes himself to his children – that is, when he does the intense, boring, repetitive work that mothers do day in, day out – it is unusual enough to require explanation. Furthermore, because of its close association with women, engaging in these acts or taking on this role may place one's masculinity in question. The author of *The Selfless Father: When a Man Says No to a Career and Yes to God and His Family* (West 2015) uses his own experience to reassure other men that 'a father can take on a non-traditional role in the household and still fulfill his God-given purpose for himself and his family'.

Radically different understandings of 'selflessness' also circulate in the anglophone world. *Selfless Persons* (Collins 1990: back cover) explains that 'the Buddhist doctrine of anatta ("not-self") denies the existence of any self, soul or enduring essence in man'; *The Selfless Mind* (Harvey 2013: back cover) presents early Buddhist thought 'in which no permanent Self is accepted'[9]; *Selfless Love: Beyond the Boundaries of Self and Other* (Birx 2014: book description) blends 'Zen parables, contemporary cognitive science, and the Christian Gospels', to help readers 'recognize that our true selves are not selves at all, that all beings are united in

Mother
[muh*th-er*] - noun
1. **A woman who loves unconditionally.**
2. **Always caring, nurturing and giving.**
3. **One person who does the work of twenty...for free.**
(See also: 'selfless', 'strong' & 'saint'.)

Illustration 1.1 Mother definition from fabulousquotes.com. Screenshot by the author.

Abortion is Selfish

Illustration 1.2 'Adoption is Selfless' poster from slideshare.net. Screenshot by the author.

unbounded, infinite awareness and love, beyond words'; and *Selfless Self* (Shaw 2015): a collection of the teachings of Shri Ramakant Maharaj, lauded as 'the Bible of our time', explains that there is 'No you, no I, just like sky . . . [the self] is everywhere. No relation to the body.'[10]

Hierarchical Relationships: Jesus versus Selfish Pigs

Structural dichotomies are conventionally represented in two parallel columns, as can be seen in Needham's collection on *Right & Left* (1973) and in MacCormack and Strathern's *Nature, Culture and Gender* (1980). Presenting terms in this way conveys an apparent equality. Both sides look the same (width and length, number of words), but almost inevitably, one set of categories is valued more highly than the other.[11] In fact, it was hierarchical evaluations of nature, culture, female and male that motivated Ortner (1972). Selfish and selfless or unselfish are likewise understood to relate to each other in a hierarchical fashion. This could not be otherwise because they are elements of a moral system in which and by which actions and people, policies and political systems are judged to be good or bad, better or worse.

Given the common anglophone associations between up/above/better and n/below/worse, a more accurate representation of the relationships would be rows rather than columns (Table 1.3).

Insults and slurs reflect this moral system of distinction. 'Selfish' works as an insult; 'selfless' and 'unselfish' do not. 'Selfish' can be used on its own or combined with other insults that may themselves connote selfishness, in which case 'selfish' serves as an emphatic. The most common such compound is 'selfish pig'. An American evangelical uses this metaphor in her book directed to young teens to encourage them to avoid becoming *Selfish Pigs* (Macaulay 2003; see also Marriott 2003).

To act selfishly is to breach social/moral norms, and this provides fertile ground for humour. British cartoonist Andy Riley provides a compendium of the types of behaviours likely to be considered selfish in *Selfish Pigs* (2009). Not surprisingly, many involve gluttony, something we attribute to pigs. A series of Riley's cartoons show the pig taking more than his fair share. If being greedy and taking food intended for others is wrong, doing so from Jesus is even worse!

Table 1.3. Dichotomy versus hierarchy.

Dichotomy		Hierarchy						
selfish	selfless	selfless	right	good	white	right	high	heaven
wrong	right	selfish	wrong	bad	black	left	low	hell
bad	good							
black	white							
left	right							

Illustration 1.3 Cover of the book *Selfish Pigs*. Andy Riley (2009), published with permission.

Illustration 1.4 'Jesus Producing Loaves and Fishes'. Andy Riley (2009), published with permission.

One cartoon shows Jesus producing enough loaves and fishes to feed the multitudes, but when the pig gets through, all that remains are a few fish bones. Another depicts the pig hogging the food at the Last Supper.

Selfish is also frequently combined with gendered obscenities: 'bitch', 'bastard' and 'cunt'. For example, 'Selfish Cunt', an all-male British rock band, was formed in 2003 (songs include 'Fuck the Poor', 'My Prerogative', 'Corporate Slut'). Like 'pig', at least in some circles, 'bastard' has come to connote selfishness. *Urban Dictionary* defines 'bastard' as 'one who is narcissistic and unknowingly frustrating', and the top definition they provide for 'selfish bastard' is an insult to be 'used when you ask your friend for something small and they refuse to give or share it with you'. It defines 'selfish bitch' as 'an accusation made by someone who doesn't get what they want, usually after causing a scene but before leaving abruptly. "Fuck you, selfish bitch! (SLAM!)"'. Illustrations from the world of consumer goods include a placard that instructs, 'Keep calm and hate greedy, selfish, talentless bitches', and a humorous birthday card that

Illustration 1.5 'Selfish Bitches' placard. KeepCalmStudio.com. Screenshot by the author.

reads, 'It's all about you isn't it u selfish bastard' (https://www.brainboxcandy.com/selfish-bastard-greetings-card/).

A simple hierarchical relationship is often found in children's books. 'Sharing is good; keeping good things for oneself is bad', is the moral of the story in Oscar Wilde's still popular children's book, *The Selfish Giant* ([1888] 2012). God punishes the giant because he won't share his garden with the local children. The giant achieves redemption when he shares with a child (the Christ Child).[12] Two de-Christianized versions of the story were published in the UK in the 2010s that make the same point using anthropomorphized animals (Charles 2014; Orami 2015).

Being Selfish, one of twenty-nine children's books in the *Help Me Be Good* series by American author Joy Berry (1988), focuses on sharing food and toys, and on developing empathy, the skill to think about how one's actions would make others feel. A note to parents assures them that this book 'will help your child understand the true meaning of . . . "It is more blessed to give than to receive"' (Berry 1988). In the text addressing the child, the author instructs:

> People who do not share are selfish. They care more about themselves than about others . . . It is important to treat others the way you want to be treated. If you want others to share with you, you need to share with them. You need to be unselfish.

Whether it be a giant and 'his garden', a crocodile and 'his river', a monkey and a banana patch, a child and her toys, the moral mandate is to share. To keep all the good things (more than one's fair share) for oneself is immoral. This is exactly what fuelled the Occupy movements of the 2010s. Since the Occupy Wall Street movement started in 2011, many Americans have reconceptualized selfishness in terms of income and wealth inequality. Assessing the success of the movement, one author posited that its greatest success was in 'changing the national conversation by giving Americans a new language – the 99 percent and the 1 percent' (Levitin 2015). Several economists (Krugman 2011) pointed out that the extent of the inequality was even greater than conveyed by the activists' slogan. The greatest increase in wealth occurred among the top .1% so it ought to read 'We Are the 99.9%' (Thompson 2014). Bernie Sanders (1992, 2015) made this the core of his 2016 presidential platform in a piece called 'Corporate Greed Must End'. 'Corporate greed' is defined by *Urban Dictionary* as 'hoarding by selfish decision-makers in large businesses: huge salaries, golden handshakes, . . . perks, tax evasion, and embezzling'.

The London Occupy protest also took place in the financial district. In both countries protesters called for an end to tax avoidance by 'the very wealthy and large corporations [and for them to] start paying their *fair share*' (Sanders 2015, emphasis added;). One British protestor explained, 'seeing our public sector decimated while corporations are effectively getting away with theft. It's legal but immoral' (McVeigh and Clark 2011). The movements in both countries and elsewhere around the world also embraced 'shared' government through

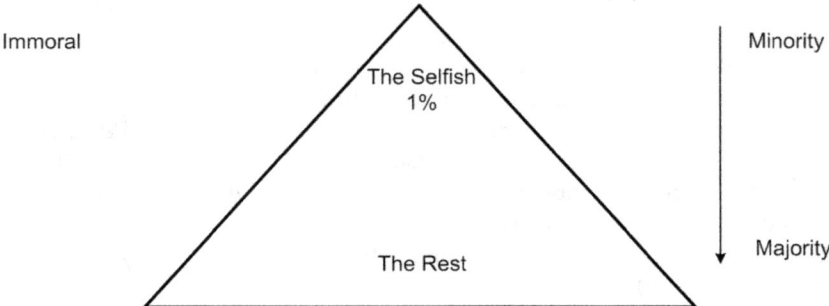

Figure 1.1 The moral landscape of the Occupy movement: 'We Are the 99'. Figure created by the author.

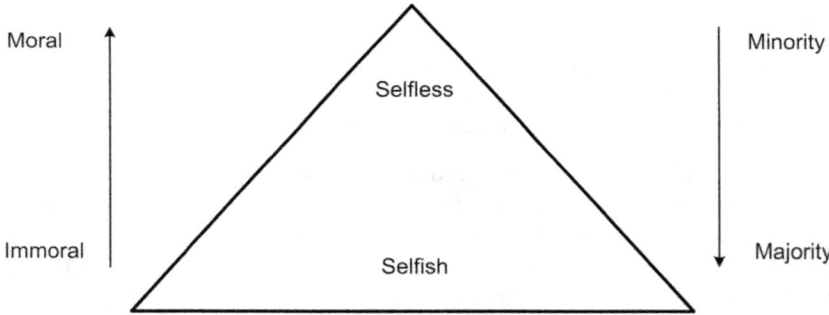

Figure 1.2 Christian moral hierarchy: 'Selfless in a Selfish World'. Figure created by the author.

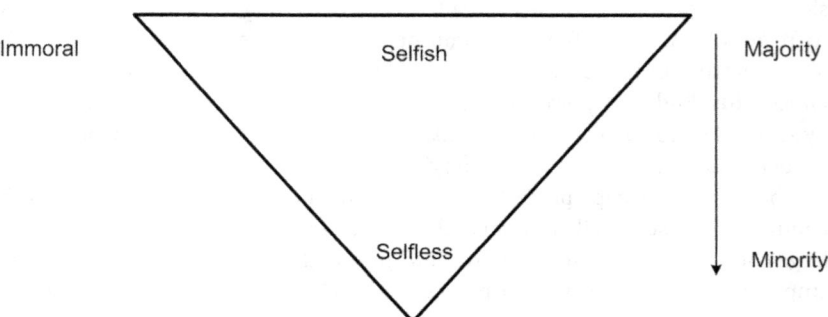

Figure 1.3 Christian moral hierarchy: 'The Upside-Down World of Selfless Faith'. Figure created by the author.

direct democracy rather than having all the power concentrated among a small number of people who can be influenced by the rich (Kelsey-Fry 2016).

Unlike the simple hierarchies discussed above using the examples of insults and children's books, some moral judgements about selfishness and selflessness are not just relative to each other as characteristics or qualities, but also relative to the rest of the population/moral universe. The Occupy movement addresses both. These dimensions are better captured by another frequent symbol of hierarchy, the pyramid.

These two dimensions are also evident in Christian instructional guides for adults.[13] As one would expect, given the differences in religiosity in the US and UK, most of these books originate in the US, where more than 70% of the population still identifies as Christian (Center for the Study of Global Christianity 2017; Pew Research Center 2019; Sherwood 2017). In fact, pastoral guides have been enjoying increasing popularity, with nonfiction Christian book sales up 8% in value in the US between 2014 and 2015 (Nielsen 2016), and religious book sales reaching a new high in the US of $593.7 million in 2018.

In books like *How to Raise Selfless Kids in a Self-Centered World* (Stone 2012), written by a pastor at a megachurch in Kentucky, and in *Selfless in a Selfie World* (Gandee 2014), by the wife of an American pastor, selfishness is understood to be the numerical norm in a 'self-centred world', and selflessness the less common but attainable moral goal to which readers should/do aspire.

Titles like *The Selfless Way of Christ: Downward Mobility and the Way of Christ* (Nouwen 2007) and *God's Gravity: The Upside-Down Life of Selfless Faith* (Borlase 2006) turn the culturally dominant hierarchy on its head and embrace the biblical paradox: 'the meek shall inherit the earth'. Most of us have our priorities all wrong, the authors say. Rather than striving for the top, 'to promote yourself above all others', to achieve fame and fortune, we should aim for the bottom, and seek to embody Christian humility (Gandee 2014). Whereas participants in the Occupy movements want their 'fair share' of the good things the super elite enjoy, in this conceptualization, one should not aspire to those kinds of 'goods' but choose instead spiritual rewards.

Continua

In *Elements of Critical Theory*, Wayne Shumaker distinguishes between pairs of terms that are 'truly dichotomous' and those that are 'merely opposites', and uses 'good' and 'bad' to illustrate the latter, noting that not all behaviours are either good or bad. 'Good' and 'bad' 'stand at opposite ends of a continuum instead of describing the two halves' of a dichotomy (Shumaker 1952: 34).

In terms of the ways in which selfish/selfless are used, the distinctions between dichotomies and continua are blurred. Within a single sentence or paragraph, what is at first presented as a dichotomy, an either/or, morphs into a continuum, with neither end being morally desirable. The goal is to achieve

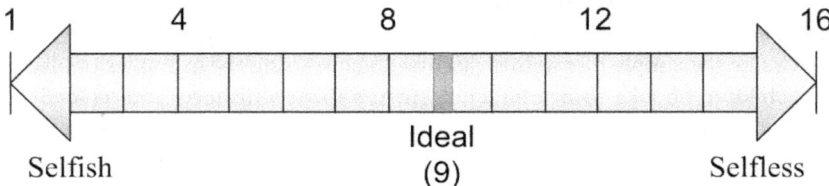

Figure 1.4 Narcissism and altruism, the ends of a moral continuum. Figure created by the author.

a moral sweet spot, to get the balance 'just right'. A clear example of this is the online quiz, 'Selfish or Selfless?' The title suggests a dichotomy, but upon completion of the quiz, readers are informed that results can range from 1 to 16, and the ideal score is 9 (not smack in the middle, but just one step towards altruism). The test providers explain that scoring 9 'suggests *a balance* between altruism and egoism. It means you are taking good care of yourself and others' (https://psychologia.co/egoism-and-altruism/, emphasis added).

Other evidence of this model is found in the frequency with which moral judgements about selfishness are made using quantifiers like 'a little', 'a bit', 'too' and 'excessive' (emphases added in the quotes below). A humorous piece suggests there should be algorithms built 'into Facebook, Twitter and Instagram to alert users' when they go too far and engage in '*excessive self-promotion*' (Chamorro-Premuzic 2014).

The model of a continuum means that an increase in one means a decrease in the other. Perceived increases in selfishness are matched by a perceived decrease in community-mindedness: British psychologist Oliver James believes the English-speaking world has become 'considerably *less generous* and *more selfish*' (2008: 5, 67); a historian reports that citizens in Reagan's America felt '*less* engaged, . . . *less* interdependent' (Troy 2005: 17).

Understanding the moral peril of selfishness to be a matter of degree distinguishes it from some other moral failings, for example thievery, adultery, bigotry, but is comparable to lying in that some lies (white, noble, mutual, paternalistic, etc.) may be considered to be good, and 'the whole truth and nothing but the truth' is considered to be an impossible goal (Bok 1978).

Selflessness, too, is judged as a matter of degree. Some is good; too much is bad. This type of distinction has been present in the anglophone world since the eighteenth century and the rise of 'the culture of sensibility' (Barker-Benfield 1992) that encouraged the cultivation of feelings and empathy. Gendered ambivalence has always dogged this realm. 'Men of feeling', that is, those who showed compassion for others, risked being judged as effete. Adam Smith (1759) distinguished between '*moderated* sensibility', the good, male kind, and the '*excessive* sensibility' of women and men of weak nerves (Barker-Benfield, this volume). In nineteenth-century America, liberal Protestant ministers, along with their educated, middle-class, mostly female congregants, were linked to what historian Ann Douglas has called *The Feminization of American Culture* (1977: 18), largely supplanting American Calvinists who had 'a toughness ... and intellectual rigor which ... then and since has been ... identif[ied] with "masculinity"'. In her book on the ambivalence of many late twentieth-/early twenty-first-century Americans towards extreme altruists, MacFarquhar notes that 'selflessness can seem soft – a matter of *too much* empathy and *too little* self-respect' (2015: 10).

Medicalization of Morality: Narcissism and Altruism

People deemed to belong on either end of the selfish–selfless continuum are frequently described in medical terms. James's play on influenza in the title of his book, *Affluenza* (2007), and its sequel (2008), provides one example of medicalization, that is, 'the expansion of medicine' into 'areas traditionally viewed in moral or religious terms' (Figert 1996: 99). In the 1970s, only one of Collier's students described 'the wrongdoer as "sick", and in need of psychiatric help' (Collier 1989: 146). The results would surely be different today.

Narcissism

At one end of the continuum we find narcissism. By the twenty-first century, narcissism had moved from the confines of clinical practice into the public domain as part of the 'psychiatrisation' of American society (Pickersgill, quoted in Tempany 2010). A rash of books have been published on the subject since 2010,[14] including one that suggests that we should think of narcissism as we do autism, as a 'spectrum disorder' (Malkin 2016). The authors of the book *The Narcissism Epidemic* (Twenge and Campbell 2009: 2) consider narcissism 'a psychocultural affliction' which has spread rapidly and had reached epidemic proportions. One reporter likens it to the obesity epidemic (Fishwick 2016). Social/medical judgements about body weight are comparable to those regarding selfishness/selflessness when construed in terms of a continuum. In both instances, moral judgements are intertwined with judgements regarding health, and both are based on matters of degree.

Narcissism has always been associated with excess. In the Greek myth, Narcissus is so smitten by his own image that he is unable to tear himself away and dies as a result; his self-obsession is literally self-destructive. At the end of the nineteenth century, the term was used to describe '*excessive* masturbation'. Part of the psychoanalytic tool kit since the early twentieth century, developed in the work of Rank, Freud, Buber and Fromm, in 1980 it was added to the American Psychiatric Association's *Diagnostic and Statistical Manual of Mental Disorders* (*DSM*) as a personality disorder defined by 'a pervasive pattern of grandiosity, need for admiration, and a lack of empathy'. Subtypes have been proposed:

'Unprincipled narcissist' – deficient conscience; unscrupulous, amoral, disloyal, fraudulent, deceptive; 'Amorous narcissist' – sexually seductive, glib and clever; disinclined to real intimacy; indulges hedonistic desires; bewitches and inveigles others; pathological lying and swindling; tends to have many affairs, often with exotic partners; 'Compensatory narcissist' – seeks to counteract or cancel out deep feelings of inferiority and lack of self-esteem; offsets deficits by creating illusions of being superior, exceptional; 'Elitist narcissist' – feels privileged by virtue of special childhood status and pseudo achievements; entitled façade bears little relation to reality; is upwardly mobile; cultivates special status and advantages by association; 'Malignant narcissist' – fearless, guiltless, remorseless, calculating, ruthless, inhumane, callous, brutal, rancorous, aggressive, biting, merciless, vicious, cruel, spiteful; hateful and jealous; anticipates betrayal and seeks punishment; desires revenge; has been isolated, and is often suicidal, and is homicidal (Wiki). Attributing the term 'collective narcissism' to Adorno, who used it to explain support for Hitler in the 1930s, a British journalist diagnoses those who support Brexit or Trump's nationalism as examples of this dangerous condition (Zavala 2017).

An American essayist reports that by 2011, narcissism had become the insult of choice, 'a derogatory *apercu* that's one-size-fits-all ... Professional pundits love it, as do bloggers, politicians, religious leaders, celebrity shrinks, cultural critics, Internet commenters and blowhards at parties' (Daum 2011). Dombek provides a witty critique of the rampant tendency to detect narcissism in others, ending with a tongue-in-cheek suggestion for a new entry in the *DSM*, 'Narciphobia' (2016: 137).

This moral panic is gendered. Women are associated with two of the frequently cited symptoms of the narcissism epidemic – cosmetic surgery and digitally mediated self-absorption. The number of cosmetic surgeries has risen dramatically in both countries since 2000 (up 124% in the US between 2000 and 2016), with more than 90% of these on women in 2015–2016 (Dunofsky 1997; Tornambe 2010; Williams 2016). In 2015, Rizzoli, a venerable New York publishing house that specializes in illustrated books, published *Selfish*, a selection of reality television star Kim Kardashian West's selfies. This book, and the expanded and updated version issued the following year promising purchasers, More Me, occupied the top-selling spot on the Amazon list for 'selfish' in both countries (ahead of *The Selfish Gene* [Dawkins (1976) 2006] and a new gay romance [Miller 2014]; see also Powers 2008). Kim's mother 'once pronounced her daughter "obsessed" for taking 1,200 selfies in one day' (The Daily Mail Reporter 2014).

The book was widely criticized, often by people who admitted to having never looked at it, but cultural critic Avi Steinberg defended Kardashian and other selfie-taking women, noting that for 'people whose bodies have been culturally marginalized there is nothing as potent, necessary and political as the self-turned gaze'. He recalled Virginia Woolf's lament from *A Room of One's Own* that 'publicity in women is detestable', and argued that Kardashian's 'genuine

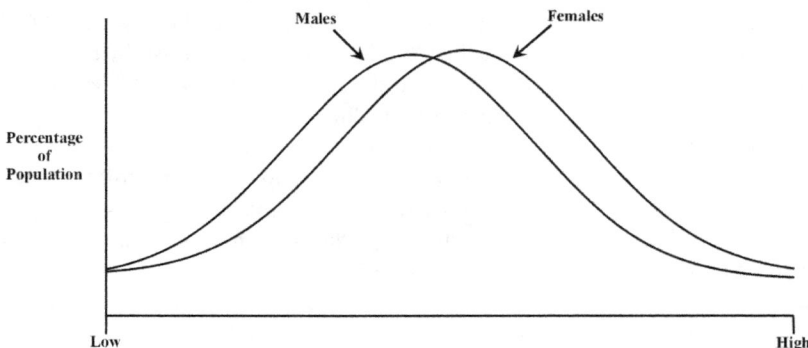

Figure 1.5 Selfishness and selflessness of men and women distributed on bell curves (adapted from Baron-Cohen 2003: 85). Figure created by the author.

achievement may be that she has become a singularly successful producer and owner of her own image' (Steinberg 2015).

Narcissism is also associated with men. A review of thirty-one years of research found that men consistently scored higher in narcissism (Kluger 2015). Cambridge psychologist Baron-Cohen believes that the *Essential Difference* (2003: 1) between men and women is that 'female brains . . . are hard-wired for empathy'. Male brains, especially 'the extreme male brain', lacks the ability to empathize. Instead of linear continua, he uses bell curves to illustrate (2003: 60, 85; see also Scull 2018: 4). 'Men are the selfish sex. It's not a feminist conspiracy, it's just science' (Mahdawi 2017) was how a journalist summarized a neurobiological study (Soutschek et al. 2017) that found 'male neural reward systems are more stimulated by self-centredness while women are more likely to get a dopamine rush when helping others' (Mahdawi 2017). She cautioned though, 'This doesn't necessarily mean men's brains are wired more selfishly than women's brains; it's likely more nurture than nature' (Mahdawi 2017, see also Davis 2017).

A psychiatrist at a London mental health hospital posits that narcissism is 'more common among men . . . because the traditional male instincts – power, aggression, a hunger for adulation – are more amenable to narcissism', but he suggests that 'with gender models changing, there is no known reason why women won't succumb to the disorder in greater numbers' (Tempany 2010) and that it will become an equal opportunity disorder.

Some believe that the dominance of men in finance and the hard sciences can be explained by the fact that men tend to score higher on 'narcissistic personality traits' (Lemaitre, quoted in Devlin 2017). An article in the *Financial Times* explained that severe narcissists are drawn to careers in finance, especially hedge funds (Tempany 2010). One of the experts featured in the article, a self-avowed narcissist and author of *Malignant Self-Love* (Vaknin 2013), had formerly owned Israel's largest stock brokerage house (see also Graeber 2018: 13).

Male politicians and/or sexual predators are also branded this way. In 2014, Governor Chris Christie was labelled 'the New Jersey Narcissist' by a reporter who tallied the number of times he used the words I, I'm, I've, Me, My/Myself (Milbank 2014). Another concluded that Christie is not capable of integrating 'the "we" into me, me, me' (Bruni 2014). Pinker associates narcissism with tyrants – 'their vainglorious monuments, hagiography iconography, and obsequious mass rallies' (2011: 628). On both sides of the Atlantic, first as candidate, then as president, Trump has been recognized as a narcissist and ridiculed as the 'narcissist-in-chief' (Kohn 2016; Lilienfeld and Watts 2015; Patterson 2018).[15] Narcissism is also attributed to many of the powerful American men who have cheated on their wives[16] and/or sexually assaulted women.[17] The same applies to Tucker Max, a pioneer of heterosexual 'seduction culture' (informed by evolutionary biology) and those who follow him (Dombek 2016: 20).

Dombek (2016: 59) reminds us that for Freud, the prototypical narcissists were women and gay men. She wryly suggests that if enough male heterosexual narcissists reform themselves as Tucker Max has, by attending his workshops or reading his books, the gender of prototypical narcissists could change again. But despite the enduring attraction of dualistic thinking, it is worth remembering that both men and women are currently tarred with this brush. Indeed, another seduction culture pioneer, Neil Strauss, recalls that at the pickup artist workshops he ran, about 80% of men in the audience believed that their mothers were narcissists (Dombek 2016: 58).

Altruism

People judged to be at the other end of the continuum may also be considered sick. MacFarquhar reports that a common reaction to the altruists who feature in her book is to suppose that they are suffering from mental illness. Their 'extreme sense of duty' is seen as 'a kind of disease – a masochistic need for self-punishment, or a kind of depression that makes its sufferer feel unworthy of pleasure' (2015: 298). D.S. Wilson asserts that as with selfishness, altruism 'comes in benign and pathological forms' (2015: 133), although this distinction, he grants, is not as widely understood for altruism as it is for selfishness, hence the book he co-authored titled *Pathological Altruism* (Oakley et al. 2011). As has been noted throughout this chapter, selflessness occupies a much smaller portion of the Anglo-American moral landscape than selfishness; the same disproportion pertains to altruism and narcissism. 'Altruist' is not an insult, but 'narcissist' is.[18] Popular books and news reports on altruism are relatively rare compared to those on narcissism.

Despite its relative lack of popular appeal, altruism has enjoyed a flurry of scholarly interest since the 1970s. Experimental and behavioural economists, game theorists, business, organizational, economic and consumer psychologists, and philosophers have worked to define it, to explain its origins, and the circumstances that foster it, collectively engaging in what some refer to as 'the science of altruism'.¹⁹ In the 1980s, following publication of E.O. Wilson's *Sociobiology* (1975) and Richard Dawkins' *The Selfish Gene* ([1976] 2006), the subject of altruism, which had been addressed by Darwin in *The Descent of Man* (1871), once again became a topic of interest in evolutionary biology. Distinctions are made between different types of altruism, and what counts as altruism and what should be labelled as something else. In evolutionary biology, 'altruistic behaviour' is often defined as 'behaviour that benefits other organisms, at a cost to itself', that is, by reducing the number of expected offspring of the giver (Okasha 2013).²⁰ Some biologists and philosophers of biology distinguish between 'strong altruism', which signifies 'absolute fitness reduction for the donor . . .', and 'weak altruism', which reduces 'the relative fitness of the donor' vis-à-vis that of the recipient (Okasha 2013). Another complicating factor for biologists in their efforts to pin down what qualifies as altruistic behaviour is the time frame. A sacrifice now may benefit one or one's offspring later.

As for behaviours that benefit both self and other, some biologists distinguish such acts from altruism and use instead the terms 'mutual benefit' or 'cooperative' to describe such behaviour. American political scientist and game theorist Robert Axelrod's *The Evolution of Cooperation* ([1984] 2006) explores the conditions needed to foster cooperation. This work earned him a MacArthur prize in 1987 and initiated a wide-ranging body of interdisciplinary work including experimental work on gendered patterns of philanthropic giving (Rigdon and Levine 2018).

Philosophers, too, have been revisiting altruism and making distinctions between different types. 'Practical ethicist' Peter Singer promotes the idea of 'effective altruism' (1993, 2015), which he contrasts with the 'feel good' altruists described by MacFarquhar (2015). He explains, 'most effective altruists are not saints but ordinary people like you and me . . .', and he places them 'somewhere on the continuum between a minimally acceptable ethical life [which he defines as 'using a substantial part of our spare resources to make the world a better place'] and a fully ethical life [defined as 'doing the most good we can']' (Singer 2015: xii–xiii). Paul Bloom makes a similar argument in *Against Empathy* (2018). He believes that empathy naturally limits the number of people who will be helped, hence the moral superiority of the 'rational compassion' approach he and Singer support. The model of a continuum pertains, but rather than aiming for the middle, as we saw in the examples above, the goal of utilitarian ethicists is to help people behave in a way that will place them near the end to be determined quantitatively. Although not made explicit, there is a gendered dimension to his position. Given the cultural association of feelings with women, and rationality/maximization with men, his normative stance privileges a male-valenced form of giving.

The work of anthropologists and historians (e.g. Bornstein 2012; Colpus 2012, 2018; Fassin 2013; Laidlaw 2000; McKearney 2016; Redfield 2013; Stuurman 2017) in the 2010s offers a very different approach to that of philosophers like Singer. They have produced insightful, ethnographically and historically grounded accounts of the multiplicity of ways in which people define and engage in what is variously called 'altruism', 'philanthropy' and 'charity'.

Some of this work investigated 'humanitarianism'. Raising questions about the universality of what Bornstein identifies as 'the liberal empathy-altruism model' (see Barker-Benfield, this volume), she contrasts 'liberal empathy which seeks to assist abstract others in need' with 'relational empathy which turns strangers into kin' (Bornstein 2012: 22). Fassin draws our attention to the potent role humanitarianism plays in 'our moral economies': in the face of glaring inequalities, 'humanitarianism elicits the fantasy of a global moral community [which may] have redeeming powers', bridging 'the contradictions of our world' to 'make the intolerableness of its injustices somewhat bearable' (2012: xii).

Selfless Moral Exemplars

Moral exemplars played an important role in late twentieth-century anglophone moral philosophy's development of 'virtue ethics' (Laidlaw 2014: 48–49) and in the anthropology of ethics (Humphrey 1997; Laidlaw 2014: 83; Robbins 2018). The exemplars that surfaced in my Amazon search provide a tantalizing starting place for thinking about the roles moral exemplars play in the US and UK.

Some of the individuals celebrated in these books are easily recognizable as icons of selflessness, for example political and civic leaders like Mahatma Gandhi, Nelson Mandela and Martin Luther King Jr. (Tanthapanichakoon 2015), and as such resemble 'the restricted range' of models 'for conscious self-fashioning' identified by Greenblatt among the Renaissance elite (Laidlaw 2014: 84). Many are Christian 'Heroes of Faith', like *Moses: A Man of Selfless Dedication* (Swindoll 2009), or the nineteenth-century Irish missionary who 'believed that if Jesus could give everything He had, she could do no less' (Wellman 2012: back cover), or the Polish friar who martyred himself in Auschwitz and is now the patron saint of 'Selfless Humility', commemorated on scented candles, bath salts, pendants and earrings sold on Amazon.[21]

'Ordinary people',[22] too, are celebrated as moral exemplars and the range of people so honoured conveys something more akin to the fluid, individualized way that the Mongolian herders identify moral exemplars (Humphrey 1997). The biographies and collections with 'selfless' in their titles illustrate 'the almost infinitely wide range' from which exemplars can be chosen, a democratization of moral exemplarity, if you will. As the authors stress, these are 'regular', 'everyday' people, not just a limited number of distinctive 'characters' (MacIntyre 1981, cited in Laidlaw 2014: 84). Examples include *Selfless Sacrifice* (Ali 2013), a self-published memoir by an Indian-Trinidadian immigrant to London, written to honour the sacrifices her mother made for her; *True Stories of Good Deeds, Charitable Acts and Selfless Service*, published by a Mormon press (Deseret Book Company 2003), featuring 'everyday people in everyday

COMPILED BY PAUL D. PARKINSON

UNSELFISH
LOVE THY NEIGHBOR AS THY SELFIE

Illustration 1.6 Unselfishness depicted by a diverse group of people joining together. In contrast to selfies, they face away from the camera. Paul D. Parkinson (2015), published with permission.

situations'; *Unselfish: Love Thy Neighbor as Thy Selfie* (Parkinson 2015), released the same day as Kardashian's book as an antidote to it, presenting the stories of ninety-nine 'regular people and celebrities' who go 'against the grain and help ... their fellow man' (Opsahl 2015); and a sequel, *Unselfish Kids*, the stories of forty elementary-age children who have done unselfish things released on Giving Tuesday, 3 December 2019.

The authors are explicit in their hopes that readers will be inspired by these selfless figures, but MacFarquhar (2015) found that many twenty-first-century Americans feel ambivalent about altruists, those who push themselves 'to moral extremity'. They make people 'uneasy', not simply because people may judge themselves negatively against such high moral standards, but also because 'selflessness is understood to be antithetical' to so much of what people value – being able to 'give to your family, to seek beauty, to work for your own purposes, to act spontaneously, to act without any purpose at all' (MacFarquhar 2015: 1, 295). She believes this stance is a relatively new, 'romantic one – one that values emotion more than reason, spontaneity more than willed intent, and the search for an original, authentic self, more than careful molding of a moral one' (2015: 296). If she is right, perhaps it is not too much of a stretch to compare the role of these moral exemplars with those identified by Robbins in Papua New Guinea, the big man and the sorcerer, who are 'exemplary characters, not in the sense of being idealized or necessarily a model ... for emulation', but more as illustrations of 'the limits of moral order'. From this perspective, such exemplars show members of society what a 'fully realized instance' of selflessness looks likes and entails. Ordinary people may value this virtue but also feel the need to 'manage and balance' it (Robbins, in Laidlaw 2014: 85).

Transformation

Both MacCormack (1980) and Strathern (1980) identify transformation as a potential type of relationship between the categories of nature and culture (in the 1980s they did not posit the transformation of genders): 'one category can transform into another, with nature becoming culture, children through socialization becoming adults ... wild becoming domesticated, and raw becoming cooked' (MacCormack 1980: 7). A similar relationship can be seen between the categories of selfishness and selflessness (or unselfishness). Children can be taught to share, Random Acts of Kindness campaigns can make the world a kinder place, new digital technologies can make people more self-absorbed, socioeconomic policies can make societies more selfish. This mode of understanding is complementary to that of a continuum in that the goal of many transformative efforts is to 'move the needle' along the continuum towards the more positively valued end. It is employed with regards to both individuals and societies.

Transforming Selves and Others: Moral Improvement and Self-Actualization

Transformation is particularly evident in moral guide books, many of which are written by self-identified Christians. The goal of many of these books is to aid the reader in self-transformation, to engage in what Faubion (2011: 4), following Foucault, describes as the project of ethical self-cultivation. One example of a guide aimed at self-transformation is by an American theologian who explains 'how ideal, selfless love' has the power to transform: 'Love enables people' to overcome their sinful natures and 'to do loving sorts of things and be loving sorts of persons' (Smedes 1978: x, 145, 147).[23]

Books on Buddhism, Hinduism and Taoism, published in about equal numbers in the US and UK, provide other models for transforming oneself from selfish to selfless. *Selfless Insight: Zen and the Meditative Transformations* (Austin 2011: back cover), by a clinical neurologist and Zen practitioner, explains 'how our maladaptive notions of self are rooted in interactive brain functions and how after the extraordinary, deep states of kensho-satori strike off the roots of the self, a flash of transforming insight-wisdom leads towards ways of living more harmoniously and selflessly'. Even within the realm of Zen, the meanings of selflessness and the proposed routes to the desired transformation vary starkly, from meditating in front of a rotting human corpse, preferably that of 'a child or young adult' (Rousseau 2016), to relaxing in a spa, enjoying a massage to the soothing sounds of 'spa Zen music' with titles like 'Selfless', 'Selflessness' and 'Selfless Thoughts'. Christian meditation, too, is promoted as a path to selflessness (Freeman 2009).

Another approach advocates self-transformation in the opposite direction, that is, towards selfishness. A cluster of self-published twenty-first-century English-language paperbacks and e-books use the slogan 'Get Selfish' in their titles.[24] The earliest one I found is *It's Time to Get Selfish* (Busfield 2006) by a female American triathlete and competitive kickboxer. Others include *Get Selfish, Get Happy* (Owen 2009) by an Australian woman who trademarked 'The Selfish Self'; and *Get Selfish* by Joanna Hunter (2015), a 'spiritual, business, life coach' who turns the Golden Rule on its head, advising readers that we should do unto ourselves what we do for others (2015: 6). Retailers have jumped on this bandwagon. Like the 'Get Selfish' movement, companies such as Dove chocolates (Dove 2010) and Pandora jewellery stores use the imperative to urge women to spoil themselves by purchasing gifts traditionally given to women by men.

Men have also adopted this approach. Nicholas Caldwell self-published three e-books to show readers how, by embracing selfishness, they can eliminate stress (n.d.a), increase success (n.d.b) and become a '*Pumped-Up, JACKED, Chiseled SEXUAL Beefcake*' in eight minutes a day (n.d.c, emphasis in original).

Others aim at the transformation of flawed others, wherein the authors adopt the role of 'ethical pedagogue' (Faubion 2011: 71). Children's books are obvious examples. In her note to parents, the author of *Being Selfish* (Berry 1988) explains the challenges of bringing about such a transformation: 'Abandoning selfishness is often the most difficult step from early childhood egocentricity towards socialization ...'. The book, she believes, will help parents transform their child 'from a self-centered, selfish person into an others-oriented, unselfish one' (1988). Another example is the book *12 Biblical Traits You Need to Raise Selfless Kids* (Cone 2016), written by a southern female radio host and former pageant winner, who wrote the book because she was so distressed by how selfish one of her daughters had become.

Some offer advice on how to transform a 'selfish husband', something I take to be a new social category. There are no comparable books aimed at reformation of 'selfish wives'. The self-published e-book, *The Selfish Husband: How to Cope with and Transform Your Selfish and Inconsiderate Husband* (Parker 2014), defines a selfish husband as one who 'would rather stay out with his friends than stay home with you; watches TV all day and does not lift a finger to help out with household chores ... or places a lot more attention and importance to his job over your well-being and your marriage' (1). The cover shows a young man slouched on a couch, phone in hand, with a look on his face that suggests that the woman facing him, holding a laundry basket, has let him know she is not pleased.

Christian books also take up this issue: one by a Baptist pastor (Lea 2015), another by a newly married Mormon man (Smith 2014), and *What to Do When He Won't Change: Saving Your Marriage When He Is Angry, Selfish, Unhappy, or Avoids You* (Ito 2011), by a Christian marriage and relationship coach who provides 'services worldwide via skype and telephone. For the same price you would pay for a weekend away, you can improve your relationship for a lifetime. $1187.80 for four 60-minute sessions. Six months of financing available' (https://coachjackito.com/).

Others adopt the stance that transformation is not always possible (Brown 2002, 2003; Loving 2015). Children who were raised by narcissistic parents are advised not to waste energy trying to change them (Brown 2008), and employees are coached on how to deal with a narcissistic boss (Shragai 2013).

Transformation of Societies: Moral Decline

Societies, too, are judged to be selfish or selfless. Communist societies are associated with selflessness by advocates and opponents. Leaders in Communist Russia and Cuba have boasted about their selflessness; critics of Communist China scold it for not living up to its avowed moral standards; and critics of communism use selflessness as a slur.[25] All of these instances project a timelessness with no suggestion of moral transformation.

In contrast, the books addressing morality in capitalist democracies describe historical transformation.[26] Unlike books directed towards individuals, which are aspirational and intended to enact a positive transformation, books about the transformation of the US and the UK report on negative transformations that have occurred in the recent past.

In the twenty-first century, a perceived rise in selfishness is often attributed to Thatcher and Reagan. When Thatcher died in 2013, this aspect of her legacy was a matter of public discussion,[27] and in 2017, Prime Minister Theresa May felt the need to distance herself from 'the "caricature" of Thatcherite conservatism': 'We reject the cult of selfish individualism' (Rayner 2017). A similar tale of moral decline in the US is attributed to Ronald Reagan (Jampole 2011). The years of his presidency (1981–1989) have been described as a period during which there was 'growing superficiality and selfishness... Going from the "Me Decade" to the "Mine, All Mine Decade"' (Troy 2005 : 17).

Several recent books by British authors address these issues. In addition to James (2008), we have *The Selfish Society: How We All Forgot to Love One Another and Made Money Instead* (Gerhardt 2011) by another British psychologist. Gerhardt concludes: 'We have come to inhabit a culture of selfish individualism that has confused material well-being with happiness' (back cover). There are also two books by British journalists: one by a controversial British columnist, who tried to figure out how he and his generation came to be *Selfish Whining Monkeys: How We Ended Up Greedy, Narcissistic and*

Unhappy (Liddle 2014); and *Selfie: How We Became So Self-Obsessed and What It's Doing to Us* by reporter Will Storr (2018), which offers a scathing critique of the misuse of science to promote 'self-esteemery' in the late 1980s and 1990s (Gottlieb 2018).

In the US, sociologist Robert Putnam (2000) focused not on an increase in selfishness, but a decrease in civic engagement, especially in the voluntary associations that Tocqueville had seen as an essential antidote to rampant, unbridled individualism. Putnam charts sharp decreases in political participation, church membership, community group participation, philanthropic activity, workplace connections, even informal socializing. Using 1992 data, he reported that 'ordinary Americans shared a sense of civic malaise' – three-quarters of the US workforce judged 'the breakdown of community' and 'selfishness' to be 'serious' or 'extremely serious' problems in America (2000: 25).

These authors differ regarding causes. James (2008) lays the blame on neoliberal economics, Gerhardt (2011) blames changes in child-rearing arrangements. Putnam (2000) identifies numerous causes, including generational distance from the socially solidifying experience of World War II, suburban sprawl which results in people spending 'alone time' on their daily commute, and the rise of television and mass-mediated home entertainment. This concern is captured on the cover of Gerhardt's book, which shows a man and a woman sitting at home 'alone together', to borrow Sherry Turkle's (2011) phrase, concentrating on their laptops instead of each other.

Many blame social media for 'a shrivelling of empathy' (Gentleman 2017); others suggest that 'for social media to have become so popular there has to have been pre-existing narcissism', and still others think we are 'simply more aware' of narcissism because of social media (Fishwick 2016). Referring to the classical myth's relevance for selfie-takers, Steinberg (2015) observed, 'Narcissus's isolation and loneliness, his inability to encounter, much less, to love, anyone in the flesh is recognizable to us as one of the core anxieties of our twenty-first century, digitally refracted existence'. This anxiety is evident in the range of reporting. Articles in the *NYT* have addressed: concern about Facebook's 'personal time line', which the author worries 'gives me borderline Digital Narcissistic Personality Disorder' (Bilton 2011); a New York politician who sexted selfies of his bulging underwear, as an example of self-destructive narcissistic behaviour (Schwartz 2013); the dis/ease caused by 'self-googling' (Kehlmann 2015); and a piece that interprets sensational reports ('Death by Selfie') about fatal accidents of people while selfie-taking as 'darkly comic morality tale[s] whose aim . . . is to police youth "narcissism"' (Steinberg 2015).[28]

Changing Patterns of and Moral Concerns about Sociality

The issue of how much time we 'ought' to give to others is a moral one. In 'Vers de Societe', a poem written in 1971, Philip Larkin carps about all the hours he has had to waste being sociable when he would rather have been on his own reading and looking out of the window. 'How sternly it's instilled, *All Solitude is Selfish . . . Virtue is Social.*' (2003: 147, emphasis in the original).

This moral judgement informs the widely held belief that mobile phone use is leading to moral decline/reduced sociality, or as Oliver Sacks (2019) puts it, 'the complete disappearance of the old civilities'. In 2008, to determine whether Americans really had become more isolated than before the rise of the internet, sociologist Keith Hampton repeated a 'street life study' in major urban nodes in Manhattan, Philadelphia and Boston using the same system of time lapse photography that another sociologist, William H. Whyte, had used in 1975. The results were surprising. Hampton found that 'our tendency to interact with others in public has improved since the 70s', and attributed this to another unanticipated change: a substantial increase in the number of women in public spaces. In three of the four test venues, their proportion increased significantly, including a whopping 33% increase on the steps of the Met. The only place women decreased proportionally was in the study cite in Boston, which was a major shopping area. Rather than finding an increase 'in aloneness or digital distraction', there was a shift towards 'gender equity' (Oppenheimer 2014: 37).

Larkin, too, ponders the issue in terms of social change. He posits, then rejects the idea that the obligation to socialize may be a substitute for going to church now that God is gone, something that bores us but that we do because, 'however crudely, it shows us what should be' (2003: 147).

More recently, such issues are being considered in the framework of another popular psychology dichotomy: extroversion/introversion.[29] The most well-known proponent of introversion is Susan Cain, author of the best-selling book *Quiet: The Power of Introverts in a World That Can't Stop Talking* (2013). According to Cain, and the group of introvert experts who publish regularly in *Psychology Today*, our culture has an 'Extrovert Ideal', the result of which is that introverts closet themselves. Her self-styled 'Quiet Revolution' aims to undo this injustice and help introverts be valued for who they are. A *NYT* columnist reported the relief this book provided, by offering a legitimate excuse to do as she wished. 'At first, saying "no" to fund-raisers and coffees brought with it a keen, almost illicit pleasure. What freedom!' (Dell'Antonia 2016). On reflection, though, she worried, 'Am I Introverted, or Just Rude? In a contest between my manners and my preferences, am I allowing my preferences to win?', and concludes that this is 'just an ordinary version of selfishness' (Dell'Antonia 2016). She makes a case for the importance of interacting not just with people we know or with whom we might develop close ties, but with others, acknowledging that such encounters are more difficult and demanding in some ways than those with people with whom we have deep connections. 'It's the looser ties, the ones that have to be created or re-created at each meeting, that are tough . . . The more we isolate ourselves from new people, the more . . . segregated our society is likely to become. Those casual interactions

... are the ones that are most likely to cross social and economic barriers' (Dell'Antonia 2016).

This is akin to the position developed by the geographer Ash Amin in his book, *Land of Strangers* (2012). Because of how heterogeneous 'modern Western societies' have become, he warns against nostalgia for 'community'. He advocates for a version of sociality that is not restricted to 'mutual obligations and strong social ties' but includes 'impersonal, respectful distance', 'principled disagreement' and 'the openly disputed'. He proposes that a 'society of strangers' which relies on 'the principle of the commons' be recognized and valued.

Part II: Shifting Categories and Contradictory Evaluations

In this next part of the chapter, I develop further my exploration of the types of relationships that are evident in current, often gendered usage of selfishness and selflessness. I draw on Sahlins' (1985) and Robbins' (2004) treatment of 'the relationships between values and values, categories and categories, and values and categories' (Robbins 2004: 6) to map variations in the moral 'categories' of selfishness and selflessness or unselfishness and the 'values' attributed to them.

Again, there are striking similarities with the multiple, often opposing meanings attributed to 'nature' and 'culture' and the purposes for which they are deployed. MacCormack accounts for the inconsistent meanings and values associated with the categories 'nature' and 'culture' by reminding us that when 'complex concepts' like these are applied to particular entities for comparison, 'specific characteristics of these phenomena ... are selected' and this creates 'great potential for ... contradiction' (1980: 9). One of the examples Strathern gives is that sometimes 'we see males as attuned to cultural needs, and females to biological ones, but also the reverse: males as ... capable of displaying base nature to the female's other-oriented ... sociableness' (1980: 183).

I have found similar reversals and contradictions in the way selfishness and selflessness are used. This includes opposing values being attributed to each category: each term is sometimes morally evaluated as good and sometimes as bad. The first two examples I offer are of this type: selfishness, normally considered bad/immoral, is in certain instances considered good/moral.

I then present an example of a reversal in the value of values: selfishness is deemed bad but bad is given high value. I end this section with three examples of reversals of meanings of the categories, or to put it a different way, in the relationship between the category and its referents. In these examples, behaviours normally associated with the category of selfishness are deemed to belong in the opposite category. In addition, these revised categories are sometimes evaluated in contradictory ways. 'Selflessness is really selfishness' and judged by some to be bad, and by others to be good, despite this.

The Relationship between Categories and Values: Selfishness Is Good if It Protects Property

The first example I give of shifting values comes from the children's book *Being Selfish*, which I used earlier to illustrate the hierarchical relationship between selfish/unselfish. If only it were so simple. The first three paragraphs of the author's note portray selfishness to be a moral failing and advise parents how to help their children overcome it. In the last paragraph, though, she changes course and instructs: 'it is important for your child and you to determine what constitutes situations in which sharing is inappropriate. Then, it is important for you to support your child's "selfishness" in these situations just as much as you support his or her unselfishness in other situations' (Berry 1988). Within the space of a page, the values accorded to 'selfish' and 'unselfish' are reversed. The default position, as it were, is selfishness is bad, which is reinforced by reference to the moral authority of the Bible. But in some unspecified situations, to be determined by the parents, sharing is bad/being selfish is good. To the primary message, you must follow the Golden Rule, another American value intervenes – the right to protect personal property. When sharing presents a risk to private property (a toy may be used 'improperly', broken, not returned), selfishness is not only condoned but advised: 'You do not have to share with anyone who is careless. Put your things away if you think they might be lost or damaged' (Berry 1988). In this example, the moral value of protecting private property trumps that of sharing with others.

The Relationship between Categories and Values: Selfishness Is Good Because It Is Natural

Another reversal in the value associated with selfishness is the idea that selfishness is good because it is human nature to prioritize what is in our self-interest; to try to stifle this inclination is not only ignorant and foolish, but immoral. Sometimes selfishness is construed as part of 'human nature', other times as part of our 'animal nature', or a conflation of the two. For example, the songwriter for a California post-hardcore band explained that his CD, *Selfish Machines*, was about 'the animal instinct that everyone has and won't admit exists ... and human nature and our selfish tendencies' (Fuentes 2010).

One strand of 'it is natural to be selfish' thinking comes from novelist and philosopher Ayn Rand. In *The Virtue of Selfishness* (1964: back cover), she sets forth the principles that 'altruism is incompatible with man's nature, with the creative requirements of his survival, and with a free society'. Rand acknowledged that her use of the term 'selfishness' was unconventional, but maintained that it was consistent with the dictionary definition of the term, 'concern with one's own interests' (1964: ix, vii).[30]

Another important source for the view that selfishness is natural comes from a misreading of the hugely influential book, *The Selfish Gene* ([1976] 2006), by English evolutionary biologist Richard Dawkins. Dawkins came to regret his choice of title. In the introduction to the 30th anniversary edition, he explains that people 'assume the book is about selfishness whereas, if anything, it devotes more attention to altruism'. What was important about his title, he argues, 'was not the word "selfish" but the word "gene" ... The critical question is what level in the hierarchy of life will turn out to be the inevitably "selfish level": species, group, organism, or the gene' ([1976] 2006: viii). As a corrective, Dawkins produced a 1986 BBC documentary film and new chapter for his second edition (1989), both entitled 'Nice Guys Finish First', to demonstrate how cooperation can evolve even in a basically selfish world.[31]

The idea that we are naturally selfish because of our genes has staying power though. In 2018, one of the consumer products available for purchase on Zazzle, an online store for personalized office products and gifts, was a t-shirt emblazoned with a colourful image of a DNA strand and the words 'My genes are selfish'.[32] It is no coincidence that the model wearing it is male given the sociobiological predilection for rationalizing male dominance.

Neurobiology and developmental psychology are also routinely drawn upon to support the naturalness of selfish behaviour. For example, a book on addiction, *The Selfish Brain* (Dupont 1997: 4), explains that 'the brain's ... pleasure center' does not 'consider other people's feelings or needs'. Our 'natures' are also used to explain unselfish behaviour, conceptualized as a battle between our reptile brain and the mammalian part of our brain (Gerhardt 2011: 23).

Whereas Rand supports pursuing self-interest to achieve self-actualization, others embrace it to exploit others. *Selfish, Scared and Stupid: Stop Fighting Human Nature and Increase Your Performance, Engagement and Influence* (Flanagan and Gregory 2014: book description), written by two 'behavioural research strategists', invites readers to 'learn how the survival of the species plays into business ... Discover how to offer customers strategic rewards, thereby making the buying process more attractive to selfish natures'.

The Relationship between Values and Values: Selfishness Is Bad but Bad Is Good

This next example represents a reversal in the value of values: the dominant evaluation of selfishness as bad is retained, but badness is evaluated as good. Here selfishness is seen as transgressive; so, too, is sexual pleasure, especially if it is women's. Selfish = indulging one's carnal desires = good. Marilyn Monroe, 'one of the most popular sex symbols of the 1950s, emblematic of the era's attitudes towards sexuality', has continued to be a pop-culture icon (Wiki). Many early twenty-first-century products, such as vinyl wall art, waterproof neoprene laptop sleeves, handbags and dog tags, are embossed with her widely distributed, but completely unsourced, self-description (Garis 2014): 'I'm selfish, impatient and a little insecure. I make mistakes, I am out of control, and at times hard to handle, but if you can't handle me at my worst then you sure as hell don't deserve me at my best'. As if the sexual meaning was not clear enough, this quote is often illustrated with her famous lipstick kiss mark, advertised as suitable for hanging over one's bed, or trimmed with black lace. Freud made the connection between selfishness and sexiness. In answer to the question 'What made . . . self-absorbed women so sexy?' Freud explained that, as with children, for 'certain animals which seem not to concern themselves about us', the charm lies in the 'narcissism', 'self-contentment, and inaccessibility' (quoted in Dombek 2016: 36).

Another example is *The Pleasure Is All Mine: Selfish Food for Modern Life* (Pirret 2009), a cookbook for single people described as '*wickedly* funny' and recommended for those who 'need a *shamelessly* selfish treat' (product description, emphasis added). The cover shows an attractive woman (possibly the author) in a seductive pose. Even though she is purportedly alone, she is wearing black stiletto heels and a low-cut, tight, sleeveless dress with a slit up the back, holding a bottle of wine, looking over her shoulder, laughing. The same year her book was published, Pirret started a widely publicized affair with a British celebrity chef, garnering headlines that dubbed her 'the hottest chef', 'saucy in so many ways . . . focused on food, sex and fame' (Clay 2011). This book should not be confused with *The Pleasure's All Mine: A History of Perverse Sex* (Peakman 2013), which was negatively reviewed by someone who objected to the title because she felt it suggested that 'perverse sex is greedy, self-indulgent' (Raven 2013).[33]

Others embrace selfishness with ironic humour and/or as part of counter-cultural transgression (Croom 2011). Since the early 1990s, numerous bands have chosen to call themselves 'Selfish'.[34] A search for 'selfish' on the US Zazzle website produced 2491 results (the UK site produced only 408), including key chains that read 'I heart selfishness' or 'Bob the Selfish Santa', mouse pads that advise one to 'Keep calm and carry on being selfish', and a line of 'Take back your shame' women's t-shirts bedecked with your choice of slogans, including 'Selfish', 'Everything I did, I did for me', or 'Be shameless – Lazy, Overweight, Selfish, Bossy'. Phone cases that brand their users as selfish are popular selfishness-endorsing products, one sporting a quotation attributed to Marilyn Monroe, another with an anime character saying 'I love Me!' on one side, and another instructing 'Fight only for yourself and love only yourself' on the flip side. Elsewhere on the web, a graphic artist sells 'Selfish Life' pictures of a heart with a razor blade through it on a variety of items including an organic baby bib. A line of stationery goods called 'Selfish Needs' is designed to help you 'elevate your ambitious intentions and narcissistic notions' 'because sometimes you gotta look out for number one'.

The Relationship between Categories: Selfishness Is Really Selflessness

In addition to reversals in the values ascribed to selfish and selfless, we also find reversals in the referents of the categories, that is, behaviours normally considered to be self-indulgent, like pedicures with wine and friends, are recategorized as selfless. Books directed to caregivers are likely places to find selfish/selfless deployed in this way: selfishness is not what it seems but is actually a means of being better able to give to others. This is based on an ethno-model of selfhood which is akin to a bank account into which recourses can be deposited or spent. One has only so much to give, and when that is expended, the self needs to be replenished. *Just for You: Selfish Sewing Projects* explains, 'busy women spend all day doing things for everyone else' and this book will give 'a hard-working woman the perfect way to relax and replenish' (Fairbanks-Critchfield and Markos 2014: back cover). An American 'Spiritual Living and Emotional Wellness Coach' tells her readers, 'You cannot give something you do not have and we all need your personal magic, so please, let your greatest path of serving the world, start with you . . . when you are happy, you naturally give more' (Zunk 2016). The author of *Selfish Mama: How to Be the Mom You Know You're Meant to Be* believes that if mothers take care of themselves, they 'can joyfully, even ecstatically' give themselves to their families (Corbett 2015: 8). The cover shows three pretty young women, dressed in bathrobes, sitting side by side on a couch, with their feet soaking in footbaths and wine glasses raised (see also the film 'Bad Moms' [Spitz 2016]). The aim is to become an even better giver. 'When I feel consistently satisfied with how I spend my time (because ultimately, it is *my* time, not anyone else's), then I have so much more to give them' (Corbett 2015: 5, emphasis in the original). Here, caring for one's children is not a moral or social duty, but an individual, free choice, something that can be given or withheld at will.

The same message is directed to those who 'provide unpaid care for disabled or elderly relatives, friends, or neighbors' in an ironically titled British book, *The Selfish Pig's Guide to Caring*, which encourages caregivers to take care of their own needs too (Marriott 2003).

The Relationship between Categories: Selflessness Is Really Selfishness

The attribution of ulterior motives to those who engage in ostensibly selfless actions is pervasive. The story goes: 'no one ever really sacrifices himself. Because every purposeful action is motivated by some value, or goal that the actor desires, one always acts selfishly, whether one knows it or not' (Branden 1964: 66).[35] A discounting of kind acts is so routine it seems almost a cultural tic.

The pop-psychology quiz discussed above provides an example: 'Some people may appear perfectly altruistic, but in reality, they are doing it for their own reasons such as desire to be liked and respected (e.g. abusing and depriving their own family while rushing to help strangers)'. Another example appears in the article on the woman who had won the New York City Marathon and had mentored up-and-coming runners. The reporter first praises, then undermines her generosity by arguing that helping her teammates is not the selfless act it may seem, but really an act of self-interest: 'This is not all selfless acts of mentorship ... the camaraderie she has fostered has served her well ... Elevating other women is actually an act of self-interest: It's not so lonely at the top' (Crouse 2017).

Pleasure is often seen as a moral disqualifier; if giving gives the giver pleasure, the good deed may be morally tainted. This type of thinking has been operative from at least the eighteenth century. Kant (1785) discussed the 'inclination' that people had for helping others because of 'the pleasure' they get from seeing others' happiness (in 2015: 186). As Barker-Benfield shows (this volume), in the eighteenth century, doing good for another was understood to provide 'exquisite fellow-feeling', and this made abolitionists vulnerable to being accused of engaging in self-indulgence. Fassin shows how in the context of humanitarianism such feelings are 'a crucial motive for action' but can also be tactically used by governments to justify self-interested military operations, as was the case of Libya (2015: 184–87).

The pleasures and self-interests, personal costs and vulnerabilities that are attendant to behaving selflessly are all brilliantly conveyed by Virginia Woolf ([1927] 1994) in Mrs Ramsay – renowned hostess, loving mother, and devoted wife to a selfish, insecure husband, 'narrow as the blade of one' ([1927] 1994: 1). As she knits by a window with her youngest in her lap, Mr Ramsay enters, declaring himself a failure. Without moving from her place, she

> braced herself, and, half turning, seemed to raise herself with an effort, and ... to pour ... into the air ... all her energies ... [a] force, burning and illuminating ... a delicious fecundity [so that he might be] assured of his genius [and] taken within the circle of life, warmed and soothed ... all the rooms of the house made full of life – the drawing room; behind the drawing room the kitchen; above the kitchen the bedrooms; and beyond them the nurseries; they all must be furnished, they must be filled with life (25).

Having been so giving, in response to the needs/desires of another, she finds herself self-less: 'there was scarcely a shell of herself left for her to know herself by; all was so lavished and spent' (25). Yet a few pages later, Mrs Ramsay doubts her motives. Was it possible 'that all this desire of hers to give, to help, was vanity. For her own self-satisfaction was it that she wished instinctively to help, to give ... ?' (28).[36]

It is also striking how frequently people who are praised for selflessness disavow the label. I present just two recent examples. A woman confessed that she was 'not being entirely selfless' when she offered to wait in line for tickets at Disneyland because the pavilion was air-conditioned (Lasky 2017), and a man who wrestled a gun out of a shooter's hands rejected depictions of himself as a selfless hero, describing his actions as 'completely ... a selfish act ... I was completely doing it just to save myself' (Wong 2018). In both cases, being honest about one's motivations is morally compelling. A third example shows people rejecting the label for different moral reasons. Live-in volunteers at a Christian home in London for people with mental disabilities reject the label of 'altruist' because altruism is 'a one-way ... unconditional kind of giving ... one that does not have any sense of reciprocity' (McKearney 2016: 131), and these 'carers' purposively try to cultivate relations of dependency, mutuality and intersubjectivity.

The rhetoric of investment and economies of scale are also sometimes used to re-label selflessness as self-interested, and therefore more normal and socially acceptable. One of the long-term breastfeeding mothers described by Faircloth (this volume) uses the metaphor of investment to make a utilitarian argument: 'People don't see that investing now will save time later'. Caplan (2011) encourages people to enjoy the economies of scale by having many children.

The Relationship between Categories and Categories and Values: Selflessness Is Really Selfishness and Selfishness Is Good Because You Get More of What You Want

The final iteration I discuss is how selflessness is promoted to others by asserting that it is really selfishness, and selfishness is good because it means you will get more of what you want. In other words, this is an illustration of a change in the relationship between the categories, and a change in the relationship between category and value.

I begin with another example from eighteenth-century Britain, when opponents of the slave trade appealed to slave owners' self-interest, making the case that ending slavery was not actually a selfless act, but a self-interested one. An early example comes from Sarah Scott, who because she believed it would be impossible to end slavery itself, argued for the amelioration of the treatment of enslaved African people. In a novel set in Jamaica (1766), her exemplary hero, a slave owner, made the case that if provided 'proper commendations and reward', slaves would work more productively (1996: 19). In 1788, Rev. Thomas Clarkson, the leading white opponent of slavery and the slave trade, argued that what might at first appear to be an act of compassion and generosity would in fact benefit slave owners' own selfish imperatives. With abolition of the trade, one's existing slaves would become more valuable, owners would be inclined to treat them better and as a result they would live longer, reproduce more and work harder, all of which would increase profits. 'Let them be treated with tenderness. Let his wants be supplied. This will operate as an incitement to his exertions: gratitude will demand a return' (Clarkson 1788: 101).

In the twenty-first century, selflessness has been promoted in business, management, leadership, personal development and marketing as an effective strategy for increasing personal health, happiness and professional success.[37] One example is *Selfless Development: How to Find Your Purpose* (Sheffer 2016), written by a self-promoting, 27-year-old 'former executive' who left the corporate world to found her company, 'Simply Free'. Doing so, she explains on her website, turned an 'already strong young woman into an unstoppable, relentless, purpose driven, powerhouse ... developing ourselves through selfless awareness of our God-given purpose is the divine design for achieving our best life'.[38]

The Random Acts of Kindness Foundation's website includes a page and a video on 'the scientifically proven benefits of being kind': increased energy, happiness, lifespan, pleasure, higher levels of oxytocin (the love hormone), serotonin (the feel-good chemical) and decreases in pain, stress, anxiety, depression and blood pressure.

Citing an experiment by consumer psychologists that supports this, a Mormon financial advisor encourages readers to 'Spend ... Your Money to Make Someone Else Happy', because doing so will make you happier than spending on yourself (Richards 2012).[39] A cover story in *The New York Times Magazine*, 'Is Giving the Secret to Getting Ahead?' (Dominus 2013: 22), features Adam Grant, an organizational psychologist and best-selling author of *Give and Take* (2014: 9), who argues that he can help readers reach the top of the success ladder, by helping them become the right type of 'giver'.

A related narrative is present in the burgeoning area of 'selfless leadership' (Brookes 2015). Numerous business blogs offer lists of traits (between four and nine) that can be used to identify such leaders. A psychologist who teaches at a US military academy contrasts selfless leaders with selfish ones, those 'who are really taken with their image in the mirror, so impressed by the power and influence they seemingly wield' (Kail 2011). Because selflessness has long been associated with effeminacy (Barker-Benfield 1992, this volume; Douglas 1977), this military man takes pains to assure the reader that 'selflessness is all about strength ... Shoulder the heaviest burden first and set it down last. Real strength is measured by what we enable our followers to accomplish through our service to them ... being selfless is one of the hardest things you'll ever do' (Kail 2011). American General 'Mad Dog' Mattis links machismo with unselfishness, declaring that the future of American democracy depends on having armed forces made up of 'cocky, macho, unselfish, ... young men and women' (Filkin 2017: 36).

Conclusions

This chapter provides what Mauss ([1938] 1985: 2) might call 'a summary catalogue of the forms' that the categories selfless and selfish have 'assumed at various times and in various places' in the late twentieth-/early twenty-first-century UK and US. Doing so provided 'a means by which to try to discover in what consists their unstable nature' (Mauss [1938] 1985: 1). The method I adopted, gathering a wide range of examples of how these categories are being employed in the public sphere, enabled me to do more than to treat them as part of a 'disembodied semiotic system' (Sahlins 1985: 151), but, again to borrow from Mauss, to see how they 'take on flesh and blood' (Mauss [1938] 1985: 2).

More broadly, these categories provide an illustration of a Sausurrian understanding of how meaning is generated through difference, a foundational premise of both structuralism and post-structuralism (Belsey 2002: 8). It is not just that the categories selfish, selfless and unselfish take their meaning by means of how they differ from each other, but as Sahlins observes, as symbolic objects, these categories 'represent a differential interest to various subjects according to its place in their life schemes' (1985: 150). When they are put to work by people, for their own particular purposes, as the examples I have provided in this chapter illustrate, what Sahlins calls their 'conceptual value' acquires 'an intentional value', which, as we have seen, particularly in the second part of this chapter, often differs from its 'conventional value' (Sahlins 1985: 150). As with gender, the 'personal meanings' of selfishness and selflessness can vary greatly yet still be easily recognizable as part of contemporary British and American moral landscapes. 'From a whole set of ideas . . . that circulate in discourse, certain elements are drawn upon by individuals in certain circumstances and in so doing . . . generate a way of inhabiting a [moral] subject position that is uniquely individual but nevertheless recognizable' in the US and UK (Chodorow, adapted by and from Long 2016: 78).

There are more than methodological similarities between Mauss's efforts to trace the social history of 'person' and 'self' and the project undertaken in this chapter and indeed throughout the volume. Mauss places the emergence of the categories 'person' and 'self' in the context of the Protestant Reformation and the sectarian movements of the seventeenth and eighteenth centuries. It is not coincidental that this was the same historical context during which words relating to selfishness and selflessness were introduced into the English language (Introduction, this volume). As Mauss explains, it was during this period that 'were posed the questions regarding individual liberty, regarding the individual conscience and the right to communicate directly with God, to be one's own priest, to have an inner God' (Mauss [1938] 1985: 21), all of which bear directly on contemporary understandings of morality, even secularized ones, including judgements about whether one's self or other persons are behaving selfishly.

One can appreciate how selflessness and selfishness rely on the liberal self by comparison with the 'abyss of slavery', a condition under which slave owners and the governments that supported them denied both liberty and selfhood to enslaved people. During the American Civil War, Black soldiers asserted their selfhood and selflessness simultaneously; they fought 'because they subscribed to the republican ideal that fighting . . . not only made men; it made citizens . . . to kill was the right of a free man just as to die for one's country was the duty and right of a citizen'. This is why the South could not 'accord Negro soldiers the rights of prisoners of war', for to do so would admit their rights as citizens and their moral selfhood (Laqueur 2008: 6, on Faust 2008).

Selfishness, too, is contingent on selfhood. In Toni Morrison's novel *Beloved* ([1987] 2004), the female protagonist illustrates that one does not have the luxury of engaging in selfishness if one does not have a self. After escaping, she marvels at the profound and novel pleasure of selfishness: '. . . selfishness I never knew nothing about before. It felt good. Good and right. I was big . . . and deep and wide'. She felt able to love her children now that they were 'hers' to love ([1987] 2004: 190).

Compare her circumstances, or those of the asylum seekers and their children in US custody on the Mexican border (summer 2018–), with the people we met in this chapter as they made judgements about sharing – things and themselves; how much and how often they could/should spend on themselves and how much on others;[40] the 'proper' amount of attention they should give themselves; their appearance, their public image; about how they should 'spend' their time – how much alone, how much in the company of others; how much they should pursue individual goals versus collective ones.

Let us return now to Collier (1989: 156). She explained her Stanford students' moral system as stemming from a particular conception of selfhood.

> They assumed a society made up of separate, autonomous, equal individuals whose relations with one another are the product of individual free choice. In their assumed world, everyone has the right to life, liberty, and happiness, that is, the right to have others not infringe on personal space, property, or feelings.

This worldview does seem to explain the kinds of moral judgements her students at an elite American university were making in the 1970s and, based on the contemporary examples given in this chapter, still informs the moral landscape on which many judgements about selfishness are made. But the material presented in this chapter exceeds this model and represents a much more diverse terrain. As was noted in the Introduction, and illustrated here, some Christian understandings of humility, devotion and service as well as understandings of the self, informed by Eastern religions, represent radical alternatives to what is often taken for the modern Western sense of self.

Furthermore, the Black Lives Matter movement (2013–) that brought attention to the police violence and systematic racism against Black people, and the MeToo movement (2017–) that exposed the extent of sexual assault and sexual harassment, make clear that not everyone in the US or UK can expect that others will treat them as they themselves would like to be treated (see also Benjamin 2018). At the same time, many of those who used to be able to do so, no longer feel confident that they can count on what had been taken-for-granted protections and freedoms. The *Angry White Men* (Kimmel 2017: x), who are the subject of a book on American masculinity, feel 'undone by a parade of others who challenged their previously unfettered access to the American Dream'.

At various points in Anglo-American history, conventional understandings of the 'proper' relationship between individuals and others, between individuals and society, have been challenged and changed. The 'others' in question have included abstract entities (God, the Publique, country) but also types of people, for example husbands, wives, daughters, bosses, and strangers we casually interact with in stores, on the street, in restaurants and on trains.

Such periods generate creative fluorescence (e.g. new words, innovations in the arts, jokes, insults, GIFs and memes). They also spawn alarmist narratives about moral decline. These narratives are nostalgic for the way people treated each other and the respect they gave social institutions in the past. As I argued in the Introduction, and have demonstrated in this chapter, the end of the twentieth century and beginning of the twenty-first is such a period, one in which 'people are likely to experience a heightened sense of moral concern' and to fixate 'on moral debate in everyday life' (Robbins 2007: 311).[41] I hope that anthropological and historical perspectives might lead to greater understanding and perhaps even strategies as we navigate and try to contribute to this moment of moral challenge and change.

Acknowledgements

Thanks to James Griesemer for direction with biological altruism; Mary Rigdon for guidance on experimental economics of gender and altruism; Nat McClennan for help with contemporary music genres; Ilana Gershom for directing me to Collier at a crucial moment; Mike Driver for building me the lovely space in which I finally finished this project; Terry Childers for the tables and diagrams and all things electronic; Fenella Cannell for an astute reading; Paola Filippucci for sharing her expertise on sacrifice. To Barbara Bodenhorn, I am grateful for her profound intellectual engagement with this chapter and the project as a whole. As for Ben (aka G.J. Barker-Benfield), it is such a gift to have a partner like you; your intellectual contribution is evident throughout and I continue to relish your 'immoral support'.

Linda L. Layne is a Bye-Fellow and Director of Studies for Social Anthropology, Girton College, and a Visiting Professorin the Reproductive Sociology group at the University of Cambridge (LL427@cam.ac.uk). She has written books on collective identity in Jordan and pregnancy loss in the US and is currently working on *All the Credit, All the Blame: An Intimate History of One American Single Mother by Choice* and *Uncanny Kinship: Absent Presences in Contemporary EuroAmerican Families*, a comparative study of SMC families, two-mom families, two-dad families, and families that have suffered a pregnancy loss.

Notes

1. A few comparable examples from history include Marx (1964), Williams (1973) and Merchant (1980).
2. See Needham (1973) on the use of left and right for such evaluative purposes in many cultures. Watterson develops the dichotomy further in the body of the book with the metaphor of taking sides, e.g. 'Which side are you on?' and advice for how to 'change sides'.
3. Novels: Roth 2011, 2012, 2013; Arand 2016. Films: Singh 2015; Roth 2014, 2015, 2016. Television: Hull and Vazquez 2013.
4. For example, Pitcher 2013; Scharlin-Pettee 2016; Wolff 2015.
5. https://en.wikipedia.org/wiki/Onward,_Christian_Soldiers (accessed 3 December 2019).
6. The Eastbourne Lifeboat Station, established in 1822 with a lifeboat named the 'Samaritan', displays the ten medals for 'gallantry'.
7. This same biblical verse is chosen as the title of a biography of Mother Teresa (Moore 2002) and yet, in both cases, it is precisely their willingness to give their lives for people who are not their friends, but strangers, that is notable.
8. Selflessness is one of the virtues entailed in 'morally idealized representations of the "Superstrong Black Mother"' (Mattingly 2014: 7).
9. See Ladwig (2009) for a compelling account of the moral ambiguities in Buddhism of 'excessive giving'.
10. https://www.selfless-self.com/Extracts.php (accessed 3 December 2019).
11. Robbins follows Dumont in his understanding of values as 'determinations of the relative importance of elements of a culture (beliefs, ideas, things etc.) and as such [they] always serve to produce hierarchies of more or less valued elements' (2007: 296).
12. I located six Christian-identified groups who had chosen 'Selfless' as their name: two bands from Florida, including one that uses its hard rock and metal-infused music to 'spread the gospel of Jesus Christ to a lost and dying world'; a male solo act who produces under the 'Humble Lifestyles' label; a foursome who are 'super nice' as the result of having been 'ignored by girls and bullied in high school'; a male solo act from New Mexico who affirms, 'Salvation is never selfish, it's Selfless'. Since 2010, Christian groups have also used 'selfless' in the titles of their CDs: K-Mor, 'God Glorifying, Inspirational, and Uplifting Gospel Rap'; and NuBridge from Louisiana. Other recording artists who use this term include: Benjah Ninjah, Malcolm Jamal Warner, The Frame Defect, Royal Auditorium and A Thousand Years. The Dakota Brown Band recorded a song entitled 'Selfless' after the eponymous singer-songwriter had a life-changing car accident.
13. Selflessness and words associated with it (self-denial, self-annihilation, self-nothingness, self-abasement, self-abnegation, self-abdication, self-renunciation) represent the 'self-denying values' of Christian morality that Nietzsche found remarkable and antipathetic.
14. Arabi 2016; Behary and Siegel 2013; Burgo 2016; Keys 2013; Kluger 2014; Loric and Grannon 2015; Malkin 2016; Payson 2010.
15. US *NYT*: Blow 2017; Brody 2016; A.C. Brooks 2016; D. Brooks 2016a, 2016b; Bruni 2015; Friedman 2017; Lilienfield and Watts 2015; Wayne 2016. UK: Hosie 2017; *The Independent* 2017; Smith 2016; Swaine, Laughland and Jacobs 2016; Valenti 2016.
16. Trump, 'Anthony Weiner, Eliot Spitzer, Mark Sanford, Kwame Kilpatrick, John Edwards, and Bill Clinton, to name only a few' (Dombek 2016: 20).

17. Trump, Dominique Strauss-Kahn, Harvey Weinstein, Bill Cosby, Bill O'Reilly, Matt Lauer (Vaknin 2011; Creager 2017; Associated Press 2015; Wemple 2015; Heitler 2017), to name a few more.
18. Some consumer products, for reasons that are not immediately apparent, take 'altruism' as their brand or model name: a woman's ring (stainless steel and Swarovski crystal), a brand of mountain bikes, and a line of silicone cookware (amazon.co.uk, amazon.com).
19. A popularization of this was produced by a British television personality in a book called *The Empathy Instinct* (Bazalgette 2018); see also Sober and Wilson 1998.
20. Biologists and philosophers of biology distinguish biological altruism from human altruism because of the role, or lack thereof, of intention. 'In biology, conscious intention is not required . . . it is the consequences of an action for reproductive fitness that determine whether the action counts as altruistic' (Okasha 2013).
21. St Maximilian Kolbe (1894–1941) was beatified in 1971 with a papal decree that invoked the same verse in John used to honour selfless firefighters and Mother Teresa. 'Greater love hath no man than this . . . Like his master, Jesus Christ, he had loved his fellow-men to the point of sacrificing his life for them' (Wiki).
22. Some are presented as both ordinary and extraordinary. For example, a missionary in Papua New Guinea is described as serving the poor with apostolic zeal and heroically dying while a prisoner of the Japanese in World War II (Reida and Maier 2012); and as 'just an ordinary nun [who] founded no order, started no movement nor did she perform miraculous deeds' (Mulcare 2013). Even Moses, we are told, was 'an ordinary human being who, by God's matchless grace, was able to do some pretty remarkable things' (Swindoll 2009: xi).
23. Christian love is also seen as a way to transform the world. For example, at the royal wedding in 2018, the sermon delivered by an African-American pastor praised the transformative power of love, using the example of Christ's sacrifice, 'Love is not selfish and self-centred. Love can be sacrificial, and in so doing, becomes redemptive. And that way of unselfish, sacrificial, redemptive love changes lives, and it can change this world' (Curry 2018), positing that it could end war and poverty.
24. A very similar title and 'philosophical' approach appears in French, in *Sauvez Votre Peau! Devenez Narcissique* (Midal 2018). Thanks to Debbie Holden and Cat Lacour for drawing my attention to this genre.
25. Examples include: Lenin's praise of a Russian socialist writer for his 'selfless devotion' to the revolution (Ignatieff 2016); a tribute to Fidel Castro, who referred to Cuba as 'this dignified and selfless country' (Ahmed 2016); a character in a spy thriller set in the former East Germany (Porter 2005: 1371), who is accused of lacking 'the selfless contribution to the state required of every responsible citizen'. Examples of those who accuse communist regimes of false advertising include: a negative review of an exhibition and film in Moscow, celebrating British spy Kim Philby, that seeks to portray 'Russia's secret police officers as selfless public servants rather than lawless goons' (Higgins 2017); a disgruntled Chinese billionaire who explains that the Chinese Communist Party 'still strives to cultivate an image of selfless service to the nation' (Forsythe 2017). An example of crediting communism with selflessness and deeming selflessness to be immoral: Ayn Rand, who witnessed the Russian revolution when she was twelve, deemed 'the communist principle that Man must exist for the sake of the State' to be 'evil' (http://aynrandlexicon.com/lexicon/communism.html, accessed 6 December 2019).
26. Long (2016: 77) describes a prodemocracy student activist who grew disillusioned and by the 2010s felt that democracy had led to the indulgence of 'self-interest' and

27. 'selfish desires' and had 'had a destructive effect upon both political and social relations'. He now aspires to a 'mode of political engagement . . . where he might be able to express his desires . . . without disrupting harmonious, hierarchical relationships' (83).
27. The editors of *The Guardian* (The Editors 2013) proclaimed her legacy as 'public division, private selfishness and a cult of greed'. A similar picture of 'her dark legacy' was shared by Young (2013; see also Carroll 2014). Sutcliffe-Braithwaite (2013) contends that Thatcher 'did not endorse the selfishness, materialism and greed . . . these were an unexpected and unwelcome by-product of her policies'. Another said it was not fair to blame Thatcher because Britain 'was already selfish' (response to The Editors 2013). Others used polling data to argue that even post-Thatcher, Britain is not selfish (Shaheen 2013): 'Britons continue to favour state responsibility over individualism . . .'. See also Delap's critique of the labelling of post-Thatcher Britain as a 'selfish society', in this volume.
28. *The Guardian* published pieces that linked Facebook to socially aggressive narcissism (Pearse 2012); that explored whether millennials are particularly vulnerable to becoming 'vain and attention-seeking narcissists' because of their use of social media during the 'necessary narcissistic stage' of development (Fishwick 2016); and provided an online quiz (*The Guardian* 2016) to help you determine if 'you [are] selfless, selfish or selfie-obsessed'.
29. Like narcissism, introversion is conceptualized in terms of a continuum or spectrum, but it differs in that it is not considered a personality disorder, but merely a personality type or temperament. An online test will help determine which one you are (www.pyschologytoday.com.gb.tests).
30. Many fellow philosophers commented on her 'paradoxical title', judging it to be either 'rhetoric excess' or an appropriate title for 'an equally provocative thesis about ethics' (Wiki).
31. Some Christian authors concerned with selfishness seek to reconcile Christianity with evolutionary biology, e.g. Messer (2007) and Foster (2009).
32. https://www.zazzle.co.uk/selfish_gene_t_shirt-235887445663076177 (accessed 6 December 2019).
33. Another example of a positive value being assigned to the transgressive act of enjoying food/drink on one's own, i.e. breaking the rules of commensality, is a tea-for-one teapot advertised as 'selfish', suggesting that the Italian company that makes and markets 'Selfish-Design-Porcelain' believes this label will attract customers.
34. A music wiki lists six bands that call themselves Selfish: a Finnish hardcore/punk band 1989–; a Czech pop-punk band circa 1997; a Swedish rock band circa 1998; a German rock band circa the late 1990s; a 'Chicago emcee/producer who embodies the reactionary essence of marginalized hip-hop artists'; a J-pop band active in early 1990s. 'Selfish Cunt' is the name of a British band 2003–, known for its 'aggressive stage shows . . . politically charged and often sexually graphic lyrics' (Wiki); an Indie/alternative band, Edinburgh 2010–, is called 'Selfish Needs', and five groups have songs with that title.
35. This narrative is criticized in an essay, 'Isn't Everyone Selfish?' included in Rand's *The Virtue of Selfishness* (1964).
36. I am indebted to Michael Hollington for drawing my attention to this passage. See also Lawrence Osborne's 'moral thriller' for a fictional account that questions the motives of would-be do-gooders. As one reviewer put it, 'For the idle elite of his novel, charity is only intermittently selfless. More frequently compromised by vanity and ego, it's the conduit for a certain kind of self-actualization' (Kitamura 2017).

William Boyd's novel about *The Many Lives of Armory Clay* (2015) allows us inside the head, to witness the 'internal argument', of a woman as she tries to decide what she is morally obliged to do/be for her grown daughters and whether those unspecified obligations mean she should not pursue her own wishes for the next phase of her life. On the one hand, she wants to see how the 'me' that had experienced war at an earlier phase of her life would respond now, to see what the newer, older, wiser self would make of it: 'My education as a person would never be complete if I didn't do this'. On the other hand, she reminded herself that she was a mother of two precious daughters. 'Were my arguments specious or genuine? Was I being true to myself or selfish?' (Boyd 2015: 351). She decides there is no way to know the answer to these questions without going there.

37. Even Christian guide books advocating Christian humility and 'voluntary self-emptying' (Nouwen 2007: 10) emphasize the personal benefits this approach will bring, such as growth and new life in Christ. Gandee (2014: back cover) assures readers that people will be rewarded for selfless behaviour: 'Not only does God delight in His people's humility, but He will bless them for it'.

38. https://www.simplysheffer.com (accessed 7 October 2018).

39. On 'Giving Tuesday', an American invention meant to counteract the shopping frenzy associated with Black Friday and Cyber Monday (two specially designated shopping days following American Thanksgiving, a holiday intended to help people pause and give thanks for all they have), a story in the business section of the *NYT* encouraged readers to do something for someone else and document it with a 'selfless selfie' to share on social media in the hope of inspiring others to do the same (Wolfe 2016). Another article reported on a marketing campaign that merged 'greenwashing' with what might be termed 'selflessness washing'. Burt's Bees (now owned by Clorox) encouraged people 'to purchase limited-edition lip balms and take "selfless selfies"' in exchange for which the company would donate funds to plant wildflowers (Levere 2017). Of course, there is also a comedic version, the #selfishie (Bradley 2014).

40. In his study of grocery shopping by residents of North London, Miller (1998: 40) observed the very common practice of buying oneself a 'treat', which stands out as an exception from the norm, i.e. that shoppers will 'subordinate their personal desires to a concern for others' and choose based on 'necessity, thrift, and moderation'. Whereas for Miller's informants, the treat is modest and limited (e.g. a chocolate bar or avocado), this is not the case for the shoppers in the US, whom marketers encourage 'to splurge on something for themselves'. This group presents an elastic market. 'Even the classic gift of affection for others – jewelry', people are now encouraged to buy for themselves. The new trend towards self-gifting is even bigger in China. A special 'lonely hearts' shopping day on 11-11 (a date consisting of 'lonely 1s') is the largest retail event in the world, four times bigger than Black Friday and Cyber Monday, the biggest shopping days in the US. In 2017, over $25 billion was spent on China's annual Singles Day (Haas 2017).

41. Rubin (2015: 2) posits that 'the morality of higher purposes' has changed into 'a morality of self-fulfillment', which accompanied the 'development of the modern administrative state'. But evidence suggests that rather than a historical sequence, these two pulls have been in tension from at least the seventeenth century (Weale 2016) and have affected men and women differently (Meyer 1987). Putnam (2000: 25) argues for a 'declensionist' narrative, a waxing and waning, a gilded age of selfishness followed by a progressive age of concern with the common good. Many of us living through the Trump era hope this is the case.

References

Abdullah, K. 2017. 'Childless in a Houseful of Children', *The New York Times*, 15 September.
Ahmed, A. 2016. 'Fidel Castro Criticizes Barack Obama's Efforts to Change Cuba', *The New York Times*, 28 March.
Ali, S. 2013. *Selfless Sacrifice: A True Story*. Milton Keynes: AuthorHouse.
Amin, A. 2012. *Land of Strangers*. Cambridge: Polity Press.
Apple, M.W. 2011. 'Doing the Work of God: Home Schooling and Gendered Labor', in M.W. Apple et al. (eds), *The Routledge International Handbook of the Sociology of Education*. Abingdon, UK: Routledge, pp. 145–54.
Arabi, S. 2016. *Becoming the Narcissist's Nightmare: How to Devalue and Discard the Narcissist While Supplying Yourself*. E-book. SCW Archer Publishing.
Arand, W.D. 2016. *The Selfless Hero Trilogy – Other Life Dreams; Other Life Nightmares; Other Life Awakenings*. E-book. William D. Arand.
Associated Press. 2015. 'Bill Cosby Accuser Calls Him "Narcissistic"', *Billboard*, 29 July.
Austin, J. 2011. *Selfless Insight: Zen and the Meditative Transformations*. Cambridge, MA: MIT Press.
Axelrod, R. [1984] 2006. *The Evolution of Cooperation*. New York: Basic.
Bacon, L. 2015. *Hero Dogs: Secret Missions and Selfless Service*. USA: Sterling Publishing.
Bakalar, N. 2017. 'Valiant in Battle, These Ants Rescue Their Wounded', *The New York Times*, 12 April.
Barker-Benfield, G.J. 1992. *The Culture of Sensibility: Sex and Society in Eighteenth-Century Britain*. Chicago: University of Chicago Press.
———. 2010. *Abigail and John Adams: The Americanization of Sensibility*. Chicago: University of Chicago Press.
———. 2018. *Phillis Wheatley Chooses Freedom: History, Poetry, and the Ideals of the American Revolution*. New York: New York University Press.
Baron-Cohen, S. 2003. *The Essential Difference: Men, Women and the Extreme Male Brain*. London: Alan Lane.
Batson, C.D. 2016. *The Altruism Question: Toward a Social-Psychological Answer*. New York: Routledge.
Bazalgette, P. 2018. *The Empathy Instinct: How to Create a More Civil Society*. London: John Murray.
Behary, W.T., and D.J. Siegel. 2013. *Disarming the Narcissist: Surviving and Thriving with the Self-Absorbed*. Oakland, CA: New Harbinger Publications.
Belsey, C. 2002. *Poststructuralism: A Very Short Introduction*. Oxford: Oxford University Press.
Benjamin, R. 2018. 'Black AfterLives Matter: Cultivating Kinfulness as Reproductive Justice', in A. Clarke and D. Haraway (eds), *Making Kin Not Population*. Chicago: Prickly Paradigm Press, pp. 41–65.
Berry, J. 1988. *Being Selfish*. Danberry, CT: Grolier Enterprises.
Bilton, N. 2011. 'Facebook Timeline Bumps Online Narcissism Up a Notch', *The New York Times*, 15 November.
Bindel, J. 2016. 'Is Not Having Children Selfish? Far from It', *The Guardian*, 26 October.
Birx, E.J. 2014. *Selfless Love: Beyond the Boundaries of Self and Other*. Boston, MA: Wisdom Publications.
Bloom, P. 2018. *Against Empathy: The Case for Rational Compassion*. New York: Vintage.
Blow, C.M. 2017. 'Trump's Madness Invites Mutiny', *The New York Times*, 15 May.

Bok, S. 1978. *Lying: Moral Choice in Public and Private Life*. London: Quartet Books.
Borlase, C. 2006. *God's Gravity: The Upside-Down Life of Selfless Faith*. Relevant Media Group.
Bornstein, E. 2012. *Disquieting Gifts: Humanitarianism in New Delhi*. Stanford, CA: Stanford University Press.
Boyd, W. 2015. *Sweet Caress: The Many Lives of Armory Clay*. London: Bloomsbury.
Bradley, B. 2014. 'Carl Reiner and Conan O'Brien Invented the #Selfishie, and the World is a Better Place', *Huffington Post*, 22 July.
Branch, J. 2016. 'Karch Kiraly Now Setting Up US Women's Volleyball Team to Succeed', *The New York Times*, 18 June.
Branden, N. 1964. 'Isn't Everyone Selfish?' in A. Rand (ed.), *The Virtue of Selfishness*. New York: Penguin, pp. 66–70.
Brockes, E. 2018. *An Excellent Choice: Panic and Joy on My Solo Path to Motherhood*. New York: Penguin.
Brody, J. 2016. 'The Narcissist Next Door', *The New York Times*, 18 July.
Brookes, S. 2015. *The Selfless Leader: A Compass for Collective Leadership*. New York: Palgrave MacMillan Intl.
Brooks, A.C. 2016. 'Narcissism Is Increasing. So You're Not So Special', *The New York Times*, 13 February.
Brooks, D. 2014. 'Introspective or Narcissistic?', *The New York Times*, 7 August.
———. 2016a. 'The Unity Illusion', *The New York Times*, 10 June.
———. 2016b. 'Donald Trump's Sad, Lonely Life', *The New York Times*, 11 October.
Brown, N. 2002. *Working with the Self-Absorbed: How to Handle Narcissistic Personalities on the Job*. Oakland, CA: New Harbinger Publishers.
———. 2003. *Loving the Self-Absorbed: How to Create a More Satisfying Relationship with a Narcissistic Partner*. Oakland, CA: New Harbinger Publishers.
———. 2008. *Children of the Self-Absorbed: A Grown-Up's Guide to Getting Over Narcissistic Parents*, 2nd ed. Oakland, CA: New Harbinger Publishers.
Bruni, F. 2014. 'The "I" in Christie's Storm', *The New York Times*, 12 January.
———. 2015 'La Dolce Donald Trump', *The New York Times*, 18 July.
Burgo, J. 2016. *The Narcissist You Know: Defending Yourself against Extreme Narcissists in an All-About-Me Age*. New York: Touchstone.
Busfield, R. 2006. *It's Time to Get Selfish: A Journey Inside of Self. A Fascinating Truth. A Life Altering Experience*. Ka'a'awa, HI: Buzzworld Publishing.
Cacciola, S. 2016. 'The Ball Is Moving, and the Lakers Are Rolling', *The New York Times*, 16 November.
Cain, S. 2013. *Quiet: The Power of Introverts in a World That Can't Stop Talking*. New York: Penguin.
Caldwell, N. n.d.a. *The Selfish Guide to Stress: How to Take Back Your Life When You're Exhausted, Overworked, and Ready for a Change (The Selfish Series Book 1)*.
———. n.d.b. *The Selfish Guide to Success: How to Use the Power of Momentum to Change Your Life and Put the Focus Back on You (The Selfish Series Book 2)*.
———. n.d.c. *The Selfish Workout Guide: The No Gym, No Weights, Fail-Proof Way to Get the Body of Your Dreams*.
Caplan, B. 2011. *Selfish Reasons to Have More Kids*. New York: Basic Books.
Carroll, D. 2014. 'Editor's Blog – The Agent of Globalization: Margaret Thatcher's True Legacy Is the "Selfish Society"', *Policy Review*, February.
Center for the Study of Global Christianity. 2017. 'Quick Facts about Global Christianity', https://gordonconwell.edu/center-for-global-christianity/research/quick-facts/. Accessed 20 November 2019.

Chamorro-Premuzic, T. 2014. 'Sharing the (Self) Love: The Rise of the Selfie and Digital Narcissism', *The Guardian*, 13 March.
Charles, F. 2014. *The Selfish Crocodile*. London: Bloomsbury.
Chrisafis, A. 2018. 'Paris "Spider-Man" Joins Fire Brigade after Citizenship Fast-Tracked', *The Guardian*, 29 May.
Clarkson, T. Rev. 1788. *An Essay on the Impolicy of the African Slave Trade in Two Parts*, 2nd ed. London: J. Phillips, Georg-Yard, Lombard-Street. A Leopold Classic Library reproduction.
Clay, X. 2011. 'Suzanne Pirret – Saucy in So Many Ways', *The Telegraph*, 15 August.
Collier, J.F. 1989. 'Whodunits and Whydunits: Contrasts between American and Zinacanteco Stories of Conflict', *Ethnographic Encounters in Southern Mesoamerica: Essays in Honor of Evon Zartman Vogt, Jr.* 3: 143–57.
———. 1997. *From Duty to Desire: Remaking Families in a Spanish Village*. Princeton, NJ: Princeton University Press.
Collins, S. 1990. *Selfless Persons: Imagery and Thought in Theravada Buddhism*. Cambridge: Cambridge University Press.
Colpus, E. 2012. 'Gaining Pleasure and Reward through Transcending the Self: British Women's Philanthropy c.1918–1939', paper presented at the Centre for Research in the Arts Social Science and Humanities (CRASSH) workshop on 'The Rhetoric of Selfishness and Selflessness', Cambridge University, 21 June.
———. 2018. *Female Philanthropy in the Interwar World: Between Self and Other*. London: Bloomsbury Group.
Cone, S. 2016. *Raising Uncommon Kids: 12 Biblical Traits You Need to Raise Selfless Kids*. Grand Rapids, MI: Baker Books.
Corbett, C. 2015. *Selfish Mama: How to Be the Mom You Know You're Meant to Be*. Self-published.
Creager, T. 2017. 'Harvey Weinstein: Sex Addict or Power Hungry Narcissist?', 9 November, http://toddcreager.com/harvey-weinstein-sex-addict-or-power-hungry-narcissist/. Accessed 9 November 2017.
Croom, A.M. 2011. 'Slurs', *Language Sciences* 33(3): 343–58.
Crouse, L. 2017. 'The Shalane Effect Works', *The New York Times*, 15 November.
Curry, M. 2018. Sermon Transcript. http://time.com/5283953/royal-wedding-sermon-transcript/. Accessed 22 October 2019.
Curtis, A. 2010. '"Giving 'Til It Hurts": Egg Donation and Costs of Altruism', *Feminist Formations* 22(2): 80–100.
Daly, I. 2012. 'Older First-Time Mothers: Smart or Selfish?', paper presented at the Centre for Research in the Arts Social Science and Humanities (CRASSH) workshop on 'The Rhetoric of Selfishness and Selflessness', Cambridge University, 21 June.
D'Arcangelo, L. 2016. 'The WNBA's Biggest Problem Isn't Lack of Interest from Men. It's Women', *Huff Post*, 14 March.
Davis, N. 2017. 'Stereotype that Women Are Kinder and Less Selfish Is True, Claim Neuroscientists: Reward System in Female Brains Geared Toward "Prosocial" Behavior', *The Guardian*, 9 October.
Daum, M. 2011. 'Narcissist – Give It a Rest', *Los Angeles Times*, 6 January.
———. 2015. *Selfish, Shallow, and Self-Absorbed: Sixteen Writers on the Decision Not to Have Kids*. New York: Picador.
Dawkins, R. [1976] 2006. *The Selfish Gene*. Oxford: Oxford University Press, with new introduction for the 40th anniversary edition.
Dell'Antonia, K.J. 2016. 'Am I Introverted, or Just Rude?' *The New York Times*, 24 September.

Deseret Book Company. 2003. *True Stories of Good Deeds, Charitable Acts and Selfless Service*.
Devlin, H. 2017. 'Science Falling Victim to Narcissism Crisis', *The Guardian*, 20 January.
Dombek, K. 2016. *The Selfishness of Others: An Essay on the Fear of Narcissism*. New York: Farrar, Straus and Giroux.
Dominus, S. 2013. 'Is Giving the Secret to Getting Ahead?', *The New York Times Magazine*, 31 March, 21–27, 36–38.
Douglas, A. 1977. *The Feminization of American Culture*. New York: Doubleday.
Dove. 2010. 'My Moment. My Dove', video advertisement. https://www.youtube.com/watch?v=UG-jaeq1rtY. Accessed 22 November 2019.
Dunofsky, M. 1997. 'Psychological Characteristics of Women Who Undergo Single and Multiple Cosmetic Surgeries', *Annals Plastic Surgery* 39(3): 223–28.
Dupont, R. 1997. *The Selfish Brain: Learning from Addiction*. Minnesota: Hazelton.
The Editors. 2013. 'Margaret Thatcher: The Lady and the Land She Leaves Behind', *The Guardian*, 8 April.
Evans, S. 2013. '25 Things Contemporary Sports Haters Say: "Women's [Insert Sport] Is Too Slow and Boring"', Complex, 1 May, https://www.complex.com/sports/2013/05/25-things-contemporary-sports-haters-say/womens-insert-sport-is-too-slow-and-boring. Accessed 22 November 2019.
Fairbanks-Critchfield, C., and S. Markos. 2014. *Just for You: Selfish Sewing Projects*. Concord, CA: C & R Publishers. Stash Books.
Fassin, D. 2012. *Humanitarian Reason: A Moral History of the Present*. Berkeley: University of California Press.
———. 2014. 'The Ethical Turn in Anthropology: Promises and Uncertainties', *HAU: Journal of Ethnographic Theory* 4(1): 429–435. doi:10.14318/hau4.1.025.
———. 2015. 'Troubled Waters: At the Confluence of Ethics and Politics', in M. Lambek, V. Das, D. Fassin and W. Keane (eds), *Four Lectures on Ethics: Anthropological Perspectives*. Chicago: Hau Books, pp. 175–210.
Faubion, J. 2011. *An Anthropology of Ethics*. Cambridge: Cambridge University Press.
Faust, D.G. 2008. *This Republic of Suffering: Death and the American Civil War*. New York: Knopf.
Figert, A.E. 1996. *Women and the Ownership of PMS*. Hawthorne: Aldine de Gruyter.
Filkins, D. 2017. 'James Mattis, The Warrior Monk', *The New Yorker*. 29 May, pp. 34–45.
Fishwick, C. 2016. 'I, Narcissist – Vanity, Social Media, and the Human Condition: Are the Likes of Instagram and Facebook Turning Us All into Vain and Attention-Seeking Narcissists, or Were We That Way to Begin With?', *The Guardian*, 17 March.
Flanagan, K., and D. Gregory. 2014. *Selfish, Scared and Stupid: Stop Fighting Human Nature and Increase Your Performance, Engagement and Influence*. Milton, Australia: John Wiley and Sons.
Forsythe, M. 2017. 'Greater Corruption in China? A Billionaire Says He Has Evidence', *The New York Times*, 15 April.
Foster, C. 2009. *The Selfless Gene: Living with God and Darwin*. London: Hodder & Stoughton.
Freeman, L. 2009. *The Selfless Self: Meditation and the Opening of the Heart*. Norwich: Canterbury Press.
Friedman, R.A. 2017. 'Is It Time to Call Trump Mentally Ill?', *The New York Times*, 17 February.
Fuentes, V. 2010. '"Pierce the Veil" Wiki', Fandom Wikia, http://pierce-the-veil.wikia.com/wiki/Selfish_Machines. Accessed 22 November 2019.

Gandee, C. 2014. *Selfless in a Selfie World: Before Honor is Humility*. Bloomington, IN: WestBow Press.

Garis, M.G. 2014. 'Marilyn Monroe's Best Quote Wasn't by Marilyn Monroe', *Elle*, 1 June.

Gentleman, A. 2017. 'Rufus Norris: "We Are Living in An Age of Extreme Selfishness"', *The Guardian*, 27 February.

Gerhardt, S. 2011. *The Selfish Society: How We All Forgot to Love One Another and Made Money Instead*. London: Simon and Schuster.

Gottlieb, A. 2018. 'How We Got to Be So Self-Absorbed: The Long Story', Review of *Selfie* by W. Storr, *The New York Times*, international edition, 28 June.

Graeber, D. 2018. *Bullshit Jobs: A Theory*. London: Allen Lane.

Grant, A. 2014. *Give and Take: Why Helping Others Drives Our Success*. London: Orion Publishing Group.

Great Britain, British Army. 2008. *Values and Standards of the British Army*. With a Forword by General Sir Richard Dannatt – Chief of the General Staff, pp. 1–8. AC 63813.

Groskop, V. 2013. '"Shelf-Help" Books Set to Fill Publishers' Coffers in 2014', *The Guardian*, 28 December.

The Guardian. 2016. 'Are You a Social Media Narcissist? Take Our Quiz', *The Guardian*, 17 March.

Haas, B. 2017. 'Chinese Shoppers Spend a Record $25bn in Singles Day Splurge', *The Guardian*, 12 November.

Harvey, P. 2013. *The Selfless Mind: Personality, Consciousness and Nirvana in Early Buddhism*. Surrey, UK: Curzon Press.

Heitler, S. 2017. 'And Now Matt Lauer . . . Why Celebrities Get Sexually Aggressive', *Psychology Today*, 29 November.

Higgins, A. 2017. 'Even in Death, the Spy Kim Philby Serves the Kremlin's Purposes', *The New York Times*, 1 October.

HM Queen Elizabeth II. 2017. Message to Acting Commissioner of the Metropolitan Police Service Craig Mackey, 23 March, https://www.royal.uk/message-acting-commissioner-metropolitan-police-service-craig-mackey. Accessed 25 March 2017.

Hosie, R. 2017. '"Malignant Narcissism": Donald Trump Displays Classic Symptoms of Mental Illness, Claim Psychologists', *The Independent*, 30 January.

Horton, A. 2019. 'Former Interpreters for US Troops Wait Out the State Department – and the Taliban – as Visas Decline', *The Washington Post*, 23 January.

Houen, A. 2016. 'Reckoning Sacrifice in "War on Terror" Literature', *American Literary History* 28(3): 574–95.

Howell, S. (ed.). 1997. *The Ethnography of Moralities*. London: Routledge.

Hull, R., and K. Vazquez. 2013. 'Selfless, Brave and True', Episode 18, Season 2, *Once Upon a Time*, dir. R. Hemecker. ABC.

Humphrey, C. 1997. 'Exemplars and Rules: Aspects of the Discourse of Moralities in Mongolia', in S. Howell (ed.), *The Ethnography of Moralities*. London: Routledge, pp. 25–47.

Hunter, J. 2015. *Get Selfish: The Way is Through*. My Inner Peace Publishing.

Ignatieff, M. 2016. 'Review of "*The Discovery of Chance: The Life and Thought of Alexander Herzen*" by Aileen Kelly', *The New York Times*, 20 May.

The Independent. 2017. 'How to Diagnose a Narcissist: With Donald Trump', Video, 30 January.

Ito, J. 2011. *What to Do When He Won't Change: Saving Your Marriage When He Is Angry, Selfish, Unhappy, or Avoids You*. Createspace Independent Publishing Platform.

James, O. 2007. *Affluenza*. London: Vermilion.
―――. 2008. *The Selfish Capitalist: Origins of Affluenza*. London: Vermilion.
Jampole, M. 2011. 'One of History's Great Puzzles: What Did People Ever See in Ronald Reagan and the Politics of Selfishness?', *Op-edge blog*, 10 November.
Japan Society. 2008. 'Former Kamikaze Pilots and Attack Survivor Attend Japan Society's NY Premiere', press release for premier of film *Wings of Defeat* (2007), 18 March.
Javid, S. 2014. 'Never Forget the Bravery and the Selfless Sacrifice', *The Sunday Telegraph*, 3 August.
Jent, K. 2017. 'Making Stem Cell Niches: An Ethnography of Regenerative Medicine in Scotland and the United States', dissertation. Sociology, University of Cambridge.
Kachka, B. 2013. 'The Power of Positive Publishing: How Self-Help Ate America', *New York Magazine*, 6 January.
Kail, E. 2011. 'Leadership Character: The Role of Selflessness', *The Washington Post*, 22 July.
Kardashian West, K. 2015. *Selfish*. New York: Rizzoli.
Kehlmann, D. 2015. 'Self-Googling in 1997', *The New York Times*, 5 June.
Kelsey-Fry, J. 2016. 'The UK Occupy Movement Five Years on and the Growth of Direct Democracy', *New Internationalist*, 14 October.
Kempton, W. 1986. 'Two Theories of Home Heat Control', *Cognitive Science* 10: 75–90.
Keys, D. 2013. *Narcissists Exposed: 75 Things Narcissists Don't Want You to Know*. Amazon Create Space self-publishing.
Kimmel, M. 2017. *Angry White Men: American Masculinity at the End of an Era*. New York: Nation Books.
Kitamura, K. 2017. 'Affluent Idlers Find a Just Cause in a Refugee Swept Ashore', *The New York Times*, 5 July.
Kluger, J. 2014. *The Narcissist Next Door: Understanding the Monster in Your Family, in Your Office, in Your Bed, in Your World*. New York: Penguin.
―――. 2015. 'Why Men Are More Narcissistic Than Women', *Time*, 5 March.
Kohn, A. 2016. 'Narcissist-in-Chief: A Psychological Take on a Political Reality', *Psychology Today*, 2 December.
Kopnina, H. 2016. 'Nobody Likes Dichotomies (But Sometimes You Need Them)', *Anthropological Forum* 26(4): 415–29.
Krasno, J. 2016. 'The United Nations' Good Works', Letter to the Editor, *The New York Times*, 21 September.
Krugman, P. 2011. 'We Are the 99.9%', *The New York Times*, 24 November.
Ladwig, P. 2009. 'Narrative Ethics: The Excess of Giving and Moral Ambiguity in Lao Vessantara-Jataka', in M. Heintz (ed.), *The Anthropology of Moralities*. Oxford: Berghahn Books, pp. 136–60.
Laidlaw, J. 2000. 'A Free Gift Makes No Friends', *Journal of the Royal Anthropological Institute* 6(4): 617–34.
―――. 2014. *The Subject of Virtue: An Anthropology of Ethics and Freedom*. Cambridge: Cambridge University Press.
Lambek, M. 2010. *Ordinary Ethics: Anthropology, Language, and Action*. New York: Fordham University Press.
―――. 2015. 'Living as If It Mattered', in M. Lambek, V. Das, D. Fassin and W. Keane (eds), *Four Lectures on Ethics: Anthropological Perspectives*. Chicago: Hau Books, pp. 5–52.
Laqueur, T. 2008. 'Among the Graves', *London Review of Books* 30(24): 3–9.

Larkin, P. 2003. *Collected Poems*, ed. A. Thwaite. New York: Farrar, Straus and Giroux.

LaRosa, J. 2018. 'What's Next for the $9.9 Billion Personal Development Industry', Marketresearch.com, 17 January.

Lasky, J. 2017. 'At Shanghai Disney Resort, Mulan, Mickey and Dumplings', *The New York Times*, 4 July.

Lea, C. 2015. *A Selfless Marriage*. Rainer Publishing.

Levere, J.L. 2017. 'Marketing Natural Body Care Products, with a Side of Activism', *The New York Times*, 16 April.

Levitin, M. 2015. 'The Triumph of Occupy Wall Street', *The Atlantic*, 10 June.

Lichtenberg, J. 2010. 'Is Pure Altruism Possible?', *The New York Times*, 19 October.

Liddle, R. 2014. *Selfish Whining Monkeys: How We Ended Up Greedy, Narcissistic and Unhappy*. London: 4th Estate.

Lilienfeld, S.O., and A.L. Watts. 2015. 'The Narcissist in Chief', *The New York Times*, 4 September.

Long, N.J. 2016. 'Why Indonesians Turn against Democracy', in J. Cook, N.J. Long and H.L. Moore (eds), *The State We're In: Reflecting on Democracy's Troubles*. Oxford: Berghahn Books, pp. 71–96.

Loric, L., and R. Grannon. 2015. *How to Take Revenge on a Narcissist: Take Your Power Back by Using the Secret Techniques of Emotional Manipulators against Them*. Self-published e-book.

Loving, C. 2015. *Selfish People: How to Deal with a Shallow, Manipulative, Controlling and Self-Absorbed Person*. Self-published e-book.

Macaulay, S. 2003. *How to Be Your Own Selfish Pig: And Other Ways You've Been Brainwashed*. Boston, MA: Summit Press.

MacCormack, C. 1980. 'Nature, Culture, Gender: A Critique', in C. MacCormack and M. Strathern (eds), *Nature, Culture and Gender*. Cambridge: Cambridge University Press, pp. 1–24.

MacCormack, C., and M. Strathern (eds). 1980. *Nature, Culture and Gender*. Cambridge: Cambridge University Press.

MacFarquhar, L. 2015. *Strangers Drowning: Grappling with Impossible Idealism, Drastic Choices, and the Overpowering Urge to Help*. New York: Penguin.

Mahdawi, A. 2017. 'If You Like Sitting in Window Seats, Believe in God and Go to the Gym, Science Says You're Probably a Self-Centred Monster', *The Guardian*, 29 October.

Malkin, C. 2016. *Rethinking Narcissism: The Bad – and Surprising Good – about Feeling Special*. New York: Harper Collins.

Marriott, S. 2003. *The Selfish Pig's Guide to Caring: How to Cope with the Emotional and Practical Aspects of Caring for Someone*. Worcester, UK: Polperro Press.

Marx, L. 1964. *The Machine in the Garden: Technology and the Pastoral Ideal in America*. Oxford: Oxford University Press.

Mattingly, C. 2014. *Moral Laboratories: Family Peril and the Struggle for a Good Life*. Berkeley: University of California Press.

Mauss, M. [1938] 1985. 'A Category of the Human Mind: The Notion of Person; The Notion of Self', in M. Carrithers, S. Collins and S. Lukes (eds), *The Category of the Person: Anthropology, Philosophy, History*, trans. W.D. Halls. Cambridge: Cambridge University Press, pp. 1–25.

Mcdonough, R. 2017. 'Safe Abortions, and the Adoption Option', letter in response to R. Sherman, 'The People to Listen to on Abortion', 21 May, *The New York Times*, 29 May.

McKearney, P. 2016. 'Enabling Ethics: L'Arche, Learning Disability, and the Possibility of Moral Agency', unpublished Ph.D. dissertation. Social Anthropology, University of Cambridge.

McVeigh, T., and A. Clark. 2011. 'UK Uncut Protesters Target Barclays over Tax Avoidance: Direct Action Highlights Barclays' Failure to Pay More than 1% Corporation Tax in 2009', *The Guardian*, 19 February.

Merchant, C. 1980. *The Death of Nature: Women, Ecology and the Scientific Revolution.* New York: Harper and Collins.

Messer, N. 2007. *Selfish Genes and Christian Ethics: Theological and Ethical Reflections on Evolutionary Biology.* London: SMC Press.

Meyer, D. 1987. *Sex and Power: The Rise of Women in America, Russia, Sweden, and Italy.* Middletown, CT: Wesleyan University Press.

Midal, F. 2018. *Sauvez Votre Peau! Devenez Narcissique.* Paris: Flammarion Versilio.

Milbank, D. 2014. 'Chris Christie, the New Jersey Narcissist', *The Washington Post*, 10 January.

Miller, C. 2014. *Selfless*. E-book. Smashwords edition.

Miller, D. 1998. *A Theory of Shopping.* Ithaca, NY: Cornell University Press.

Millar, E. 2014. 'Abortion, Selfishness and "Happy Objects"', in A. Brooks and D. Lemmings (eds), *Emotions and Social Change: Historical and Sociological Perspectives.* New York: Routledge, pp. 196–213.

Moore, T. 2002. *No Greater Love: Mother Teresa.* Novato, CA: New World Publishing.

Morales, R. 2016. 'Chris Paul, Sensational and Selfless, Credits Clippers Defense', *Los Angeles Daily News*, 27 February.

Morrison, T. [1987] 2004. *Beloved.* New York: Vintage Books.

Moull, Z. 2015. 'Breaking the Rules: An Interview with Playwright Morris Panych', *The Play Guide for the Shoplifters*. Theatre Calgary.

Mulcare, D.J. 2013. Review of *Selfless: The Story of Sr. Theophane's Missionary Life in the Jungles of Papua New Guinea*, by Sr. Immolata Reida, SSpS. 27 June. https://dmulcare.wordpress.com/2013/06/27/selfless-the-story-of-sr-theophanes-missionary-life-in-the-jungles-of-papua-new-guinea-by-sr-immolata-reida-ssps/. Accessed 22 November 2019.

Needham, R. 1973. *Right & Left.* Chicago: University of Chicago Press.

Nielsen. 2016. *Nielsen Book Research: 2015 in Review*, https://quantum.londonbookfair.co.uk/RXUK/RXUK_PDMC/documents/9928_Nielsen_Book_Research_In_Review_2015_The_London_Book_Fair_Quantum_Conference_2016_DIGITAL_FINAL.pdf?v=635995987941118341. Accessed 22 November 2019.

Nouwen, H.J.M. 2007. *The Selfless Way of Christ: Downward Mobility and the Way of Christ.* Maryknoll, NY: Orbis Press.

Nygren, A. 1999. 'Local Knowledge in the Environment–Development Discourse: From Dichotomies to Situated Knowledges', *Critique of Anthropology* 19(3): 267–88.

Oakley, B., et al. 2011. *Pathological Altruism.* Oxford: Oxford University Press.

Obama, M. 2018. *Becoming.* New York: Viking.

Okasha, S. 2013. 'Biological Altruism', *The Stanford Encyclopedia of Philosophy*, ed. E.N. Zalta, http://plato.stanford.edu/archives/fall2013/entries/altruism-biological/. Accessed 20 November 2019.

Oppenheimer, M. 2014. 'Technology Is Not Driving Us Apart After All', *New York Times Magazine*, 18 January, 34–37.

Opsahl, K. 2015. 'Cache Valley Author's Book "*Unselfish*" Getting National Attention', *HJ News*, 7 May.

Orami, L.Z. 2015. *Micha Is Being Selfish*. E-book. Amazon.

Ortner, S. 1972. 'Is Female to Male as Nature Is to Culture?', *Feminist Studies* 1(2): 5–31.
——. 1973. 'On Key Symbols', *American Anthropologist* 75(5): 1338–46.
Owen, H. 2009. *Get Selfish, Get Happy*. Australia: A&A Book Publishing.
Parker, J. 2014. *The Selfish Husband: How to Cope with and Transform Your Selfish and Inconsiderate Husband*. E-book. Amazon, Kindle edition.
Parkinson, P.D. 2015. *Unselfish: Love Thy Neighbor as Thy Selfie*. New Kensington, PA: Whitaker House.
Parkinson, P.D. and S. Parkinson. 2019. *Unselfish Kids*. USA: Unselfish Stories, LLC.
Patterson, R.N. 2018. 'Our Narcissist in Chief', *Huff Post*, 7 January.
Payson, E.D. 2010. *The Wizard of Oz and Other Narcissists: Coping with the One-Way Relationship in Work, Love, and Family*. Julian Day Publications.
Peakman, J. 2013. *The Pleasure's All Mine: A History of Perverse Sex*. London: Reaktion Press.
Pearse, D. 2012. 'Facebook's "Dark Side": Study Finds Link to Socially Aggressive Narcissism: Psychology Paper Finds Facebook and Other Social Media Offer Platform for Obsessions with Self-Image and Shallow Friendships', *The Guardian*, 17 March.
Pew Research Center. 2019. *Religious Landscape Study*. http://www.pewforum.org/religious-landscape-study/. Accessed 22 November 2019.
Pinchevsky, T. 2016. 'Devils Look for Offense in Taylor Hall's Absence', *The New York Times*, 18 November.
Pinker, S. 2011. *The Better Angels of Our Nature: A History of Violence and Humanity*. London: Penguin.
Pirret, S. 2009. *The Pleasure Is All Mine: Selfish Food for Modern Life*. William Morrow & Company.
Pitcher, J. 2013. 'Magic: The Gathering Director Addresses Player Gender Disparity', *Polygon*, 21 July.
Porter, H. 2005. *Brandenburg*. London: Orion Publishing Group. E-book.
Powers, M. 2008. *Selfless*. Dreamspinner Press.
Putnam, R.D. 2000. *Bowling Alone: The Collapse and Revival of American Community*. New York: Simon and Schuster.
Rand, A. 1964. *The Virtue of Selfishness*. New York: Penguin.
Rapport, N. 1997. 'The Morality of Locality: On the Absolutism of Landownership in an English Village', in S. Howell (ed.), *The Ethnography of Moralities*. London: Routledge, pp. 74–97.
Raven, C. 2013. 'Review: *The Pleasure's All Mine: A History of Perverse Sex*', *The Independent*, 13 December.
Rayner, G. 2017. 'May's Manifesto for the Mainstream', *The Daily Telegraph*, 19 May.
Redfield, P. 2013. *Life in Crisis: The Ethical Journey of Doctors without Borders*. Berkeley: University of California Press.
Reida, I., with G.J. Maier 2012. *Selfless: The Story of Sr. Theophane's Missionary Life in the Jungles of Papua New Guinea*. USA: Missionary Sisters Servants of the Holy Spirit.
Richards, C. 2012. 'Spending Your Money to Make Someone Else Happy', *The New York Times*, 10 September.
Rigby, R. 2013. 'How Britons Became Suckers for Self-Help: Britain Is Awash with Personal Improvement Books, from the Worthy to the Whacky', *Management Today*, 25 April.
Rigdon, M.L., and A.S. Levine. 2018. 'Gender, Expectations, and the Price of Giving', Review of Behavioural, *Economics* 5: 39–59.

Riley, A. 2009. *Selfish Pigs*. London: Hodder & Stoughton.
Robbins, J. 2004. *Becoming Sinners: Christianity and Moral Torment in a Papua New Guinea Society*. Berkeley: University of California Press.
———. 2007. 'Between Reproduction and Freedom: Morality, Value, and Radical Cultural Change', *Ethnos: Journal of Anthropology* 72(3): 293–314.
———. 2018. 'Where in the World Are Values? Exemplarity, Morality and Social Process', in J. Laidlaw, B. Bodenhorn and M. Holbraad (eds), *Recovering the Human Subject*. Cambridge: Cambridge University Press, pp. 174–92.
Roth, V. 2011. *Divergent*. New York: Harper Collins. Film adaptation 2014, Summit Entertainment.
———. 2012. *Insurgent*. New York: Harper Collins. Film adaptation 2015, Summit Entertainment.
———. 2013. *Allegiant*. New York: Harper Collins. Film adaptation 2016, Summit Entertainment.
Rousseau, B. 2016. 'Corpses, Pythons, Sleep Deprivation: Meditation Rituals in Thailand Can Be Intense', *The New York Times*, 31 August.
Rubin, E.L. 2015. *Soul, Self, and Society: The New Morality and the Modern State*. Oxford: Oxford University Press.
Sacks, O. 2019. 'The Machine Stops: The Neurologist on Steam Engines, Smartphones, and Fearing the Future', *The New Yorker*, 11 February.
Sahlins, M. 1985. *Islands of History*. Chicago: University of Chicago Press.
Sandberg, S., and A. Grant. 2016. 'On the Myth of the Catty Woman', *The New York Times*, 23 June.
Sanders, B. 1992. 'Rep. Bernie Sanders (I-VT): A Small Step for the 99%', clip from C-Span, https://www.c-span.org/video/?c4544765/rep-bernie-sanders-small-step-99. Accessed 22 November 2019.
———. 2015. 'Corporate Greed Must End', *Huff Post*, 24 June.
Scharlin-Pettee, H. 2016. 'On the Grind with the Women of Magic: The Gathering', 16 January, https://broadly.vice.com/en_us/article/the-women-of-magic-the-gathering. Accessed 22 November 2019.
Schwartz, T. 2013. 'The Antidote to Emptiness', *The New York Times*, 26 July.
Scott, S. 1996 [1766]. *The History of Sir George Ellison*. Lexington: The University Press of Kentucky.
Scull, A. 2018. 'All You Need Is Not Love: Are We Really Hard-Wired to Feel Other People's Pain?', *Times Literary Supplement*, 13 April, 3–4.
Shaheen, S. 2013. 'Did Thatcher Make Britain a More Selfish Country?', *Left Foot Forward*, 15 April.
Shane, S. 2016. 'Combative, Populist Steve Bannon Found His Man in Donald Trump', *The New York Times*, 27 November.
Shaw, A. (ed.). 2015. *Selfless Self: Talks with Shri Ramakant Maharaj*. Selfless Self Press.
Sheffer, K. 2016. *Selfless Development: How to Find Your Purpose*. Createspace Independent Publishing Platform.
Sherwood, H. 2017. 'Nearly 50% Are of No Religion – But Has UK Hit "Peak Secular"?', *The Guardian*, 14 May.
Shragai, N. 2013. 'Life with a Narcissistic Manager', *The Financial Times*, 28 October.
Shumaker, W. 1952. *Elements of Critical Theory*. Berkeley: University of California Press.
Singh, T., dir. 2015. *Self/Less*. Endgame Entertainment.
Singer, P. 1993. *Practical Ethics*, 2nd ed. Cambridge: Cambridge University Press.
———. 2015. *The Most Good You Can Do: How Effective Altruism Is Changing Ideas about Living Ethically*. New Haven, CT: Yale University Press.

Smedes, L.B. 1978. *Love within Limits: Realizing Selfless Love in a Selfish World*. Grand Rapids, MI: William B. Eerdmans Publishing Company.

Smith, D. 2016. 'Donald Trump: The Making of a Narcissist', *The Guardian*, 16 July.

Smith, S.A. 2014. *Your Life Isn't for You: A Selfish Person's Guide to Being Selfless*. San Francisco: Berrett-Koehler Publishers.

Sober, E., and D.S. Wilson. 1998. *Unto Others: The Evolution and Psychology of Unselfish Behavior*. Cambridge, MA: Harvard University Press.

Soutschek, A., C.J. Burke, A. Raja Beharelle et al. 2017. 'The Dopaminergic Reward System Underpins Gender Differences in Social Preferences' *Nat Hum Behav* 1, 819–827. doi:10.1038/s41562-017-0226-y.

Spanier, G. 2016. 'Amazon UK's Annual Sales Hit £6.3 Billion', *Campaign*, 1 February.

Spitz, M. 2016. 'What Would Mrs. Brady Do? "Bad Moms" Takes on Modern Motherhood', *The New York Times*, 28 July.

Steinberg, A. 2015. 'The Murky Meaning of the Killer Selfie', *The New York Times*, 11 December.

Stone, D. 2012. *How to Raise Selfless Kids in a Self-Centered World*. Nashville, TN: Thomas Nealson, Inc.

Storr, W. 2018. *Selfie: How We Became So Self-Obsessed and What It's Doing to Us*. London: Picador.

Strathern, M. 1980. 'No Nature, No Culture: The Hagen Case', in C. MacCormack and M. Strathern (eds), *Nature, Culture and Gender*. Cambridge: Cambridge University Press, pp. 174–222.

Stuurman, S. 2017. *The Invention of Humanity Equality and Cultural Difference in World History*. Cambridge, MA: Harvard University Press.

Sutcliffe-Braithwaite, F. 2013. 'Margaret Thatcher, Individualism and the Welfare State', *History and Policy*, 15 April.

Swaine, J., O. Laughland and B. Jacobs. 2016. 'Entering the Orbit of a "Total Narcissist": Who's Who in Donald Trump's Inner Circle', *The Guardian*, 15 April.

Swindoll, C.R. 2009. *Moses: A Man of Selfless Dedication*. Nashville, TN: Thomas Nealson, Inc.

Tanthapanichakoon, W. 2015. *World's Selfless Leaders – Mahatma Gandhi, Mother Teresa, Nelson Mandela, Martin Luther King Jr.: How Selfless Leadership Moved the Whole Nation and Its People without Money and Political Power*. Self-published.

Tempany, A. 2010. 'When Narcissism Becomes Pathological', *Financial Times*, 4 September.

The Daily Mail Reporter. 2014. 'Kris Jenner Blasts Daughter Kim Kardashian for Taking 1,200 Selfies during Thailand Trip', https://www.dailymail.co.uk/tvshowbiz/article-2710132/Kris-Jenner-blasts-daughter-Kim-Kardashian-taking-1-200-selfies-Thailand-trip.html.

Thompson, D. 2014. 'How You, I, and Everyone Got the Top 1 Percent All Wrong: Unveiling the Real Story Behind the Richest of The Rich', *The Atlantic*, 30 March.

Tornambe, R. 2010. 'Under the Knife or on the Couch? When Narcissism and Plastic Surgery Collide', *Huffington Post*, 17 November.

Troy, G. 2005. *Morning in America: How Ronald Reagan Invented the 1980s*. Princeton, NJ: Princeton University Press.

Turkle, S. 2011. *Alone Together: Why We Expect More from Technology and Less from Each Other*. New York: Basic Books.

Twenge, J. 2006. *Generation Me: Why Today's Young Americans Are More Confident, Assertive, Entitled – and More Miserable than Ever Before*. New York: Simon Schuster.

Twenge, J.W., and K. Campbell. 2009. *The Narcissism Epidemic: Living in the Age of Entitlement*. New York: Simon Schuster.
Vaknin, S. 2011. 'Narcissists and Hotel Maids: The Strauss-Kahn Affair and Beyond' mentalhealthmatters.com, 1 August.
_____. 2013. *Malignant Self-Love: Narcissism Revisited*. Czech Republic: Narcissus Publications.
Valenti, J. 2016. 'Jill Harth's Allegations against Trump Paint a Picture of an Entitled Narcissist', *The Guardian*, 20 July.
Watson, A. 2019. 'Religious books sales revenue in the U.S. 2017–2018', 30 October, https://www.statista.com/statistics/251467/religious-books-sales-revenue-in-the-us/. Accessed 22 November 2019.
Watterson, E. 2010. *Selfish or Selfless: Which One Are You?* Self-published e-book. SON Enterprises.
Wayne, T. 2016. 'Voting Narcissistic Sociopath – Until Now', *The New York Times*, 27 August.
Weale, A. 2016. 'Self-Centred: The Tension between the Morality of Higher Purpose and the Morality of Personal Fulfilment – A Review of Edward L. Rubin's *Soul, Self, and Society*', *Times Literary Supplement*, 29 July, 29.
Wellman, S. 2012. *Amy Carmichael (Heroes of the Faith)*. Uhrichville, OH: Barbour Publishing.
Wemple, E. 2015. 'When Narcissists Hug: O'Reilly and Trump Light Up Fox News Air', *The Washington Post*, 30 September.
West, J. 2015. *The Selfless Father: When a Man Says No to a Career and Yes to God and His Family*. Indianapolis, IN: Dog Ear Publishing.
Wilde, O. [1888] 2012. *The Selfish Giant*, illustrated by R. Voutila. Australia: Allen & Unwin.
Williams, R. 1973. *The Country and the City*. Nottingham, UK: Spokesman Books.
Williams, Z. 2016. 'Me! Me! Me! Are We Living through a Narcissism Epidemic? From Attention-Seeking Celebrities to Digital Oversharing and the Boom in Cosmetic Surgery, Narcissistic Behaviour Is All Around Us. How Worried Should We Be about Our Growing Self-Obsession?', *The Guardian*, 2 March.
Wilson, D.S. 2015. *Does Altruism Exist?* New Haven, CT: Yale University Press.
Wilson, E.O. 1975. *Sociobiology: The New Synthesis*. Cambridge, MA: Harvard University Press.
Wolfe, J. 2016. 'New York Today: Giving Tuesday', *The New York Times*, 29 November.
Wolff, M. 2015. 'Women in Magic: The Gathering', starcitygames.com, 15 June.
Wong, H. 2018. 'James Shaw Jr. on Why He Rushed the Waffle House Shooter: "He Was Going to Have to Work to Kill Me"', *The Washington Post*, 22 April.
Woolf, V. [1927] 1994. *To the Lighthouse*. Ware, Herts, UK: Woodsworth.
Young, H. 2013. 'Margaret Thatcher Left a Dark Legacy that Has Still Not Disappeared', *The Guardian*, 8 April.
Zavala, A.G. 2017. 'Welcome to the Age of Collective Narcissism: A Certain Mentality Has Been on Display in Western Democracies of Late – and We Don't Really Understand It', *The Independent*, 26 January.
Zembiec, P. 2014. *Selfless beyond Service: A Story about the Husband, Son and Father behind the Lion of Fallujah*. USA: Outskirts Press.
Zunk, J. 2016. 'Why Being Selfless Is Actually Selfish', *Huff Post*, 16 February.

Websites

https://en.wikipedia.org/wiki/Amazon.com
https://en.wikipedia.org/wiki/Narcissism
https://en.wikipedia.org/wiki/Narcissistic_personality_disorder
https://en.wikipedia.org/wiki/Me_generation
https://en.wikipedia.org/wiki/Me_Too_movement
https://en.wikipedia.org/wiki/The_Virtue_of_Selfishness
https://en.wikipedia.org/wiki/Marilyn_Monroe
https://en.wikipedia.org/wiki/Nathan_Hale
https://en.wikipedia.org/wiki/History_of_Wikipedia#2016
https://en.wikipedia.org/wiki/We_are_the_99%25
https://www.urbandictionary.com/define.php?term=corporate%20greed
https://en.wikipedia.org/wiki/Second_Great_Awakening
https://en.wikipedia.org/wiki/Urban_Dictionary
https://en.wikipedia.org/wiki/Onward,_Christian_Soldiers
https://www.japansociety.org/former_kamikaze_pilots_and_attack_survivor_attend_japan_societys_ny_premeire_documentary_screening
https://www.randomactsofkindness.org/the-science-of-kindness
http://plato.stanford.edu/entries/altruism-biological/
http://plato.stanford.edu/entries/biology-philosophy/
http://www.memecenter.com/tag/selfishness
https://www.pinterest.com/explore/selfish
http://www.last.fm/music/Selfish/+wiki
https://cosmicloti.com/.../thatchers-funeral-reply-with-the-light-that-drives-away-dark
http://www.newsworks.org.uk/The-Guardian
http://www.alexa.com/siteinfo/nytimes.com
https://www.zazzle.co.uk/s/selfish+abortion+bumperstickers
https://www.amazon.co.uk/Brandani-55243-Selfish-Design-Porcelain/dp/B009XT8AOC
https://rnli.org/find-my-nearest/lifeboat-stations/eastbourne-lifeboat-station
https://en.wikipedia.org/wiki/Selfish_Cunt
https://www.urbandictionary.com/define.php?term=selfish%20bitch
https://www.amazon.co.uk/Brandani-55242-Selfish-Design-Porcelain/dp/B009XT8AGU
http://occupylondon.org.uk/about/about-2/

2

'Sentiment Has Struggled with Selfishness'
Selfishness, Sensibility and Gender in the Late Eighteenth-Century British Antislavery Campaign

G.J. Barker-Benfield

During the four and a half centuries after 1492, twelve and a half million Africans were enslaved by Europeans, in collaboration with Africans on the coast (Eltis and Richardson 2010: xvii). James Walvin (2007: xv) writes that, 'by about 1750, slavery had established itself as an unquestioned institution in the British way of life. Hundreds of British ships, thousands of British sailors, tens of thousands of British settlers, not to mention British workers, merchants, financiers – and millions of consumers all depended on, or benefitted from slavery'. Notions of selfishness and selflessness were of central importance to those who opposed and those who defended the slave trade and slavery. The amount of slave-produced sugar, the most important of slave-produced goods, enjoyed annually by the average Briton went from 4 lbs in 1400 to 18 lbs by 1800 (Tomkins 2007: 77). How were metropolitan British consumers made significantly more aware of the terrible origins of what they consumed? How did many thousands of white Britons join the fifteen thousand or so of their black fellow inhabitants in seeing the enslavement of Africans as profoundly selfish and immoral? How was that view translated into political action, into abolition? In response, how did defenders of slavery turn the charge of selfishness against their critics?

Anglophone campaigners against slavery couched their argument in the language supplied by a culture of sensibility (Carey 2005). The word sensibility and its cognates had longstanding connotations of unselfishness. Generally speaking, the word sensibility meant a highly developed capacity for what speakers and writers called 'feeling'. This indicated the emotions invoked by consciousness of others – what can be called an instinctive relationship to other people. This sympathy might, at its best, motivate benevolent acts to relieve the distress of others. Cultivators of sensibility constantly attributed moral values to it; they saw themselves locked in opposition to selfish, immoral men (Barker-Benfield 1992).

The Origins of Sensibility versus Selfishness

The ideology of sensibility came into existence in opposition to the worldview expressed by the English philosopher Thomas Hobbes, above all in *Leviathan*, published in 1651. Hobbes wrote that man was 'in that condition which is called Warre': if 'not actually fighting', he was in 'the known disposition thereto' with no 'notion of Right or Wrong . . . Justice and Injustice are none of the Faculties neither of the Body or Mind'. In 'such a condition every man has a Right to every thing, even to one another's body', and thus could enslave another ([1651] 1968: 185, 186). Of all 'the voluntary acts of every man', in this state, and under the government formed to control such perpetual struggle, 'the object is some Good to himself'. Hobbes ([1651] 1968: 190) thus postulated a fundamental selfishness in human nature and affairs. In his introduction to *Leviathan*, C.B. MacPherson points out that Hobbes was using 'a mental model of society which . . . corresponds only to a bourgeois market society' ([1651] 1968: 37–39). It was a society, MacPherson continues, 'in which there are legal ways by which men can transfer some of the power of others to themselves, and in which everyone is peacefully engaged in seeking to get or resist this transfer and the capitalist market model is the only one that fits these requirements' (48). The state he advocated 'was designed not to deny men a life of competition and acquisition, but to ensure they could have it' (52). In Christopher Hill's words, 'Hobbes's man . . . is selfish' and Hobbes can be seen as 'the high priest of capitalism, stripping bare the essence of capitalist society' (1972: 313–14).

Hobbes stirred up a hornet's nest of clerical opposition fundamental to the rise of sensibility. Quentin Skinner (1966: 297) has pointed out that this was because Hobbes's was 'a point of view which was itself gaining increasingly in fashionable circles and in ideological importance'. In 1658, 'Hobbean' principles were said to 'destroy all relations between man and man' (314), a charge of particular relevance to our topic. A group of Anglicans known as Cambridge Platonists, followed by still more Anglicans known as Latitudinarians, created what R.S. Crane (1934: 221) called 'the propaganda of benevolence and tender feeling' to combat the dangerous political and moral doctrines of Thomas Hobbes. They were 'great preachers of the social virtues', declaring man 'good' (211). This was in direct refutation of Hobbes, who had said that 'men take pleasure to behold from the shore the danger of them that are at sea in a tempest, or in a fight', out of a passion for 'novelty and remembrance of our own security present' (219). His Latitudinarian opponents preached that God made man's nature 'to be affected with the Grief and with the Joy of those of his own kind; and to feel the Evils which others feel, that we may be universally disposed to help and relieve one another' (212). The word they frequently used for this disposition was 'humanity', a word which, in the eighteenth century, became virtually synonymous with having sensibility (Barker-Benfield 2010: 115–18).

Latitudinarians exhorted 'their hearers and readers to consider how enjoyable the benevolent emotions may be'. John Tillotson, the Latitudinarian

Archbishop of Canterbury, preached that there was 'no sensual Pleasure in the world that is comparable to doing good' (quoted in Campbell 1987: 103). Implicitly, that kind of pleasure had to compete with the alarming increase in the number of sensual pleasures made available to many more people by the consumer revolution. The pleasure of doing good was constantly emphasized by humanitarians eager to gain public support. One minister termed it a 'pleasing Anguish that sweetly melts the Mind and terminates in a self-approving Joy' (Crane 1934: 217). Such talk made advocates of 'humanity' vulnerable to the charge of self-indulgence, indeed, of selfishness.

The preaching of benevolence, that is, of charitable activity based on sympathy, was part of continuous campaigns for the 'reformation of manners', rooted in the Protestant reformation. From the later seventeenth century through to the nineteenth, it was pushed by statute, proclamation and formally constituted societies, by sermons, and by a range of literature. Reformers attempted to stop blasphemy, swearing, perjury, drunkenness and profaning the Sabbath, and the cruel treatment of animals and all kinds of distressed people (Bahlman 1957). A primary concern was men's abusive treatment of women. Reformers of manners sought to combat mere self-interest – mere selfishness – by considering the circumstances of other people and eventually the social costs of unabashed commerce. It was part of a cultural struggle, one in which religious values were always prominent, and which continued well into the Victorian era. The antislavery campaign, 1780–1840, must be set in this context (Barker-Benfield 1992: ch. 2; Gatrell 2006: chs. 14–17).

One of the earliest critics of slavery and the slave trade, the Rev. Richard Baxter, illustrates that the contrast between selfishness and selflessness was not a simple one. Baxter was taken by Max Weber ([1920] 1958: ch. V) and R.H. Tawney ([1926] 1962: 219–24) to exemplify the Protestant ethic, itself a moral outlook associated with self-interest, even selfishness. Reflecting Calvinist precedents, Baxter (2000: I, chs. 9, 10) saw God as 'our owner, ruler, and benefactor, or absolute Lord, our most righteous governor, and our most loving father, or benefactor'. The repetition of benefactor, along with the attribution of lovingness, reminds us that Baxter was also one of Crane's divines, preaching the importance of the social affections. Baxter's encyclopaedic *Christian Directory*, published in 1673, urged his audience to 'ascetic' work, that is, devoted to God's glory. He adjured his congregation: 'Do all for God, and walk in holiness with him, and keep out selfishness, (the poison of your callings)' (2000: I, ch. 10).

Baxter wrote his book soon after Charles II chartered what became the Royal Africa Company. Its purpose was to trade in enslaved Africans, sold to men who were thereby relieved of having to work at all. Baxter declared slavers pirates and thieves, and those who bought slaves 'fitter to be called incarnate devils than Christians'. Those who kept 'their negroes and slaves ... from becoming Christians' openly declared 'that their worldly profit is their treasure and their god' (2000, vol I: 461). The slave trade was a component of the transatlantic system feeding the consumer revolution, already well established in Baxter's lifetime. As Walvin (2007: 7) explains, 'exotic items' were 'transformed from dazzling luxuries of the rich to the essentials of the common folk: tea, porcelain, and spices from Asia; ivory, wax, and gum from Africa; rice, tobacco, sugar and rum from the slave plantations of the Americas'. Many of these goods, made into commercial items, flowed into houses, transforming women's lives, depending, of course, on class. Among the fruits of consumerism was the proliferation of print and its corollary, literacy, sustained by the increasing manufacture of books and the establishment of bookstores and subscription libraries. Increasing numbers of women wrote and read poetry and fiction, and this propagated the domestic maternal ideology central to the culture of sensibility. Men were urged to be better husbands and fathers, civilized – softened – by and to sensibility (Barker-Benfield 1992: chs. 4, 5). Men who sympathized with women in these efforts at reform, however, were liable to the charge of 'effeminacy'. One 1675 writer had asked, in the context of the anti-Stoical compassion preached by Latitudinarians, 'Must we be guilty of effeminacy, to perform Acts of Generosity?' (quoted in Crane 1934: 216). The reform of men – making them into 'men of feeling' – was accompanied by the insistence that they were still manly, with greater mental power than women, who were seen as naturally more susceptible to feeling and less able to control it (Barker-Benfield 1992: chs. 3, 5, 6). Male opponents of slavery would feel this vulnerability very keenly even as they drew on the extraordinary support of female opponents. Female opponents of slavery were also vulnerable to charges of giving in to their feelings, by definition leading to a lack of sexual self-control.

Gendered Sensibility Enters the Debate over the Slave Trade

The Rev. Francis Hutcheson ([1728] 2002: 22), a leading opponent of Hobbesian 'selfishness', asserted that human nature included a 'moral sense'. As in the case of other senses, human beings experienced it as an immediate feeling: it was a central tenet of sensibility. Hutcheson applied this 'ethics of feeling' to slavery, thereby overthrowing 'the entire classical rationalization for slavery' (Sypher 1939: 263, 277). That rationalization had been developed and perpetuated by men who enjoyed the privilege of formal education. To base ethics on feeling instead was of immense value to those long denied such an education. Popular sentimental literature, significantly written and read by women, propagated the ethics of feeling (Barker-Benfield 1992: 258–66). The Scots' philosophical school of 'moral sense' was named for this psychological principle (Hirschman 1977: 100; see also Barker-Benfield 1992: 132–48).

Among Hutcheson's students was Adam Smith. Prior to *The Wealth of Nations* (1776), in which he is seen to have rationalized self-interest as a major motive in modern, anglophone capitalism, Smith published *The Theory of Moral Sentiments* (1759). This represented the most elaborate, philosophical account of sensibility, reflecting the dialectic between selfishness and selflessness.

Together, Smith's two books demonstrated his view that improved material conditions allowed parents to nourish sensibility in their children. It was a view shared by his fellow Scottish moralists, who, in the words of John Dwyer (1987: 5), 'elevated private life and the domestic circle, both as a protection against a commercial "society of strangers" and as an ideal environment for the stimulation of interactive sensibility'. In effect, their vision of childrearing and family dynamics attempted to harmonize and render moral the individualism that it also encouraged.

The first chapter of *The Theory of Moral Sentiments*, entitled 'Of Sympathy', opens with a refutation of inevitable, Hobbesian selfishness. 'How selfish so ever man may be supposed, there are evidently some principles in his nature, which interest him in the fortune of others, and render their happiness necessary to him, though he derives nothing from it except the pleasure of seeing it' ([1759] 1982: 9). This was the pleasure which Latitudinarians had declared was part of human nature. Smith illustrates such un- or anti-selfish, pleasurable principles with 'pity or compassion, the emotion which we feel for the misery of others, when we either see it, or are made to conceive it in a very lively manner' (9). Smith's invocation of the non-blood kin relation of the brotherhood of all drew on the enlightenment ideal, the 'universal family held together by affection ... blunting the force' of individualism, in the face of the rise of commercial capitalism (9). Sentimental novels also hypostasized non-blood kinship, among women too, and they were celebrated when they extended 'maternal' emotional qualities beyond their own families. Nonetheless, the second paragraph of Smith's *Theory of Moral Sentiments* warned that even though 'our brother is upon the rack, as long as we ourselves are at our ease, our senses will never inform us of what he suffers' (9).

Smith's warning of the insensibility into which 'ease' can lull us was to be picked up by antislavery writers. The audience for the debate over the slave trade enjoyed not only 'selfish ease', in antislavery poet Hannah More's ([1784] 1787: 182) phrase, but luxury goods produced by the slave labour of Africans. How, then, to break through? 'Our senses', Smith ([1759] 1982: 9) had continued, 'never can carry us beyond our own person, and it is by the imagination only that we can form any conception of what are his sensations'. Imagination must act, 'by representing to us what would be our own [sensations] if we were in his case ... By the imagination we place ourselves in his situation, we conceive ourselves enduring all the torments, ... and even feel something, which though weaker in degree, is not altogether unlike them'. Impelled, then, by what Smith, among many others, held to be a natural human quality, simple selfishness could be transcended, and one might identify with another human being in his happiness but, more insistently, in his sufferings.

The words 'brother', 'we' and 'his body' alert us to Smith's gender inflection, although he sees his subject as human nature. Later in the book he turns more expressly to gender. First, he praises 'moderated sensibility', in contrast to 'excessive sensibility', and declares that moderated sensibility 'to the misfortunes of others does not disqualify us for the performance of any duty'. Smith has males in mind, telling his readers, 'Our sensibility to the feelings of others, far from being inconsistent with the manhood of self-command, is the very principle upon which it is founded' (Smith [1759] 1982: 143, 152). This was in keeping with the reformation of male manners (Barker-Benfield 1992: 109–19; Gatrell 2006: 20).

Smith contrasts this manly, moderated sensibility with the uncontrollable kind in men of weak nerves. This can be compared to what Smith ([1759] 1982: 143) then writes of women. Grouping generosity, public spirit and justice together, he asserts, 'Generosity is different from humanity . . . Humanity is the virtue of a woman, generosity of a man. The fair sex, who have commonly more humanity than ours, have seldom so much generosity'. Smith pursues his invidious definition of 'humanity', as consisting 'merely in the exquisite fellow-feeling which the spectator entertains with the sentiments of the person principally concerned, so as to grieve for their sufferings, to resent their injuries, and to rejoice at their good fortune'. He explains 'merely': the most humane actions required no self-denial, no self-command, male qualities. Women's apparent humanity is instinctive, the unmediated reflexes of their nervous systems. 'They consist only in doing what the exquisite sympathy would of its own accord prompt us to do' (152). The pronoun tells the reader that men are capable of sympathy, too, but they are also capable of self-denial, that is, of subordinating feeling to will. While they were capable of sympathy, women were incapable of unselfish actions (156, 190–91). The gendering of sensibility long predated Smith, but he elaborated it and his theory was widely influential in the period of the debate over slavery. His gender distinction would prove a problem for the women of sensibility who accused slave owners and slave traders of selfishness. It allowed pro-slavery writers to accuse such women of mere self-indulgence, mere selfishness, themselves.

Sterne and Sancho's Application of Smithian Sympathy to Antislavery

Lawrence Sterne, a Latitudinarian minister as well as a great novelist, was the writer most influential in making sensibility the dominant literary fashion in the last third of the eighteenth century (Howes 1971: ch. 2). The letter that African Briton Ignatius Sancho wrote to him in 1766 to ask him further to raise his influential literary voice on behalf of slaves illustrates the application of Smithian sympathy to antislavery. Sancho quotes Sterne's sermon on Job: 'Consider how great a part of our species – in all ages down to this – have been trod under the feet of cruel and capricious tyrants, who would neither hear their cries, nor pity their distresses – consider slavery – what it is – how bitter a draught – and how many millions are made to drink of it'. Sterne, 'of all my favorite authors', is the only one 'to draw a tear in favour of my miserable black brethren', importuning him to 'think in me you behold the uplifted hands of my brother Moors' (Sancho [1982] 1998: 73–74). It is 'our species' to which Sterne and Sancho both belong, and here he asks Sterne to extend his sympathy to his brothers as Sancho himself has, Smith-style.

Another sermon Sancho called to Sterne's attention clearly reflects Smith's *Theory of Moral Sentiments*. Calling Sterne 'an epicurean in acts of charity', Sancho declares, 'Philanthropy, I adore', that is, Sterne's charity sermon, 'Philanthropy Recommended' (Sancho [1982] 1998: 73–74). Its subject is Christ's parable of the Good Samaritan, whereby an ethnic enemy of the Jews crosses the street to succour a Jew, lying robbed and injured in the street, after two of his own kind have passed him by. The parable's moral is 'that we should worship the Lord our God with all our hearts, and love our neighbour as ourselves', a moral which Smith's urging 'us' to enter our brother's body resembles and perhaps echoes (Sterne 1996: 21).

Sterne putting himself in the shoes – or body – of the distressed Jew held particular meaning for Sancho, whose other letters expressed his consciousness of his blackness of complexion, even as they asserted the common ground of human feeling. Sterne's Samaritan continued: 'he is a Jew and I am a Samaritan – But are we not both men? partakers of the same nature – and subject to the same evils? – let me change conditions with him for a moment and consider, had his lot befallen me . . .'. Then, still more germane to Sancho's imagining Sterne's sympathy for him and his suffering black, West Indian brethren: 'misfortunes are of no particular tribe or nation, but belong to us all, and have a general claim upon us, without distinction of climate, country or religion' (Sterne 1996: 28). As Sancho had praised Sterne for already having drawn a tear in favour of his black brethren, so Sterne's philanthropic Samaritan says of the member of the different 'tribe' he helps, 'I shall soften his misfortunes by dropping a tear of pity over them' (22). This is an example of 'universal benevolence', and an exhortation 'to kindness and humanity', those terms reminding us of the Rev. Sterne's Latitudinarian predecessors' views (21). In fact, Crane (1934: 229) links Sterne's alter ego, Parson Yorick, the person under whose name Sterne published his *Sermons*, to these predecessors. According to Sterne, when we witness the kind of misfortunes the Samaritan came across, 'at first sight we generally make them our own . . . from a certain generosity and tenderness of nature which disposes us for compassion, abstracted from all consideration of self' (1996: 21). This is a virtual paraphrase of Smith; so, too, 'one would think it impossible for man to look upon misery, without finding himself in some measure attached to the interest of him who suffers it'. But there were those who passed by the victim in distress. Sterne presents such people as unnatural, inhuman, 'formed either of such impenetrable matter, or wrought by habitual selfishness to such an utter insensibility of what became of their fellow creatures, as if they were not partakers of the same nature or had no connection with the species' (1996: 23). The contrary behaviour to such selfishness 'is represented by our Saviour operating like the warm zeal of a brother . . .'. That the 'propensity to pity the unfortunate' is called 'humanity' stands for the fact that it is 'inseparable from our nature', and 'instances of selfish tempers' do not contradict that fact: 'a man must do great violence to himself, and suffer . . . painful conflict, before he has brought himself to a different disposition' (29).

Women, Sensibility and Selfishness

So far, I have referred to the self-assertiveness of men: the selfish competitors described by Hobbes and those who opposed them. What of women's self-assertiveness? The 'autonomous hedonism' of modern consumerism described by sociologist Colin Campbell (1987) was available to women as well as men. Public activities sponsored by the consumer revolution (depending on income) included shopping, visiting, attending assemblies, balls and masquerades, displaying styles of dress and hair, their preparations enjoyed privately, in all of which women could be seen either as following fashion or literally taking pleasure in themselves, as well as entering the marriage market. These activities should be borne in mind when considering the charge of 'self-indulgence' made against exponents of sensibility, or that it was merely a fashion (Barker-Benfield 1992: chs. 4, 6).

Above all, the cultivation of sensibility could lead to greater self-consciousness, publicly registered in art, in the novels of Richardson and Sterne, and in the literature published by so many women (Barker-Benfield 1992: 127–8, 191–99, 236–37, 270; Brissenden 1974; Meyer 1987: Introduction and *passim*; Spencer 1986; Watt 1963). According to Campbell (1987: 156), reading and writing such literature could be 'totally subjectivist; an individual's intuitive sense was unique to him' – or to her. Some of these writers asserted the moral and intellectual equality of women and therefore may be called feminists.

Whenever women raised their heads above the parapet by entering the public sphere personally, and especially by publication, they were accused of sexual self-assertion. After all, the explanation for their subordination was sexual difference. Women's reading was uncontrollable and readers were seen to be inflamed in accordance with the psychophysiology of sensibility, and thereby prone to masturbation, seduction, adultery and prostitution (Smith [1776] 1979: 81–82).[1] Historian Margaret Jacob (1993: 165) notes evidence suggestive of the acknowledgement of women's own appetite for sexual pleasure, and not just male writers' fantasies. It seems, too, that some women took greater control of their reproductive lives in the Revolutionary era (Barker-Benfield 1992: 326–30; Klapp 2009).

Women (and men) could be corrupted by the fashion of sensibility. That this was the case and that these dangers were identifiable with selfishness was expressed in 'On the Affectation of Sentiment and Sensibility', published in the *Universal Magazine of Knowledge and Pleasure* in London in February 1791. The author, C.W., wrote that 'fashion is not less consulted in the embellishments of sentiments and opinion than in the furbelows and gewgaws that disguise the sex they are intended to beautify and adorn'. He looked back to Richardson's heroines, Pamela and Clarissa, as early inspirations for women to 'expose themselves to temptation'. Still more dangerous were the subsequent 'school' of sentimental novelists, above all the Rev. Sterne who, in *A Sentimental Journey* (1768), included a series of virtually sexual encounters presented in the language of sensibility by its narrator, Yorick, with whom Sterne identified himself. According to C.W., Sterne had poisoned 'his age and his country with the most universal affectation of sensibility' (C.W. 1791: 128–29).

C.W. writes that Sterne's relationship with Eliza Draper,[2] manifest in posthumously published letters, heightened 'the stolen enjoyments of adultery with scraps of morality'. Both sexes imitated Sterne's characters, and were led to sexual intercourse: 'soft-sighing virgins melting without compassion', that is, merely with sensuality. This, wrote C.W., was the abuse of 'heavenly Sensibility!' which he apostrophizes: 'And though vanity may ape thy fair deportment, the fine vibration of thy soul accord not with the wild tumults of licentious guilt; nor can the delicate softness of thy nerves endure the rude changes of intemperate pleasure, or the giddy whirl of dissipated affectation' (C.W. 1791: 128–29).

The trouble was that genuine and affected sensibility operated according to the same, material, psychophysiological model. Sensibility could either sponsor sincere sympathy and then action on the part of the distressed, or it could be merely 'selfish', self-indulgently 'sensual'. Virtuous, unaffected sensibility was relational, unselfish, in contrast to the affected, self-pleasuring selfishness of affected sensibility.

In fact, Sterne himself had presented the 'strait-hearted wretch', who is 'confined within himself, – feels no misfortunes, but those which touch himself', as an illustration of 'selfishness and meanness'. To characterize the whole human race that way, he had continued, 'could serve no end but the routing out of our nature all that is generous, and planting in the stead of it such an aversion to each other, as must rob us of one of the greatest pleasures in it, the mutual communications of kind offices' (Sterne 1996: 67).

On the one hand, proponents of 'sensibility' urged women and men to be unselfish. On the other hand, they were vulnerable to accusations of selfishness. Because of the prominence of women among reformers, and because they challenged men's treatment of women (which traditionally was hard and selfish), the accusations levelled at them were fraught with sex. All of this was central to the debate over the slave trade and slavery.

Antislavery Bluestockings Counter Smith's View of Women, Ambivalently

Sancho had praised one other writer, in addition to Sterne, for arousing sympathy for enslaved blacks. She was the anonymous author of the sentimental novel, *The History of Sir George Ellison* (1766), in fact Sarah Scott, who in that novel and others wished to demonstrate that women – well-educated ladies – were as capable of relieving the distressed as men. While she made the distinction between active and inactive compassion, she argued that both sexes were capable of either. This directly contradicted Adam Smith's view of women.

With predecessors dating back to the later seventeenth century, Scott and her contemporary feminists were called 'Bluestockings' from the 1750s. They came from the middle and upper classes and endorsed patriarchal hierarchy, but they asserted intellectual equality of women and its corollary, the improvement of female education. Along with other writers and preachers, all proponents of sensibility, they attacked the double standard and urged husbands and fathers to treat wives and children with respect and sympathy (Kelly 2001; Scott [1976] 2001: 11–46; Scott [1766] 1996: 25). This was part of what Paul Langford (1989: 463–67) calls 'the Sentimental Revolution', promulgating a galaxy of reforms to aid distressed people, and extending to animals, of which the antislavery campaign was the culmination.

Later Bluestockings included Hannah More and Mary Wollstonecraft, both antislavery writers, although they differed fundamentally over women's public roles and the equality of the sexes (Mellor 2000; Stott 2003; Sutherland 1991). Although More remained unmarried and raised her voice publicly against slavery, her 1784 poem 'Sensibility' suggests the domestic sphere was where other women belonged.

> From the large aggregate of little things;
> Of these small cares of daughter, wife, or friend,
> The almost sacred joys of Home depend:
> There SENSIBILITY, thou best may'st reign,
> HOME is thy true legitimate domain.

'Feeling' was to be generated there by mothers who embodied self-subordination, if not self-effacement. Such domesticity depended on prosperity, generated in large part by self-interest, by slavery, and by men's exploitation of paid workers, too, the poor from whose labours More benefitted and whom she wished to evangelize, even as she believed in keeping them in their place.

Her poem makes explicit the identification of 'Sensibility' with unselfishness, and reveals the vulnerability of those who presented themselves as upholders of sensibility to charges of mere affectation, of self-indulgence, in fact of selfishness, a vulnerability intensified by gender. More poses divine sympathy against 'the boast', 'the false feeling', which she personifies as female, versus the qualities of genuine sensibility she calls 'manly':

> While her fair triumphs swell the modish page,
> She drives the sterner virtues from the stage;
> While feeling boasts her ever-fearful eye
> Fair Truth, firm faith, and manly justice fly;
> Justice, prime good! From whose prolific law,

> All worth, all virtue, their strong essence draw.
> ...
> The sterling attribute [justice] we scarcely own,
> While spurious Candor fills the vacant throne.

Smith had included justice in his account of the sterner virtues with which men could temper their humanity, enabling them to behave unselfishly. Wollstonecraft ([1792] 1978: 121), who knew Smith's *Theory* well, declared indignantly that women 'have been stripped of the virtues which should clothe humanity', calling for the single, ungendered standard that the word 'humanity' could connote. In her poem, More maintains a 'we', identifying herself and women with justice against mere boast of feeling, although she believed strongly that all women were more susceptible to feeling than men. 'SWEET SENSIBILITY' is, More wrote, an 'Unprompted moral', the result of delicacy of nerves:

> Perception exquisite! Fair virtue's seed.
> The quick precursor of the lib'ral deed!

This was the vital connection, from the instinctive sympathy prompted by the moral sense, to action.

Compromise between Sensibility and Self-Interest: Antislavery Enters Parliament

More belonged to the evangelical group of reformers called the 'Teston circle' (Brown 2006). The early public voice of its antislavery efforts was the Rev. James Ramsay's. He attempted to reconcile humanity with self-interest, or, it can be said, a degree of selflessness with modified selfishness. Ramsay's *Essay on the Treatment and Conversion of African Slaves in the British Sugar Colonies*, published in 1784, became a turning point in the antislavery campaign: it made the issue the subject of a parliamentary enquiry which, in the long run, eventuated in the end of the slave trade. Ramsay had been an eyewitness of plantation slavery, having lived on the West Indies island of St. Christopher for many years (Brown 2006: 366–76).

But it is important to recognize that it was a woman, Lady Margaret Middleton, the wife of Ramsay's official patron, Sir Charles Middleton, who directed Ramsay to his antislavery project, writing to him about the Christianization of his slaves. His reply was the nub of his *Essay*, published after his return to England where Elizabeth Bouverie, Lady Margaret's close collaborator in evangelical reforms, gave Ramsay his living at Teston. Lady Margaret asked Sir Charles, who passed on the request to William Wilberforce, a fellow MP, to bring the issue of slavery into parliament. He became the leading parliamentary voice until the passage of the Act for the Abolition of the Slave Trade in 1807 (Brown 2006: 346–47; Tomkins 2007: 55).

Christopher Leslie Brown judges Lady Middleton's impact to have been 'decisive'. He suggests that like other reform-minded women, 'her triumph lay in finding a male authority figure to carry on her work so that the issues involving salvation and black potential would not be clouded with what she saw as empty controversy over who or what sex acted'. Some key ideas in Ramsay's book were expressed by Lady Middleton in her letters. Brown quotes a later visitor to Barham Court who told his daughter that the 'abolition of the slave trade was . . . the work of a woman' (Brown 2006: 350–52, 349).

Lady Middleton working behind the scenes in this way may be aligned with other women's contributions to the antislavery campaign. Their role, scholars now declare, was 'absolutely central' (Davis 2007: 11). Yet in this 1780s phase, women did not sign the petitions delivered to the all-male MPs because women's signatures would 'delegitimize' them (Drescher 2009: 217). More told women that 'the legitimate domain' for the operation of their gendered 'SENSIBILITY' was 'HOME'. It was because of More's view of sharply gendered sensibility that she and other evangelicals, writes Claire Midgley, 'encouraged female contributions to antislavery literature to take the form not of tracts directed to the intellect but of poetic appeals to the heart' (Midgley 1997: 29). Forty years on, in the decisive phase of the campaign for the emancipation of slaves, women's signatures were accepted by parliament. In May 1833, 187,000 of them, termed by commentators 'one vast and universal expression of feeling from all the females of the United Kingdom', was 'hauled into the House [of Commons] amidst shouts of applause and laughter' (Drescher 2009: 250). Laughter should be historicized, in this case, men laughing at women's massive, decisive entry into politics. One MP there that day was a man of feeling, however: Irish MP Daniel O'Connell commented, 'Assuredly the crying grievance of slavery must have sunk deep into the hearts, and strongly exerted the feelings of the British nation before the females of this country could have laid aside the retiredness of their character to . . . interfere with political matters'. O'Connell juxtaposed those feelings with the violence of male overseers: the man 'who taunts the females of Great Britain with having petitioned Parliament . . . was almost as great a ruffian as the wielder of the cart-whip'. Drescher makes the point that women defeated male laughter with an apparent paradox: 'The perceived attributions of femininity were used to rationalize women's self-assertion' (2009: 250, 249). Those attributions included gendered sensibility, which connoted selflessness, yet was here turned to public purposes.

Throughout his *Essay on the Treatment and Conversion of African Slaves* (1784a: xv, 86, 88, 92, 147, 161, 19), Ramsay describes slave masters and white overseers as 'unfeeling' in their treatment of slaves, in contrast to himself and to the humane readership to whom his work is addressed. Ramsay tells them that slavery 'needs only to be laid open or exposed in its native colours, to command the abhorrence and opposition of every man of feeling and sentiment' (1784a: xv, 86). Masters are 'our countrymen' but, 'without law or religion', are left, 'each to be guided by his own changeable temper, and to be influenced by . . .

self-interest . . .' (1784a: 19, 108–9). Ramsay repeatedly presents slave masters as selfish, without the capacity to put themselves in the place of others, to sympathize with them, the very definition of sensibility and humanity. Their selfishness is literally opposed to any common good. Ramsay writes that in 'order to become a good member of society', man 'must be inspired by religious principles that he may not counteract the common views, out of secret fraud, malice, or selfishness, but be carried on to every generous exertion by which the public happiness may be effected' (1784a: 190, 142–43, 151).

It is not surprising, given the historical origins of the values the antislavery writers brought to bear on a system they saw motivated entirely by greed, that their pictures of slave society resembled the worlds Hobbes had depicted. In his widely distributed *An Essay on the Slavery and Commerce of the Human Species, Particularly the African* ([1786] 2010), Thomas Clarkson wrote that enslaved Africans were 'perpetually at war in their hearts with their oppressors and are continually cherishing the seeds of revenge', although this was because they were made so by being 'forcibly torn from their country, and are retained . . . by violence'. On the master's side, '*Self-preservation* . . . demands the most rigorous *severity*', given the disproportion between, say, '*one* master and *fifty* slaves. Masters must adopt a system of tyranny and oppression' ([1786] 2010: 114, emphasis in original).

Ramsay held that 'conformity with revealed religion supposed a conquest over the selfish passions', but even disregarding the 'irreligion' of forcing slaves to work on Sundays, 'to fill the bags of avarice, to supply the funds of luxury', he exclaimed with outrage, 'what impudence respecting society, doth it imply, when a private man sets his selfish opinion up against the laws of his country, and dares to insult them publickly, by acting in direct opposition to our express statute' (1784a: 277, 146–47).

Ramsay's proposal is in fact a compromise with the selfishness he believes is inevitable. He argues repeatedly that humanity and self-interest go together. It was an idea that Lady Middleton had expressed to him. She 'rejected the suggestion that gospel preaching should interfere with the accumulation of profits' (Brown 2006: 350–51). Like the preceding Latitudinarians, she was willing to reconcile religion with commercial, individualistic capitalism. She insisted, in her words, that the gospel 'would be the most profitable means of making slaves diligent and faithful for it would awaken conscience in them to be a strict overseer, and a severe monitor, whom they could not evade'. She expressed the corollary that to treat slaves in a Christian – humane – way, to 'cooperate with [God's] benevolence in promoting the happiness of his fellow creatures', would preserve slave owners' investment. Ramsay published this letter (written in 1768) in his *Essay*.

In some places, however, Ramsay denies the effectiveness of 'self-interest' in motivating slave masters' treatment of their slaves. But elsewhere he argues that masters will find that the humane treatment of slaves, for example cutting Sunday work hours, feeding them properly, increasing the size of gangs, and thereby 'the vigour and industry of the slaves ... would in time improve his property greatly'. That improvement included a natural increase in numbers. If instead of wearing slaves out, their 'animal powers' are increased 'with proper care and nourishment', slave owners will not have 'to make constant demands on the slave market' (Ramsay 1784a: 44–45, 186–87, 91n, 58–59). He elaborated this point the same year in a briefer work, *Inquiry into the Effects of Putting a Stop to the African Slave Trade*, which Brown (2006: 375) notes was 'the first sustained attempt in twenty years to describe abolition as wise commercial policy'. Ramsay's combination of humanity and the language of sensibility with more reasoned, more political argument is noteworthy, parallel to the combination of humanity and self-interest.

To reform the unfeeling, physical brutality of slavery was one aspect of the more humane treatment of Africans urged by Ramsay, which would prepare them for their conversion to British Protestantism, the major goal of Ramsay and Lady Middleton. A second was the establishment of the kind of family life that reformers in Britain (including Smith) upheld; it was the location for the generating of sensibility, of greater selflessness in human relationships. Very early in his *Essay*, Ramsay writes: 'Even in the savage state, custom, which leaves men on a footing of equality have enslaved wives' (1784a: xv). That marriage enslaved women had been a persistent theme among English writers for over a century at least. We can see its perpetuation not just in Bluestocking feminism but as the express purpose of the whole culture of sensibility, to reform men (Barker-Benfield 1992: ch. 2).

Ramsay's next sentence, after the word 'wives', goes to the related dimension of the culture of sensibility, its assertion of the social significance of marriage, here applied to African slaves in Britain's sugar colonies. 'Among our negro slaves, he who cannot attach to himself, a wife, or subdue any other creature, buys some half starved dog, over whom he may exercise his tyrannic disposition'. Ramsay wishes to show the reader the necessity of advancing the slave 'in the scale of social life, before we offer him a participation of our religion'. These 'creatures' ... only motive of action is present feeling'. The 'negroes' are immersed in sense, their intellectual powers wholly employed in service of the body, unchecked, for example, by the kind of marriage that Ramsay assumed was a mark of civility and religion. This characteristic reflects their inhumane treatment, where they 'have no reputation to support, no lasting interest to care for'. At present, the enslaved African man 'may have what wives he pleased, and either of them may break the yoke at their caprice'. Slavery meant the slave had no more 'ties' than the master, and was, in this sexual respect at least, able to act entirely selfishly. Ramsay has the male slave in mind to implement this metropolitan, bourgeois ideal: 'Nothing would more humanize slaves, and improve their conditions, than their acquiring property in their wives and families' (Ramsay 1784a: 153, 173–75, 284). I leave aside the irony of this.

'Marriage', wrote Ramsay, 'or a family, is the embryo of society'; it 'contains the principles and seeds of every social virtue'. It was, as Smith had said, the place where children could be raised to consider others, African children, then, like their fathers, made sensitive to their 'dear relatives; even as in polished society'. Ramsay imagines African 'savages to be so far civilized' that 'their women [would be] treated with the regard that women generally receive in polished life, eased of labour, employed only in regulating their family', the desirable path, although such progress also could support mere 'idleness and amusement', the temptations to selfish behaviour with which selfless mothering had to compete. But, properly 'treated', socialized in fact, the precondition for the conversion that Ramsay and Lady Middleton saw as their chief goal, some qualified 'negroes' could preach 'feelingly' to their fellows (Ramsay 1784a: 284, 227, 185).

Those unfeeling, selfish, white, West Indian managers of slaves could also be reformed by marriage. Slavery would thus be made more humane: married managers alone could take proper care of the sick slaves. They 'stay more constantly at home, and have numberless advantages over single men in point of character, faithfulness and applications'. Such domesticated, self-disciplined slave masters, moreover, worked slaves more profitably. 'Yet planters have determined it to be better to employ perhaps a dissipated, careless, unfeeling young man, or a grovelling, lascivious old bachelor (each with his half score of black or mulattoe pilfering harlots . . .) rather than allow a married woman to be entertained at the plantation' (Ramsay 1784a: 82). It was a widespread view that marriage made bachelors more feeling, first towards their wives and then to their children (Barker-Benfield 2010: 181–82).

Ramsay found it necessary to tell his audience that 'he is not sensible of anything, sinister, selfish or censorious in view', in urging this 'reformation' of slavery. He had bemoaned that, 'We are exceedingly ready, it is the turn of the age, to express ourselves sorrowfully, when any act of oppression or unjust suffering, is related before us; the generous sentiment flows glibly off our tongues, charity seems to dictate every sympathizing phrase, and vanity comes cheerfully forward to make her offering'. More's poem, 'Sensibility', detailed such expressions of false sensibility, its sexual connotations laid out by C.W., the Sterne critic described above (Ramsay 1784a: 296).

Evidently, Ramsay and More, and all the others who levelled the charge of false feeling, hoped to provoke those who affected sensibility to make style into substance, turn self-indulgence into at least a degree of selflessness. Ramsay asks, 'who shall we find willing to sacrifice his amusements or his pleasures to obey the cause of humanity? Who to relieve the sufferings of the wretched slave . . . or to offer up selfish interest at the altar of mercy?' (Ramsay 1784a: 10).

Fostering Ties across the Colour Line

Ramsay had answered those last two questions about who was to sacrifice pleasures for humanity by saying that religion made earthly happiness depend on his doing all the good in his power 'to his brethren around him' (Ramsay 1784a: 151–52). The Society for Effecting the Abolition of the Slave Trade, formed in 1787, took for its motto, 'Am I Not a Man and a Brother?', the words placed around the figure of an enchained, supplicating, African man, together forming the Society's seal (Tomkins 2007: 60). In his *Essay* on slavery (1786), Clarkson wrote that Ignatius Sancho's 'letters are too well known to make any extract', and it is very plausible that in designing the seal, the committee, one of whose purposes was to distribute Clarkson's *Essay* (he was its 'most influential member') had in mind Sancho's words to Sterne: 'think in me you behold the uplifted hands of the thousands of my brother Moors' (Sancho [1982] 1998: 74). Clarkson's *Essay* ([1786] 2010: 126) stated emphatically that 'the first doctrine' that Christianity 'inculcates in us is brotherly love'. Most of the committee were Quakers, influenced, as was Clarkson, by Benezet, his city (Philadelphia) named for brotherly love by William Penn (Walvin 2011: 169).

Of course, the Quakers themselves were avatars of the Protestant ethic, among other enterprises engaged very profitably in the slave trade, before Woolman and Benezet decisively reformed them (Soderlund 1985). Weber, who coined the term 'the Protestant Ethic', and described its propagation by Calvinism, suggested that it was 'brotherly love' that helped make work 'ascetic', somehow redeeming the fact that Calvinism tended 'to tear the individual away from the closed ties with which he is bound to this world'. Brotherly love evinced 'the wonderfully purposeful organization of this cosmos ... designed by God to serve the utility of the human race' (Weber [1920] 1958: 108–9). One can see here the relationship between such a view and Smith's in *The Wealth of Nations*, juxtaposed with what he had said of the natural, inner dynamic towards brotherhood in *The Theory of Moral Sentiments*. Modern men, famously motivated by the self-interest that liberates economic energies, would unconsciously benefit socially from the 'Hidden Hand', operating within human nature like the Protestant God of predestination. It would moderate the selfishness associated with Hobbes, as well as Calvin and the Protestant ethic. Ramsay's remarks on self-interest and selfishness seem influenced by Smith ([1776] 1979: 11, 27).

So, too, is Clarkson's *Essay*, and it seems clear that the Abolition Society's motto referred to Smith's exemplary operation of sympathy, as well as connoting the enlightenment, non-kin familial ideal which had informed it. The committee and Clarkson extended this resonant trope to enslaved Africans, as Sancho had in that 1766 letter to Sterne, subsequently published in Sterne's *Letters* (1775) and Sancho's *Letters* (1782). Given the dramatic impact on the antislavery campaign of the sensational trial in 1783 of the master of the slave ship, the *Zong*, who had murdered 132 Africans by throwing them into the Atlantic for the insurance money, dramatizing the routine killings of Africans that was part of the process of enslavement, the motto may also have invoked God's question to the fratricide Cain: 'Where is Abel, thy brother?' (Walvin 2011: 10–11; Genesis, 4:9–10).

To this should be added the perspective of More's poem 'Slavery', published in 1788. She adjured her readers to imagine the actions of the 'petty tyrants', slaving on the African coast, 'See the fond links of feeling nature broke', contrasting them with the actions of men of feeling, Captain Cook and William Penn:

> . . . thy social hands
> Had link'd dissever'd worlds in brotherhood,
> Careless, if colour, or if clime divide.

More, like Ramsay, still looked to a British empire, but one of liberty and Protestantism, to which Ramsay added transatlantic free trade, including Africans in Africa supplying raw materials and a market for Britain's manufacturing goods, replacing the now lost mainland America (1784a: 295; 1784b: 15–20, 33, 39).

Clarkson's friend and fellow abolitionist, Josiah Wedgwood, pioneer manufacturer and advertiser, reproduced the 1787 seal on a jasper, cameo medallion, donating hundreds to the Society (McKendrick 1988). Clarkson recorded: 'Ladies wore them in bracelets, and others had them fitted up in an ornamental manner as pins for their hair'. The seal was put on snuff boxes and cufflinks, too, as well as printed on posters and in magazines. He continued: 'At length the taste for wearing' those pins and bracelets, 'because general and thus fashionable, which usually confines itself to worthless things, was seen for once in the honorable office of promoting justice, humanity, and freedom'. Women, debarred from formal political action, some of them finding resources for self-assertion in fashion – but all liable to being figures of self-indulgence – advocated Smithian anti-selfishness on behalf of African slaves (Tomkins 2007: 65).

Throughout his 1786 *Essay*, Clarkson attempts to stimulate the process Smith had described, arousing 'the principle of nature' against selfishness. So, Clarkson presented the enslavement of Africans in 'the form of a narrative', and has himself and his readership 'suppose ourselves . . . on the shore of Africa, and relate a sense . . . presumed to have been presented to our view, had we been really there'. Accompanied by an African commentator, and watching a dusty procession of enslaved Africans, 'we indulged our imagination' to see a 'father, in another a husband, and in another a son'. If, as Clarkson tells the African, Christian Britain is, 'of all nations, the most remarkable for humanity and justice', why, the African asks, do they allow Africans to be enslaved 'to administer to . . . luxury and greatness?' Clarkson's answer expresses the intention of his *Essay*, and that of the antislavery campaign in general, to break through ease and selfishness by way of imaginative identification.

> Alas . . . can the cries and groans, with which the air now trembles, be heard across this extensive continent? . . . If they could reach the generous Englishman at home, they would pierce his heart . . . He would sympathize with you in your distress. He would be enraged at the conduct of his countryman and resist their tyranny. (Clarkson [1786] 2010: 93, 96, 97)

Another obvious question emerged from the application of Smithian sympathy to slaves: how were whites, so different in appearance from their African brother, 'to enter as it were into his body and become in some measure the same person with him', including bringing his 'agonies . . . home to ourselves', so that 'we then tremble and shudder at the thought of what he feels' (Smith [1759] 1982: 9). Didn't this body question, in context, call for a particular act of selflessness (one can say something identical regarding women's responsiveness)? Ramsay wrote, 'there is no difference between the intellects of whites and blacks, but such as circumstances and education naturally produce'. And God's purpose in creating differences in 'complexion and features' is somehow 'the binding of tribes and families together', ready for the ultimate 'union', as Christians and in heaven: all souls are made of 'the same simple substance', regardless of outward appearance and social status (Ramsay 1784a: 203). Clarkson devoted considerable space to the subject, countering the argument 'that the Africans are an inferior link of the chain of nature, and are designed for slavery' because of '*colour*, and those other marks, which distinguish them from the inhabitants of Europe' (emphasis in original). Clarkson said from the outset that slaves 'have the same feelings with ourselves', and having assessed current theories, concluded that 'climate is the cause of the difference of colour which prevails in the different inhabitants of the globe'. All 'mankind, however various their appearances are derived from the same stock', and he quotes the Bible: 'God, who hath made the world, hath made of one blood all the nations of men . . .' (Clarkson [1786] 2010: 126, 29, 139, 129, ch. VIII). Race, then, was no barrier to countering selfishness, as one entered the body of one's brother. It was not until the 1820s, apparently, that women adopted the motto, 'Am I Not a Woman and a Sister?' (Yellin 1989: 8–12).

Ramsay's Scheme Called Selfish

Ramsay called on parliament and the Church to implement the amelioration of slavery (resulting, he hoped, in the eventual ending of the slave trade, and even the emancipation of slaves), on the basis of that combination of humanity and self-interest to which I have referred. From the outset, he calls on his reader's 'benevolence, his conscience, his interest . . . in carrying on the work'. This signified politics in the large, out-of-doors sense. 'The people', half a million slaves, 'whose improvement is here proposed, toil for the British state'. The 'public' therefore, 'has an interest in their advancement in society'. Ramsay hoped that an increased number of Anglican ministers in the sugar colonies, improved and strengthened by metropolitan statute and funding, would mediate between masters and slaves, ministers and masters collaborating to ameliorate treatment of slaves, followed by their conversion. The combination of benevolence and self-interest, Ramsay believed, would procure for his 'scheme' a general prepossession in favour. 'While the man of feeling finds every generous sentiment indulged in the prospect which it opens, the politicians, the selfish, will all have their little wishes of opulence and accumulation realized'. Similarly, Ramsay is sure that 'the system taught by revelation' 'for the equal and gradual improvement' of mankind's 'common nature' will gain 'a favourable . . . hearing equally from the politician and philanthropist'. That last distinction was of fundamental significance to evangelical reformers (Ramsay 1784a: v, 208).

Ramsay acknowledges in his last chapter that what he proposes is not 'the best possible, but . . . the most practicable method, having respect to the selfishness and prejudices of the age'. He concedes in his Conclusion 'that he has not laid before the public . . . all I have thought . . . all I have written'. He has had to face a conflict between his moral feelings and a painful reality: 'sentiment has struggled with the selfishness of the age, and been obliged to suppress many a generous wish'. Ramsay added parallel contrasts: 'the feelings of benevolence have been forced to give way to the suggestions of narrow policy; and even a sense of the public interest has been forced to yield to private prejudice' (Ramsay 1784a: 264, 291).

But Ramsay found it necessary to defend himself against the accusation of selfishness. He declared he was not 'sensible of anything . . . selfish . . .' in urging the reformation of selfish slave owners. In acknowledging that affected sensibility was 'the turn of the age', Ramsay said of his whole plan, 'At the worst, it adds only one more to the many Utopian schemes that volunteer reformers produce for a heedless public' (Ramsay 1784a: 264). James Tobin, from the West Indies colony of Nevis, who was Ramsay's first and most persistent proslavery adversary, seized this as an opening (Brown 2006: 367–70). He presented himself and his 'friends', the West Indian sugar planters, as genuine men 'of sensibility'. According to Tobin, sugar planters treated their enslaved Africans with much greater humanity than British lords treated their peasants, a contrast he couched in conventionally sentimental terms, to draw sympathy for his views from his readers. He insisted on the innate inferiority of Africans (Tobin 1785: Preface, 5, 85–91). In fact, Tobin charged Ramsay with prejudice against white planters. Just as young ladies, particularly those of volatile disposition, can 'imbibe the most romantic notions', so Ramsay, a self-confessed 'speculative man', 'by indulging his own ideas, can bring forth the most chimerical projects even for the apparent good of mankind, though we are tempted to admire his philanthropy, we cannot but compassionate his ignorance of human nature', that is, of Africans. In short, Tobin explains Ramsay's misrepresentations by saying he has been led away by the warmth of his feeling to self-indulgence, detached from reality, the conventional way of denigrating unchecked sensibility. Tobin wished both to undercut the rhetoric of feeling that, typically, Ramsay brought to bear on slave owners, and to reverse his characterization of them as selfish (Tobin 1785: 148, 114–15).

On Selfishness and Effeminacy

Ramsay's contrast between politicians and philanthropists (figures associated respectively with selfishness and selflessness) represented an existential conflict for evangelicals thinking of acting politically. Brown addresses it in connection with the Teston circle, including Middleton, Ramsay, More and Wilberforce, to which Clarkson was also attached. The prime minister, William Pitt, wrote to Wilberforce, his friend, 'Can one be a serious Christian and retain public standing? Can a serious Christian act in the world without compromising faith?' Brown comments that this apparent conflict 'haunted' Wilberforce. To persuade him to take up antislavery politically, Pitt wrote, 'Surely the principles as well as the practice of Christianity are simple, and lead not to meditation only but to action' (Brown 2006: 383). This was another version of inactive versus active compassion that Sarah Scott had expressed.

In addition to that internal conflict, men who argued against slavery on the basis of feeling faced the charge of effeminacy that men of feeling had faced from the beginning (Alter 1788: 11; Carey 2005: 91). Wilberforce, an opponent said, had 'an effeminate face' (Williams [1941] 1994: 181). James Boswell's satirical 1791 poem, 'No Abolition of Slavery, or the Universal Empire of Love', impugned the manhood of antislavery MPs. Addressing one of them, he asked:

> Shall Thou, a Roman free and rough,
> Descend to weak *blue-stocking* stuff
> And cherish feelings soft and kind
> Till you emasculate your mind.

While there were other candidates, the 'blue-stocking stuff' may well refer to More, who wrote of her fellow women writers in 'Bas-bleu', 1786, two years before her 'Slavery'.

The title of Boswell's poem indicated that his subject was his own appetitive heterosexuality. It celebrated the purported sexual freedom of enslaved male Africans, contrary to Ramsay's wish to regulate it by marriage. Tobin had shared this ostentatiously playful and unreformed male perspective, contrary to his avowal of sensibility: he wrote of the 'young negro' inclined 'to take an additional wife or two', although 'the sable ladies' are 'not exempt from the troublesome passion of jealousy', so 'the few libertines of the *ton* who take advantage of this licence, have cause to repent . . .' (Tobin 1785: 95). Boswell was a man who delighted in 'venereal pleasures', in his own phrase, proud that he 'sallied forth like a lion after girls, blending philosophy and raking'. He carefully tallied his many seductions and purchases, although Boswell's tallies 'were accompanied by [expressions of] remorse towards his wife' (Gatrell 2006: 26, 31).

We might bear Boswell's characterization of anti-slave trade MPs in mind when reading Prime Minister Pitt's 1791 speech on behalf of Wilberforce's anti-slave trade bill. It seemed to express a compromise between the philanthropically inclined man of feeling and the politician. Pitt began by asserting that of every question in which he had taken 'a share' since entering parliament (January 1781), until the present (18 April 1791), 'there had never been one in which his heart was so deeply interested as the present', but yet, 'however forcibly he might appeal to the natural and unerring feelings of every man upon this subject, and however strong an argument he might therefore draw even from this consideration . . . this was not the ground in which he was about to rest the determination of the present question' (Williams 1954: 6). The issue was before his all-male, political audience because of the feelings 'excited' on its behalf, to quote Clarkson, who, writes Walvin (2011: 190), had 'led and organized' the extraordinary 'public agitation' of the antislavery campaign, 'a national clamour' cutting 'across boundaries of class and region – and gender'. But, as we have seen, that 'feeling' to which Pitt referred was profoundly disturbing, at bottom rousing questions about manhood. And from the other, sentimental angle, the antislavery Wollstonecraft, writing her *Vindication of the Rights of Woman* contemporaneously, referred in it to Pitt's talking of 'the interest his heart takes', while continuing to sanction 'this abominable traffic', but she also took the opportunity to link such hypocrisy with unmanliness by punning on Pitt's reportedly homosexual pleasures (Wollstonecraft [1792] 1978: 256).

In the same speech, Pitt continued: 'The present was not a mere question of feeling: it was not for the sake of exercising humanity, as has often been falsely imagined, that the abolition of the trade in slaves was pressed upon the committee', that is, the parliamentary committee established to enquire into the slave trade, 'but it was quite another principle, which ought . . . to determine their minds'. Smith had called 'sympathy' a principle in man's nature that could counteract selfishness, a view Ramsay reluctantly and ambivalently was forced to dismiss. Pitt's casting aside of humanity as an 'exercise' recalls the distinction Smith had made between 'humanity', 'consisting merely in the exquisite fellow feeling' which was 'the virtue of a woman', and the 'generosity' male minds were able to couple with it, exerting it in the public interest, and in politics, as Pitt went on to urge. Pitt then drew on the invidious potential in linking sensibility with masculinity, as Tobin had in attacking Ramsay's motives. He addressed the slave owners' MPs in front of him: 'the West India gentlemen had used very strong language' in claiming the necessity of continuing the slave trade, but Pitt 'could not help thinking, there was an over great degree of sensibility among those gentlemen'. He laid out Ramsay's case that 'no permanent mischief would follow from the abolition, not even hurt or inconvenience', but that 'it would lay the foundation for a more solid improvement of all the various interests of these colonists'.

Active, Unselfish Sensibility Triumphant

After a dozen years of repeated defeats in parliament, the anti-slave trade bill was finally passed in 1807. Wilberforce had been its indefatigable proponent, sustained by a religious feeling defined by the opposition to selfishness (Tomkins 2007: 173).

To Wilberforce and his fellow evangelicals, 'feeling' in their form of Christianity was fundamentally important, as he explained in his *A Practical View of the Prevailing Religious System of Professed Christians in the Higher and Middle Classes in this Country, Contrasted with Real Christianity* (1797), particularly in the section entitled 'On the Admission of the Passions into Religion'. It had been a view propounded by those anti-Hobbesian, Latitudinarian preachers from the later seventeenth century. Not in the least coincidentally, Wilberforce, like More and the Teston circle centred on Lady Middleton and Elizabeth Bouverie, was deeply committed to the same reformation of manners as those long-ago predecessors, manners that were the deeply entrenched expressions of powerful, male-oriented culture. Reformers opposed, in Wilberforce's words, 'idolatry ... swearing, drinking, fornication, lasciviousness, sensuality, and dissipation' (Wilberforce 1797: 33, 100). It was the culture of which Boswell can be seen as a spokesman, which Tobin shared, and which Ramsay, Clarkson and More had attacked. Wilberforce himself had been reformed and converted in 1785–1786 from his participation in this drinking, gambling male culture (Tomkins 2007: chs. 3, 5). He said in October 1787, 'God Almighty has set before us two great objects, the suppression of the slave trade and the reformation of manners' (Tomkins 2007: 59). The earlier tradition of opposition to Hobbesianism and the elevation of fellow-feeling that contributed to the rise of sensibility were eventually followed by sensibility's mere fashionability. Religious passions must 'manifest themselves by prompting the active discharge of the duties of life, the personal, and domestic, and relative, and professional, and social, and civil duties' (Wilberforce 1797: 32, 35). Their exercise should be constant and total. This vision answered that hesitation over politics confronted by Wilberforce in the 1780s. Wilberforce's implementation of the anti-slave trade bill, and of the reformation of manners also through parliamentary action, was the practical translation of sensibility's concern for others, instead of mere self-indulgence.

Conclusion

The antislavery campaign necessarily had to express the values of the white British audience it reached: for the first time, that huge public audience was decisively composed of women as well as men. That its targets were male slave owners, susceptible to being portrayed in a way that touched a familiar nerve, that is, as unfeeling males, inflected how the case was made. To persuade MPs to vote to end slavery and the slave trade, opponents had to make their case in hard economic and legal terms of empire and self-interest, too. In the end, a critical mass of eighteenth-century, middle-class women, together with men of feeling, were galvanized to that dramatically decisive level by the gendered culture of sensibility, whereby antislavery was identified with selflessness and slavery with selfishness.

G.J. Barker-Benfield is Professor Emeritus in the History Department, State University of New York at Albany and a Life Member at Clare Hall, University of Cambridge (benfield@albany.edu; bb106@cam.ac.uk). He is the author of *The Horrors of the Half-Known Life: Male Attitudes toward Women and Sexuality in Nineteenth-Century America* (Harper & Row, 1976; reprinted Routledge, 2000), *The Culture of Sensibility: Sex and Society in Eighteenth-Century Britain* (University of Chicago Press, 1992), *Abigail and John Adams: The Americanization of Sensibility* (University of Chicago Press, 2010) and *Phillis Wheatley Chooses Freedom* (New York University Press, 2018).

Notes

1. See the stories of seduction and abandonment in Scott ([1760] 2007).
2. C.W. (1791: 130) accused Sterne of having abandoned his wife and daughter, and another critic criticized him for having let his aged mother languish in debtor's prison (Howes 1971: 53–54, 89).

References

Aldridge, A.O. 1949. 'The Pleasures of Pity', *English Literary History* 16(1): 76–87.
Alter, P. 1788. 'Reflections on the Slave Trade', *Gentleman's Magazine* 58: 11.
Bahlman, D.W.R. 1957. *The Moral Revolution.* New Haven, CT: Yale University Press.
Barker-Benfield, G.J. 1992. *Culture of Sensibility: Sex and Society in Eighteenth-Century Britain.* Chicago: University of Chicago Press.
——. 2010. *Abigail and John Adams: The Americanization of Sensibility.* Chicago: University of Chicago Press.
Baxter, R. 2000. *The Practical Works of Richard Baxter*, 4 vols. Vol. I, *A Christian Directory* [1673]. Morgan, PA: Soli Deo Gloria Publications.
Boswell, J. 1791. *No Abolition of Slavery, or the Universal Empire of Love.* London: R. Faulder.
Brissenden, R.F. 1974. *Virtue in Distress: Studies in the Novel of Sentiment from Richardson to Sade.* New York: Harper and Row.
Brown, C.L. 2006. *Moral Capital: Foundations of British Abolitionism.* Chapel Hill, NC: University of North Carolina Press.
C.W. 1791. 'On the Affectation of Sentiment and Sensibility', *Universal Magazine of Knowledge and Pleasure* 68 (February): 128–33.
Campbell, C. 1987. *The Romantic Ethic and the Spirit of Modern Consumerism.* Oxford: Basil Blackwell.
Carey, B. 2005. *British Abolitionism and the Rhetorical of Sensibility: Writing, Sentiment, and Slavery, 1760–1807.* Basingstoke, Hampshire: Palgrave MacMillan.

Clarkson, T. [1786] 2010. *An Essay on the Slavery and Commerce of the Human Species, Particularly the African.* Charleston, NC: Bibliobazaar.

Crane, R.S. 1934. 'Suggestions Toward a Genealogy of the "Man of Feeling"', *English Literary History* 1(3): 205–30.

Davis, D.B. 2007. 'Declaring Equality: Sisterhood and Slavery', in K.K. Sklar and J.B. Stewart (eds), *Women's Rights and Transatlantic Antislavery in the Era of Emancipation.* New Haven, CT: Yale University Press, pp. 1–18.

Drescher, S. 2009. *Abolition: A History of Slavery and Antislavery.* Cambridge: Cambridge University Press.

Dwyer, J. 1987. *Virtuous Discourse: Sensibility and Society in Late Eighteenth-Century Scotland.* Edinburgh: John Donald.

Eltis, D., and D. Richardson (eds). 2010. *Atlas of the Transatlantic Slave Trade.* New Haven, CT: Yale University Press.

Gatrell, V. 2006. *City of Laughter: Sex and Satire in Eighteenth-Century London.* New York: Walker.

Grimsted, D. 1989. 'Anglo-American Racism and Phillis Wheatley's "Sable Veil," "Length'ned Chains" and "Knitted Heart"', in R. Hoffman and P.J. Albert (eds), *Women in the Age of the American Revolution.* Charlottesville, VA: University Press of Virginia, pp. 338–444.

Hill, C. 1972. *The World Turned Upside Down: Radical Ideas during the English Revolution.* New York: Viking Press.

Hirschman, A.D. 1977. *The Passions and the Interests: Political Arguments for Capitalism before Its Triumph.* Princeton, NJ: Princeton University Press.

Hobbes, T. [1651] 1968. *Leviathan*, ed. C.B. MacPherson. London: Penguin.

Howes, A.B. 1971. *Yorick and the Critics: Sterne's Reputation in England, 1760–1868.* New Haven, CT: Yale University Press.

Hutcheson, F. [1728] 2002. *An Essay on the Nature and Conduct of the Passions and Affections, with Illustrations on the Moral Sense*, ed. A. Garrett. Indianapolis, IN: Liberty Fund.

Jacob, M. 1993. 'The Materialist World of Pornography', in L. Hunt (ed.), *The Invention of Pornography: Obscenity and the Origins of Modernity, 1500–1800.* Cambridge, MA: MIT Press, pp. 157–202.

Kelly, G. 2001. 'Sarah Scott, Bluestocking Feminism, and Millenium Hall', introduction to Scott, *Millenium Hall.* Peterborough, ON: Broadview Press, pp. 11–46.

Klapp, S.E. 2009. *Revolutionary Conceptions, Women's Fertility, and Family Limitation in America, 1760–1820.* Chapel Hill, NC: University of North Carolina Press.

Langford, P. 1989. *A Polite and Commercial People: England, 1727–1783.* Oxford: Oxford University Press.

MacPherson, C.B. 1962. *The Political Theory of Possessive Individualism: Hobbes to Locke.* Oxford: Oxford University Press.

McKendrick, N. 1988. 'Josiah Wedgwood and the Commercialization of the Potteries', in N. McKendrick, J. Brewer and J. Plumb (eds), *The Birth of a Consumer Society: The Commercialization of Eighteenth Century England.* Bloomington, IN: Indiana University Press, pp. 100–41.

Mellor, A. 2000. 'Hannah More, Revolutionary Reformer', in *Mothers of the Nation: Women's Political Writing in England, 1780–1830.* Bloomington, IN: Indiana University Press, pp. 13–38.

Meyer, D. 1987. *Sex and Power: The Rise of Women in America, Russia, Sweden, and Italy.* Middletown, CT: Wesleyan University Press.

Midgley, C. 1997. *Women against Slavery: The British Campaign, 1780–1870*. London: Routledge.
More, H. [1784] 1787. 'Sensibility: A Poem', in *Sacred Dramas Chiefly Intended for Young Persons*. Philadelphia: Thomas Dobson, 1, 182.
———. 1786. *The Bas-Bleu*. London: T. Cadell.
———. 1788. *Slavery, A Poem*. London: T. Cadell.
Ramsay, J. 1784a. *Essay on the Treatment and Conversion of African Slaves in the British Sugar Colonies*. London: James Phillips.
———. 1784b. *Inquiry into the Effects of Putting a Stop to the African Slave Trade*. London: James Phillips.
Sancho, I. [1982] 1998. 'Ignatius Sancho to Lawrence Sterne [21 July 1766]', in V. Carretta (ed.), *Letters of the Late Ignatius Sancho, An African*. New York: Penguin.
Scott, S. [1760] 2007. *The Histories of Some of the Penitents in the Magdalen House, as Supposed to Be Related by Themselves*. London: Pickering and Chatto.
———. [1762] 2001. *Millenium Hall*. Peterborough, ON: Broadview Press.
———. [1766] 1996. *The History of Sir George Ellison*. Lexington: University Press of Kentucky.
Skinner, Q. 1966. 'The Ideological Context of Hobbes's Political Thought', *The Historical Journal* 9(3): 286–317.
Sklar, K.K., and J.B. Stewart (eds). 2007. *Women's Rights and Transatlantic Antislavery in the Era of Emancipation*, New Haven, CT: Yale University Press.
Smith, A. [1759] 1982. *The Theory of Moral Sentiments*, ed. D.D. Raphael and A.L. Macfie. Indianapolis, IN: Liberty Press.
———. [1776] 1979. *The Wealth of Nations*, ed. A. Skinner. New York: Penguin.
Soderlund, J.R. 1985. *Quakers and Slavery: A Divided Spirit*. Princeton, NJ: Princeton University Press.
Spencer, J. 1986. *The Rise of the Woman Novelist: From Aphra Behn to Jane Austen*. Oxford: Basil Blackwell.
Sterne, L. 1996. *The Sermons of Lawrence Sterne*, vol. 4. *The Florida Edition of the Works of Laurence Sterne*, ed. M. New. Gainesville: University Press of Florida.
———. [1768] 1968. *A Sentimental Journey*, ed. I. Jack. Oxford: Oxford University Press.
Stott, A. 2003. *Hannah More: The First Victorian*. Oxford: Oxford University Press.
Sutherland, K. 1991. 'Hannah More's Counter-Revolutionary Feminism', in K. Everset (ed.), *Revolution in Writing: British Literary Responses to the French Revolution*. Milton Keynes: Open University Press.
Sypher, W. 1939. 'Hutcheson and the "Classical" Theory of Slavery', *Journal of Negro History* 24(3): 263–80.
Tawney, R.S. [1926] 1962. *Religion and the Rise of Capitalism*. Gloucester, MA: Peter Smith.
Tobin, J. 1785. *Cursory Remarks Upon the Reverend Mr. Ramsay's Essay on the Treatment and Conversion of African Slaves and Sugar Colonies, by a Friend to the West India Colonies and their Inhabitants*. London: G. and T. Wilkie.
Tomkins, S. 2007. *William Wilberforce: A Biography*. Oxford: Lion House.
Walvin, J. 2007. *The Trader, the Owner, and the Slave: Parallel Lives in the Age of Slavery*. London: Vintage.
———. 2011. *The Zong: A Massacre, the Law and the End of Slavery*. New Haven, CT: Yale University Press.
Watt, I. 1963. *The Rise of the Novel: Studies in Defoe, Fielding and Richardson*. Harmondsworth, UK: Penguin.

Weber, M. [1920] 1958. *The Protestant Ethic and the Spirit of Capitalism*, trans. Talcott Parsons. New York: Charles Scribner's Sons.
Wilberforce, W. 1797. *A Practical View of the Prevailing Religious System of Professed Christians in the Higher and Middle Classes in this Country, Contrasted with Real Christianity*. London: T. Cadell.
Williams, E. 1954. *The British West Indies in Westminster, 1789–1823, Extracts from Debates in Parliament*. Westport, CN: Negro University Press.
———. [1941] 1994. *Capitalism and Slavery*. Chapel Hill: University of North Carolina Press.
Wollstonecraft, M. [1792] 1978. *Vindication of the Rights of Woman*. New York: Penguin.
Yellin, J.F. 1989. *Women and Sisters: The Antislavery Feminists in American Culture*. New Haven, CT: Yale University Press.

3

Selfless Advocacy?
Profeminist Men's Movements in Late Twentieth-Century Britain

Lucy Delap

Commentators have often been tempted to explain moral change using broad-brush categories and linear narratives. Conjuring categories of 'Respectables', 'Puritans' or 'Mutualists', they have tended to offer sweeping accounts of the forces of permissiveness or convention (Collins 2003, 2007; Fisher 1993). One such narrative has asserted that late twentieth century Britain – sometimes characterized as 'Thatcher's Britain' – saw a turn to selfishness, operationalized through acquisitiveness and individualism. Recent scholarship has challenged this narrative, and identified more politically diverse forms of popular individualism and entitlement (Lawrence 2019; Robinson et al. 2017; Sutcliffe-Braithwaite 2018). This chapter similarly decentres the neoliberal or Thatcherite sources of thinking about selfishness, and instead traces some diverse discourses of selfishness and selflessness that were influential in organizing intimate lives and social movements. Through surveying the moral categories and judgements historical actors made about themselves, their politics and their society, I hope to shed some light on how morality has figured in historical landscapes, and how our methodologies might be more explicit in thinking about moral change.

The discussion that follows centres on the naming of selves and practices as selfish by men in the late twentieth century, in response to a historically specific moment of feminist critique, circa 1971 to 1991. Through periodicals, pamphlets, oral histories and memoirs, I chart a critique of 'selfish masculinity', understood by anti-sexist (or profeminist) men and feminist women as an important component of male hegemonic power over women. This is juxtaposed to profeminist men's attempts to develop a selfless form of politics – a giving up of male power and privilege in favour of women's empowerment.

A 'selfless' men's politics was simpler to announce than to achieve, and many women involved in women's liberation were profoundly sceptical about the extent to which selfless motives underlay men's anti-sexism. Over time, many anti-sexist men themselves began to be sceptical about the utility of political selflessness. A strand of men's activism emerged in the late 1970s which called on men to act 'selfishly' and ask themselves: 'anti-sexism, what's in it for me?' The resulting development of ideas of men's liberation proved extremely divisive for men's feminist activism, and led to the dispersal of the coalition that had been built around a 'selfless' male anti-sexist agenda. Examining this moment will, I hope, allow us to capture the lived experience and politics of post-1968 radicalism, and chart the politics that it produced, not just at that moment of social critique 'around 1968' (Gildea et al. 2013), but over a longer period that witnessed adaptation and political reaction. It also allows us to flesh out and analyse for adequacy the idea of a transition over the second half of the twentieth century towards a more individualistic and 'selfish' society in Britain.

An Anatomy of Selfishness

Late twentieth-century Britain is sometimes understood as representing a relatively secular, individualist and diverse society, marked by a diminishing consensus around moral norms (Black, Pemberton and Thane 2013; Robinson et al. 2017). The sense of profound social change associated with postwar 'permissiveness', migration and 'affluence', and later with deindustrialization and economic restructuring, was sometimes depicted as a moral dislocation as much as a socioeconomic one. This perceived moral change was multidimensional. It had a prominent spiritual dimension, for example. As Sam Brewitt-Taylor has argued, secularization seemed inevitable in a 'modern' society, and there was deep anxiety and debate about what moral values would take the place of the predominantly Christian mores of the earlier twentieth century (Black 2010; Brewitt-Taylor 2013). Secular values also seemed in transition; intergenerational reciprocity and care were challenged by the confident or angry young people produced by the postwar baby boom, and their cultural predominance. Ethics of service and self-sacrifice that had fuelled an active voluntary sector seemed to be in decline. Arguably, the hedonism associated with postwar affluence, and the rise of youth cultures centred on consumption, lent themselves to forms of selfishness. Arthur Marwick associates postwar European and American youth cultures with an ethic of 'doing your own thing', which was individualistic and even self-indulgent. Youth cultures seemed premised on the idea that 'a person not only could but should aggressively seek the enhancement of the self' (Collier 1991: 232; Marwick 2006). While historians and sociologists have acknowledged that this nonetheless still led to activism and ethical commitment, many commentators of this period feared that the developed world had become more selfish (Bocking-Welch 2016; Giddens 1991; McLeod 2010; Thomson 2006). A political pamphlet produced by the British Liberal Party in 1968 talked in typical terms of 'the selfishness and complacency of our society', and called for a crusade against it: 'Without acceptance of an unselfish society we will have increasing world hunger, increasing world conflict, and even in those countries, such as ours, which may be lucky ... we will suffer from a society which will increasingly turn sour.' (Beaumont 1968).

The visibility of assertive feminists after 1968 was also part of this debate about morals. Women's moral and political values were widely thought to be transformed by feminism and individualism, evidenced in rising rates of divorce and women's workplace participation. For critics, this was due to women's misplaced putting of self above family or marital commitments. Nonetheless, the women's liberation movement sometimes deliberately deployed a language of selfishness. Women, it was argued, had been socialized to express selfless behaviour in relation to sexual partners and families. Mid-twentieth-century feminists such as Winifred Holtby had written of women's tendency to self-sacrifice as being 'one of the most formidable handicaps confronting women'; Virginia Woolf argued that women were haunted by the phantom of the self-sacrificing 'angel of the house' (Dyhouse 1981: 36, see also chapter 1, this volume). Post-1968 feminists still recognized these constraints of socialization, and argued that women had a moral duty to cultivate selfishness and repudiate men's needs. As one argued in 1977, 'I loved women in every way and I had to break the chains of my commitment to men and come out for *myself*. My commitment to men was merely an extension of my need as a woman for acceptance and security in a male world' (Ettore 1977: 2–3). This lent itself to separatist sentiments (Graham and Layne, this volume), as a necessary and politically productive form of 'self-focus', though many on the left saw this as a form of 'self-indulgence'.[1] As Helen Bailey declared in the *Anti-Sexist Men's Newsletter*, 'Many feminists feel that the only way forward is through severing themselves completely from men, looking towards themselves and other women for support and energy. In this way alone, they believe, women can gain the necessary self-respect and confidence needed to fight for their rights and survive in the male-dominated world'. This need to cultivate 'selfish' autonomy, she believed, accounted for the deep suspicion many feminist women felt concerning practices of mixed sex political organization, and indeed of profeminist men (Bailey 1984).

Selfishness was not only a resource for the dissident and politically rebellious. By the 1970s and 1980s, moral schema were being reworked by politicians, economists and geneticists in ways that offered new ways of thinking about selfishness. In some dimensions, selfish behaviour remained problematized in the 1970s. Right-wing politicians, for example, used stereotypes of selfish trade unionists to great effect during the industrial conflicts of that decade. But others on the Right had begun to portray 'selfish' market behaviour – the striving for individual gain – as economically rational and collectively beneficial. They were clearly drawing on Austrian and neoclassical economics in doing so, but also on more diverse sources. In the United States, Michel Novak developed a neo-Conservative Catholic defence of modern capitalist competition based on ideas of the 'innate selfishness' of humans (Novak 2001: 14). And from a more libertarian perspective, Ayn Rand had gained a following with an egoist philosophy that celebrated selfish behaviour. She described mankind as in a state of 'arrested moral development' due to its habit of judging selfishness to be inherently morally evil. Instead, she celebrated a morally neutral selfishness that simply meant 'concern with one's own interests'. This kind of selfishness, she believed, could be better understood as a form of self-respect (Rand 1964: ix, x).

An alternative re-reading of selfishness was found within evolutionary biology, and was given popular purchase by Richard Dawkins' account of the genetics of social behaviour in *The Selfish Gene*, first published in 1976, in which he declared, 'let us try to teach generosity and altruism because we are born selfish' (Dawkins 1978).[2] As Dawkins' critics summarized the implications of this work, 'all men and women are basically selfish. Our ruthless genes, according to a modern formulation which rules out any gene for altruism, structure us that way'. This vision, the British social democrats Marianne Rigge and Michael Young argued, meant that

> People can detach themselves from others and struggle to advance themselves . . . They can cushion themselves and the others for whom they accept responsibility in their own families with more of the fruits of their selfishness. The consequence is that at its worst modern society seems to be only a well-heeled yob . . . The legitimators of greed are everywhere in evidence. They crowd our mind with their messages about the standard of living which has only one standard to it, that of self-interest. (Young and Rigge 1979: 7)

While there was no direct link between Dawkins' presentation of ruthless evolutionary motives underlying human behaviour and the cultivation of a more individualistic and entrepreneurial ethic by the political Right, both resonated with an apparent revaluation of selfishness as a viable, even admirable ethic that has been taken as a key characteristic of the 1980s. Thatcher's critics, such as the Marxist Martin Jacques, talked of 'the age of selfishness . . . the credo of the self, inextricably entwined with the gospel of the market, has hijacked the fabric of our lives' (Gerhardt 2011: 11).

It is clear that Thatcher's policies and beliefs cannot be taken as characteristic of British society more generally; the recent historiography of the late twentieth century has begun to go beyond talk of 'Thatcher's Britain' and offer a more plural view of this period. James Hinton, for example, has charted the diversity of lives lived in late twentieth-century Britain, while Jim Phillips has explored the moral economy of the Scottish coalfields during the 1984–5 miners' strike (Hinton 2016; Phillips 2012). This chapter takes what has become a typical 'Thatcherite' label, selfishness, and explores the work it did outside of the purview of Thatcherite policies, in an attempt to think beyond the confines of the frame of 'Thatcher's Britain'. I return to this question of how to characterize late twentieth-century British society more generally in the concluding section.

Encounters with Feminism and Anti-sexist Identities

The British 'men's movement' can be discerned as an active social movement that grew out of the women's liberation movement from the early 1970s, mostly among men who had been involved in leftist political or counter-cultural scenes (Delap 2017). It drew heavily on ideas and texts from the United States, and to a lesser extent Australia and continental Europe. Alongside transnational influences, anti-sexist men were also aware of the historical precedent for 'male feminism', particularly the Edwardian male support for women's suffrage (John and Eustance 1997).

In Britain, anti-sexist men developed a space for rethinking masculinity and supporting feminist goals, initially in men's groups on university campuses and within progressive circles in the early 1970s. The later 1970s and 1980s saw a broader flourishing of local and national anti-sexist periodicals, networks of groups, national conferences, activism and agreed national goals. What this meant in practice was very disparate, and although common themes emerged, many of the groups involved were quite inward looking. Many participant men rejected the terminology of movement and preferred to see themselves as supporters of the women's movement. One participant refered to it as 'an emerging community-in-movement' (Motherson 1979). As Mark Long, a Liverpool-based crèche organizer put it, 'Didn't feel like a liberation movement, in fact I wouldn't use, I wouldn't describe what we were doing then as "men's movement", I didn't see us as being men with separate interests, we were very clear, we called ourselves anti-sexist from the very beginning' (Long, interview 2012). Nonetheless, the numbers of individuals involved, the high visibility, combined with the level of activity and the networked nature of men's groups supports a retrospective analysis of men's activism as a distinct social movement in its own right.

Estimates of the size of the movement vary and must always be provisional; men's groups were often short-lived, and numbers attending fluctuated. Many operated informally and did not seek public recognition, thus leaving very few historical traces. The lists of men's groups published in the October 1979 issue of the *Anti-Sexist Men's News* suggest a modest nine men's groups in London, as well as a coordinating London Men's Centre. *Achilles Heel*, a collectively produced anti-sexist men's magazine, published a national list in their third issue, also in 1979, listing seventeen London groups, and another eighteen dispersed around the country. The *Anti-Sexist Men's News* in its summer 1985 issue listed forty-one groups nationally, plus seven in London, supported by four additional periodicals and numerous subgroups (covering those working with crèches, disabilities, music, male violence, bisexuality and so on). This included four groups in Northern Ireland and three in Wales, including one for Welsh speakers. Men's groups outside of Britain corresponded enthusiastically with the British men's periodicals; anti-sexist periodicals from a range of countries (chiefly the United States, Australia, Holland and Denmark) were circulating. Two major television series publicized the movement ('About Men' on Channel 4 in 1983, and 'Men . . .' on BBC2 in 1984), and men's groups were widely depicted in the media. There was a widespread perception that the feminist movement had implications for men, and that some men were trying to respond constructively.

The relationship between anti-sexist men and women's liberation activists was diverse, fluid and sometimes acrimonious. Some women welcomed anti-sexist men, and acknowledged that feminism needed to change men as well as women. A writer to the women's liberation periodical *Shrew* argued in 1971:

> It seems to me that we need to begin, in dialogue with any men who are interested, to try to define new patterns, to build new structures and relationships, FROM OUR OWN POLITICS, for their participation and contribution to the battle for a new society. Isn't it inconsistent to say we are for men sharing more in the raising of children and not to give any lead to how this sharing can be done? (Anon 1971: 6)

In the early 1970s, many feminist groups were operating on a mixed sex basis, although women-only and men-only spaces were being explored. Women influenced by socialism were largely open to working with men. Many found radical feminist talk of separatism troubling, although they acknowledged the difficulties of the relationship. Sheila Rowbotham argued in a 1971 pamphlet, 'The decision to exclude men should be made on the basis of the experience of each group. It may be necessary in the early stages for women to discuss the situation without men because their nervous hostility or benevolent patronage are precisely the points at which we become hysterical or dry up through lack of confidence as a group . . .'. Nonetheless, she was reluctant to support separatism over the longer term: 'Some women may simply drop into the "male" aggressive role.' Perhaps most disturbingly, women-only groups left no way to include men in visions of social change: 'The way is not open for men to redefine themselves' (Rowbotham 1971: 26).

In this same year, however, the national women's liberation conference held at Skegness resolved that all future conferences should be women only, 'so that [men] do not act as scape-goats preventing us seeing the nature of our rage, and partly because one or two clearly do act in male-chauvinist leadership ways towards the women in their group' (Mitchell and de Winter 1971: ii). As Anna Coote and Beatrix Campbell later wrote, 'invariably it was found that the presence of men altered the *quality* of discourse between women and diluted its potency, absorbing their attention and stilling their imagination' (Coote and Campbell 1987, emphasis in the original).

Radical and revolutionary feminisms offered a set of ideas that largely rejected joint work with men. *Catcall*, a British 'feminist discussion paper' produced between 1976 and 1981, reprinted articles from the American radical feminist Redstockings group that were directly critical of men. They rejected the feminist tendency that 'absolves men from any but psychological responsibility (if that) for the oppression of women, and blames it all vaguely on "sex roles" or "society". . . . This theory, by promoting a "Sex Role Revolution" instead of a real feminist revolution papers over the class antagonism between men and women and substitutes cultural change for power change' (*Catcall* 1976: 16). The growth of revolutionary feminism in Britain from the mid 1970s led to even stronger statements of rejection of men. Linda Bellos, a revolutionary feminist and Black activist, wrote: 'Yes I hate men; I don't want to work or live with them' (Bellos 1981: 31; see also Rees 2010). Men's anti-sexism was greeted with hostility, and seen as inadequate. A Leeds woman wrote an angry letter to the *Anti-Sexist Men's News* in 1980, asking men to be more active in their support for feminism, stop saying sorry, and challenge other men's sexism more publicly: 'Start seeing yourselves as collaborators in a war against your own kind', she concluded (Sarah 1981: 6–7).

Anti-sexist men had an ambivalent relationship to these sorts of statements and politics. Some found them disheartening; others found them frightening, or as one put it, 'shattering'. Others read radical and revolutionary feminism as justified, or polemical – one Cambridge anti-sexist man relished the SCUM manifesto as a 'wonderful' text, while another found it scared him (Spiegelhalter and Sugg, interview 2012). Paul Smith (b. 1950) noted that the first time he saw a feminist magazine, 'I was horrified, I must admit [laughs] . . . it was so shocking [laughs]. I'd never thought about anything like that before. [laughs] It really – and I felt, urghhhh, like I was a bit under attack . . .' (Smith, interview 2012).

Despite the challenge of radical feminists' critical orientation to men, this strand of feminism remained important to men. Misha Wolf (b. 1949), an anti-sexist activist influenced by anarchism and based in London, demonstrates something of the tensions for 'feminist' men. During an oral history interview, he spoke of his attraction to radical feminism, despite its position on men:

> I know it's peculiar, but I . . . I felt much more sympathetic to the radical feminists than to the socialist feminists, partly because their view was much sort of purer and I [laughs], as I said, if you're going to do something, you may as well do it to the full.

Wolf identified strongly with women's culture and lesbianism:

> In a way it's not surprising that I was listening to lesbian music, because I, I could identify with the lesbians more than I could with women who were living with men, because I felt that if I was one, I wouldn't want to live with men, so why should they? (Wolf, interview 2012)

Nonetheless, this powerful sense of identification with radical and lesbian feminism did not lead to any confidence in Wolf's dealings with feminists: 'I remember once being on a tube and reading *Spare Rib* and a woman sitting next to me smiled at me, so I shut my eyes and I kept my eyes shut for the rest of my journey 'cos I just didn't know, I had no idea how to deal with that' (ibid. See also Delap 2018).

Selfish Masculinities

One of the elements of feminism that men found 'shattering' was its portrayal of the unreconstructed male ego as fundamentally selfish. Women identified male selfishness, and pointed out its impact on women. One wrote a supportive letter to the *Anti-Sexist Men's News* in 1984, looking forward to the replacement of 'undesirable' elements of masculinity – 'aggression, dominance and selfishness' – by new qualities of 'tolerance, co-operation and compassion' (Bailey 1984). Most believed that while individual men might be personally selfish, the real problem was more institutional. The belief that men were structurally rendered selfish by their socialization, and more fundamentally by patriarchy, was widely expressed. This proved very powerful and troubling to some men. An early statement of belief in the selfishness of patriarchal masculinity can be found in an article written in 1971 in a Cambridge-based women's liberation movement magazine, *Women Are People*. Hugo Blake, a graduate student, argued in an article on 'the role of men in women's liberation' that men had to 'give up their selfish cosiness . . . and recognise he is confined to a role, can lead a fuller, more exhilarating life by liberating himself and by living with a liberated woman' (Blake 1971). Mick Cooper, a counsellor and men's movement activist, wrote a brief history of the anti-sexist men's movement in 1982, and also made selfishness a prominent area of critique:

> Power is conferred on men by institutions: however much they attempt to reject this power, as a man they will always have it. Selfishness is taught to men at a very early age; however much men attempt to change their role there will always be unconscious 'selfishness' at the basis of it. Only by directly attacking the patriarchal structure which puts them in a position of power, can men depart from their masculine straightjacket, for it is their class position which creates their role and not the role that creates the class. (Cooper 1990: 10)

This was a political moment, however, when abstract statements about patriarchy were often distrusted as 'theory'. There was an enormous emphasis on founding politics on experiences of intimate and everyday life. As the *Achilles Heel* collective argued in 1978, 'we have developed an aversion to the abstraction and rhetoric in which so much theory on the Left seems to have got stuck . . .' (*Achilles Heel* 1978). Selfishness was understood as both a structural component of patriarchy, and a critical category in evaluating experiences of family life and intimate relationships. Andy Barrow (b. 1947), an ex-soldier and teacher who became involved in men's groups in Cambridge, described his memories of his working-class father:

> Dad was an appalling man. Um . . . He . . . I – I couldn't have said this until relatively later on – but I now know that he was acutely narcissistically damaged. He'd been fostered by a very, very selfish mother, um, fostered out . . . um . . . his father had died when he was very young. Without going into all of that, he was an intensely selfish man. Very, very childlike. Um . . . appalling tantrums if he couldn't get his

own way. Um. And did everything he possibly could to keep us as children . . . as long as we were the children he could think of himself as being the man and it was the only way he could view himself as being a grown-up, 'a man'. (Barrow, interview 2012)

After his father's verbal and physical violence, Andy rejected this model of 'selfish manhood', and adopted instead a pacifist, anti-authority masculinity that eventually led to him being ejected from the army, and training as a counsellor.

The idea of selfish masculinity was not only perceived in relation to other men, but for some men was also perceptible within their self-identity. One wrote that having been part of a men's group in Brighton in the late 1970s, 'I feel that I am full of contradictions – indeed, I know I am. I'm accused of being both warm and aggressive, understanding and intolerant, giving and selfish, sexist and anti-sexist. All are true!' (Bennell and Firth 1979). More specifically, others perceived that they might be described as selfish by women in relation to sexual practices. Misha Wolf, for example, had a revelation of his sexual selfishness upon reading the *Hite Report on Female Sexuality*, a survey of sexual behaviour in the United States, first published in 1976. Wolf recalled that:

> I had a terrible time [when I read the Hite report] . . . About not just being a fool – discovering that I had been a fool . . . And selfish. . . . I had no idea of women's sexuality at all, and I had been having sex with women and not having a clue whether they were getting anything out of it, and not doing anything to find out and all that stuff. And not having a clue what to do to enable them to get anything out of it and so on. (Wolf, interview 2012)

Wolf's sense of his 'selfishness' was later painfully enlarged when his sister committed suicide in 1981. His own need for emotional support had, he felt, blinded him to her needs. His experience of paralysing guilt led to his withdrawal from political activism among anti-sexist men. But his sense of shock, guilt and surprise in rethinking his relationship to women was fairly typical. As Paul Smith confirmed,

> the shock for me was I always thought of myself as . . . a liberated male [laughs], whatever that meant, I thought I was really good with women, because erm, I always treated women with complete respect . . . So it was a huge shock to . . . to be challenged both personally and intellectually by this literature, erm, but directly personally as well. (Smith, interview 2012)

Selfless Activism

While the perception of selfish masculinity was widely expressed, there was also an optimism among anti-sexist men that a selfless masculinity could be developed through their support for women's liberation. Nonetheless, for many men, their feelings of guilt at their complicity in women's oppression led to a particularly passive or self-renunciating form of political engagement with feminism.

Many believed that their role should be simply to respond unquestioningly to women's demands. Keith Motherson, a prominent anti-sexist writer and activist who co-founded the feminist-socialist grouping Alternative Socialism, wrote of his desire that men should not bargain with women about their position, but offer 'unilateral disarmament, unconditional, without strings'. The ability to do this represented a shift in the male psyche, understood by Motherson as a 'male ego death process' (Motherson 1979).

For those who felt they could sustain 'selfless' activism as men working on behalf of women, the content of what this would mean was often opaque. As Fidelma Ashe (2004) has argued, many feminists had come to believe that feminist knowledge could only be based on women's experience. Linda Bellos, for example, declared, 'we want and need to share our experience of oppression, to understand it. How can a man talk about what it feels like to be an oppressed woman? You can't; that's why you were and are excluded' (Bellos 1981: 30). For many women, male support for feminist goals was best expressed through renunciation – giving up political profile and 'limelight', deferring to women, and listening to them. Indeed, for many male profeminists, their cultivation of skills of listening and empathy proved to be durable and cherished outcomes of the men's movement.

There were other, more practical forms in which this 'selfless' praxis might be cashed out. Some men understood it as an imperative to redistribute material resources, and in particular to acknowledge the patriarchal basis for male earning power. Keith Motherson argued that 'our patriarchal/class surplus money isn't really ours – it only gets passed to us first because of institutional sexism.' (Motherson 1981: 10). Some wrote of their commitment to making quite substantial percentages of their income available for the women's movement – Misha Wolf, who was in relatively well-paid employment, gave 10% during his years of activism. Others gave money from other sources; one had inherited wealth from a business that predominantly employed women, and felt that he should be giving this money back to women's politics. He supported women's bookshops and other causes, setting up an informal grouping termed 'Cash against Sexism' (anon., interview 2012).

Others could not give money because they were unemployed, and opted instead to give up their time. The major way in which this evolved was through the 'Crèches against Sexism' movement. On an ad hoc or sustained basis, men frequently provided childcare at conferences or meetings held by women's organizations. Bristol Crèches against Sexism reported in 1980 that forty men were providing childcare in the city, and there were similar groups in Edinburgh, Oxford and London. In 1981, Mark Long recalled that a group of anti-sexist men in Liverpool 'settled on childcare as being the single most practical and supportive activity we could think of, because that would unlock those women's participation, or women's participation in other activities without in any way challenging their leadership' (Long, interview 2012). Feminist women insisted that men acknowledge their indebtedness through practical action;

Asphodel [Pauline Long], also prominent in Alternative Socialism, the London Matriarchy Study Group and later in the Goddess Movement, appealed to men to help her repair and decorate her house: 'In doing so you are acknowledging that you have a debt to pay to women, even though you may not feel that you knowingly or willingly incurred that debt. We have nurtured you and we suffer because of your privileges. Now here is an opportunity to return some of that nurture' (Asphodel 1981: 24–25).

Alongside material wealth or time, men also sought to divest themselves of other traditional patriarchal or gendered privileges. Some chose, for example, to renounce their names; one Cardiff-based activist changed his name to '5' or 'Five' in 1977, partly to subvert others' ability to identify his gender. The artists Ray Barrie and Mary Kelly named their son, born in 1973, Kelly Barrie, to acknowledge their shared parenting and preference for a gender-neutral name. Men's movement activist Keith Paton changed his surname to 'Motherson', acknowledging his maternal origins and rejecting the patriarchal passing on of paternal surname (see Bodenhorn, this volume and 2006 for a different take on the power of naming). However, these strategies of effacement and divestment of privilege were difficult to sustain, and a very different vision of men's politics became more visible in the late 1970s and 1980s.

Masculism and Men's Liberation

Many men found that the adoption of a more selfless, egalitarian mode of sexual and emotional being required profound commitment and self-insight, and was not easy to attain. A Brighton activist acknowledged after more than a year of participating in a men's group that he was 'furtive' about his anti-sexist politics, which still felt 'odd' (Bennell and Firth 1979). It was particularly hard where the giving up of privilege was perceived as a genuine loss. Most anti-sexist men, however, preferred to see their politics as directly benefiting men. As Motherson argued, 'surrendering our gut-sexism and social privileges as men is in our/their best interests' (Motherson 1981: 10). Like many others in the men's movement, Motherson was searching for a language that could legitimately claim that men had an interest in, and something to gain from, anti-sexism. This, however, was to give rise to a new political framing of anti-sexism, renamed as men's liberation or 'masculism'. Five Cram, an activist in Cardiff men's groups, attempted to develop a version of 'masculism' in the early 1980s, through his discomfort with the identity 'feminist'. Its content was presented as compatible with and sympathetic to feminism; Five called for men to disengage from the competitive world of work and instead connect to childcare. For Five, 'the goals of masculism complement those of feminism despite springing from a separate and apparently selfish motivation'. It could produce a movement that was 'founded in male experience ... yet sympathetic and parallel to the sister movement of feminism ... Putting their own house in order may yet prove to be men's most effective contribution to feminism' (Cram 1983: 10–11). For Five, this was not so much about a 'selfish' need for a direct personal benefit for men, but rather about creating a politics that could reach much wider audiences. He argued strongly that the men's movement could only impact the patriarchal order by involving greater numbers of men, and could not be smug about its own actions:

> Despite the obvious dangers of being just more men's voices in a world dominated by men's voices, it is clearly a cop-out simply to keep quiet and congratulate ourselves on 'opting-out' of sexism. To try to wash our hands of guilt in this way is to be guilty of evading responsibility for positive action. (Cram 1982: 12)

This led to a strong polemical statement of the need to prioritize self-interest within anti-sexism:

> Instead of concentrating on how sexism benefits men, let's concentrate on how *antisexism* benefits men. Then we'll know what reasons other men might have to recognise and support antisexist ideas. Every antisexist man needs to ask himself the question: Antisexism: What's in it for me? (Ibid.: 13)

Ultimately, the men's movement itself, striving to establish an *unselfish* masculinity and support the women's movement, came to be viewed by many of its participants as narrow and deeply unsatisfying. This was sometimes framed as a form of selfishness in its own right, through the self-indulgence of clique politics. Chris Tribble (b. 1948), a single parent who attended men's groups in Rochdale during the late 1970s, acknowledged that: 'You could say that we retreated into a bunker and were selfish because of that' (Tribble, interview 2012). Despite the strong Asian presence in the Rochdale area, for example, his group did not make connections with Asian men, and remained predominantly white and middle class. Chris felt that his sense of his own problems and needs meant that he had little spare energy to devote to selfless forms of engagement, though he did volunteer in crèches. Like many other men, he was looking for something positive and affirming from his gender politics. John Hoyland (b. 1942), a member of the original Achilles Heel Collective in 1978 and a playwright, reworked Rebecca West's aphorism, that to be a feminist was to express 'sentiments that differentiate me from a doormat':

> I never liked the view in the men's movement, that, you know, it was a movement against sexism, and our only role was to serve, as it were, the women's movement. I never liked that, you know I thought there were very positive things that we could do about questioning the nature of masculinity, actually, which were about us ... simply to be there, as it were, as a doormat for the women's movement, I never actually liked that very much. (Hoyland, interview 2012)

These tendencies were evident from the late 1970s, and the launch of the widely circulating and outward-facing *Achilles Heel* magazine represented an attempt to move on from 'guilty' politics, and to think more positively about masculinities. A founding Achilles Heel Collective member, Paul Atkinson

(b. 1944), noted that around this time, 'men were going in different directions ... I couldn't really identify with men who were ... going into some sort of guilty ... position, in relation to women, and that was their duty to change their behaviour and stop using certain words' (Atkinson, interview 2012). When a group of anti-sexist men, including Keith Motherson, attempted to draw up a list of '10 Commitments' that codified anti-sexist men's commitment and accountability to women, the 1980 national conference in Bristol refused to validate them. Instead, another Achilles Heel Collective member, Paul Morrison (b. 1944), drew up a 'minimum self definition' of anti-sexist men which, in his words, was about substituting 'the old politics' for a new commitment to 'personal change' (Morrison, interview 2012). The nature of men's gender activism changed, with a stronger emphasis on men-only spaces and therapeutic journeys, eventually leading to more ritualistic and spiritual emphases. Robert Bly's well-known text *Iron John*, published in 1990, captured an experimental men's movement that was already in motion in both Britain and the United States in the 1980s. Much of the infrastructure of the movement adjusted to the new focus on men's politics. The *Anti-Sexist Men's Newsletter* changed its name to *MAN*. As one contributor put it, 'Anti-sexism is the point I started from but does not reflect the hope I feel for change' (Peter 1986). It was widely felt that a movement that was founded on opposition – *anti*-sexism – could not have a positive appeal. Selflessness had become seen as an unattractive political ethic.

Conclusions

Discussion of the place of selfishness and altruism in men's and gender politics offers a means of unpacking the powerful sense of change in late twentieth-century Britain, and supplements the established narrative of a 'selfish society' created by Thatcherism. It provides us with valuable insights into the moral basis on which both political activism and intimate lives were conducted. A complex double shift can be perceived; initially, progressive men came to feel or acknowledge the justice of the feminist critique of male selfishness – emotional, sexual or material. They responded with dismay, guilt, and sometimes with an altruist or selfless politics of renouncing their privilege. Ironically, this could lead to either smug or cliqueish politics that could in turn be perceived as selfish in its narrowness.

Yet attempts to cultivate 'selfless' anti-sexist politics were fraught, and led to a rejection of guilt by those more interested in new masculinities, often understood in therapeutic or spiritual terms. The potentials for alliances between profeminist men and feminist women diminished, and there were increasing overlaps between the men's movement and the child custody activism of this same period, some of which had strong anti-feminism overtones. Keith Motherson (1981: 10) noted pessimistically that 'it often seems that our male egos are able to recuperate themselves and reform around practically anything – "anti-sexism" too can be grist to our ego mill.' He feared that 'men's "liberation"' would substitute personal growth for political activism, and thus come to represent simply 'traditional male-bonding, "men-ism".'

Men's liberation, however, was not the last word. The fluid and unsettled nature of men's politics continued, with further reactions and renunciations sparked by the 'men's liberation' of the 1980s. In 1991, a dismayed younger activist in Sheffield, Dave Gauntlett, founded a new magazine called *Powercut*, which tried to reconnect men's activism to 'things which are on the feminist agenda': 'It seemed that the men writing in that magazine [*Achilles Heel*] had got so involved in all their "men's" stuff that they had forgotten quite what they were fighting, or that they were fighting at all (having settled into more cosy and less difficult debates like whether to have a vasectomy or not, instead)' (Gauntlett 1991). There was a raw energy to this publication, with its critique of the spiritual elements of what had become the mythopoetic men's movement. Gauntlett described one such text as written by 'the lazy guilty liberal Guardian-reader *extraordinaire* . . . it makes me feel *sick*, all this bloody crap standing between real people and real change. . . . Men *must* change but I really don't think a lifetime trip into outer space with this shit will help' (ibid., emphasis in the original). The accusations of men's politics as fuelled by guilt were repetitively applied by successive waves of men active in gender politics.

Powercut is representative of some characteristic and revealing changes in very late twentieth-century gender politics. This periodical represented a major shift in the nature of social movement activism, away from a consciousness-raising model influenced by feminism, Black activism and gay liberation. Instead, British radical politics of this later period witnessed a flourishing of 'zine' type publications that were far more engaged with, though also critical of, popular culture. *Powercut* debated pop culture, hip hop and class politics, aiming to provide 'accessible & relevant sexual politics' (Gauntlett 1992). It was also a publishing genre that refused the rotating collectives and collaborations that had marked earlier feminist and profeminist periodicals. Dave Gauntlett wrote of the satisfaction of producing a zine alone: 'I think when you do things by committee it all gets watered down: things tend to lack a central vision and co-ordination and one central anger isn't there'. Instead, 'I throw everything into it while I'm sticking it together (typing, designing, illustrating – *making* the pages, which is what I do), hardly see anyone . . .'. To some extent this was in keeping with his pessimism about the power to effect change in a more individualistic, consumer-oriented society: 'Producing a magazine isn't doing much . . . a lot of the time there's not much you *can* do. I challenge things in my own life but I can't run anyone else's – the best I can is this mag . . .' (ibid., emphasis in the original). Nonetheless, *Powercut*'s first issue sold out, and eight hundred copies were produced of the second issue in late 1992; zines became a very significant site of new developments and innovations in feminism (Duncombe 2008).

Powercut helps us to see the ways in which British gender politics, and arguably political culture more generally, had become more individualistic, and to some extent more pessimistic, in the 1990s. But to brand this as a more selfish society is probably too simplistic. It is more useful to note that, as Sonya Rose argues, 'outpourings of moral discourse mark the times when questions of group or national solidarity and homogeneity become highly charged' (Rose 1999). We can see the debates over what or who is selfish, or what modalities of selflessness can be politically effective, as indicative of the profound rethinking of political or personal loyalties, political practices and forms of selfhood in the upheavals of post-1968. This was a long-lasting moment of political upheaval – it was not just 'around 1968', but was reworked in subsequent decades, despite their reputation for political disengagement. Thatcherism had no exclusive role in ushering in social and moral change; instead, there were many autonomous ways in which morality was already at play in social movements and individual lives that were far removed from the political Right. I remain unconvinced of the adequacy of terming this a shift to a 'selfish society'. As we have seen, selfishness was used in complex ways, and for all its individualistic pessimism, *Powercut* remained committed to an angry, accessible politics, that was 'fighting all that stands in the way of real change' (Gauntlett 1991). Moreover, as Angela McRobbie and Sarah Thornton (1995) have argued in another context, it seems unlikely that moral or emotional categories that are more typically used to assess individuals can be usefully applied to societies. A 'selfish society' can only be a highly superficial characterization of complex, multivalent late twentieth-century Britain.

Acknowledgements

I am enormously grateful to the men who have been interviewed as part of the project 'Unbecoming Men: Men and Women's Liberation in Late Twentieth Century Britain', whose reflections on their experiences are drawn on in this chapter. Some names have been changed. The original interviews are archived at the British Library Sound Archive.

Lucy Delap is a Reader in Modern British and Gender History at the University of Cambridge and a Fellow of Murray Edwards College, and an editor of *History & Policy* (lmd11@cam.ac.uk). Her book *The Feminist Avant-Garde: Transatlantic Encounters of the Early Twentieth Century* (Cambridge University Press, 2007) won the 2008 Women's History Network Prize. Her monograph, *Knowing Their Place: Domestic Service in Twentieth Century Britain*, was published by Oxford University Press in 2011. Other publications include *The Politics of Domestic Authority in Britain from 1800* (Palgrave, 2009), *Feminist Media History* (Palgrave, 2010) and *Men, Masculinities and Religious Change in Twentieth Century Britain* (Palgrave, 2013).

Notes

1. A document produced by an early men's group in Dalston in 1977, titled 'the Dalston theses', was at pains to reassure its readers that 'the forms of sexual trade unionism adopted by men and women affected by sexual politics are not a self-indulgence'. The group was dominated by members of the International Socialists, and clearly felt the need to defend their interest in sexual politics, which, they believed was 'not in itself revolutionary' (unpublished paper, in the possession of the author)
2. In the 30th anniversary edition of this book, Dawkins wrote of his regret at using the term selfish, and claimed that this sentence was 'misleading' (Dawkins 1978: ix).

References

Interviews

Interviews cited in this chapter were conducted in 2012 with the following:
Paul Atkinson
Andy Barrow
Five Cram
John Hoyland
Mark Long
Paul Morrison
Paul Smith
David Spiegelhalter
Willie Sugg
Chris Tribble
Misha Wolf

Published Sources

Achilles Heel. 1978. Issue 1, editorial statement.
Anon. 1971. 'People's Liberation', *Shrew* 3(3).
Ashe, F. 2004. 'Deconstructing the Experiential Bar: Male Experience and Feminist Resistance', *Men and Masculinities* 7(2): 187–204.
Asphodel. 1981. *Anti-Sexist Men's News*, issue 16.
Bailey, H. 1984. *Anti-Sexist Men's Newsletter*, issue 20.
Beaumont, T.W. 1968. *The Liberal Crusade against the Selfish Society*. London: Prism Publ.
Bellos, L. 1981. 'Madness and Rage, or Why I Won't Write an Academic Essay on Madness', *Catcall*, issue 12.
Bennell, P., and R. Firth. 1979. 'Notes from a Men Against Sexism Group, Brighton . . . 14 Months On', *Anti-Sexist Men's News*, no page numbers.
Black, L. 2010. *Redefining British Politics: Culture, Consumerism and Participation, 1954–70*. Basingstoke: Palgrave Macmillan.
Black, L., H. Pemberton and P. Thane, eds. 2016. *Reassessing 1970s Britain*. Manchester: Manchester University Press.

Blake, H. 1971. 'The Role of Men in Women's Liberation', *Women Are People*, April, no page numbers, Girton College Archives, CGIP CWLA 0/4.
Bocking-Welch, A. 2016. 'Youth against Hunger: Service, Activism and the Mobilisation of Young Humanitarians in 1960s Britain', *European Review of History: Revue Européenne d'histoire* 23(1–2): 1–17.
Bodenhorn, B., and G. vom Bruck, eds. 2006. *An Anthropology of Names and Naming*. Cambridge: Cambridge University Press.
Brewitt-Taylor, S. 2013. 'The Invention of a "Secular Society"? Christianity and the Sudden Emergence of Secularization Discourses in the British Media, 1961–4', *Twentieth Century British History* 24(3): 327–50.
Catcall. 1976, 'The Retreat to Cultural Feminism', issue 2.
Collier, J.L. 1991. *The Rise of Selfishness in America*. New York: Oxford University Press.
Collins, M. 2003. *Modern Love: An Intimate History of Men and Women in Twentieth-Century Britain*. London: Atlantic.
———. 2007. *The Permissive Society and Its Enemies: Sixties British Culture*. London: Rivers Oram.
Cooper, M. 1990. 'Searching for the Anti-Sexist Man', *Achilles Heel* 10: 10–13.
Coote, A., and B. Campbell. 1987. *Sweet Freedom: The Struggle for Women's Liberation*. Oxford: Basil Blackwell.
Cram, F. 1982. 'Anti-Sexism: What?', *Anti-Sexist Men's News*.
———. 1983. 'Are We Not Feminists? We Are Men', *Anti-Sexist Men's News*.
Dawkins, R. 1978. *The Selfish Gene*. Oxford: Oxford University Press.
Delap, Lucy. 2017. 'Uneasy Solidarity: The British Men's Movement and Feminism', in Kristina Schulz (ed.), *The Women's Liberation Movement: Impacts and Outcomes*. New York: Berghahn, pp. 214–36.
———. 2018. 'Feminism, Masculinities and Emotional Politics in Late Twentieth Century Britain', *Cultural and Social History* 4: 571–593.
Duncombe, S. 2008. *Notes from Underground: Zines and the Politics of Alternative Culture*. Bloomington, IN: Microcosm.
Dyhouse, C. 1981. *Girls Growing up in Late Victorian and Edwardian England*. London: Routledge & Kegan Paul.
Ettore, B. 1977. 'Some Reflections on the Past in the Struggle for Autonomy', *Catcall*, issue 6.
Fisher, T. 1993. 'Permissiveness and the Politics of Morality', *Contemporary Record* 7(1): 149–65.
Gauntlett, D. 1991. *Powercut*, issue 1.
———. 1992. *Powercut*, issue 2.
Gerhardt, S. 2011. *The Selfish Society: How We All Forgot to Love One Another and Made Money Instead*. London: Pocket.
Giddens, A. 1991. *Modernity and Self-Identity: Self and Society in the Late Modern Age*. Cambridge: Polity Press.
Gildea, R., et al. 2013. *Europe's 1968: Voices of Revolt*. Oxford: Oxford University Press.
Hinton, J. 2016. *Seven Lives from Mass Observation: Britain in the Late Twentieth Century*. Oxford University Press.
John, A.V., and C. Eustance. 1997. *The Men's Share? Masculinities, Male Support, and Women's Suffrage in Britain, 1890–1920*. London: Routledge.
Jones, T.W. 2013. *Sexual Politics in the Church of England, 1857–1957*. Oxford: Oxford University Press.

Laite, J. 2012. *Common Prostitutes and Ordinary Citizens: Commercial Sex in London, 1885–1960*. London: Palgrave Macmillan UK.
Langhamer, C. 2013. *The English in Love: The Intimate Story of an Emotional Revolution*. Oxford: Oxford University Press.
Lawrence, J. 2019. *Me, Me, Me: The Search for Community in Post-War England*. Oxford: Oxford University Press.
Marwick, A. 2006. 'Youth Culture and the Cultural Revolution of the Long Sixties', in A. Schildt and S. Detlef (eds), *Between Marx and Coca-Cola: Youth Cultures in Changing European Societies 1960–1980*. Oxford: Berghahn Books.
McLeod, H. 2010. *The Religious Crisis of the 1960s*. Oxford: Oxford University Press.
McRobbie, A., and S.L. Thornton. 1995. 'Rethinking "Moral Panic" for Multi-Mediated Social Worlds', *The British Journal of Sociology* 46(4): 559–74.
Mitchell, J., and de Winter, A. 1971. 'Report on Skegness Conference', *Shrew*, no. 9.
Motherson, K. 1979. 'Devolving Our Power – Thoughts towards the Huddersfield Weekend of Commitments', *Anti-Sexist Men's News* 5: no page numbers.
———. 1981. 'Pressure to Grow', *Anti-Sexist Men's News*, issue 16: 10.
Novak, M. 2001. *Three in One: Essays on Democratic Capitalism, 1976–2000*. Lanham, MD: Rowman & Littlefield Publishers.
Peter. 1986. *Man*, issue 23.
Phillips, J. 2012. 'Material and Moral Resources: The 1984–5 Miners' Strike in Scotland'. *The Economic History Review* 65(1): 256–76.
Rand, A. 1964. *The Virtue of Selfishness: A New Concept of Egoism*. New York: New American Library.
Rees, J. 'A Look Back at Anger: The Women's Liberation Movement in 1978'. *Women's History Review* 19(3) (2010): 337–356.
Robinson, E., et al. 2017. 'Telling Stories about Post-War Britain: Popular Individualism and the "Crisis" of the 1970s', *Twentieth Century British History* 28(2): 268–304.
Roodhouse, M. 2013. *Black Market Britain: 1939–1955*. Oxford: Oxford University Press.
Rose, S. 1999. 'Cultural Analysis and Moral Discourses: Episodes, Continuities, and Transformations', in L. Hunt and V.E. Bonnell (eds), *Beyond the Cultural Turn: New Directions in the Study of Society and Culture*. Berkeley: University of California Press.
Rowbotham, S. 1971. *Women's Liberation & the New Politics*. 'Spokesman' Pamphlets, no. 17. Nottingham: Bertrand Russell Peace Foundation for 'The Spokesman'.
Sarah. 1981. *Anti-Sexist Men's News*, issue 14.
Sutcliffe-Braithwaite, F. 2018. *Class, Politics, and the Decline of Deference in England, 1968–2000*. Oxford: Oxford University Press.
Szreter, S., and K. Fisher. 2010. *Sex before the Sexual Revolution: Intimate Life in England 1918–1963*. Cambridge: Cambridge University Press.
Thomson, M. 2006. *Psychological Subjects: Identity, Culture, and Health in Twentieth-Century Britain*. Oxford University Press.
Tomlinson, J. 2011. 'Re-Inventing the "Moral Economy" in Post-War Britain', *Historical Research* 84(224): 356–73.
Young, M., and M. Rigge. 1979. *Mutual Aid in a Selfish Society: A Plea for Strengthening the Co-Operative Movement*. London: Mutual Aid Press.

4

'Doing the Right Thing for My Child'
Self Work and Selflessness in Accounts of British 'Full-Term' Breastfeeding Mothers

Charlotte Faircloth

This chapter emerges from a research project involving a network of mothers in London[1] who breastfeed their children to 'full term'. Typically, this would be up to the age of three or four, though in this case it ranged from one to eight years old. In line with what is termed an evolutionary-based 'hominid blueprint', other typical practices among this sample of mothers include breastfeeding 'on cue', bed-sharing and 'baby-wearing' as part of a philosophy of 'attachment' parenting (Sears and Sears 2001).

Women frequently talk about their practices as 'doing the best thing for my child', whether in terms of physical, emotional or psychological health. Yet these mothers also face considerable public opprobrium over their decision to continue breastfeeding, with accusations that they are 'selfish' or doing it 'for their own sake' (often with the implication of sexual gratification). By way of rebuke, attachment mothers frequently frame their accounts of feeding as an act of *selflessness*, or at least as child-centred. This chapter explores some of the ways in which mothering practices might be considered part of individuals' 'self work', within the context of contemporary UK parenting culture. At the same time, it addresses some of the contradictions inherent to framing these debates through a dualistic self/other.

Background and Methods

The research for this study involved long-term ethnographic fieldwork (over the course of 2006–2007) with women in La Leche League International (LLL) groups, the world's foremost breastfeeding support organization. The group was founded in 1956 in the United States by a group of seven mothers, to support all women who wanted to breastfeed their babies, at a time when bottle feeding was prevalent. It has now become a global organization offering breastfeeding support through publications, telephone helplines and local meetings. While it offers support for all women who want to breastfeed, it is known among the various breastfeeding groups to be supportive of women who breastfeed for 'extended' periods, and has a significant proportion of members who practise what is known as 'attachment parenting'. This was a term coined by William and Martha Sears (the husband and wife paediatrician team) in the 1980s, and is a style of care that endorses long-term proximity between infant and care-taker (most typically, the mother). Drawing on the work done by Bowlby on attachment and Klaus and Kennell on bonding, as well as a wealth of evolutionary arguments, the logic is that babies have certain physiological expectations that must be met if they are to mature into healthy, productive, happy people (Bobel 2002: 61; Faircloth 2013, 2015).

Feeding is arguably one of the most conspicuously moralized elements of mothering today. Because of its vital importance for the survival and healthy development of infants, feeding is a highly scrutinized domain where mothers must counter any charges of practising unusual, harmful or morally suspect feeding techniques (Murphy 1999). Strong feelings about feeding are derived from the fact that it operates as a 'signal issue' which boxes women off into different parenting 'camps' (Kukla 2005). The World Health Organization (WHO) states that breastfeeding in developed countries should be exclusive for six months and continue 'for up to two years, or beyond' in conjunction with other foods (2003). There are no statistics for the number of children breastfed beyond one year in the UK, though by six months 75% of children are totally weaned off breastmilk, and only 2% of women breastfeed exclusively for the recommended six months (Department of Health 2005). So women breastfeeding to what they call 'full term' are non-conventional, and engage 'accountability strategies' to explain why they do what they do (Faircloth 2013; Strathern 2000).

Participant observation at ten local LLL groups was complemented by twenty-two semi-structured interviews and twenty-five questionnaires with individual women. Mothers were in the vast majority white, aged in their thirties (on average, thirty-four), well-educated (to university level or equivalent), not currently working, and married. Those who were identified as 'full-term' breastfeeders and attachment parents made up just over half of the sample, and it is their accounts on which I focus here.[2] Certainly not all mothers in the organization breastfeed to full term, though I engage particularly with the accounts of those who do, and with the values they promote and enact. In taking their feeding practices to an extreme, they magnify mainstream issues around motherhood and the construction of the self. These accounts do not represent official LLL philosophy, but are rather particular women's understandings of their breastfeeding experiences, equally influenced by broader philosophies of 'natural' or 'attachment' parenting (Faircloth 2015).

Theoretical Rationale: Selfhood and Motherhood

The concept of personal identity has had a long trajectory in the social sciences (see, for example, Giddens 1991; Jenkins 1996; Mead 1934; Strathern 1992b; Stryker 1968), where the term is typically used to denote an individual's comprehension of selfhood.

Many of the discussions around identity or 'the self' have aimed at destabilizing the notion that it is a natural, fixed or objective criterion, asserting that identity itself is instead a political project in which individuals and groups engage in accordance with social and historical contingencies (Giddens 1991). In their critique of 'identity' as a concept, for example, Brubaker and Cooper (2000) note that there remains a tendency in scholarly writing to confuse identity as a category of practice and as a category of analysis, leaving it a somewhat ill-defined term floating between the poles of reification and ambiguity. For that reason, the focus here is on 'identity' or 'self work' rather than on 'selfhood' per se. This is intended to highlight the active processes by which selfhood is constructed, as well as the inherently social nature of this enterprise (as opposed to it being simply a means of self-expression). Thus, while selfhood itself may be an abstract entity, its manifestations and the ways it is exercised are often open to view: in language, dress, behaviour, use of space and so forth. During social encounters, individuals assert elements of their identity through these mechanisms; in this sense, self work refers to the range of activities in which individuals engage to create, present and sustain their personal identity or selfhood (Goffman 1959).

In this study, women's self work is examined in the accounts they articulated during interviews or in questionnaires concerning their infant feeding practices, especially long-term breastfeeding. Many scholars have emphasized the role of language in the constitution of selfhood, arguing 'that human beings actually live out their lives as "narratives", [and] that we make use of the stories of the self that our culture makes available to us to plan out our lives . . . to account for events and give them significance, to accord ourselves an identity' (Rose [1989] 1999: xviii).

For Beck and Beck-Gernsheim (1995), our biographies are increasingly choice biographies. In the contemporary age, they argue, we must reflexively make our own narratives as traditional structures such as class, gender and racial constraints fall away. Indeed, they argue that in this context, having children is increasingly connected with hopes of being rooted and of life becoming meaningful, and with a 'claim to happiness' based on the close (and understood to be permanent) relationship with the child. Having a child is a meaningful experience, because it is an experience of the self:

> The desire for children [is] ego-related and connected with the present: parents want to . . . get something for themselves from giving birth, nursing, raising and providing for their children. . . . Hope of discovering oneself through one's children

is more widespread ... it is [typical] of a large number of parents that having children is no longer primarily understood as a service, a kind of devotion of social obligation. Instead it is admitted to be a way of life in which one pursues one's own interests. (Beck and Beck-Gernsheim 1995: x)

Strathern echoes this, in using a vignette drawn from the work of Miller, who worked with mothers in National Childbirth Trust (NCT) groups in North London. He illustrates how mothers are occupied by risk avoidance and optimization for their children, the means of which are a constant subject of debate. Strathern observes:

> the young mother is placed in a position of responsibility *by her knowledge of* the effects of these substances and toys on the growing body, and on the growing mind and sets of behaviours ... the child seems to embody the conscientiousness with which the mother has acted on her knowledge and stuck to her principles ... its development reflects the application of her own knowledge. (Strathern 2005: 4–5, emphasis in original)

Why is this so critical for the mother? Strathern notes that a parent shares a body with the child twice over:

> First is the body of genetic inheritance, a given, a matter regarded colloquially as of common blood or common substance. Second is the body that is a sign of the parent's devotion – or neglect – and it is in this middle class milieu above all through the application of knowledge that the parent's efforts make this body ... [Miller] jokes that the child grows the mother. (Strathern 2005: 5)

Thus, parenting is not only about how adults try to shape their children; it is also about how adults make statements about themselves (Furedi 2002: 107). In deciding how to dress, feed, put to sleep and transport their children, adults do not simply live their lives through children but, in part, develop their own selfhood through them.

Contextualizing Full-Term Breastfeeding: Selfish Mothers?

Typically, whenever I discuss my research – with peers, colleagues or friends – a frequent response is surprise, if not outright disgust. ('Breastfeeding a five-year-old? That's gross!') The majority of people I speak to don't know that a woman can lactate for such an extended period of time, let alone that anyone would want to. There is generally a sense that there is something strange – possibly even perverted – in women's 'need to be needed' (see also Dowling 2009a and 2009b on the stigmatization women experience when breastfeeding for extended periods of time). An example of this attitude is found in a *Daily Mail* article on the subject, published in June 2008:

> Her friends are horrified, but the woman who still suckles her five-year-old insists: I'll breastfeed till they're EIGHT! (*Daily Mail*, 13 June 2008)

Illustration 4.1 Picture accompanying *Daily Mail* article. Alistair Heap / Solo Syndication, published with permission.

> Stella Onions doesn't worry about people staring.
> Whether sitting outside a cafe or walking round the park, whenever she breastfeeds her two children, she ignores the women gawping and men brazenly pointing her out to their friends.
> Even in her own home – the only place she now lets her son and daughter feed from her – she barely cared when one friend turned away, unable to watch as they suckled. But such reactions are hardly surprising; the babes sucking at this middle-aged mother's breasts are toddlers aged five and three years old. For many, breastfeeding at this age is unnatural, crossing the boundaries of normal maternal behaviour.

A picture was published (Illustration 4.1), with the caption 'Mother knows best: Stella Onions breastfeeds daughter Josephine, aged five, who says she does not want to stop until she's married, and four-year-old Zac [sic]'.

In a similar vein, the comments below come from a BBC Radio 1 internet forum, following the screening of a Channel 4 documentary, 'Extraordinary Breastfeeding', in 2006, which featured Veronika Robinson, editor of *The Mother Magazine* (a natural parenting magazine), LLL member and prominent figure in the attachment parenting community breastfeeding her seven-year-old daughter. Radio 1 is the BBC's 'New Music' station, with a young target audience.[3]

> [Emphasis added] *Women who keep going until their kids are nine years old [sic] feature in Channel 4's documentary Extraordinary Breastfeeding ... Does that thought freak you out? Or are we too uptight?*

> *Leila:* I think breastfeeding beyond 1–2 yrs. is a bit bizarre and *becomes more about the mother's psychological want, not a child's biological need.* Women continue to lactate because of the stimulation through feeding, not because of a nutritional need of their offspring.
> *Gaz: This is sick!* How exactly do these mothers think they are helping their children's development? You wouldn't let your 10-year-old walk round with a bottle with a teat on it would you? *Here's an idea – get all their friends and their parents round to show them what they do – let's see how normal they feel then.*
> *Jenny: This is just wrong,* ok fair enough babies need nutrients and the goodness that comes from a mother's milk when they are born but past 6 months they are perfectly capable of producing the nutrients through other means and *this is just abuse to a certain extent.* Who in their right mind would think that it is 'right' and 'necessary' for a 3-year-old or worse 8- or 9-year old drinking from their breast?! It's absolutely disgusting.

In a more sober fashion, one mother I spoke to in the course of research – who had gone to an LLL meeting but decided it wasn't for her – sums up many of these concerns:

> *Charlotte:* Why isn't it for you [breastfeeding to full term]?
> *Sarah [breastfed both daughters for a year]:* Well, I just question sometimes [are] the mother[s] doing it for [themselves] and [their] emotional need, or are they doing it for the child's needs? And I think, I don't think the child needs it nutritionally, you know it provides a very strong bond, but then I think it can become a sort of a crutch ... but also, also sorry, sorry this is sort of challenging all my prejudices and stuff, but I have sort of read about it in the case of the single mother and her only boy child, you know, which I always feel a little strange about, and I think in some ways the boy child has replaced a partner, I mean, I don't sort of think that every woman that is breastfeeding is sitting there thinking sexual thoughts, because it just isn't like that, I don't think that is at all what happens, and I just think, I wonder if it is emotionally beneficial to the child.

As we can see, many of the comments include an undertone of sexual gratification on the part of mothers, with the implication that they might be 'selfishly' keeping their children 'attached' for their own pleasure.

Accounting for Full-Term Feeding: Selfless Self-Making

What emerged in the accounts from mothers who make this choice was – perhaps not surprisingly – a lot less sensational. Indeed, most long-term breastfeeders, as a way of countering these accusations, tended to focus on the benefits to their child in their explanations as to why they engage in this practice which runs against the social norm. These were both physiological and psychological.

When I asked my informants why they were 'still' breastfeeding, for example, 'attachment mothers' would usually answer by turning my question around: why would you stop? Breastmilk – and the immunity and nutrition it provides – continues to be beneficial at whatever age it is consumed, they told me:

> *Jane [25, LLL Leader Applicant, breastfeeding her 16-month-old son]:* It's just as nutritious as the day they were born, so that is great. And just things like, last week I was really ill, and I couldn't get out of bed, and we just stayed in bed and breastfeeding, and he was still getting all the nutrition he needed, and that would probably apply if he was a bit older too . . . and when he is upset or anything, or poorly, it is just such a comfort . . . Mmm. Yeah, there are lots of health benefits there for the mother as well, and for the child.

There was also a definite sense that women felt that by mothering in this way, they were building 'secure emotional foundations' for their children:

> *Sally [42, breastfeeding her 1-year-old daughter]:* . . . we really hope that by the time she is a teenager, she will have had her fill of being held and touched and breastfed, and be quite a secure person.

Being able to comfort a toddler having a tantrum, or a hurt child, was said to be the most gratifying reason for continuing to breastfeed, and one that made the work of mothering considerably easier. Women also frequently mentioned the fact that it was an advantage that older children could talk about breastfeeding, given that it was such an important part of their relationship. They hoped that since they continued to breastfeed their children when they were old enough to talk, they would also be able to remember this happy time:

> *Charlotte:* So, you said that when you were pregnant you would feed probably for six months . . . ?
> *Judy [39, breastfeeding her 4- and 2-year-old daughters]:* My mother breastfed for nine months, and my reference was that really, she said 'once you were big enough to start undoing my buttons I knew it was time to stop'. And so every month I did after that, with [child] really, as I had more time to think about it, I thought it's a bit sad my mother didn't experience this. Because an older child communicates about it, talks more about it, it's likely she will remember it . . . we spend so many hours doing it, and there is so much conversation around it . . .

What is also clear, however, is that these responses form part of women's construction of selfhood (or 'self work') in the narrativization of themselves *as* mothers. Alice – a 47-year-old mother to 25- and 15-year-old sons, and a five-year-old daughter, who had just weaned (herself, as is ideal according to the philosophy) – says, for example, as to why she breastfed, that:

> It is what nature intended and any other way of feeding is a very different experience for a child. I don't know what adverse effects there could be for a child not breastfed, and was not going to take the responsibility of denying them the experience.

The ways in which morality and 'doing as nature intended' intersect is the subject of other publications (Faircloth 2015), but suffice to say here that, as Cronon notes, the attraction of nature 'for those who wish to ground their moral vision in external reality is its capacity to take disputed values and make them seem innate, essential, eternal, and non-negotiable' (1996: 36).

Later, in the same questionnaire, in line with a focus on sel*fless*ness, Alice mentions several times 'owing it to her children' to not 'withhold the best'. Anastasia [38, 5- and 2-year old daughters, breastfeeding 20-month-old daughter] went further in described breastfeeding as 'the ultimate expression of motherhood'.

So, while these women's accounts are 'child-centred', they are also part of their own 'self work'. Ultimately, however, they point to one of the inherent problems with approaching this as either 'mother-centred' or 'child-centred' and reveal that continued breastfeeding was something considered mutually beneficial and pleasurable:

> *Signe [30, LLL Leader Applicant, breastfeeding her 3-year-old son]:* I guess I continue to do it because it is important for [my son] and, and because he asks for it . . . it obviously makes him feel better, he talks about it a lot, and says a lot of really sweet things about it. And because I find it an easy way to comfort him and to calm him down, and if he is feeling bad about something and doesn't always know how to talk about it, we can just take the time to sit down . . . and it's totally different to a year ago . . . I guess, I enjoy it [too], I enjoy the chance to sit down and in the evenings [while breastfeeding] I can sit down and read a book or something.

Breastfeeding, Body Boundaries and Individuality

For my informants, who were well aware that many viewed them as 'sick' or even 'abusive', full-term breastfeeding and attachment parenting in contemporary Britain are hard because 'separation is endemic to our society' (Sally). When I asked why it was that people might have a problem with the sight (or idea) of a child breastfeeding beyond infancy, Veronika Robinson, the 37-year-old LLL member and mothering magazine editor who featured in the documentary mentioned earlier, who was at the time of our interview still breastfeeding her daughter, aged seven, told me that 'to have a baby attached to the mother through breastfeeding is just the opposite of what our society is encouraging'. This is not confined to older children but is an anxiety that intensifies over time if the child is not considered to be 'separating' from its mother:

> *Veronika:* It's a cultural thing. If you look at our society everything is designed to separate mother from child; it happens, you get pregnant and you have a scan, and that is the first thing, that separation, it is telling the mother not to trust her own intuition, you know a mother has to rely on something outside to tell her about herself. And then the baby is born and the cord is cut straight away . . . everything right from those beginning stages, 'get the mother away from the baby'. It's everything; the sleeping, the walking – we celebrate milestones of separation. So if you have a baby that is attached to the mother through breastfeeding, that is just the opposite of what our society is encouraging.

Leticia added that mothers who do not 'separate properly' from their children are considered suspect (and selfish). I asked her whether there was a pressure on women to stop breastfeeding after a certain age, and she replied:

> *Leticia [36, 3-and-a-half-year-old son, breastfeeding her 2-year-old daughter, my emphasis]:* I think socially there is a pressure to 'get out and get your life back'. I think there is a pressure there, to get the baby in its own room at a certain point, to get it out of the bed at a certain point. To create a certain distance between you and the baby, *I think that is thought of as very healthy and if you are not doing that you are considered to be depriving your child, or not quite adjusted somehow.*

For Strathern, the individuality of persons is the first fact of English kinship (1992b: 14). She says, 'it is when persons become visible as individuals that the English feel they "relate" to one another' (49). To follow her argument (and without wanting to either reify it or claim its uniqueness to the English example), one might say that to 'relate' to each other, separation of the mother from the child (as part of this process of individuation) must be cultivated so that 'attachment' can begin. This separation is catalysed through techniques of visualization typical of foetal scans (Petchesky 1987), as much as in the moment of birth. Indeed, this is not a transition confined to a moment; rather, it is processual. In 'Parts and Wholes', Strathern notes that people do not arrive as individuals, but are made so through processes of socialization (and, arguably, separation), which in turn enables their participation in social life (a plurality of individuals):

> The English person conceptualised as an individual was in one important sense incomplete ... There always appeared to be 'more than' the person in social life. When the singular person was taken as a unit, relationships involved others as like units. Social life was thus conceptualised as the person's participation in a plurality. As a result, an individual person was only ever part of some more encompassing aggregate and thereby less than the whole. Where a prototypical Melanesian might have conceptualised the dissolution of the cognatic person as making incomplete an entity already completed by the actions of others, our prototypical English took the person – powerfully symbolised in the child that must be socialised – as requiring completion by society. (Strathern 1992a: 86–87)[4]

Making Selves: Separation and Attachment

A book frequently referred to by 'attachment mothers' as they spoke about maternal-infant subjectivity was Kaplan's *Oneness and Separateness: From Infant to Individual* (1978). The book is a mix of psychoanalytic insights and parenting advice. It opens by saying:

> In the first three years of life every human being undergoes yet a second birth, in which he is born as a psychological being possessing selfhood and a separate identity. The quality of self an infant achieves in those crucial three years will profoundly affect all of his subsequent existence. (Kaplan 1978: 15)

A well-adjusted child, it is argued, should separate from its mother gradually (as is in keeping with the philosophy of attachment parenting), rather than rushing through it, as is more typical in wider society. Kaplan argues that individuation in the child (from seeing oneself as an extension of the mother, towards seeing oneself as an agential, separate entity) comes from an appreciation of 'the inner mother', imprinted in the child through early experiences of mothering. Not allowing this imprinting to happen can leave the child in a state of limbo – between oneness and separateness:

> When this process goes wrong, a human being will have difficulties loving others, nurturing the young, taming his own aggression, knowing the boundaries of immediate time and space, mourning the dead and caring about the destiny of the human species. (Kaplan 1978: 19)

For Strathern, English people arrive attached, are 'separated' through socialization, and thereby able to 'relate' to others as individuals. Being able to (re)attach themselves autonomously to others allows them to participate in society. For the women in LLL groups in London, however, breastfeeding is a primary means by which to prolong the attachment of their children (and yet, as I discuss below, it is by preventing this separation that they open themselves up to the charge of selfishness). They would talk actively of the mother-infant dyad as something that needed 'protection' from society. For them, separation need not be cultivated (or, at least, rushed), as being attached to the mother serves as a template for being attached to others (and, in due course, a secure sense of self). In other words, the same end is aspired to (an 'individual self'), but reached by different means.

The interesting question is why 'attachment mothers' resist so strongly the separations they associate with normal perinatal practices – such as cutting the umbilical cord, bottle feeding or separate sleeping. Borrowing an idea from Miller (1997), it is arguable that this language of individuation and attachment is not only about creating the child's sense of self, but also that of the mother, which is embodied in a 'dual persona'.

Miller (1997) describes the 'semi-cultic' practices of the National Childbirth Trust groups he attended as *rites de passage* through which women negate their previous values and purify themselves in preparation to become new beings. He inverts traditional psychoanalytic theory from Klein to ask whether the stages a child is said to undergo (paranoid-schizoid, depressive or otherwise) might not best be applied to the development of new mothers. Klein ([1936] 1975), for example, argued that the paranoid-schizoid position occurs in infants when the child cannot understand how the mother can be both the 'good breast' and the 'bad breast' – the source of all things good, and all things bad. Miller says the same is true for the mother, for whom the child is at once the source of all things good, and all things awful. Breastfeeding is but one example of where the child's perceived need is both enjoyable and constraining:

> The infant's constant demands are accepted as essential priorities and at no point should the mother's own desires prevent them being attended to ... All her skills of self-construction through agency become negated. This negation is acceptable because the baby is not viewed as another, but as part of the newly recycled dual persona of mother-infant. This may be related to Freud's observation that 'Parental love, which is so moving and at bottom so childish, is nothing but the parents' narcissism born again, which, transformed into object-love, unmistakably reveals its former nature'. (Freud [1914] 1984: 85, in Miller 1997: 72–73)

Indeed, within psychoanalytic literature there is a focus on the transformation of the mother during the process of birth and post-partum life. It is considered a time of psychic crisis that prompts her to work through her own infantile issues (Baraitser 2006). Typically, there is a suggestion that although a mother extends herself (literally, she reproduces), she also loses something. Naomi Wolf writes, for example:

> When I spoke to new mothers, it seemed to me that although a child and new love has been born, something else within them had passed away, and the experience was made harder because at some level, underneath their joy in their babies, these women were quietly mourning for this part of their earlier selves. (Wolf 2001: 6)

The implication here is that a mother's self is changed irrevocably, demanding that a woman leave behind her previous, unified self, and embrace a dyadic existence (however illusory the unified self might have been). Generally, 'attachment mothers' had a mixture of feelings on this issue. Amelia said, for example: 'Sometimes we have a great time and cooperate and other times I shout or feel dominated by my child'. Another said, in answer to my question, 'Is it hard to balance your own needs with those of your child or children?':

> *Claudine [24, breastfeeding her 17-month-old daughter]*: Not really because I am not the self-sacrificing type at all! First, most of my needs do not exclude her or contradict hers, second, I do always take the time to fill my own needs for as I say I am not the self-sacrificing type at all, and also she seems to understand my needs and gives me the space to fill them. But I guess this is also because her dad is a great father, which allows me to have my own space. I suppose it might be more difficult with two or more children, or no daddy on hand.

Miller's observations are largely confined to the early period of the child's life (typically, before six months of age). There comes a time, he says, when the child pushes the boundaries of the 'newly recycled dual persona', and 'intervention' is required – such as when the child needs to be told, for example, to wait to be breastfed. This is when the child starts being seen as an 'individual'.

Indeed, a topic that came up frequently at meetings was at which point a child's 'needs' become their 'wants' – and therefore at what point a child could be asked to wait, for example, before being breastfed, or whether a mother could put her own 'need' to sleep through the night above that of her child's by ceasing night-time feeding.[5] These tensions are not confined to attachment parents, of course, but are part of wider realities that parents must negotiate. Veronika Robinson notes, about full-term breastfeeding in particular, however:

> It depends on the age of the child. Around two or three they are emerging in the world, and starting to see themselves as separate from the mothers, and so as a mother you have to let them explore, and sort of let them push the boundary; other times you have to create that boundary, that is what parenting is about.... And so, yeah, I mean, child-led weaning doesn't mean that the child determines every time they are going to breastfeed ... it is different to when you have a tiny baby. Their wants are their needs at that point ... it might be that you say 'we are not going to do it in the day' or 'in the night', whatever the mother's thing is, and I don't think there is anything wrong with it ... I think once they are moving around it's important to say that, you know, because you will have some children that will have you on the couch all day breastfeeding!

Defending Self and Other

The link between the body with definable boundaries and selfhood is long established in Western philosophy. These bodies, which are the property of the subjects who inhabit (or 'are') them, maintain a distinction from other bodies by managing the transgression of their boundaries (such as in the flow of substance between them). Breastfeeding is therefore a challenge to the notion of the individual body, since the ejection of milk from the breast does not sit easily with the 'fortress' metaphor of the body/self (Martin 1998).

Martin (1998) has written about the inability of women to be an 'individual' (one who cannot be divided) as a deeply political fact. Quoting Franklin and Haraway, she says:

> pregnancy is precisely about one body becoming two, two bodies becoming one, the exact antithesis of individuality (Franklin 1991: 203). Donna Haraway (1991: 253n) explains: 'Why have women had so much trouble counting as individuals in modern western discourses? Their personal, bounded individuality is compromised by their bodies' troubling talent for making other bodies, whose individuality can take precedence over their own'. (Martin 1998: 134–35)

In pregnancy, a woman's body/self becomes doubled – and breastfeeding, particularly for 'extended' periods, serves as a reminder of this ability to reproduce and transgress these boundaries. Martin continues:

> not only the state of motherhood but also women's state of health in general, their failure in many ways to achieve the male norm of the self as a defended castle, leads to the same effect. Whether leaking fluids through ducts and membranes (which simultaneously allows penetration of the foreign into the body) or permitting the body to turn against itself, this porous, hybrid, leaky, disorderly female self is the antithesis of the sharp-edged man ... (Martin 1998: 135)

Thus, most mothers in my sample perceived the problem with long-term breastfeeding 'in society' as one where people understand it as (bodily) evidence of the child not really being separate from the mother: a relic from the time at which a baby is unable to act autonomously and therefore precluding, one could argue, either the mother or the child from participating in the plurality of society as individuals.

Perhaps not surprisingly, then, 'judgement' was the most commonly cited challenge women mentioned to their full-term breastfeeding, often with the implication that women have selfishly 'kept the child for themselves':

> *Charlotte:* We were talking at the group about the documentary [that featured Veronika Robinson].
> *Sandra [Leader, 35, breastfeeding her 4-year-old daughter]:* I did see it, yes. My in-laws were a bit like 'that's disgusting', especially with the older children. They are still a bit uncomfy about the fact I still do it. 'Don't do it in front of us, and we won't comment' sort of thing. It [the documentary] has been quite good in terms of generating discussion; you know, a way for us to broach it and explain why we're doing this.

Many women simply lied to people, or at least kept their breastfeeding as discreet as possible. As Katy put it, 'I do tell people if they ask me directly, but to be honest, I find it easier to avoid the topic'. This included health professionals. Others used jokes to divert the attention – such as about *Little Britain's* 'bitty' sketch (a comedy show featuring a character who breastfeeds as an adult) or to suggest their children would still be breastfeeding when they went to university. By contrast, some women talked about being 'strong-minded' and the criticisms being 'like water off a duck's back'.

La Leche League operates as a network offering women support for their full-term breastfeeding, and a social identity formed around a shared set of mothering values. Although the LLL leaders interviewed insisted that La Leche League was a space for all breastfeeding mothers, many were aware that LLL had a reputation in the wider community for being 'extreme'. One leader, talking about how LLL was perceived in the wider community, commented:

> *Annette [Leader, breastfeeding her 7-year-old son]:* I suppose they probably just think that it is over-zealous really. And, erm, the earth mother sort of thing, of a woman who gives all to her children and wastes her own life, because they can't see the value in what the mothers are doing.

Kanter, a sociologist of utopian communities, notes that the idea of sacrifice and/or renunciation is central to group coherence in such communities (Kanter 1972: 72). In the questionnaire, women were asked to list some of the reasons they thought other women did not breastfeed their children. Their answers highlight the sacrifices other women are not willing to make. Just over half said it was because they 'wanted their bodies back' for themselves and their partners. Others thought they were 'too selfish' to breastfeed. These comments were typical:

Claire [38, 7-year-old son, breastfeeding 11-month-old son]: They put themselves before their babies/children but babes only need us like this for a relatively short time overall in breastfeeding, it's no real hardship is it?
Debbie [46, 8-year-old son, breastfeeding 4-year-old son]: A lot of women want a life away from their children and you cannot do both.

Women who have given up careers, as many of my informants had, might be said to have a greater investment in motherhood as a source of selfhood than those who had not. Several women pointed out that work is not possible if one wants to be able to breastfeed to full term (and, we could infer, parent in an attachment parenting style). The implication is that one cannot parent according to a child's needs unless one is also willing to make this sacrifice. These women said, in a joint interview:

Lila [37, breastfeeding her 4-year-old son]: And people make out [full-term breastfeeding] is such a long time, and so tedious, and you think . . . it really is not that long a period, it's just a few years. People are more selfish today. People still have this idea of self-sacrifice with breastfeeding . . . So they have to promote it in terms of losing weight . . . this 'me' thing comes through, they have to watch what they eat, can't drink. People have such a drive towards selfishness.
Rachel: My sister-in-law wanted to go out drinking! So she stopped at six months!
Lila: People have such a drive for individuality. They see it as a sacrifice. People don't see that investing now will save time later. It is a fraction of their lives. It is just too much for people. People find it too hard to not watch telly, or not have something for a few days. We can't deal with not having things now. Everything is a race . . . Other people are too selfish to mother like we do – we are all too much part of the 'me' generation.

We see here, then, how the discourse around selfishness is taken up by some attachment mothers and used as a means of judging 'other mothers' in the course of bolstering their own 'self work'.

Conclusion

'Accountability' takes on a particularly moralized edge in the context of mothering, because mothers share not one but *two* bodies with their children (Strathern 2005). To this extent, the child becomes a symbol of maternal devotion, and a reflection of her diligence. Mothers do not simply encourage the development of their child's social self through mothering, but develop their own 'selves' in this process, both in relation to their child and in relation to others.

It is interesting, then, that methods of childcare are so often framed as a trade-off between the needs of the mother and those of the child. As soon as methods of care are defined as either child-centred or mother-centred, then one 'side' logically has to lose out. Accounts of attachment parenting (or indeed, any kind of parenting) that portray women as sacrificing their 'selves' to be subsumed by the self of their child are simplistic, and problematic. It seems almost inevitable that by becoming a mother, a woman's 'self' changes. Whether a woman's devotion to her child constitutes a diminution of her autonomous selfhood or an extension of it will long be a source of debate. Bristow (2007) comments:

> When individuals become parents they don't subsume themselves but extend themselves – in a sense, they become more than what they were before. The act of raising children, loving them, caring for them, setting them on a trajectory through life, is an act of selfhood, and people do it because they sense it is ultimately more rewarding and meaningful than the accomplishments they might make on their own, as individuals. To pretend that this impulse isn't there, that as a parent you are doing something despite your own interests rather than because of them, is a dishonest conceit.[6]

The 'attachment mothers' here are confronted with a need to justify what is seen to be anti-social, selfish behaviour (to use Strathern's definition of society). Yet 'child-centred' approaches to parenting should better be understood as part of these mothers' struggle for self-identity, and a prominent part of their self-fashioning. This process is not necessarily experienced by 'attachment mothers' as a form of sacrifice for an other or 'oppression' to their individualized selves, but rather as an extension of agency, when understood through the more relational model. Ironically, however, in accusing other mothers of not being 'selfless' enough to provide the 'best' form of care for their children, the power of this dualistic discourse remains unchallenged.

Charlotte Faircloth is Associate Professor in the Sociology of Gender at the Thomas Coram Research Unit, Department of Social Science, University College London (Charlotte.Faircloth@ucl.ac.uk). She was a founding member of the Centre for Parenting Culture Studies (CPCS) at the University of Kent. Her book *Militant Lactivism? Attachment Parenting and Intensive Motherhood in the UK and France* (Berghahn Books, 2013) was shortlisted for the BSA Philip Abrams Memorial Prize 2014. She is co-author of *Parenting Culture Studies* (Palgrave, 2014) and co-editor of *Parenting in Global Perspective: Negotiating Ideologies of Kinship, Self and Politics* (Routledge, 2014), in addition to numerous other special issues and journal articles. Her current research explores the intersections of gender, intimacy and equality in parenting.

Notes

1. Parallel research was also conducted in Paris, but those data are not referred to here.
2. These are women who practise an 'attachment parenting' philosophy in addition to being members of LLL. Classification is based on statistics and responses derived from the questionnaire – that is, those women breastfeeding their children beyond

a year – as well as the author's observations at group meetings and interviews. All names have been anonymized.
3. http://www.bbc.co.uk/radio1/news/newsbeat/060201_extraordinarybreastfeeding.shtml (accessed 20 December 2006). The page has since expired.
4. I do not enter into a discussion here about the over-simplification of a Euro-American, bounded self and an othered 'relational' one. See Carsten's *Cultures of Relatedness* (2000: 83) for a good summary.
5. It is debatable at what point a child is reflexive enough to have a 'want' rather than a 'need'. This raises questions of autonomy and informed consent, the parameters of which are managed by mothers.
6. Of course, Bristow's comment can only be understood in the context of widely available contraception and abortion.

References

Baraitser, L. 2006. '"Oi Mother, Keep Ye' Hair On!" Impossible Transformations of Maternal Subjectivity', *Studies in Gender and Sexuality* 7(3): 217–38.

Beck, U., and E. Beck-Gernsheim. 1995. *The Normal Chaos of Love*. Oxford: Polity Press.

Bobel, C. 2002. *The Paradox of Natural Mothering*. Philadelphia: Temple University Press.

Bristow, J. 2007. 'Jennie Bristow's Guide for Subversive Parents. Lesson 2: It's Not All About You', https://www.spiked-online.com/2007/04/11/rule-2-its-not-all-about-you/. Accessed 15 May 2007.

Brubaker, R., and F. Cooper. 2000. 'Beyond "Identity"', *Theory and Society* 29: 1–47.

Buskens, P. 2001. 'The Impossibility of "Natural Parenting" for Modern Mothers: On Social Structure and the Formation of Habit', *Association for Research on Mothering Journal* 3(1): 75–86.

Butler, J. 1997. *The Psychic Life of Power: Studies in Subjection*. Stanford, CA: Stanford University Press.

Carsten, J. (ed.). 2000. *Cultures of Relatedness: New Approaches to the Study of Kinship*. Cambridge: Cambridge University Press.

Cronon, W. 1996. *Uncommon Ground: Rethinking the Human Place in Nature*. New York: W.W. Norton & Co.

Daily Mail. 2008. 'Her Friends Are Horrified, But the Woman Who Still Suckles Her Five-Year-Old Insists: "I'll Breastfeed Till They're EIGHT!"', 13 June.

Department of Health. 2005. *Infant Feeding Survey 2005*. London: Department of Health. http://www.ic.nhs.uk/webfiles/publications/breastfeed2005/InfantFeedingSurvey190506_PDF.pdf. Accessed 17 September 2008.

Dowling, S. 2009a. 'Women's Experiences of Long-Term Breastfeeding', *The Practising Midwife* 12(10): 22–25.

———. 2009b. 'Inside Information: Researching Long-Term Breastfeeding', *The Practising Midwife* 12(11): 22–26.

Faircloth, C. 2013. *Militant Lactivism? Attachment Parenting and Intensive Motherhood in the UK and France*. Oxford: Berghahn Books.

———. 2015. 'Full-Term Breastfeeding: Nature, Morality and Feminism in London and Paris', *Ethnos: Journal of Anthropology* 82: 19–43, special issue on Nature and Ethics, ed. K. Dow and V. Boydell.

Furedi, F. 2002. *Paranoid Parenting: Why Ignoring the Experts May Be Best for Your Child*. Chicago: Chicago Review Press.
Giddens, A. 1991. *Modernity and Self-Identity: Self and Society in the Late Modern Age*. Cambridge: Polity.
Goffman, E. 1959. *The Presentation of Self in Everyday Life*. New York: Doubleday.
Hays, S. 1996. *The Cultural Contradictions of Motherhood*. New Haven, CT: Yale University Press.
Jenkins, R. 1996. *Social Identity*. London: Routledge.
Kanter, R. 1972. *Commitment and Community Communes and Utopias in Sociological Perspective*. Cambridge, MA: Harvard University Press.
Kaplan, L. 1978. *Oneness and Separateness: From Infant to Individual*. New York: Touchstone Press.
Klein, M. [1936] 1975. *Love Guilt, Reparation, and Other Works 1921–1945*. New York: Delacorte Press.
Kukla, R. 2005. *Mass Hysteria, Medicine, Culture and Women's Bodies*. New York: Rowman and Littlefield.
Lee, E., and J. Bristow. 2009. 'Rules for Feeding Babies', in D. Sclater, S. Ebtehaj, F. Jackson and M. Richards (eds), *Regulating Autonomy: Sex Reproduction and Family*. Oxford: Hart, pp. 73–91.
Martin, E. 1987. *The Woman in the Body: A Cultural Analysis of Reproduction*. Boston, MA: Beacon Press.
———. 1998. 'The Fetus as Intruder: Mothers' Bodies and Medical Metaphors', in R. Davis-Floyd and J. Dumit (eds), *Cyborg Babies: From Technosex to Techno-Tots*. New York: Routledge, pp. 125–42.
Mead, G.H. 1934. *Mind, Self, and Society*. Chicago: University of Chicago Press.
Miller, D. 1997. 'How Infants Grow Mothers in North London', *Theory, Culture and Society* 14: 67–88.
Murphy, E. 1999. '"Breast is Best": Infant Feeding Decisions and Maternal Deviance', *Sociology of Health and Illness* 21(2): 187–208.
Petchesky, R. 1987. 'Foetal Images: The Power of Visual Culture in the Politics of Reproduction', in M. Stanworth (ed.), *Reproductive Technologies: Gender, Motherhood and Medicine*. Oxford: Polity, pp. 57–80.
Robinson, V. 2007. *The Drinks Are on Me: Everything Your Mother Never Told You about Breastfeeding*. East Grinstead: Art of Change Press.
Rose, N. [1989] 1999. *Governing the Soul: The Shaping of the Private Self*. London: Routledge.
Schmied, V., A. Sheehan and L. Barclay. 2001. 'Contemporary Breast-Feeding Policy and Practice: Implications for Midwives', *Midwifery* 17: 44–54.
Sears, W., and M. Sears. 2001. *The Attachment Parenting Book: A Commonsense Guide to Understanding and Nurturing Your Baby*. London: Little, Brown and Company.
Strathern, M. 1992a. 'Parts and Wholes: Refiguring Relationships in a Postplural World', in A. Kuper (ed.), *Conceptualising Society*. London: Routledge, pp. 25–103.
———. 1992b. *After Nature: Kinship in the Late Twentieth Century*. Cambridge: Cambridge University Press.
———. (ed.). 2000. *Audit Cultures: Anthropological Studies in Accountability, Ethics and the Academy*. London: Routledge.
———. 2005. *Kinship, Law and the Unexpected: Relatives Are Always a Surprise*. Cambridge: Cambridge University Press.

Stryker, S. 1968. 'Identity Salience and Role Performance: The Importance of Symbolic Interaction Theory for Family Research', *Journal of Marriage and the Family* 30: 558–64.

Wolf, N. 2001. *Misconceptions: Truth, Lies and the Unexpected on the Journey to Motherhood*. London: Chatto and Windus.

World Health Organization (WHO). 2003. *Global Strategy on Infant and Young Child Feeding*. Geneva: WHO. https://www.who.int/nutrition/publications/infantfeeding/9241562218/en/. Accessed 27 September 2007.

5

Sexism, Separatism and the Rhetoric of Selfishness
Single Mothers by Choice in the US and UK

Susanna Graham and Linda L. Layne

Selfishness and Separatism

Selfishness is the most common accusation levelled against Single Mothers by Choice (SMCs), women who choose to make a family without the involvement of a man to fill the role of father. In this chapter, we (Linda L. Layne, an anthropologist from the US, and Susanna Graham, an anthropologist from the UK) map the rhetoric of selfishness in the discourse about, and of, heterosexual SMCs in the US and UK and probe why it is that this negative moral judgement is so often applied. Most SMCs create their families using donor sperm and are judged to be selfish in contrast to single mothers who become single via divorce, separation or widowhood. They are also more likely to be called selfish than lesbian and gay parents. The reason for this difference, we conclude, is that SMCs' choice is understood to deprive heterosexual men – would-be sexual partners and co-parents – of the pleasures of procreation and parenting, pleasures they may feel are rightfully theirs.

Writing in the early 1980s, the American feminist philosopher Marilyn Frye observed that 'heterosexuality, marriage and motherhood . . . are the institutions which most obviously . . . maintain female accessibility to males'.[1] She noted that the degree of 'defensiveness, nastiness, violence, hostility and irrationality' of men's reactions to feminism tends to correlate with how blatant it is that women are choosing to separate themselves from men. Some of the examples she gives in which the separation is 'pretty dramatic' are 'women leaving homes, marriages and boyfriends' (Frye 1983: 105). Choosing to be a single mother by choice is equally dramatic.

As we saw in the Introduction to this volume, ever since the term entered the English language, 'selfish' has implicitly referred to the existence of virtuous, entitled 'others' to whom one is morally obliged to devote one's 'self'. In the seventeenth century, it was to 'God' and the 'Publique' good that people were exhorted to give themselves. In the case of single mothers by choice, it is neither God nor the public who are seen as morally deserving of the gift of self, but rather heterosexual men – would-be husbands and fathers – and children. SMCs whole-heartedly give themselves to their children. It is their choice to pursue pregnancy and parenthood without a man, and in so doing to withhold these previously taken-for-granted rights of heterosexual men, that triggers opprobrium. Gay and lesbian parents are not subject to the charge of selfishness, we argue, precisely because they are not seen as potential sexual and parenting partners by heterosexual men. As Frye (1983: 96) puts it, 'men's access to women is the Patriarchal Imperative', and 'no-saying' by women, that is, denying men access, represents 'a substantial removal (redirection, reallocation) of goods and services . . .' (cf. Delap, this volume).

We also document when and how the rhetoric of selfishness appears in SMCs' own narratives and find it most salient during the 'thinking' phase, that is, while they consider creating a family in this way. Potential SMCs worry about their motives, but those who go through with it ultimately decide that their motives are no more selfish than those of other parents, that buying sperm is less selfish and more respectful of men than several of the alternatives, and that becoming a mother is much less selfish than remaining single. Once SMCs have a child, whatever concerns they may have had about their motives or fairness to the child are supplanted by the rigours of intensive, child-centred, some would say 'selfless' parenting.[2]

The material for this chapter is derived from media coverage of SMCs, their how-to books, memoirs and online forums, and Graham's ethnographic study undertaken between November 2010 and January 2012 exploring the decision-making and experiences of twenty-three single heterosexual women in the UK who were thinking about and embarking upon solo motherhood through the use of donor sperm (Graham 2012, 2014, 2018).[3] We also draw on Layne's intensive case study of one American SMC (Layne 2013a, 2014, 2015, 2016), and contextualize our findings with those of Layne on gay parents based on media coverage, how-to books and published memoirs (Layne 2013b).

Background

The term 'Single Mother by Choice' was coined in the early 1980s by Jane Mattes, who established the first peer support group for such women in New York. A second organization, Choice Moms, was founded by American Mikki Morrissette in 1999. In the UK, SMCs are sometimes referred to as 'solo' or 'lone' mothers or mums, but the British media often refers to them using the American terms and the US-based groups are commonly-used sources of support and knowledge for women in the UK. Several UK-based organizations (the Donor Conception Network and Fertility Friends, for example) also serve UK SMCs.[4]

Although there are no official statistics for the methods used by SMCs, it is estimated that between 60 and 75% of US SMCs use sperm purchased from a sperm bank (Harmon 2005; Jadva et al. 2009). In the UK, the use of donor sperm also appears to be the preferred method. According to the UK regulatory body, the Human Fertilitisation and Embryology Authority (HFEA), in 2011, 860 single women had fertility treatment using donor sperm at a UK licensed clinic,[5] whereas only about one-third of that number of single women adopted.[6] In 2016 17% of the 5,446 donor insemination treatment cycles were done for women who registered as having no partner (HFEA 2017: 6).

Among American SMCs there is a growing preference for 'identity-release' or 'yes' donors who consent to being contacted by the resulting children if they so choose once they are eighteen years old. In the UK, since the HFEA's removal of anonymity in 2005, sperm from identity-release donors has been the only option available for women seeking treatment in licensed clinics. However, British women are still able to get anonymous donor sperm or eggs abroad, although Graham's data suggest that for many the use of anonymous donation is a consequence of seeking cheaper treatment abroad, rather than an actual preference for anonymous donors. Indeed, many participants imported identity-release sperm from large American and European sperm banks in order to secure more information about the donor, rather than less (Graham 2014).

Because the 'medically infertile' have had priority over those who are 'practically infertile' (i.e. lesbian couples and SMCs), in 2014 the UK opened the National Sperm Bank – a joint project by the National Gamete Donation Trust (NGDT) and Birmingham Women's Fertility Centre, supported by a start-up grant from the Department of Health. This, the world's first national sperm bank closed after one year due to lack of funding. Laura Witjens, Chief Executive of the NGDT, had hoped it would generate enough 'surplus sperm' to meet the demand among same-sex couples and single women, which has 'grown exponentially' as it has 'become more socially acceptable to say, "I haven't found a guy yet, don't want to wait for him, still want a child"' (Manning 2014). One rationale for this programme was to discourage such family-makers from attaining unregulated sperm locally via the internet or using services abroad. In 2014 almost a quarter of all donated sperm samples were imported from abroad 'up from 1-in-10 in 2005' (Akinyemi 2014) and by 2016, 39% of newly-registered sperm donors were from outside of the UK, of which 49% were in the US and 45% in Denmark (HFEA 2017: 4).

On both sides of the Atlantic, SMCs tend to be heterosexual, white, over thirty-five, highly educated and financially independent (Graham 2014;[7] Jadva et al. 2009; Murray and Golombok 2005). Their level of education and wage-earning abilities are characteristics that can be credited to second-wave feminism (Layne 2015). SMCs are among those who benefited from legislation in the 1960s and 1970s in both countries which resulted in dramatic increases in women's educational[8] and occupational attainment.[9] Although women still suffer a significant wage gap,[10] the fact remains, thanks to second-wave successes in creating opportunities for women in higher education and the skilled labour force, that significantly more women now feel they can afford to bring up children on their own. Being able to do so is a major factor in SMCs' decisions to go it alone (Mattes 1994; Morrissette 2008).

During the decades when American and British women were enjoying expanding opportunities, many men in these countries saw their position weaken. Their relative earning power and educational achievements diminished, marriage rates dropped and divorce rates rose. Writing in the early 1980s, Frye (1983: 96) concluded that men were right to panic at the thought of being abandoned by women, citing social scientific evidence that men's physical and mental health suffers 'when deprived of the care and companionship of a female mate, or keeper'. A similar argument was made by conservative British commentator Doughty in 2014.

Globalization and the recessions of the 1990s hurt the mostly male industrial working class and undermined the role of the male breadwinner in both countries (Faludi 1999; Heartfield 2002). A 2011 British article, 'The Survival Guide for Breadwinning Wives', reported that 'a quarter of women now earn more than their husbands [and this] can place huge pressure on a marriage' (Carey 2011). In 2013, the American Pew Research Center issued a report on 'Breadwinner Moms' that reports that in the US, 'Mothers Are the Sole or Primary Provider in Four-in-Ten Households with Children' (Wang et al. 2013). According to some, these changes have created a 'crisis of masculinity'.[11] The recession of the early twenty-first century is thought to have resulted in higher rates of job loss for men than women, leading some to label it a 'man-cession' (Carey 2011), and rekindled the notion of 'a crisis of masculinity' (Hardman 2014). As one author put it, 'Men are really searching for a role in modern society; the things we used to do aren't in much demand anymore' (McAllister quoted in Rogers 2010).

Increases in women's levels of academic achievement and financial independence are linked to a number of changes in family patterns in the US and UK, including an increase in numbers of working mothers, a decline in marriage rate, later age at marriage, later age of first child, high divorce rates, higher rates of births outside of wedlock, and the growth of single-parent households including single mothers by choice (Bailey 2007). We argue that the accusations of selfishness levelled against SMCs are fuelled by the feeling that their choices represent yet another loss of conventional heterosexual male privilege.

'That's Selfish': Accusations of 'Selfishness' in Discourse about SMCs

British SMC Ruth Yahel (2006) writes, 'the main accusation levelled at women who, like myself, have chosen to be single mothers, is that we are selfish'. The

American who founded 'Single Mothers by Choice', Jane Mattes, reports that one of the questions she is 'most often asked is if we aren't being selfish to bring children into the world without a father' (1994). Online articles pose questions like, 'Choice Moms – single women choosing to become mothers – is gaining in popularity but are Choice Moms being selfish?' and invite readers to comment, knowing that this question will generate heated commentary. For example, Choice Moms' founder, Mikki Morrissette, debated this question with Robert Franklin, a member of the board of directors of Fathers and Families (2010) and the women's magazine *Marie Clare* published a piece titled 'More Women Choosing to Have Babies Solo: A Good Thing?' which poses the question, 'Is it selfish to have babies just for "the joy" of having them?' (Kelly 2010). Louise Sloan, the American SMC who wrote *Knock Yourself Up*, recalls watching 'a fairly negative talk-show segment on single moms by choice and read[ing] several scathing opinion columns calling moms like me selfish, man-hating, immoral meanies. Ouch' (Sloan 2007).

The most elaborate and vehement condemnations of SMCs seem to come from heterosexual men. One bitterly complains:

> Is this then the real point of feminism, not equality to men but to actually replace them. To take men completely out of the family unit and make them replaceable drones when you need some dirty work done? Maybe the real problem is that a lot of women talk a good game about equality but can't get past their Cinderella mentality and marry a man who makes less then [sic] them. (Reagan 2012)

A report published in 1990by the UK's Institute for Public Policy Research, *The Family Way*, argued that 'it cannot be assumed that men are bound to be an asset to family life, or that the presence of fathers in families is necessarily a means to social harmony and cohesion' (Coote, Harman and Hewitt, quoted in Poole 2013). Fathers 4 Justice, a British direct action fathers' rights organization, singled out two of the authors, Harriet Harman and Patricia Hewitt, both Labour MPs who served as Minister of Women.

The HFEA's removal of the clause that required consideration of a 'child's need for a father' in 2008 was another flash point. Critics described it as 'another nail in the coffin of traditional family life' (Davies 2009), and as 'the feminist dream comes true ... What are men meant to do now? If they're not needed as responsible fathers, as providers, what is their role in life now? What is their status?' (respondent to Davies 2009).

One of the comments posted online in response to an article reporting on 'single career women who [now] wish their donor babies had fathers' (Hardy 2013) read:

> For Gods sake -if these women didn't put their jobs first they would have had time to go out and meet a man, get married and have the children the proper way these women are selfish and only thinking of their own needs probably another reason they couldn't get a man. (fedupreigate, Reigate; spelling and grammatical errors in original)

In the UK, figures from the 2011 census indicated that the number of men in their 30s and 40s living alone had risen to 64% and was greater than the number of women in this age group doing so. A *Daily Mail* correspondent (Doughty 2014) reporting on these figures dubbed this a 'lonely generation of men'[12] and illustrated the piece with pictures of solitary, downcast white men.

Like SMCs, members of the fathers' rights groups that emerged in the US and UK in the 1990s tend to be white and heterosexual. While their primary target is family law, which privileges mothers (Crowley 2008), they also routinely criticize single mothers. Given their premise that 'children need two parents' and that 'children have a fundamental human right to an opportunity and relationship with both their mother and father'[13]), it is not surprising that some fathers' rights activists would also be SMC critics.

Tony Fantetti, founder of the Ohio Council for Father's Rights, which appears to be one of the many 'one-man bands' (O'Connor 2007: 47) that constitute the fathers' rights movement, portrays SMCs as an extreme example of the selfishness which he attributes to single mothers. In a piece on his website he writes:

> the most selfish and self-centered type of 'single mom by choice' ... are those women who have that 'you go girl' attitude and thereby aren't just proud about bringing fatherless children into the world, they're incredibly ostentatious and extremely dogmatic as they pontificate their reasons why fathers 'aren't needed' to raise children. (2011)

A similar attitude is found among some participants of the 'manosphere' such as the 'anti-feminist blog' 'Eternal Bachelor: Give Modern Women the Husband They Deserve: None', founded in 2005 by a thirty-year-old bachelor from England who adopts the persona of Duncan Idaho, a character in the *Dune* novels who is depicted as a handsome man whom women find attractive.[14] Idaho responded to Yahel's (2006) *Daily Mail*[15] piece with a post entitled 'Selfish Cunt'. The most salient reason for which he deems SMCs 'selfish' is that they sexually rejected men like him.

> If women want the benefit of good hardworking men to provide for them financially and give them children, then they have to give those men their prime years. [Because] women have ... let ... men rot all alone while they are in their late teens and early 20's, in return once men get financially stable (mid 20's–early 30's) ... men like me will be the ones who will run the show not them! (Idaho 2006)

One respondent explains that he plans on getting his revenge by 'visiting Latin American Countries and Asian Countries and meet[ing] gorgeous women in their prime years'.[16]

Idaho (2006) also accuses SMCs of being selfish because they entered the workforce rather than allowing men like him to support them as full-time wives and mothers: 'Women chose to throw away the generous way men worked and provided for them so they, women, could stay at home to be full-time mothers.

Women chose to storm into the workplace'. He calls Yahel a 'selfish single career-gal who left it too late because she fell for feminism'.

Idaho and his supporters also fault SMCs for selfishness because they deprive children of their fathers ('A bunch of selfish skanks wanting to get knocked up and have a pet baby but can't be bothered establishing a relationship to ensure the child has a father') and because they deprive fathers of their children ('many ... get pregnant by random guys and have no intention of letting the father see the child. Or use a sperm bank for this purpose') (Idaho 2006).[17] A year later he wrote a piece, accusing a single woman who was undergoing a fifth IVF cycle in her quest to have a child of being 'selfish ... for leaving motherhood far too late (2007).[18]

A number of fathers' rights advocates in the US, including David Blankenhorn, have come out against the US's 'free market in sperm', which allows the selling of sperm to single women. John Smoot (2013a, 2013b), a former US family court judge, opposes sperm donation, noting that SMCs are one of the primary groups who use sperm banks. He blames the emergence of SMCs (i.e. women who look beyond men when they are ready to start their families) on 'male self-absorption' fostered by 'an excess of recreational sex, pornography, and video games' (2013a).

In both countries, critics draw on sexist stereotypes to make the case that SMCs are selfish for choosing to get pregnant and parent on their own rather than share the pleasures of baby-making and parenting with men.

Sexist Stereotype: Women Indulge Themselves by Shopping

One such stereotype is that shopping is a major source of pleasure for women. See, for example, the comic depiction of a 'female brain' complete with a 'shopping lobe' along with lobes for 'binges and cravings', 'chocolate' and 'maternal urges'.[19] In contrast to Miller's (1998) finding that women of North London shopped primarily as an expression of love for their families, the negative stereotype depicts women as self-indulgent shoppers, with an insatiable appetite for items with which to adorn themselves, especially designer handbags and shoes.[20] When used to criticize SMCs, their children are likened to accessories, 'an article or set of articles of dress, ... that adds completeness, convenience, attractiveness' (Dictionary.com).

This stereotype has been employed by a number of SMC critics. For example, American author/SMC Louise Sloan reports, 'People have accused me of being selfish, that I bought a baby as an accessory in much the same way I might buy an expensive handbag (Weathers 2007). A respondent to an article provocatively titled, 'Daddies Be Damned! Who Are the British Women Who Think Fathers Are Irrelevant?' (Davies 2009) views the choice to parent alone as 'selfish', and likens parenting this way to loveless 'designer breeding'. The chief executive of the new national British sperm bank refers to single women as 'customers rather than patients' (Manning 2014), and Church of England Bishop Michael Nazir-Ali (2014) predicts that the bank will result in hundreds of fatherless 'designer families'. Another critic, responding to Davies' article (2009), wrote, 'Stories such as this make me despair at the total selfishness of some people ... Money, money, money, career, career, money ... Ooh I need to have children, I'll buy one'.[21]

Sexist Stereotype: Women Are Driven by Irrational Desires

Another, related, sexist stereotype deployed by SMC critics is that women are driven by their emotions and irrational desires, most notably a hard-wired drive to become a mother. In his sympathetic review of SMC Nina Davenport's documentary *First Comes Love*, Alan Scherstuhl (2013) tries to understand the negative reaction he got from men he told about the film – 'Two hours about this unmarried woman's decision to have a baby? How narcissistic!' Scherstuhl counters, 'No more narcissistic than Proust', and goes on to describe how Nina's 'drive to mother surges with such power ... a longing so deep' it is hard to put into words, a 'biological compulsion' that is beyond rational comprehension.

SMC critics often cast women's selfish, irrational 'desires' for a baby against the 'rights' of a potential child. This is well-trod territory in the ongoing fight over abortion in the US (Collins 2014), where 'Right-to Lifers' depict 'Pro-Choicers' as irresponsible women who indulge their carnal desires and then selfishly choose abortion, ignoring the inalienable rights of the potential child. In both cases, women's reproductive desires/choices are deemed to be selfish/immoral and understood to be personal and subjective, whereas a potential child's 'rights' are understood to be morally privileged, objective and permanent. In her book, *Choosing Single Motherhood: The Thinking Woman's Guide*, Morrissette recalls a good friend saying, 'How can you purposely bring children into the world knowing they won't have a dad? That's selfish. You're only thinking of yourself, not the child' (2008: 64). She explains that her friend's reaction is a common one, and that this argument is 'based on the idea that a child's *right* to have two parents is more important than a woman's *desire* to parent'[22] (Morrissette 2008: 64, emphasis added). Anglican Bishop Nazir-Ali argues against lesbians and single heterosexual women having babies, saying, 'It is not enough to "want" a child' (2014, emphasis in original).

Morrissette also quotes a respondent to a 2001 *Newsweek* article who condemned SMCs for making 'a selfish *choice* that would intentionally disadvantage the next generation, with only the goal of *pleasuring* the mother' (2008: 68, emphasis added). In the US, the verb 'pleasuring' is used as a sex-positive euphemism for masturbation.[23] Given that most SMCs get pregnant without having sex with a man, likening their choice to masturbation has special resonance. Getting pregnant without male intercourse can be construed by some critics to be a selfish act that deprives men of their rightful pleasures.

Sexist Stereotype: Women Get Pregnant in Order to Get Social Benefits

One other charge of SMC selfishness, much more prevalent in the UK than the US, is that they avail themselves of publicly funded social benefits. Within days of arriving in Cambridge in 2011 to study SMCs, Layne was told several times – by taxi drivers and used-bike sellers, among others – that single mothers get pregnant to jump the queue for council housing. According to Jones, this is one of the most common false stereotypes about the English working class (2011: 218).[24]

The British anti-feminist blogger quoted above writes, 'They just want that lovely Child Support... They are invariably parasites and a drain on the country. Even if they work they will use tax-subsidised child-care'. He condemns the government for giving them

> the right to whelp illegitimate bastards with (taxpayer subsidised) IVF treatment ... these women are expropriating resources from male taxpayers without offering anything in return ... subsidising old unfertile women with tens of thousands of dollars to have one pet child. (Idaho 2006)

Mail Online runs frequent stories on this theme. An unauthored piece, ('How Handouts Tempt Single Mothers' (28 August 2006) led with 'Generous state handouts encourage women to become single mothers, research has found'.[25]. Steve Doughty, the social correspondent for the *Mail* quoted earlier, published two articles in 2010 on this subject: 'Half of Single Mothers Never Live with Partner after Being Enticed by Benefits "Lifestyle Choice"' (2010a); and 'Three Generations ... All of Them Single Mothers: Growth of Extended "Man-Free" Families Who Rely on State Handouts' (2010b).

In 2014, the *Mail*'s headline reporting on the National Sperm Bank trumpeted 'New Generation of Fatherless Families ... Paid for by YOU' (Manning 2014). Another headline read: 'Jobless Mum Advises Her Daughter, 19, to Get Pregnant – for an Easy Life on Benefits' (Wilkes 2014).

The women in Graham's study were keen to distance themselves from such claims. Only one participant had her fertility treatment funded by the National Health Service (NHS), and all participants felt it was important that they would be able to provide for themselves and their child without resorting to state benefits. Indeed, specifically because they were 'choosing' to become mothers in this way, they didn't feel others should 'pick up the tab' for that choice.

'Am I Being Selfish?' Selfishness and Selflessness in the Discourse of SMCs

It is not just opponents who use the rhetoric of selfishness. Among SMCs this rhetoric is found most prominently among 'thinkers', that is, women who are considering becoming a mother this way.[26] For example, it is in the first chapter of Morrissette's *Choosing Single Motherhood: The Thinking Woman's Guide*, the one directed to 'thinkers', that the question of selfishness appears.

'No More Selfish than Other Parents': A Human Drive

According to Morrissette, one of the things women are likely to consider while deciding whether or not they are 'Single Mother Material' is whether they have 'the proper motivations' (2008: 7).

> Some realize they wish to replicate the loving relationship they had with a parent. Others understand they don't want to grow old alone – they see how happy their parents are to have kids and grandkids around them. Or they see the lonesome aunt and want to avoid a similar fate. . . . Wanting to nurture a child in order to make yourself happy sounds selfish to some people. But it's generally the same reason a married person might give if asked. (Morrissette 2008: 8)

SMCs know 'they will need to justify their decision to others' (Morrissette 2008: 8). Much like the nursing women studied by Faircloth (this volume), many SMCs justify their actions by referring to human nature. Morrissette (2008: 8) asserts that what SMCs are doing is 'fulfil[ing] a human need for family and companionship'. Yahel also uses the 'it's a human drive' argument in her defence.

> I was no more selfish than any other woman conceiving. We all want to feel our baby in our arms, hold them close, smell their sweet skin, relish their triumphs and watch as others coo over our child. In the end, we are all selfishly driven as parents. We are driven by our own need to procreate, and we feel it's something that as human beings we should do. (Yahel 2006)

Anna, a 43-year-old woman in Graham's study, expressed a similar view. After several failed cycles of IVF, Anna had decided that she would not undergo any further treatment. She reflected upon the desire for motherhood that had initially pushed her pursuit of single motherhood by choice:

> [sometimes] I feel so selfish thinking, 'Was that all it was about?' That it was my need? Well it is my need. And it's not selfish because it is my need. Even if you are in a couple and you make a child in a normal way it is your need; it's not for another person you are doing it. You are doing it for yourself.

Non-mothers Are the Ones Who Are Selfish

The label 'selfish' is also used by SMCs to describe women who choose not to have children and describe their own lives before making the decision to become a mother. In a subsection entitled 'Am I too selfish?', Morrissette reports that 'this is a big question for many single women who have become accustomed to doing things how they want to, when they want to'. She herself recalls wondering how she would 'handle being at the mercy of a child when I hadn't had to mesh with anyone else's life since leaving my marriage six years earlier' (2008: 8). One 'thinker' told her she was reluctant 'to give up the life I have now. No more spur-of-the-moment weekends away, no more theatre subscriptions, no more long dinners out, no more peace and quiet when I close my door' (2008: 9).

The before/after contrast between the plethora of luxury goods and services SMCs enjoyed as single women, versus their tight budgets and altered spending patterns after they become mothers is a frequent theme. For example, Robin Bergman recalls that she 'was used to spending money on myself . . . I went on vacation every year, and I bought artwork and I bought jewellery and I bought beautiful furniture, and I ate out a lot' (Torrieri 2013). Another woman reports, 'I was spending a lot of money, I was traveling extensively, I was in Paris for a while, I was going to St. Bart's'. After she gave birth to twins at age forty-one, she gave up her high-powered job and her closet 'lined with Couture garments . . . I don't do any of those things. I don't really spend money on myself' (Torrieri 2013).

In a piece posted on the SMC website titled 'On Selfishness' (Coffee 2014), a woman who is trying to conceive asserts, 'My life as a single person is selfish. My money, time and energy go to things that please me and to do things I enjoy. Just one year ago I hopped on a plane and went to Nicaragua to learn to surf. Everything I do every single day is for me. Every single day is selfish and self centered'. She contrasts her current selfish life with the 'complete selfLESSness that comes from being a mom – and I cannot wait to sacrifice so many things to focus on my kid. I think having a child, being a mom, in whatever format, is the most unselfish thing a person can do'. Other SMCs also depict motherhood as the antithesis of selfishness. For example, according to Dawn Alexander, 'Being a mother is never selfish!' and Margie Manietta asserts, 'Clearly being a Mother is not for selfish people'.[27]

Concern about the Effects on the Child

Concerns about the effects of their decision on the welfare of their future child loomed large among Graham's study participants. Although they believed that children can flourish without a physically present father, they were concerned that their child would not know, or in many cases even know *about*, their biological father. This led some participants to question whether their decision to become a single mother through sperm donation was 'selfish':

> Throughout the whole thing my main concern . . . has always been whether I am being selfish and whether a child, a teenager, an adult is at some point going to turn round to me and ask why did you do that? You've denied me knowing my

father. (Sally, 33, reflecting upon her decision to pursue motherhood through donor sperm)

This concern seemed to stem from a belief that a lack of information about one's biological father could be detrimental to a child's sense of identity and belonging (Graham 2014). It was this importance placed on knowing one's 'genetic origins' that caused all but one participant to initially choose to use sperm from an identity-release donor. Moreover, eleven participants imported sperm from identity-release donors at large European or American sperm banks so they would be able to provide their child with more information about their biological father than the limited amount available about UK donors; not only would the child be able to gain access to identifying information about their donor at the age of eighteen, but s/he would be able to know about the donor, specifically what he was *like*, while growing up (see Graham 2014 for a further discussion). For the three participants who conceived with sperm from an anonymous donor, there was some regret. Although their decision to use anonymous donors was, for the most part, driven by financial constraints,[28] they fretted that they may have compromised what they believed was 'best' for a child and put their own 'need' for a child over their child's potential desire to have identifying information about their donor.

> I guess this is the part that, even now, sits a little bit uncomfortably with me because after all that, all that time and all that effort and energy into doing what I believed all the way through was absolutely the best thing for the child [using identity-release sperm], kind of at the final hurdle, in a way, I think I probably made a decision that was slightly more in favour of what was best for me. And whilst I don't think it is, you know, it's not like it is disastrous for the child, I think it was the first time in the whole process where, you know, the pendulum had slightly swung and instead of it being every decision I made was absolutely about what was right for the child, it became, this is kind of ok for a child but more importantly this is what it is going to take for me to get pregnant. (Emma, 40, pregnant after IVF with anonymously donated sperm and eggs)

SMCs find reassurance in social-scientific research on child outcomes in SMC families. For example, Jessica Olien (2012), a woman who chose to become an SMC via adoption, explains that although her choice may sound 'selfish to some people, ... there is no conclusive evidence that I would be giving a child any less possibility for success than a kid with two parents, as long as I am mature and have the financial means'. Indeed, studies exploring the psychological well-being of children conceived to single women using donor sperm indicate that the children of SMCs seem to be functioning not only as well as but somewhat better than those born via donor insemination to heterosexual couples (Murray and Golombok 2005, Golombok 2015, Golombok et al. 2016).

Alternative Routes to Single Motherhood: More or Less Selfish? Adoption

A question often levied at SMCs is 'why didn't you adopt?' Indeed, adoption was considered by all participants and initially pursued by two of the twenty-three women in Graham's study. Many saw adoption as a morally superior and more socially acceptable route to motherhood: it would give a loving home to 'children who are already alive and need parents' rather than 'creating something that is just for me'. Although still not seeing raising a child without a father as ideal, Sally, a 33-year-old who spent a long time weighing up whether to pursue single motherhood through adoption or sperm donation, believed adoption could be seen as preferable as she would be 'taking a child who would otherwise potentially have no family and therefore giving them something [an upbringing with no father] that would be better than their other options'. Ultimately, however, adoption was seen as a last resort by the vast majority of participants, and both of the women who initially pursued adoption decided to halt their application and explore sperm donation when realizing they wanted to experience pregnancy and have 'a child of my own'.

Loveless Marriages

One common form of counter-argument to the charge that being an SMC is selfish is to compare this form of family-building with alternatives. For example, Morrissette suggests it 'is more selfish – and harmful – to marry a man you don't love in order to build a family', and given that the divorce rate is over 50%, one could argue that 'it is selfish to have children in a marriage knowing that statistically you are likely to divorce, thereby destroying the family your child has come to know' (2008: 65).[29]

Casual Sex

Several of the women in Graham's study compared their route to motherhood with the alternative of casual sex. Christina, a 42-year-old who was now pregnant, reflected upon her initial decision to pursue single motherhood through sperm donation and described how she thought that it was because she had had to make so many conscious decisions in order to get pregnant, that she found herself questioning her motives and wondering 'am I being selfish?' She went on to speculate, 'if I just went down the pub and got drunk and met some bloke and got pregnant, if I was that type of person, I wouldn't even ask myself if I was being selfish'.[30]

Most of Graham's study participants had been asked, albeit often flippantly, why they didn't just go out and have a 'one-night stand' rather than pay the vast sums of money entailed in clinic-based treatments. Three of the participants were particularly surprised that some friends and family, at least initially, seemed to think that getting pregnant through casual sex would be preferable to conceiving at a clinic with donor sperm. Although a child conceived through casual sex would be unlikely to be raised by his or her biological father, and therefore in many ways would be similar to a child conceived via donor sperm, casual sex was deemed more 'natural' than the 'preconceived', 'calculated' and 'clinical' route to single motherhood by choice.

Juliana, a 39-year-old embarking upon intra-uterine insemination (IUI) with donor sperm in the UK, explained that it was her male friends who seemed to be the most uncomfortable with her decision:

> I think they feel *redundant* in some way that you are going out and doing this when you could go out and meet someone in the pub to do this. It would be better if I had a one-night stand. It would be better. Everyone would be like, 'oh that was the guy you met at Max's or wherever'. (Emphasis added)

Purchasing Sperm

The women Graham interviewed felt that purchasing donor sperm was preferable to 'selfishly' cheating a man into fathering a child he doesn't know about or doesn't want; better than giving a child an 'absent father' who doesn't want to be involved in her/his life. They construed their chosen method as representing a conception between two consenting adults, and felt this would make for a better 'conception story' to tell their children.

A single-mother family formed through accidental pregnancy, separation, divorce or bereavement may not be socially perceived as an ideal family, but Graham's informants believed such families were viewed more favourably than single motherhood by *choice* because they hadn't actively chosen to go against the nuclear family held as ideal but had instead found themselves departing from it through circumstance.

SMCs Reject Men?

It is not surprising, then, that all participants in Graham's study were eager to stress that they were not *choosing* to become single mothers. They had always imagined they would become mothers in a long-term, stable relationship. Single motherhood was never the plan, but an option that had to be incorporated into their life trajectory if they were to become mothers at all (see Graham 2012 for a further discussion of the ambivalence in pursuing this 'choice').

Although all could see that single motherhood by choice had feminist connotations, they certainly did not feel as if they were rejecting men:

> I don't deny that what I am doing has its basis in feminism. In the respect that women can do whatever they choose, just as men can do whatever they choose. So I don't deny that, but I would actually consider myself anti-feminist in some respects, in that I would much rather prefer to have got married first, been married a few years and then got pregnant and had what you might call 'the normal family' whatever 'normal' is these days. (Natasha, 36, embarking on IVF with donor sperm in the UK)

They were keen to stress that their decision to pursue motherhood alone was not about their independence or because they were 'anti-men'[31] but, as Anita, a 35-year-old undergoing IVF with donor sperm described, because it's 'just something I want. I don't *not* want a man, but I *do* want a baby'.

It Is Men Who Are Selfish

The women in Graham's study counter the depiction of the 'selfish career woman' who put off motherhood until it was too late by asserting that, in many cases, it was men's selfishness that was to blame. It was the fact that men had 'let them down' regarding having children that was central to these discussions. Although many of the participants were highly successful in their chosen profession, they saw their success to be a consequence of, rather than the cause of, life without children.

Nearly all the participants in Graham's study had been in long-term relationships and they described how they had not been able to start the family they so desired because their partner did not feel 'ready'. Rachel, thirty-eight, who was pregnant after IVF with donor sperm, described how before she made the decision to pursue motherhood on her own she had been in long-term relationships where she had been very open about wanting to become a mother. She described how each of several partners had assured her he felt the same way, only to change his mind or declare he was not yet 'ready' to become a parent a couple of years later; she felt she had no control over realizing her desire for motherhood:

> Women, you know, are just in this really tricky, not completely powerless but in this really sort of, you know, you're at the beck and call of someone else's whim aren't you? Your whole future depends on that and I began to feel very powerless in that situation.

Contrary to the view that those women contemplating single motherhood by choice have been selfish for not pursuing relationships and children earlier, Rachel went on to describe how she believed she was in the position of having to pursue solo motherhood because she had actually 'not been selfish enough':

Yeah, it's because I haven't pushed my needs enough, that's why I haven't got what I have wanted, because I have been willing to sit around and wait for someone else to be happy. I just thought Ok, I'm going to be a bit selfish now.

Conclusions: Some Reflections on Separatism and Power

In this chapter, we have argued that the accusations of selfishness levelled against SMCs are fuelled by heterosexual men's feelings of entitlement to the pleasures of sex and fatherhood for which they are dependent on heterosexual women, noting that this moral failing is much less often attributed to lesbian mothers or gay fathers. Neither are women (regardless of their marital status) who adopt or become pregnant via casual sex as likely to be so labelled. In both cases, unlike SMCs who purchase sperm, heterosexual intercourse is required.

The concept of selfishness is premised on the idea that people are morally obliged to give of themselves/share themselves with others. The types of people who are obliged to do the giving, and the people to whom they are obliged to give, are dictated by gendered norms and roles. Accusations of selfishness directed at SMCs highlight the extent to which women in the UK and US are still considered by many to be morally obliged to give themselves sexually to heterosexual men.

Frye (1983: 95) argues that all feminists 'practice some separation'[32] from males and male-dominated institutions', noting that they generally do so not because they hate men but 'for the sake of something else like independence, liberty, growth, invention . . .'. Such separations often 'evolve, unpremeditated, as one goes one's way . . . sometimes the separations are . . . necessary prerequisites or conditions for getting on with one's business'.[33] This describes well the experience of many single mothers by choice. By their own accounts, they are not rejecting men, but simply getting on with the business of starting a family. Once they do, SMCs engage in mothering that involves constant, sustained giving.

Acknowledgements

The idea for this chapter was hatched while Layne and Graham were both affiliated with Cambridge's Centre for Family Research, which under the aegis of Susan Golombok and M.P.M. Richards was a congenial environment for considering such issues. Layne worked on this chapter while employed at the US National Science Foundation. She would also like to thank Lucy Delap for excellent editorial guidance; Sarah Franklin for the generous use of her office and computer; and, as always, Ben Barker-Benfield, an exemplary step-father, and an utterly generous, transatlantic man.

Susanna Graham is a Research Associate at the Centre for Family Research, University of Cambridge (smg57@cam.ac.uk). Graham holds a Wellcome Trust Research Fellowship in Society and Ethics. Her current research explores the perceptions and experiences of sperm donors, a comparative study of men donating sperm through a licensed clinic or a connection website. Her PhD was also funded by the Wellcome Trust and explored the experiences and decision-making of single women embarking upon motherhood through sperm donation.

Linda L. Layne is a Bye-Fellow and Director of Studies for Social Anthropology, Girton College, and a Visiting Professorin the Reproductive Sociology group at the University of Cambridge (LL427@cam.ac.uk). She has written books on collective identity in Jordan and pregnancy loss in the US and is currently working on *All the Credit, All the Blame: An Intimate History of One American Single Mother by Choice* and on *Uncanny Kinship: Absent Presences in Contemporary EuroAmerican Families*, a comparative study of SMC families, two-mom families, two-dad families, and families that have suffered a pregnancy loss.

Notes

1. See Delap (this volume) on feminist separatism in the same period in the UK.
2. As Faircloth's chapter (this volume) shows, devoting oneself to one's children can also be cause for moral opprobrium.
3. The participants were recruited from the Donor Conception Network (DCN), the Fertility Friends website and the London Women's Clinic. Through multiple semi-structured interviews and informal email correspondence with these women over a fifteen-month period, Graham explored how their thoughts and decision-making changed over time.
4. The Donor Conception Network has a special section for single women, who make up nearly a third of their membership; Fertility Friends has a forum for single women undergoing donor conception.
5. The HFEA provided these figures to Graham on 22 November 2013 in line with the Authority's obligations under the Freedom of Information Act 2000 (Response ref: F-2013-00276).
6. In England in 2011, 280 single women adopted (Department of Education 2013), fifteen in Wales (Stats Wales 2013), thirty (including step-mothers) in Scotland (General Register Office for Scotland 2011) and five in Northern Ireland (personal communication with the Community Branch Officer about Department of Health Social Services and Public Safety 2012). The number of children adopted from the state system peaked in 2015 at 5,360 and has since been falling down to 3,820 in 2018.
7. Graham's (2014) study participants were between thirty-three and forty-six years of age; the vast majority were white, and all were highly educated, professionally employed and financially independent.
8. In the US, more women than men were earning associate's, bachelor's and master's degrees by 1988, and by 2005 they were also earning more doctorates, https://www.

statista.com/statistics/185167/number-of-doctoral-degrees-by-gender-since-1950/ (accessed 25 November 2019). In the UK, a greater number of women were attending college (53.7%) and participating in the labour force by 1999 (Heartfield 2002: 9).
9. By 2004, 59.3% of American mothers with children under age six were employed (Bailey 2007: 204).
10. By 2017 the pay gap in the US, full-time, year-round employed women had decreased to 20%, that is women were earning 80c on the dollar (American Association of University Women); in the UK women earn 80p on the pound, and at the rate by which the gap is being reduced, it will be another sixty years until equal pay is achieved (Green and Wright 2014). In fact, although the gap had diminished steadily between 2000 and 2012 in the UK (Topham 2014), in 2013 the gap widened (Green and Wright 2014).
11. Heartfield (2002) argues that there is no masculinity crisis, but that what is really going on is a working-class crisis, whereas MacInnes (1998: 11) argues that masculinity has been in a chronic state of crisis because of a 'fundamental incompatibility between the core principle of modernity that all human beings are essentially equal (regardless of their sex) and the core tenet of patriarchy that men are naturally superior to women and thus destined to rule over them'.
12. Several commentators point out that there is no evidence presented to support the claim that these singles are lonely.
13. https://en.wikipedia.org/wiki/Fathers%27_rights_movement (accessed 27 November 2019).
14. His blog is for 'us sensible guys who have decided that marriage is a losing proposition here in the Matriarchal West'. https://eternalbachelor.wordpress.com/about/ (accessed 5 December 2019).
15. The *Daily Mail* has published several articles on SMCs. This politically conservative 'middle-market tabloid' is the UK's second biggest-selling daily newspaper, and has been 'from the outset, a newspaper for women, being the first to provide features especially for them. It is the only British newspaper whose readership is more than 50 percent female' ('Daily Mail', Wikipedia). Articles on SMCs have also appeared in other UK newspapers, including *The Guardian*, *The Times* and *The Observer*, but accusations of 'selfishness' are much less frequent than in the *Daily Mail* articles.
16. This anger resonates with that expressed by supporters of Donald Trump, the misogynist American president who ran against a woman in 2016. His supporters are primarily white men without a college education. His 'campaign slogan, "Make America Great Again," is in fact an inverted admission of loss – lost primacy, lost privilege, lost prestige. And who feels that they have lost the most? White men . . . He appeals to a regressive, patriarchal American whiteness in which white men prospered, in part because racial and ethnic minorities, to say nothing of women as a whole, were undervalued and underpaid, if not excluded altogether' (Blow 2016). Another columnist also commented on these Trump supporters: 'The men's sexual revolution, in which freedom meant freedom to take your pleasure while women took the pill, is still a potent force, . . . among men who were promised pliant centerfolds and ended up single with only high-speed internet to comfort them, the men's sexual revolution has curdled into a toxic subculture, resentful of female empowerment in all its forms' (Douthat 2016).
17. Idaho is what is now known as 'incel', i.e. the involuntary celibate, an online subculture which made the headlines after a young man drove a van onto a sidewalk in Toronto on 23 April 2018, killing ten people, most of whom were women, shortly after having declared on his Facebook account, 'The Incel Rebellion has already

begun!' and invoking Elliot Rodger, another self-identified incel mass murderer. They are now a recognized phenomenon in the UK (Tait 2018).

18. https://eternalbachelor.wordpress.com/2007/09/20/selfish-woman-wants-sympathy-for-leaving-motherhood-far-too-late/ (accessed 29 November 2019)

19. An internet search for women/shopping cartoons or clip art produces a wealth of other examples of this negative stereotype.

20. This stereotype can be vividly seen in the moral judgements and ridicule levelled at Imelda Marcos's and Michele Duvalier's collections of designer shoes and handbags, as opposed to the admiration for rich men's luxury spending which tends to be viewed as morally admirable (Goldstein 1987). As Barker-Benfield (1992, 2010) documents, this stereotype has existed in the UK and the US since the rise of consumer culture, which coincided with 'the rise of women' (and resistance to it) in the eighteenth century. Critics in eighteenth-century Britain (including Wollstonecraft) observed that women 'had a peculiar fondness for dress' and were 'the most avid consumers of fashion' (Barker-Benfield 1992: 173). Special disparagement was given to the very type of consumption targeted by SMC critics, i.e. that of accessories such as 'Ribands, Ruffles, Necklaces, Fans, Hoop Petticoats and all those Superfluities in Dress' (McKendrick 1982: 95, quoted in Barker-Benfield 1992: 174).

21. The derogatory association between women, style and (consumer) choice is also made by labelling single mothering by choice a 'lifestyle choice'. The term 'lifestyle choice' entered the popular lexicon during the late twentieth century and was used to contrast the morally sound 'traditional life course' with the proliferation of morally suspect, post-1960s alternatives.

22. Yahel (2006) also uses the language of desire, noting that 'the desire to have a child doesn't go away because a woman is single'.

23. See, for instance, the 101-day video journal of Jaiya, founder of NewWorldSexEducation and 'creator of the art of female self pleasuring', each episode of which has between 9000 and 95,000 views.

24. The UK does have the highest teenage pregnancy rate in Western Europe. However, the average age for a single parent is thirty-six, and over half had the children while married. Despite this, the caricature of 'crafty, benefit-seeking teenage mums' prevails (Jones 2011: 218).

25. For example, https://www.dailymail.co.uk/news/article-402541/How-handouts-tempt-single-mothers.html (accessed 29 November 2019).

26. Selfishness appears in the discourse of British heterosexual (Dow 2013) and non-heterosexual (Pralat 2016) young people thinking about whether or not to have children in many of the same ways as it does in these potential SMCs – concerns about proper motivations for having a child, distinction between the relative selfishness of different routes to parenthood, and description of the pre-parent stage of life as one characterized by selfishness.

27. See Dow (2013: 43) for a similar line of reasoning among the single career women in Scotland whom she studied as they considered parenthood: 'They assume that they will display self-abnegatory levels of maternal responsibility in caring intensively for their [future, imagined] children'.

28. After a long, unsuccessful treatment in the UK, one woman saw going abroad for anonymously donated eggs as a way to maximize her chances of pregnancy, believing the younger egg donors in the Czech Republic, who were also paid for their anonymous 'donation', would be more likely to be capable of producing a viable pregnancy than the eggs of the older 'egg-sharers', themselves using fertility treatment, available to her in the UK. Because she was opting for anonymous eggs,

she felt compelled to use anonymous sperm too – emphasizing the importance of having equal amounts of information about both donors.
29. Another woman writes that SMCs 'are viewed by some as being selfish, having too much fun to settle down, not accepting that they can't have it all, being too picky to marry, being too successful' (Morrissette 2008: 72).
30. SMC critics tend to agree. Many critics are explicit in their view that the selfishness lies in the *choice* to become single mothers. In response to an article in *Parenting* magazine (Hochwald 2012), Brooke Johnson countered one respondent's assertion that being an SMC was inherently selfish by specifying that, for her, it was the choosing that made it so: 'It is one thing to accidentally get pregnant, but to purposely go and get pregnant and be a single mother . . . sounds very selfish' (Johnson 2012, 13 April, 9:51 pm).
31. In contrast with some of the women quoted in Delap's chapter in this volume.
32. Women's increasing ability to separate themselves from men is, in the words of British fathers' rights activist Matt O'Connor, creating a 'new, insidious gender apartheid' (O'Connor 2007: 34). He accused MPs Harriet Harman and Patricia Hewitt of being 'two early practitioners' of this apartheid.
33. This dynamic is reflected in a passage by Toni Morrison ([1973] 2004: 92). Sula, the young protagonist of an eponymous novel, declares that she does not want to get married and start having babies, 'I don't want to make somebody else. I want to make myself', to which Big Mamma replies, 'Selfish. Ain't no woman got no business floating around without no man'. When Sula points out that that is what both Big Mamma and her own mother did, the response is, 'Not by choice . . . It ain't right to want to stay off by yourself'.

References

Akinyemi, A. 2014. 'New National Sperm Bank Aims to Meet UK Demand from Gay Couples and Ethnic Minorities', *International Business Times*, 3 August.

American Association of University Women. 2019. The *Simple Truth About the Gender Pay Gap | Fall 2018 Edition*. Washington DC: AAUW.

Anne, L. 2012. 'Abortion, "God's Plan," and "Selfish" Women', *Patheos Atheist Newsletter*, 7 February.

Bailey, C.J. 2007. 'Social Change, Families and Values: Morality Politics in Contemporary America', in P. Davies and I. Morgan (eds), *America's Americans: Population Issues in the US Society and Politics*. London: Institute for the Study of the Americas.

Barker-Benfield, G.J. 1992. *The Culture of Sensibility: Sex and Society in Eighteenth-Century Britain*. Chicago: Chicago University Press.

———. 2010. *Abigail & John Adams: The Americanization of Sensibility*. Chicago: Chicago University Press.

BBC News. 2018. 'Elliot Rodger: How Misogynist Killer Became "Incel Hero"', 26 April.

Bland, A. 2014. 'Is Masculinity in Crisis?', *The Independent*, 30 January.

Blow, C.M. 2016. 'Trump Reflects White Male Fragility', *The New York Times*, 4 August.

Borba, M. 2004. 'Curbing Selfish Behavior', *Parents Magazine*. https://www.parents.com/toddlers-preschoolers/development/behavioral/selfish-behavior/. Accessed 20 January 2005.

Carey, T. 2011. 'The Survival Guide for Breadwinning Wives', *Mail Online*, 13 October. https://www.dailymail.co.uk/femail/article-2048459/Survival-guide-breadwinning-wives-1-4-earn-husbands.html. Accessed 25 November 2019.
Coffee. 2014. 'On Selfishness', Single Mothers by Choice, 22 February. http://www.singlemothersbychoice.org/2014/02/22/on-selfishness/#sthash.bKLen8ey.dpuf. Accessed 18 March 2014.
Collins, G. 2014. 'The Eggs and Us', *The New York Times*, 27 June.
Coote, A., H. Harman and P. Hewitt. 1990. *The Family Way: A New Approach to Policy Making*. London: Institute for Public Policy Research.
Crowley, J.E. 2008. *Defiant Dads: Fathers' Rights Activists in America*. Ithaca, NY: Cornell University Press.
Daniels, C.R. (ed.). 1998. *Lost Fathers: The Politics of Fatherlessness in America*. New York: St. Martin's Griffin.
Davies, B. 2009. 'Daddies Be Damned! Who Are the British Women Who Think Fathers Are Irrelevant?', *The Daily Mail*, 31 October.
Department for Education. 2013. 'Children Looked After by Local Authorities in England, Including Adoption'. https://www.gov.uk/government/statistics/children-looked-after-in-england-including-adoption--2. Accessed 29 November 2013.
———. 2018. Children looked after in England (including adoption), year ending 31 March 2018. 15 November. https://assets.publishing.service.gov.uk/government/uploads/system/uploads/attachment_data/file/757922/Children_looked_after_in_England_2018_Text_revised.pdf. Accessed 25 November 2019.
Doughty, S. 2010a. 'Half of Single Mothers Never Live with Partner after Being Enticed by Benefits "Lifestyle Choice"', *Mail Online*, 26 February. https://www.dailymail.co.uk/news/article-1253635/Quarter-mothers-single-parents-enticed-benefits-lifestyle-choice.html. Accessed 25 November 2019.
———. 2010b. 'Three Generations . . . All of Them Single Mothers: Growth of Extended "Man-Free" Families Who Rely on State Handouts', *Mail Online*, 4 March. https://www.dailymail.co.uk/femail/article-1255288/Three-generations---single-mothers-Growth-extended-man-free-families-rely-state-handouts.html. Accessed 25 November 2019.
———. 2011. 'Single Mother Britain: UK Has Most Lone Parents of Any Major European Nation', *Mail Online*, 1 April. https://www.dailymail.co.uk/news/article-1372533/Britain-lone-parents-major-Euro-nation.html. Accessed 25 November 2019.
———. 2012. 'The "Have It All" Generation of Women May Have to Learn How to Die Like Men', *Mail Online*, 30 August. https://www.dailymail.co.uk/debate/article-2195805/The-closing-gap-male-female-life-expectancies-shows-educated-liberated-women-start-learning-die-like-men.html. Accessed 25 November 2019.
———. 2014. 'Lonely Generation of Men in 30s and 40s: Family Break Up Behind Rise in Those Living Alone', *Mail Online*, 18 December. http://www.dailymail.co.uk/news/article-2878402/Lonely-generation-men-30s-40s-Family-break-rise-living-alone.html#ixzz3MH7A3nn6. Accessed 25 November 2019.
Douthat, R. 2016. 'A Playboy for President', *The New York Times*, 13 August.
Dow, K. 2013. 'Building a Stable Environment in Scotland: Planning Parenthood in a Time of Ecological Crisis', in C. Faircloth, D. Hoffman and L. Layne (eds), *Parenting in Global Perspective: Negotiating Ideologies of Kinship, Self and Politics*. London: Routledge, pp. 36–50.
Faircloth, C. 2013 *Militant Lactivism? Attachment Parenting and Intensive Motherhood in the UK and France*. Oxford: Berghahn Books.

Faludi, S. 1999. *Stiffed: The Betrayal of the American Man*. New York: William Morrow and Co.
Fantetti, T. 2011. 'Are "Single Moms by Choice" Heroines or Villains?' 10 January. *Ohio Council on Fathers' Rights*. http://www.ocffr.org/blog/2011/01/10/are-single-moms-by-choice-heros-or-villains/. Accessed 5 December 2019.
Frye, M. 1983. 'Some Reflections on Separatism and Power', in *The Politics of Reality: Essays in Feminist Theory*. Crossing Press, pp. 95–109.
Gamble, N. 2009. 'Considering the Need for a Father: The Role of Clinicians in Safeguarding Family Values in UK Fertility Treatment', *Reproductive Biomedicine Online* 19: 15–18.
Garcia-Navarro, L. 2018. 'What's an "Incel"? The Online Community behind the Toronto Van Attack', *National Public Radio*, 29 April.
Gavanas, A. 2004. *Fatherhood Politics in the United States: Masculinity, Sexuality, Race, and Marriage*. Chicago: University of Illinois Press.
General Register Office for Scotland. 2011. 'Adoptions by Type of Adoption and Type of Adopter(s)'. http://www.gro-scotland.gov.uk/statistics/theme/vital-events/general/ref-tables/2011/section-2-adoptions.html. Accessed 29 November 2013.
Gismondi, M.J. 2018. 'Why Are "Incels" So Angry? The History of the Little-Known Ideology behind the Toronto Attack. Men No Longer Have Unfettered Access to Women's Bodies. Not Everyone Is Happy about That', *The Washington Post*, 27 April.
Goldstein, J.L. 1987. 'Lifestyles of the Rich and Tyrannical', *The American Scholar* 56(2): 235–47.
Golombok, S. 2015. *Modern Families: Parents and Children in New Family Forms*. Cambridge: Cambridge University Press.
Golombok, S., S. Zadeh, S. Imrie, V. Smith and T. Freeman. 2016. 'Single Mothers by Choice: Mother-Child Relationships and Children's Psychological Adjustment', *Journal of Family Psychology* 30(4), 409–418.
Graham, S. 2012. 'Choosing Single Motherhood? Single Women Negotiating the Nuclear Family Ideal', in D. Cutas and S. Chan (eds), *Families: Beyond the Nuclear Ideal*. London: Bloomsbury Academic, pp. 97–109.
———. 2014. 'Stories of an Absent "Father": Single Women Negotiating Relatedness through Donor Profiles', in T. Freeman, S. Graham, F. Ebtehaj and M.P.M. Richards (eds), *Relatedness in Assisted Reproduction: Families, Origins and Identities*. Cambridge University Press, pp. 212–31.
———. 2018. 'Being a 'Good' Parent: Single Women Reflecting on 'Selfishness' and 'Risk' When Pursuing Motherhood through Sperm Donation'. *Anthropology & Medicine* 25(3): 249–264.
Green, C., and O. Wright. 2014. 'Equal Pay Is "60 Years Away," Claims New Research', *The Independent*, 8 August.
Hardman, I. 2014. 'Save the Male! Britain's Crisis of Masculinity', *The Spectator*, 3 May.
Hardy, F. 2013. 'Middle-Class Motherhood in Crisis: The Single Career Women Who Wish Their Donor Babies Had Fathers', *Mail Online*, 8 May. http://dailymail.co.uk/femail/article-2321587/Middle-class-motherhood-crisis-The-single-career-women-wish-donor-babies-fathers.html#ixzz2WedgqX78. Accessed 19 June 2013.
Harmon, A. 2005. 'First Comes the Baby Carriage', *The New York Times*, 13 October.
Hearn, J. 1999. 'A Crisis in Masculinity, Or New Agendas for Men?', in S. Walby (ed.), *New Agendas for Women*. London: Palgrave Macmillan, pp. 148–68.
Heartfield, J. 2002. 'There is No Masculinity Crisis', *Genders* 35: 1–15.
HFEA. 2013. Letter to Susanna Graham. Ref: F-2013-00176, 1 August. Neil McComb, Register Information Officer.

———. 2017. 'Trends in Egg and Sperm Donation', https://www.hfea.gov.uk/media/2808/trends-in-egg-and-sperm-donation-final.pdf. Accessed 25 November 2019.

Hochwald, L. 2012. 'Single Mothers by Choice: These Women Wanted a Baby, and They Didn't Let Being Single Stop Them from Becoming Parents', *Parenting*.

Idaho, D. 2006. 'Selfish Cunt', Eternal Bachelor Website 17 November. https://eternalbachelor.wordpress.com/2007/08/08/selfish-cunt/. Accessed 2 June 2012.

———. 2007. 'Selfish Woman Wants Sympathy for Leaving Motherhood Far Too Late', 5 April. https://eternalbachelor.wordpress.com/2007/09/20/selfish-woman-wants-sympathy-for-leaving-motherhood-far-too-late/. Accessed 29 November 2019.

Jadva, V., S. Badger, M. Morrissette and S. Golombok. 2009. '"Mom by Choice, Single by Life's Circumstance . . .": Findings from a Large-Scale Survey of the Experiences of Single Mothers by Choice', *Human Fertility* 12: 175–84.

Jaiya. '101 Days of Self-Pleasure', video blog. https://101daysofpleasure.com/. Accessed 25 November 2019.

Johnson, B. 2012. Comment posted in response to Hochwald 2012 in *Parenting*. Accessed 12 April 2013.

Jones, B.D. 2003. 'Single Motherhood by Choice, Libertarian Feminism, and the Uniform Parentage Act', *Texas Journal of Women and the Law* 12: 419–50.

Jones, O. 2011. *Chavs: The Demonization of the Working Class*. London: Verso.

Kelly, M. 2010. 'More Women Choosing to Have Babies Solo: A Good Thing?', *Marie Claire*, 7 May.

Kimmel, M. 2008. *Guyland: The Perilous World Where Boys Become Men*. New York: Harper Collins.

Layne, L. 2010. 'Donors and Daddies, Fathers and Lovers: The Presence of (Mostly) Absent Men in Narratives of Single Mothers by Choice', *Phoebe: Gender & Cultural Critiques* 21(2): 1–20, special issue on Men and Motherhood, ed. S. Han.

———. 2013a. 'Intensive Parenting Alone: Negotiating the Cultural Contradictions of Motherhood as a Single Mother by Choice', in C. Faircloth, D. Hoffman and L. Layne (eds), *Parenting in Global Perspective*. London: Routledge, pp. 213–28.

———. 2013b. '"Creepy," "Freaky," and "Strange": How the "Uncanny" Can Illuminate the Experience of Single Mothers by Choice and Lesbian Couples Who "Buy Dad"', *Journal of Consumer Culture* 14(2): 140–59, special issue.

———. 2014. '"I Have a Fear of Really Screwing It Up": The Fears, Doubts, Anxieties, and Judgments in the Experience of One American Single Mother by Choice', *Journal of Family Issues* 36(9): 1154–70.

———. 2015. 'A Changing Landscape of Intimacy: The Case of Single Mothers by Choice', *Sociological Research Online* 20(4): 7, special section on 'Gender, Equality and Intimacy: (Un)comfortable Bedfellows?', ed. C. Faircloth and K. Twamley.

———. 2016. '"What Kind of a Family Do We Want to Be?": One American Single Mother by Choice Family as a Case Study of Neo-Liberal Self-Regulation and the Cultivation of Entrepreneurial Subjects'. Paper presented at the workshop 'Parenting and Personhood: Cross-cultural Perspectives on Family-Life, Expertise, and Risk Management', University of Kent, Canterbury, 22 June.

MacInnes, J. 1998. *The End of Masculinity: The Confusion of Sexual Genesis and Sexual Difference in Modern Society*. Philadelphia: Open University Press.

Malin, B.J. 2005. *American Masculinity under Clinton: Popular Media and Crisis of Masculinities in the Nineties*. New York: Peter Lang.

Manning, S. 2014. 'NHS to Fund Sperm Bank for Lesbians: New Generation of Fatherless Families . . . Paid for by YOU', *Mail Online*, 2 August. http://www.

dailymail.co.uk/news/article-2714321/NHS-fund-sperm-bank-lesbians-New-generation-fatherless-families-paid-YOU.html#ixzz39XFC97wz. Accessed 22 November 2019.

Mattes, J. 1994. *Single Mothers by Choice: A Guidebook for Single Women Who Are Considering or Have Chosen Motherhood*. New York: Random House.

Miller, D. 1998. *A Theory of Shopping*. Cambridge: Polity Press/Cornell University Press.

Morrison, T. [1973] 2004. *Sula*. New York: Vintage.

Morrissette, M. 2008. *Choosing Single Motherhood: The Thinking Woman's Guide*. Boston, MA: Houghton Mifflin.

Morrissette, M. and Robert Franklin. 2010. 'Choice Motherhood: Is It Harmful to Children?' A four part debate. 9 April. https://www.publicsquare.net/2010/04/choice-motherhood-harmful-children/. Accessed 29 November 2019.

Murray, C., and S. Golombok. 2005a. 'Going It Alone: Solo Mothers and Their Infants Conceived by Donor Insemination', *American Journal of Orthopsychiatry* 2: 242–53.

Nazir-Ali, M. 2014. 'COMMENT: Designer Babies Are a Disaster for Society, Writes Bishop Michael Nazir-Ali', *Mail Online*, 3 August. http://www.dailymail.co.uk/news/article-2714321/NHS-fund-sperm-bank-lesbians-New-generation-fatherless-families-paid-YOU.html#ixzz39XIxk95V. Accessed 25 November 2019.

O'Connor, M. 2007. *Fathers 4 Justice: The Inside Story*. London: Weidenfeld and Nicolson.

Olien, J. 2012. 'I Want to Be My Kid's Only Parent: I Crave the Closeness of Single Motherhood – Without the Complications a Husband Can Bring', *Slate*, 23 February. http://www.slate.com/articles/life/family/2012/02/single_motherhood_by_choice_i_don_t_want_the_complication_of_a_partner_.html. Accessed 25 November 2019.

Payne, L. [1985] 1995. *Crisis in Masculinity*. Grand Rapids, MI: Hamewith Books.

Pralat, R. 2016. 'Thinking and Talking about Parenthood: Lesbian, Gay and Bisexual Perspectives', PhD dissertation. Sociology, University of Cambridge.

Poole, G. 2013. 'From the Tories' "Feckless Dads" to the "Crisis in Masculinity": Can Labour Go Father?' *New Statesmen* 17 May.

Reagan, A.T. 2012. Comment posted in response to Hochwald 2012 in *Parenting*. Accessed 15 April 2013.

Rogers, T. 2010. 'The Dramatic Decline of the Modern Man', *Salon*, 15 November. https://www.salon.com/2010/11/14/manthropology_interview/. Accessed 29 November 2019.

Schers, A. 2013. 'Crowning Achievement: First Comes Love – Nina Davenport Births a Son – and a Great Doc', *Village Voice*, 24 July. http://digitalissue.villagevoice.com/publication/?i=168318&article_id=1462287&view=articleBrowser&ver=html5#{%22issue_id%22:168318,%22view%22:%22articleBrowser%22,%22article_id%22:%221462287%22}. Accessed 3 August 2014.

Sloan, L. 2007. *Knock Yourself Up: No Man? No Problem*. New York: Penguin.

Smoot, J.M. 2013a. 'Why Sperm Donation is Bad for Dads and Kids', *Public Discourse*, 12 February. http://www.thepublicdiscourse.com/2013/02/7571/. Accessed 13 January 2014.

———. 2013b. 'Why and How We Should Tackle the Sperm-Sale Industry', *Public Discourse*, 13 February. http://www.thepublicdiscourse.com/2013/02/7574/. Accessed 13 January 2014.

Stats Wales. 2013. 'Adoptions of Looked After Children during Year Ending 31 March by Gender and Marital Status of Adopters'. https://statswales.wales.gov.uk/Catalogue/Health-and-Social-Care/Social-Services/Childrens-Services/Children-

Looked-After/Adoptions/AdoptionsOfLookedAfterChildrenDuringYearEnding31 March-by-Gender-MaritalStatusOfAdopters. Accessed 29 November 2013.

Tait, A. 2018. 'Rise of the Women Haters: Inside the Dark World of the British "Incels"', *The Telegraph*, 18 August.

Terzo, S. 2014. 'Abortion Clinic Worker Counsels Women to "Be Selfish" and Abort', *Live Action News*, 23 May. http://www.lifesitenews.com/opinion/abortion-clinic-worker-counsels-women-to-be-selfish-and-abort. Accessed 25 November 2019.

Topham, G. 2014. 'UK Urged to Close Gender Pay Gap and Improve Participation Rates', *The Guardian*, 2 March.

Torrieri, M. 2013. 'Here's the Real Cost of Being a Single Mom', 6 September. https://www.businessinsider.com/the-real-cost-of-being-a-single-parent-2013-9?r=US&IR=T. Accessed 25 November 2019.

Tyler, I. 2005 'Who Put The "Me" In Feminism? The Sexual Politics of Narcissism', *Feminist Theory* 6(1): 25–44.

———. 2007a. 'The Selfish Feminist', *Australian Feminist Studies* 22(53): 173–90.

———. 2007b. 'From "the Me Decade" to "the Me Millennium": The Cultural History of Narcissism', *International Journal of Cultural Studies* 10(3): 343–63.

Wang, W., K. Parker and P. Taylor. 2013. *Breadwinner Moms: Mothers Are the Sole or Primary Provider in Four-in-Ten Households with Children.* Pew Research Center. 29 May.

Weathers, H. 2007. 'Who Needs Dads? The Single Mum's Guide to Having a Baby without a Man', *Mail Online*, 29 November. http://www.dailymail.co.uk/femail/article-497045/Who-needs-dads-The-single-mums-guide-having-baby-man.html#ixzz1wpSGLe00. Accessed 5 December 2019.

Wikipedia. 'Daily Mail', https://en.wikipedia.org/wiki/Daily_Mail. Accessed 20 June 2013.

Wikipedia. 'Duncan Idaho', http://en.wikipedia.org/wiki/Duncan_Idaho. Accessed 8 August 2014.

Wikipedia. 'Fathers' Rights Movement', https://en.wikipedia.org/wiki/Fathers%27_rights_movement. Accessed 8 August 2014.

Wilkes, D. 2014. 'Jobless Mum Advises Her Daughter, 19, to Get Pregnant – For an Easy Life on Benefits', *Mail Online*, 16 April. http://www.dailymail.co.uk/news/article-2605677/Mother-two-never-worked-encouraged-daughter-pregnant-council-house-easy-life-benefits.html#ixzz39bSpMorL. Accessed 5 December 2019.

Yahel, R. 2006. 'Motherhood Is My Right', *Daily Mail*, 16 November. http://www.dailymail.co.uk/femail/article-416733/Motherhood-right.html#ixzz1wpTH7knF. Accessed 5 December 2019.

6

Selfish Masturbators?
The Experience of Danish Sperm Donors and Alternatives to the Selfish/Selfless Divide

Sebastian Mohr

When men make the decision to donate semen, their motivations are frequently questioned: are they doing it for the money? Do they seek sexual pleasure? In media productions, for example, it is often assumed that donating semen is an easy way to earn additional income, while at the same time enjoying the pleasures of sexual stimulation (Mohr 2013; Schneider 2010; Thomson 2008). This image of the selfish masturbator is the result of certain moral landscapes (Helgason and Palsson 1997; Pálsson and HarÐardóttir 2002) in which debates about the use of reproductive biomedicine are embedded. In these moral landscapes, sperm donation is problematized as a questionable part of contemporary reproductive biomedicine because it involves payment for a bodily substance that is the result of sexual indulgence. A 2010 report by the conservative British think tank 2020health on the use of pornography by NHS fertility clinics (Manning 2010), for example, mobilized moral concerns about sperm donors using publicly financed pornography to pleasure themselves. Yet despite the moral outrage about sperm donors as selfish masturbators, nearly nothing is known about sperm donors' experience of masturbation and their masturbatory practices. What it means to be a sperm donor seems not to be of concern. Rather, the supposedly corruptive force of money paired with the self-indulgent aura of masturbation marks men who donate semen as suspicious individuals no matter what.

I complicate this picture by attending to Danish sperm donors' experiences of masturbation. I open up the stereotypical portrayal of sperm donors as selfish and incentive driven by showing how sperm donors' gendered and sexual self-perceptions come into play with the regulatory mechanisms of sperm donation. Instead of making assumptions about how easy it is to donate semen, since it 'only' involves masturbation, I turn the analytical gaze towards Danish sperm donors' experiences of masturbation to argue that controlling male masturbation is a central mechanism of contemporary reproductive biomedicine (Mohr 2018). Through regulation of the affective spaces of male masturbation, reproductive biomedicine appropriates men and their bodies.

First, I discuss some of the existing literature on sperm donors and the ways in which it has contributed to the understanding of the sperm donor as a selfish individual while at the same time also challenging this image. Here it will become apparent that a too-narrow focus on sperm donors' motivations, and an analytical preoccupation with commodification, characterizes much of the existing literature. I then turn to Danish sperm donors' sense-making of masturbation as part of sperm donation based on interviews with twenty-six men who donate their semen. These men's narratives reveal the intricate interplay between biomedical regulation and the affective spaces of masturbation in which men performatively remake themselves as specific moral and gendered individuals.

The Selfish Donor: Motivations and Commodification

Public images of sperm donors can be understood as projections of moral debates connected to the use of reproductive technologies in general, and of sperm donation and donor assisted reproduction specifically. Whereas the image of the selfish masturbator alludes to moral debates revolving around sexuality and responsible male (sexual) conduct, images of the sperm donor as the caring individual, as Michael Thomson (2008) sees them emerging in the United Kingdom during the 1990s, in the debates about donor anonymity reflect attempts to integrate donor conception into dominant societal discourses about what it means to be a family. Research on sperm donors has had its share in creating public perceptions of what men who donate semen are like.

Much of the existing work on sperm donors is comprised of quantitative studies. Qualitative and ethnographic work on sperm donors emerged relatively late considering that sperm donation and donor insemination are reproductive practices on record since at least the end of the eighteenth century (Ombelet and Robays 2010) and bearing in mind that engagements with reproductive biomedicine have been central to feminist anthropology since at least the late 1970s (Franklin and McNeil 1988; Thompson 2005). Whereas most of the quantitative work is characterized by a focus on the so-called 'motivations' of sperm donors (Mohr 2014; Van den Broeck et al. 2013), qualitative work tends to focus on issues of commodification.

Many of the surveys concerning sperm donors' motivations and attitudes stem from professional fields either involved in or somehow related to reproductive biomedicine (Bay et al. 2014; Handelsman et al. 1985; Lalos et al. 2003; Thorn, Katzorke and Daniels 2008). An interest in sperm donors from this field does not come as a surprise, since if the objective is to recruit men as sperm donors, then knowledge about them is helpful. This research recognizes money as sperm donors' so-called 'primary motive'. In countries like Denmark or the US, where a commercial scheme guarantees the supply of donor semen, this argument could be used to defend the commercial organization of sperm donation. The image of the incentive-driven donor might here serve as a political argument for upholding a system in which private sperm banks are guaranteed to generate profit. At the same time, an interest in money within the field of reproductive biomedicine may also be about calculating costs. Being able to pinpoint just how much or how little money it takes to motivate men to donate their semen provides grounds to calculate some of the costs of making donor semen available. Yet money's importance in surveys about sperm donors' motivations may very well also be related to the moral superiority of altruistic donation models (Titmuss 1971). Pleas for a non-commercial organization of sperm donation have been put forward, arguing that donating semen altruistically would allow for more ethically permissible engagements (Daniels and Hall 1997; Daniels and Lewis 1996), pointing to the underlying assumption that money somehow could corrupt the so-called gift of life (Spar 2006).

One of the most prominent quantitative scholars on sperm donors is Ken Daniels (1987, 1989, 1991, 1995, 1998a, 1998b; Daniels, Curson and Lewis 1996; Daniels, Lewis and Curson 1997). Daniels developed a critique of viewing sperm donors only as a means to an end within the field of reproductive biomedicine. In his attempt to value the contribution of sperm donors beyond the supply of semen, Daniels argued for referring to 'sperm donors' as 'semen providers' (1998a, 1998b). This term, he argued, would better represent the engagements of men who provide 'the gift of life'. He involved the larger field of fertility service providers and especially sperm banks in discussions about the ethics of compensating sperm donors (Daniels and Lewis 1996). Yet his attempt to rehabilitate the status of the sperm donor was limited by his methodological and epistemological approach. A quantitative framework limits the range of meanings donating semen may have for a man, and a focus on sperm donors' motivations restricts analytical attention to incentives. It is an irony, then, that the term 'semen provider' Daniels had chosen in order to give more weight to sperm donors' contribution beyond the supply of semen would come to represent the opposite, namely the reduction of men who donate semen to incentive-driven and selfish individuals (Mohr 2014; Van den Broeck et al. 2013).

Qualitative work on sperm donors complicated this image of the sperm donor (Baumeister-Frenzel et al. 2010; Hammarberg et al. 2014; Kirkman 2004; Kirkman et al. 2014; Mohr 2010, 2013, 2014, 2015, 2016, 2018; Riggs 2008, 2009; Riggs and Scholz 2011; Speirs 2007, 2012; Steiner 2006). At the same time, though, a strong focus on commodification in early American scholarship on sperm donors again positioned money at the heart of sperm donation. Diane Tober undertook fieldwork at three American sperm banks and conducted interviews with staff, recipients and donors during the 1990s (Tober 2001). She analyses the function of altruistic rhetoric for the appropriation of men, their bodies and their semen at American sperm banks. While not offering a detailed analysis of sperm donors' own accounts, Tober compares sperm donors' reproductive labour with the work of sex workers and argues that the image of the selfless and altruistic sperm donor is misplaced since the act of masturbation and the compensation sperm donors receive void any kind of altruistic incentive. Instead, Tober argues, the image of the selfless sperm donor is used to successfully market the commodity donor semen, thereby making donor insemination and sperm donation more acceptable. Moreover, the employment of altruistic rhetoric has performative effects in that sperm banks' selection of donors is based on a vague notion that an altruistic incentive makes for a better donor than a selfish interest in monetary compensation.

Following this interest in commodification, Rene Almeling interviewed sperm donors and egg donors also in the US (Almeling 2006, 2007, 2009, 2011). Deliberately playing with the notion of selling egg cells and semen as well as sex in the title of her book *Sex Cells: The Medical Markets for Eggs and Sperm* (2011), Almeling approaches the analysis of donor interviews from an interest in how participation in compensation-based donation programmes influences men and women differently in their meaning-making of reproductive donation. Analysing men's bodily experiences of donating semen, Almeling argues that 'the social process of commodification ... influences ... men's embodied experiences of donation' (2011: 109). She interprets men's accounts of disciplining their bodies and their narratives of limited pleasure while masturbating at the sperm bank as the result of a job routine since men get paid for their semen samples. This analysis of donor narratives within a commodification framework highlights that paying sperm donors might lead to experiences of objectification and alienation among sperm donors. Focusing on the monetary aspects of sperm donation, Almeling's work makes clear that understanding sperm donors' meaning-making of reproductive donation within a selfless-selfish divide might be too simplistic a model. She points out that the organizational logic of sperm banks has a profound influence on what men's experiences of donating semen are.

Qualitative accounts of sperm donors are limited to Euro-American countries, for example the US, the UK, Australia, Germany and Denmark. Even though these countries have differing historical trajectories and differing approaches to regulating sperm donation, they are also very much alike in the sense that they share many notions of kinship, gender and, not least, a capitalistic mode of production. Analytical attention to how capitalism and commodification interplay with gendered identities as part of sperm donation is thus warranted and necessary.

Yet I want to extend this analytical interest to another particularity of donating semen: masturbation. The procurement of semen for purposes of donor insemination involves masturbation as an intimate sexual act through which men confront their self-conceptions as men in the affective spaces of masturbation. This claim is supported by examples in which donating semen is even more profoundly equated with sexual pleasure, and donor insemination with adultery, such as Bob Simpson reports from Sri Lanka and for Pakistani Muslims living in the UK (Simpson 2004, 2013). Masturbating for reproductive donation opens up a space in which men meet their gendered and sexual selves. Continuous encounters with one's own desires, semen, and the desires and semen of other men in a biomedically regulated context is only possible through sperm donation. Making sense of sperm donation thus goes beyond monetary incentives and commodification. The meaning of donating semen also emerges in encounters with substance, masculinity and sexuality as they take place in the affective spaces of masturbation at sperm banks (Mohr 2014, 2015, 2016, 2018).

By turning to Danish sperm donors' experiences of masturbation, I will pursue this analytical avenue. Following the argument of Marcia Inhorn (2007, 2012), Steve Garlick (2014) and other scholars (Rosenfeld and Faircloth 2006; Wentzell 2013) concerned with the appropriation of men and their bodies through reproductive biomedicine, I will look at how the regulation of the affective spaces of masturbation works and how it is made meaningful by Danish sperm donors. This will complicate the picture of the sperm donor as a selfish masturbator even further by pointing to those experiential dimensions of sperm donation that provide grounds for meaning-making beyond monetary incentives or commodification.

Making Sense of Masturbation: Danish Sperm Donors' Narratives

When Danish men become sperm donors, they are subjected to a rigorous regulatory regime. A central mechanism of this regime is the control of men's sexual practices. During the initial screening process, candidates whom sperm bank staff regard as not responsible enough to become donors are screened out (Mohr 2010, 2016, 2018). The assessment of responsibility thereby rests on assumptions about acceptable sexual conduct: men suspected to engage in risky or unacceptable sexual practices are dismissed as donors, including promiscuous men, gay men, and men exhibiting what sperm bank staff call 'weird' sexual preferences. Once accepted into the donor corps, men's sexual practices are monitored through recurring questionnaires, informal conversations and physical examinations carried out by physicians. In addition, all donors at Danish sperm banks are required to abstain from ejaculation for at least forty-eight hours before delivering a semen sample. This is regarded as the minimum time period in which sperm cells can replenish to an acceptable level. Whereas the average Danish man has between 40 and 50 million sperm cells per one millilitre of semen (Jørgensen et al. 2012), men who want to be sperm donors need to have at least 200 million. Since most men donate semen twice a week and some even three times, sperm donors do not have much extra sexual spare time. For some men, masturbating at the sperm bank becomes their only sexual activity while being a sperm donor.

Oliver, single and in his late twenties, reflected on how this control regime impacted his life:

> The only thing that I pay attention to is that I need to plan my sexuality, you know. I cannot just, for example I couldn't just masturbate if I felt like it, if I were at home alone one evening, and now I would actually like to see a porno movie and masturbate, I can't do that. Well, I can, of course, but that would cost me 300 crowns, so, of course I don't do that. In that regard, I think that this is limiting.

William, in his mid twenties and in a long-term relationship, looked forward to the time when he would cease to be a sperm donor:

> I want to stop at some point because the biggest price you pay is, and as a guy I can tell you this, you are really restricted by the fact that you have to go down there and have to ejaculate [at have udløsning] and that there are supposed to go forty-eight hours before that. I don't live together with my girlfriend, but that doesn't mean that you don't miss this freedom, you know, you can't fall asleep at night or whatever, and then this becomes the biggest sacrifice. Sometimes, I also think about this when I am together with my girlfriend. It is just really hard to avoid those kinds of thoughts, you know, thinking about the money and then wondering if it is worth it. But as soon as I get these thoughts I try to suppress them. Sometimes though I can't help it; you can't always stop yourself from keeping an eye on this. But in a strange way, somehow I think all of this has also been good for our sex life. I mean, we have been together for almost four years and somehow, just as if, when I have to wait a little longer, in that way that has been good for us. But it is nevertheless a small sacrifice. Sometimes, I have money on my mind, you're thinking: oops, there you go, 300 crowns.

Oliver's and William's descriptions paint a picture of how far the grip of biomedical regulation extends into sperm donors' lives. Being subjected to a regime that controls their orgasms, Oliver and William both experience this control as a limitation of personal freedom, William even to the degree of articulating that he wants to stop being a donor. At the same time, both men evoke the image of a sacrifice. Masturbating at home when one feels like it or having sex with one's partner become matters of evaluation rather than lustful indulgence. Oliver and William find themselves pondering which sacrifice is bigger: losing compensation for a semen sample or missing out on intimate pleasures, something that at least for William becomes, as he terms it, the biggest sacrifice.

This talk about limitations and sacrifices is embedded in the experience of doing something that is frowned upon or even taboo. As a recent survey among Danish sperm donors reveals, only very few of them feel comfortable talking about being a sperm donor (Bay et al. 2014). In interviews, men would often reiterate this inhibition. Oscar, single and in his mid twenties, talked about the boundary-breaking experience he has as a sperm donor:

> Well, actually it is very boundary breaking [grænseoverskridende], you know, sometimes when you are there [at the sperm bank] and you come with your sperm in a small glass, and then you are supposed to hand it over, well, I feel a little bit stupid

[halvdum]. . . . It is very, well, it is one's sexuality that all of a sudden is so, what is the word, that is so exposed all of a sudden, and that is very boundary breaking.

Victor, in his late thirties, remarried and father of one daughter, voiced that being a sperm donor is not only boundary breaking but also something that one should keep for oneself:

> This is a little bit, how can I phrase this, sleazy [lummert] maybe. There is something suspect in it, something, well, it is not anything criminal, but it can feel a little bit, I don't want to say frightening [afskrækkende], neither disgusting [afskygeligt], but I think as I said before this is a very personal thing. That's why it is nothing one talks about a lot. It is a little bit shady, maybe that is the right word.

This feeling of participating in something shady was to some degree part of every donor's narrative. For some men, like Victor, this feeling was a constant companion. For others, the shadiness would fade over time. The professionalism of staff and the atmosphere at the sperm bank thereby played an important role in men's narratives of becoming comfortable with being a sperm donor. Emil, in his late thirties, married and a father of two, described this in the following way:

> It is a really nice little place, you know, very tidy and neat. It feels, in regards to that, you are supposed to go in there and do what you have to do, it feels, and this is totally strange [vildt mærkeligt], you get up there and there are two sweet girls behind the desk, and you are supposed to go into this toilet sized room and do what you have to do, and they are just two metres away from you, you know. I know that the door is locked, and that it is soundproof and all those things, but it just feels kinda strange. So, that is strange. But also, you know, I am a very private person to begin with, and it was a little bit awkward to come up there and, well, yes, masturbate inside of this small shack [biks] there, but, I mean, they are all very sweet and friendly, and there is nothing, when you hand over your small cup, nobody makes a face, that's how it is. I think, I feel very welcome there, you are treated nicely, they are lovely people, and the place is neat and tidy.

Making sense of masturbation as part of being a sperm donor thus relies very much on a space in which masturbation is nonchalantly accepted as a given that does not need to be discussed. If masturbation were a topic of conversation between sperm bank staff and sperm donors, sperm donors would feel more uneasy about being a sperm donor. Many donors voiced that they appreciate the short and impersonal encounters with staff, suggesting to me during interviews that a more personal involvement would be inappropriate. Simultaneously, sperm banks rely on this self-disciplining on the donors' side in order to control men's adherence to company policies with regards to abstinence and donors' sexual responsibilities. An interrogative and unpleasant talk about why a donor fails to provide good quality semen is presented during donor candidate interviews as a sanctionary measure, reminding donors that they can only avoid this shameful situation if they successfully discipline themselves and deliver samples with good semen quality.

As intrusive as this control regime is, most donors did not mind the regulatory measures that they have to endure as sperm donors. During interviews, men referred to the screening process and the ongoing assessment not so much as a nuisance but rather as proof of quality and professionalism. Most of them had internalized the organizational logic of sperm banks which posits continuous (self-)control as a sign of quality. When asked, for example, whether excluding gay men and drug users as donors was reasonable, most men were convinced that sperm banks had a responsibility to minimize health risks. Jeppe, for example, single and in his late teens, argued:

> I think, you could say, the things which you risk with for example sex with other men or when you use needles [for drugs], that is, you could say, a fatal thing that could happen to an eventual donor child if it is born with HIV or something like that. So, I think that it is actually okay to have that kind of requirement [to exclude gay men and drug users as sperm donors]. You can say, there is also an economic reason in that: you don't need to check, you don't have to be paranoid; and it also gives assurance to those who receive the donation that there are rules for this and that certain measures are taken.

Continuous control of lifestyle and sex life are thus seen by sperm donors as a necessary means in order to guarantee the legitimacy of sperm donation, and by accepting these kinds of interventions, donors come to understand themselves as individuals who have all the mandatory qualities and characteristics. They understand themselves as responsible and healthy men who can make a difference, or as Malthe, married, in his late thirties and father of two, put it:

> I like exams to begin with, but there is always this element of surprise, how should I say, you are under pressure when you have to take a test. And one thing is to take an exam where your professional competences are tested, and you prepare for it and so on. Another is to go for a test where you are tested as a person, physically, and you can't really do anything [to make it better], then you think: what if I fail? Am I not a healthy enough person? I remember, they told me that I was about 5 kilos overweight and that I should lose some of my weight, and I did. I am not chubby anymore.

This narrative reveals how much of men's self-worth is at stake when they become sperm donors. Not only are donors reassured that they have what it takes; they also make the biomedical logic of sperm banks their own and incorporate it into the way they perceive themselves. For Malthe, this meant altering his body in order to be a better sperm donor. Taking on the challenge of losing weight made Malthe into a responsible man who takes his obligation as a sperm donor seriously, and enduring control of one's sexual practices becomes just another part of turning oneself into the responsible man sperm banks seek.

However, conceiving of masturbatory control at Danish sperm banks as a necessary sacrifice alludes only to one way in which this kind of regulation becomes effective. If the regulation of the affective spaces in which donors experience themselves as men through masturbation were only understood as an outside control of their agency, it would unlikely be successful. Men also need to regard sexual self-discipline as an individual matter. It has to be incorporated into donors' gendered and sexual self-perceptions. As Michel Foucault (1990) has argued, biopolitical governance rests on self-governance, on the individual's identification with the idea that restraining and disciplining oneself to achieve an abstract good is also of personal value, a project of the self. What I call the *boost experience* (Mohr 2014, 2018) describes how Danish sperm donors make the regulatory regime of sperm banks meaningful by integrating it into their performativity of masculinity: they enact sexual restraint and biomedical regulation in their ways of being a man, constituting themselves as men by incorporating this form of governance as a positive experience. Felix, in his early twenties and single, described his interest in becoming a sperm donor in the following way:

> I think, my life was a bit boring somehow, a bit too rigid [stringent] in one way or another, and I thought, I should try, I mean, of course it is nice to get money and so on, but I also just thought that it would be fun to try something boundary breaking, in one way or another. And this was the wisest thing I could think of instead of parachute jumping or something like that.

Anton, in his early thirties, married and a father of two, also described the first few times of delivering a semen sample at the sperm bank as exciting. When I asked him why it was exciting, he said:

> Well, it was boundary breaking, you know, in regard to masturbation. That is something, you know, something that you normally do in private. But now, you receive a small glass from a receptionist, and then you go into this little box, and the whole world knows that you are doing what you are doing when you're in there.

Pleasure is thus an important part of how the regulation of sperm donors is made effective. Rather than only being seen as a restraint or hindrance, the controlling gaze by sperm bank staff and the prescribed ejaculatory abstinence also figure as measures that evoke lust and pleasure, something that one donor called 'the forbidden fruit'. Invoking this sense of a forbidden fruit, Storm, in his late twenties and single, talked about sexual restraint in the following way:

> Well, the way it works is that at the sperm bank it [masturbation] happens every other day while at home it happens every day. That means you built up something, and then you are looking forward to it the hours before you go down there [to the sperm bank]. So, it becomes more fun. But I can't use it as a way to fall asleep anymore at home. So, I use it differently somehow, but that doesn't bother me.

While ejaculatory control and masturbation at a sperm bank might be regarded as something pleasurable by sperm donors, thereby contributing to the success of biomedical regulation through self-disciplining, the act of masturbating itself was nevertheless often described as compromising pleasure. Routines men use at home are altered and, most importantly, the purpose of reproductive donation requires men to collect the semen sample in a specimen cup, something that requires the coordination of bodies and their affective states and the handling of semen as a bodily substance. When I asked Noah, in his mid twenties and single, what the difference was between masturbating at home versus doing it at the sperm bank, he said:

> Well [laughing], the whole thing about that you need to hit the cup, that doesn't really, I really think that you can enjoy it more when you don't need to hit the cup. It is a little bit of a deal breaker. You know, you can very well, your thoughts can follow two lanes instead of only being focused on lust, you also need to coordinate that you get all of it into the cup and that kind of thing. So, in this regard it is very different from when I do it at home. . . . But I also have to say, I can also, what do you call that, well, there is something about, I have the feeling that when I can hold on a little bit longer [keep on masturbating] then I also donate more. So, I try, I am just as relaxed [as at home], but I try to perform better in that way, you know, I try to hold on a little bit longer, so that I also can deliver a proper [ordentlig] donation. I mean, at home I don't really care how much it is.

In Noah's narrative, coordinating ejaculation so that semen can be collected properly compromises pleasure, while he simultaneously also tries to control his affective states of excitement and pleasure in order to produce a good semen sample. This dynamic was characteristic for all donors. They all had to learn how best to masturbate at the sperm bank, and they all had to train their body to perform when it was needed. For some, like Noah, this meant coordinating the moment of ejaculation to fit with collecting semen in a specimen cup. For others, like August, in his early twenties and single, it meant tuning out all possible outside disturbances:

> I try to think about the things that I am watching, I think. I mean, especially when you compare this [watching porno movies] to the magazines, it is a lot easier to concentrate on it, because there are all kinds of noises, and all of your senses are alert, so in this way you can concentrate on that a lot easier than if you only had a magazine. I mean, then you would probably hear them talking at the reception or you could hear that another one [sperm donor] is going to the toilet or the box next to you.

As August makes clear, using pornographic movies to masturbate at the sperm bank helps him to be able to perform. Sperm donors need to be able to ejaculate. If they cannot accomplish ejaculation, they are worthless as donors. Using pornography thus helps men to perform properly by providing the means to control affective bodily states.

Over time, this control of bodily states often becomes a form of routinization. Most men I talked to donated semen twice a week, some even three times. As a routine performance, masturbating at sperm banks thus easily becomes something ordinary the longer a man has been a sperm donor, and, as a result, its boundary-breaking appeal transforms into a usual occurrence more comparable to a job or a professional engagement. Mathias, in his early twenties and in a committed relationship, described his visits to the sperm bank as follows:

> It is nothing special, you go up there, you do what you have to do, and then you leave again. I don't think this is anything where you're thinking: oh my god, this was some experience, or something like that. It is just as if you were going to the doctor's or something like that, and then you leave again. I don't think this is anything special.

And when I asked him what happened after he got accepted as a donor, he said:

> Well, after I had the interview with the physician, and after everything had been tested and was fine, well, then I was actually just a sperm donor. After that I could come up there, write my personal registration number onto a cup, go inside and do it and then leave again, and then that is that.

For men like Mathias, masturbating at the sperm bank is not worth discussing. It is a routine that they engage in twice or three times a week. It is part of their obligation as a sperm donor; as he puts it, 'you do what you have to do'. Alfred, in his mid twenties and single, talked similarly about masturbation at the sperm bank as something that one just needs to get over and done with. Yet despite masturbation being a routine, his narrative also alluded to how his performance as a sperm donor is tied to his self-image as a man. Talking about the difference having to masturbate at the sperm bank twice a week has made to his life, he said:

> You are supposed to abstain, you know, you should not have had emission [sædafgang] during the last seventy-two hours, and if you are in such a rhythm, where you do it twice a week, that means that the only times you do it, are when you are there. And when you have done that for three weeks, then the only time that you did it was there [at the sperm bank]. And then you just want to get it over with, so you do it really fast, and then you leave and don't do it for another three days, until you come up there again, and then you just do it fast. And I can feel, that this, when I am together with a girl, then you don't last as long. So, I keep thinking about that, I mean, this is embarrassing, to ejaculate too early because you don't get to practise it since the only time you get to do it you do it as fast as possible because you don't feel like being at the sperm bank.

Alfred positions premature ejaculation during intercourse as an embarrassing experience. Routinized masturbation as a sperm donor undermines his sexual performance, causing moments of embarrassment for him. Being able to control his sexual life in order to produce semen samples, Alfred lives up to his obligations as a donor. Yet doing so compromises his obligation as a sexual partner, a lover, a man who knows how to pleasure women, something that in his narrative is connected to being able to control one's orgasm to the point of not ejaculating too early. Thus, being a sperm donor and forced to routinized masturbation also alters his masculine self-image.

Conclusion

Masturbation as part of sperm donation has many facets. What in public often only figures as indulgence in sexual pleasure for monetary compensation is far from only being a selfish endeavour. As I have argued throughout this chapter, the control of male masturbation serves as a central mechanism of contemporary biomedicine. With a discussion of how Danish sperm donors make sense of providing semen samples through masturbation for purposes of reproductive donation, I have shown how regulatory practices interplay with men's gendered and sexual self-conceptions. The narratives I presented in this chapter point to the fact that the appropriation of men and their bodies through reproductive biomedicine is assured by regulating the affective spaces of male masturbation.

Masturbating at sperm banks is experienced as a boundary-breaking event, which might be enticing but which can also figure as a taboo, a shameful necessary evil connected to being a sperm donor. Beyond being a transgressive event, masturbation in the context of sperm donation is also experienced as limiting personal (sexual) freedom. Since Danish sperm donors have to abstain from ejaculation for at least forty-eight hours before delivering a semen sample, strict orgasmic control characterizes the regulatory regime sperm donors are subjected to. For some men, having to abstain from ejaculation becomes the biggest sacrifice since it intervenes in their freedom to choose when and how they want to have sex. Here, the biomedical logic of good semen quality (Mohr and Hoeyer 2018) intervenes in men's intimate relationships. For other men, being forced to exercise ejaculatory control is a lustful experience that becomes part of how they experience themselves as men. Adhering to the regulatory regime at Danish sperm banks, these men enact themselves as responsible, healthy men who have all the desired qualities.

Moreover, the control and regulation they have to endure is regarded by most donors as a sign of good business practice and professionalism. The fact that they are being screened, checked and controlled reassures many donors that Danish sperm banks take their obligations seriously. They thus not only feel that they are among a selected few with the desired qualities, but they also feel they are part of a morally responsible endeavour worth participating in. Being regulated makes sperm donors feel at ease with having to masturbate, a dynamic that helps to counter the popular image of the sperm donor as a selfish masturbator with which sperm donors are confronted. Additionally, sperm donors come to integrate self-disciplining and self-control as part of their subjectivation processes. Disciplining oneself in order to deliver good semen samples therefore not only figures as a form of control from the outside but rather becomes part of how men understand themselves and what they deem important. Thus, besides possibly being enticing, ejaculatory self-discipline figures for some donors also as an important part of being a responsible individual.

While controlling the affective spaces of masturbation at Danish sperm banks requires the voluntary collaboration of donors, and while Danish sperm donors' experiences of regulation point to an incorporation of regulatory logics into self-images, masturbation at sperm banks also clearly figures as just another technical matter in what it means to be a sperm donor. Masturbation at sperm banks becomes a regular engagement with corresponding habits and routines. Having to ejaculate into a specimen cup turns into a routinized practice without much of an indulgent quality to it. This routinization over time, however, alters the ways in which sperm donors understand themselves as men. Whereas for some men continuous masturbation at the sperm bank might represent a chance to relive themselves as virile men with good semen quality over and over again, for others routinized masturbation undermines their ability to perform as a sexual partner, thereby infringing on a definitive part of their gender identity.

Producing semen samples on a regular basis for purposes of reproductive donation is certainly an experience limited to a few men, even on a global scale. Yet despite the fact that only a few men have this experience, understanding what it means to masturbate as a sperm donor is important beyond acknowledging these men's contribution. Asking what it means to masturbate in the context of sperm donation enables us to understand how biomedical regulation works, since, as Steve Garlick argues, 'men's bodies appear as prominent sites' of biopolitics (2014: 65). Whereas some would claim that transnational policies, globalized markets or international standards secure the success of reproductive biomedicine, based on my research on the experiences of Danish sperm donors, I would argue that biomedical regulation will only ever be effective if it is capable of involving the affective and bodily states of individuals. The global supply of donor semen and the success of infertility procedures such as Intra-Cytoplasmic Sperm Injection (ICSI) and in-vitro fertilization are only possible if men's bodies are appropriated. This appropriation, as I have demonstrated throughout this chapter, happens by regulating the affective spaces of masturbation in which men enact and experience themselves as men.

Sebastian Mohr is Senior Lecturer in Gender Studies and the Director of the Centre for Gender Studies at Karlstad University, Sweden (sebastian.mohr@kau.se). He works as an ethnographer of gender, sexuality and intimacy in the fields of (reproductive) biomedicine, the military and militarization, and technology. He is vice-chair of the Sexuality Research Network of the European Sociological Association, co-editor of NORMA: International Journal for Masculinity Studies, a member of the editorial board of Women, Gender & Research and former co-convener of the EASA European Network for Queer Anthropology. Sebastian is the author of *Being a Sperm Donor: Masculinity, Sexuality, and Biosociality in Denmark* (Berghahn Books, 2018).

References

Almeling, R. 2006. '"Why Do You Want to Be a Donor?": Gender and the Production of Altruism in Egg and Sperm Donation', *New Genetics and Society* 25(2): 143–57.
———. 2007. 'Selling Genes, Selling Gender: Egg Agencies, Sperm Banks, and the Medical Market in Genetic Material', *American Sociological Review* 72: 319–40.
———. 2009. 'Gender and the Value of Bodily Goods: Commodification in Egg and Sperm Donation', *Law and Contemporary Problems* 72: 37–58.
———. 2011. *Sex Cells: The Medical Market for Eggs and Sperm.* Berkeley: University of California Press.
Baumeister-Frenzel, K., et al. 2010. 'Gespräche Mit Spendern', in M. Knecht et al. (eds), *Samenbanken – Samenspender: ethnographische und historische Perspektiven auf Männlichkeiten in der Reproduktionsmedizin.* Berliner Blätter. Berlin: Lit Verlag, pp. 81–112.
Bay, B., et al. 2014. 'Danish Sperm Donors across Three Decades: Motivations and Attitudes', *Fertility and Sterility* 101(1): 252–57.
Daniels, K.R. 1987. 'Semen Donors in New Zealand: Their Characteristics and Attitudes', *Clinical Reproduction and Fertility* 5(4): 177–90.
———. 1989. 'Semen Donors: Their Motivations and Attitudes to Their Offspring', *Journal of Reproductive and Infant Psychology* 7(2): 121–27.
———. 1991. 'Relationships between Semen Donors and Their Networks', *Australian Social Work* 44(1): 29–35.
———. 1995. 'Information Sharing in Donor Insemination: A Conflict of Rights and Needs', *Cambridge Quarterly of Health Care Ethics* 4: 217–24.
———. 1998a. 'The Semen Providers', in K.R. Daniels and E. Haimes (eds), *Donor Insemination: International Social Science Perspectives.* Cambridge: Cambridge University Press, pp. 76–104.
———. 1998b. 'The Social Repsonsibility of Gamete Providers', *Journal of Community & Applied Social Psychology* 8: 261–71.
Daniels, K.R., R. Curson and G.M. Lewis. 1996. 'Semen Donor Recruitment: A Study of Donors in Two Clinics', *Human Reproduction* 11(4): 746–51.
Daniels, K.R., and D.J. Hall. 1997. 'Semen Donor Recruitment Strategies: A Non-Payment Based Approach', *Human Reproduction* 12(10): 2330–35.
Daniels, K.R., and G.M. Lewis. 1996. 'Donor Insemination: The Gifting and Selling of Semen', *Social Science & Medicine* 42(11): 1521–36.
Daniels, K.R., G.M. Lewis and R. Curson. 1997. 'Information Sharing in Semen Donation: The Views of Donors', *Social Science & Medicine* 44(5): 673–80.
Foucault, M. 1990. *The History of Sexuality. Volume 1: An Introduction.* New York: Vintage Books.
Franklin, S., and M. McNeil. 1988. 'Reproductive Futures: Recent Literature and Current Feminist Debates on Reproductive Technologies', *Feminist Studies* 14(3): 545–60.
Garlick, S. 2014. 'The Biopolitics of Masturbation: Masculinity, Complexity, and Security', *Body & Society* 20(2): 44–67.
Hammarberg, K., et al. 2014. 'Proposed Legislative Change Mandating Retrospective Release of Identifying Information: Consultation with Donors and Government Response', *Human Reproduction* 29(2): 286–92.
Handelsman, D.J., et al. 1985. 'Psychological and Attitudinal Profiles in Donors for Artifical Insemination', *Fertility and Sterility* 43(1): 95–101.
Helgason, A., and G. Palsson. 1997. 'Contested Commodities: The Moral Landscape of Modernist Regimes', *The Journal of the Royal Anthropological Institute* 3(3): 451–71.

Inhorn, M.C. 2007. 'Masturbation, Semen Collection and Men's IVF Experiences: Anxieties in the Muslim World', *Body & Society* 13(3): 37–53.

———. 2012. *The New Arab Man: Emergent Masculinities, Technologies, and Islam in the Middle East*. Princeton, NJ: Princeton University Press.

Jørgensen, N., et al. 2012. 'Human Semen Quality in the New Millennium: A Prospective Cross-Sectional Population-Based Study of 4867 Men', *BMJ Open* 2(4): e000990.

Kirkman, M. 2004. 'Saviours and Satyrs: Ambivalence in Narrative Meanings of Sperm Provision', *Culture, Health & Sexuality* 6(4): 319–34.

Kirkman, M., et al. 2014. 'Gamete Donors' Expectations and Experiences of Contact with Their Donor Offspring', *Human Reproduction* 29(4): 731–38.

Lalos, A., et al. 2003. 'Recruitment and Motivation of Semen Providers in Sweden', *Human Reproduction* 18(1): 212–16.

Manning, J. 2010. 'Who Said That Pornography Was Acceptable in the Workplace? An Investigation into the Use of Pornography by NHS Fertility Clinics'. London: 2020health.

Mohr, S. 2010. 'What Does One Wear to a Sperm Bank? Negotiations of Sexuality in Sperm Donation', *kuckuck.notizen zur alltagskultur* 25(2): 36–42.

———. 2013. 'Ordnede forhold: Sæddonorer og sæddonation i danske medier', *Kritik* 209: 72–83.

———. 2014. 'Beyond Motivation: On What It Means to Be a Sperm Donor in Denmark', *Anthropology & Medicine* 21(2): 162–73.

———. 2015. 'Living Kinship Trouble: Danish Sperm Donors' Narratives of Relatedness', *Medical Anthropology* 34(5): 470–84.

———. 2016 'Containing Sperm – Managing Legitimacy: Lust, Disgust, and Hybridity at Danish Sperm Banks', *Journal of Contemporary Ethnography* 45(3): 319–42.

———. 2018. *Being a Sperm Donor: Masculinity, Sexuality, and Biosociality in Denmark*. New York: Berghahn Books.

Mohr, S., and K. Hoeyer. 2018. 'The Good Sperm Cell: Ethnographic Explorations of Semen Quality', *Tecnoscienza* 9(2): 9–28.

Ombelet, W., and J. v. Robays. 2010. 'History of Human Artificial Insemination', in W. Ombelet and H. Tournaye (eds), *Artificial Insemination: An Update*. Wetteren: Universa Press, pp. 1–5.

Pálsson, G., and K. HarÐardóttir. 2002. 'For Whom the Cell Tolls: Debates about Biomedicine', *Current Anthropology* 43(2): 271–301.

Riggs, D.W. 2008. 'Lesbian Mothers, Gay Male Sperm Donors, and Community: Ensuring the Wellbeing of Children and Families', *Health Sociology Review* 17(3): 226–34.

———. 2009. 'The Health and Well-being Implications of Emotion Work Undertaken by Gay Sperm Donors', *Feminism & Psychology* 19(4): 517–33.

Riggs, D.W., and B. Scholz. 2011. 'The Value and Meaning Attached to Genetic Relatedness among Australian Sperm Donors', *New Genetics and Society* 30(1): 41–58.

Rosenfeld, D., and C.A. Faircloth. 2006. *Medicalized Masculinities*. Philadelphia: Temple University Press.

Schneider, K. 2010. 'Das öffentliche Bild des Samenspenders in Fernsehserien und im Film', in M. Knecht et al. (eds), *Samenbanken – Samenspender. Ethnographische und historische Perspektiven auf Männlichkeiten in der Reproduktionsmedizin*. Berliner Blätter. Berlin: LIT Verlag, pp. 68–80.

Simpson, B. 2004. 'Acting Ethically, Responding Culturally: Framing the New Reproductive and Genetic Technologies in Sri Lanka', *The Asia Pacific Journal of Anthropology* 5(3): 227–43.

———. 2013. 'Managing Potential in Assisted Reproductive Technologies: Reflections on Gifts, Kinship, and the Process of Vernacularization', *Current Anthropology* 54(S7): S87–96.

Spar, D. 2006. *The Baby Business: How Money, Science, and Politics Drive Commerce of Conception*. Boston, MA: Harvard Business School Press.

Speirs, J. 2007. 'Secretly Connceted? Anonymous Semen Donation, Genetics and Meanings of Kinship', dissertation. University of Edinburgh.

Speirs, J.M. 2012. 'Semen Donors' Curiosity about Donor Offspring and the Barriers to Their Knowing', *Human Fertility* 15(2): 89–93.

Steiner, C.B. 2006. 'En Eller Anden Forbindelse. En Etnografi Om Danske Sæddonorer i Et Slægtskabsperspektiv', dissertation. Institut for Antropologi, Københavns Universitet.

Thompson, C. 2005. 'Fertile Ground: Feminists Theorize Reproductive Technologies', in C. Thompson, *Making Parents: The Ontological Choreography of Reproductive Technologies*. Cambridge, MA: MIT Press, pp. 55–75.

Thomson, M. 2008. *Endowed: Regulating the Male Sexed Body*. New York: Routledge.

Thorn, P., T. Katzorke and K. Daniels. 2008. 'Semen Donors in Germany: A Study Exploring Motivations and Attitudes', *Human Reproduction* 23(11): 2415–20.

Titmuss, R. 1971. *The Gift Relationship: From Human Blood to Social Policy*. New York: Pantheon Books.

Tober, D. 2001. 'Semen as Gift, Semen as Goods: Reproductive Workers and the Market in Altruism', *Body & Society* 7(2–3): 137–60.

Van den Broeck, U., et al. 2013. 'A Systematic Review of Sperm Donors: Demographic Characteristics, Attitudes, Motives and Experiences of the Process of Sperm Donation', *Human Reproduction Update* 19(1): 37–51.

Wentzell, E.A. 2013. *Maturing Masculinities. Aging, Chronic Illness, and Viagra in Mexico*. Durham, NC: Duke University Press.

7

Inroads into Altruism

Marilyn Strathern

> [As an] approach to 'integration in the society of strangers . . .
> [it is always possible] that a politics of care . . . can be decentred from considerations of interpersonal obligation and civic orientation'.
> —Amin, *Land of Strangers*, phrases transposed

Despite the numerous qualifications that particular cases bring, there seems an irrepressible momentum to the type of thinking that opposes self-interest to other-interest. It spills over into contrasts between interests that are short or long term, are mobilized for individual or for social and public benefit, or are self-explanatory traits of the human being against virtues that have to be upheld. Conceptually speaking, the antithesis is self-organizing, insofar as each element makes inroads into the other only to have its distinctiveness from the other reasserted. This is no less so than in an intriguing area of UK biomedical policy, intriguing for its indication that what might be rhetorically – or politically – persuasive is less than adequate as an interpretation of the lived state of affairs. That state of affairs involves a commoning of sorts.

Supply and Demand

Introducing reflections on what she calls 'the transplant imaginary', the American anthropologist Sharp (2014: 8) speaks of the efforts of medical science 'to generate [technological] alternatives to organs of human origin such that transplant surgeons might one day bypass altogether the capricious supply of those derived from altruistic strangers, kin, friends, coworkers, and acquaintances who donate parts of themselves to patients dying of organ failure'. 'Might one day bypass altogether': the Hardin of nearly fifty years ago would chuckle at such faith in technical solutions, not at the impossibility of trying but at the impossibility of demand being satisfied. However, the vocabulary of supply and demand is as persistent in UK as in US attempts to meet patient need. By contrast with the issues raised by Fannin (2016), scarcity remains the overt economic logic, and with the concept of organ shortage comes something not unlike the delineation of a resource at once limited and of access to all.

The phrase supply and demand[1] refers to the proportions of transplants, organs and still unmet need. The UK NHS Blood & Transplant service (NHSBT) regularly publishes the numbers of those who have benefited, who have contributed as living or deceased donors, and who are on the transplant waiting list. In 2009–10, when achieved transplants stood at 3700, some 8000 potential recipients were waiting for an organ, with 2000 suspended from the list; in 2013–14 with 4600 transplants, there were 7000 people waiting, with 3100 suspended. Donors, both living and deceased, had increased from roughly 2000 to 2450.[2] Gains are counterbalanced by factors that keep up the level of demand: frequently mentioned are people living longer and particular health problems on the rise (notably obesity and diabetes). Equally pertinent, as medical developments introduce more kinds of treatments, new demands are created. This is not the place to weigh up these issues; my interest is in the notion that the flow of organs is blocked by something else in seemingly short supply, although it cannot be computed in numbers.

The availability of body organs does indeed seem capricious. Deceased donations of non-storable body parts depend on the medical conditions under which organs are removed, only a fraction of those on the Organ Donor Register (ODR) dying in circumstances where their organs are viable, and only some of those being suitable for cases in hand. The issue of immunological matching is also relevant to living donations. However, the caprice Sharp put in the mouths of enthusiasts for technological solutions lies elsewhere: it is an attribute of the chancy and uncertain social process that turns strangers, kin, friends and co-workers into donors. In the eyes of professionals and clients/patients alike, the obvious reason is because donors are persons. If on the one hand lie their state of health and the usability of their body parts, on the other hand lie their state of mind and willingness to donate.

Much has been written, popular and academic, on the concept of body parts. From the professionals' point of view, it matters that they are interchangeable, and Tsing's (2012) discussion of 'scalability' is apposite. Her example is the early modern experimentation with growing uniform crops that drove colonial sugar plantations, although she could as well have been talking about the agricultural revolution at home: with the correct conditions, the 'same' crop can be grown anywhere. So too, provided the requirements for the correct medical and physiological conditions are met, one person's body part can be replaced by another's. As an ontological premise,[3] the continuity of the natural world is re-enacted in every transplant. The nature of the body imagined thereby has been the subject of cross-cultural comment: Lock (2002: 226) quotes a Japanese cultural critic contrasting the assumption that organs are replaceable parts with the Japanese assumption that in every part of a deceased body one may find a fragment of the person's mind and spirit.[4] This does not mean that those who occupy the former position[5] use body parts without thought for the person, but rather that the person's mind and spirit are brought to bear on them in very specific ways. Indeed, a person has a distinct interest, we may call it, in his or her body.

An ethical sensitivity in medical or clinical practice is built by law into transplant procedures themselves, both in UK regulation and in numerous global regulatory frameworks, all presuming medical intervention by consent. When it comes to using bodily material, establishing the consent of the person (colloquially known as the 'donor') from whose body a part will be taken is a crucial initial step. For living donors, it is necessary to verify that the circumstances under which they wish to donate are free of coercion; for deceased donors, to verify that they had made their wishes known in their lifetime, by signing the national register (ODR), say, or that a person in a 'qualifying relationship'[6] is ready to give consent from what he or she knows is likely to have been the deceased's wishes. What is in short supply, then, are not just organs in an appropriately healthy state ('well cared for during procurement' [Lock 2002: 49]) but organs for which consent has been properly obtained. And here, deceased rather than living donations present, in the view of some, certain untapped possibilities.

Time and again diverse advocates, professional and non-professional, including those speaking on behalf of the British Medical Association, have argued strenuously for procedures that would dramatically transform the question of numbers: a universal opt-out system. The arguments have made some headway in one part of the UK, and I return later to recent Welsh legislation. At this point it is the protagonists' arguments that are interesting. A universal system would do away with the need for persons to specifically register consent (that is, to opt-in). It is taken for granted that the deceased have no personal use for their organs and the ancillary proposition is that they would be content to have them taken to save the lives of others. Three things are of note. First, potential donors are being regarded as part of a population of like-minded people; it is assumed that unless they explicitly say otherwise everyone shares these views. Second, individual interest survives death, in a form of the deceased's 'will' to allocate the body to medical use. Third, above all, the donor's consent is not obliterated but is being presumed. What is significant is that this consent does not need to be re-established at the time of death:[7] the organs would have *already* been made available. This would be done through the opt-out system itself, a kind of enabling infrastructure pre-empting further decision-making. It is almost as though embodied organs could be conceived as some kind of national resource in which an individual person had lifetime usufructuary rights that death releases for dispersal.

Would this shift a sense of the body as, precisely, a resource for exploitation, as critics argue? If so, the suggestions for an opt-out system envisage it as a resource that is non-commodifiable; on the contrary, they point to certain aspects of the whole arena of transplantation that are distinctly commons-like. We may compare this arena with public service provision in the National Health Service at large, which shares the overarching presumption that distribution of health care is based on patient need. Yet the public goods of the NHS (medication, care procedures, surgical apparatus, all commodities researched, planned, funded) are so evidently finite that they cannot prevent such expectations being constantly shrunk by economic and financial considerations, postcode lotteries, management reforms and the like. On the other hand, organ transplantation may affect only a few but it emerges as a relatively high-profile arena for restating a commonality of interest in a resource whose scarcity seems equivocal: potentially limitless in nature, scarce for technological and social reasons.[8] In their embodied state, the body's organs are not goods, let alone commodities.[9] Are arguments for opt-out one consequence of a transplant imaginary that sees organs, up until the moment of extraction, as natural entities, material unclaimed, in the 'wild'?

To ask the question obviously leaves the vernacular voice I have until now been trying to convey. However, this is the juncture at which to step to one side of the policy-oriented language in which organ transplantation has been discussed in order to open up a particular theoretical interest in it. What is the social counterpart to such an imaginary – that is, what kind of sociality, what kind of concern or disregard for others, is presumed in such an imagining of organ availability? Scarcity may be the overt preoccupation of those involved in transplantation procedures. However, a point long established in anthropological discussions of property, applied by Demian (2004: 65–66; see also Gibson-Graham, Cameron and Healy 2016) to a discussion of the non-excludable nature of common resources, emphasizes that it is relations between persons that identify resources in the first place. Here we might turn to something else in seemingly short supply. This is 'altruism'.

Altruism

The issue is the concept of altruism as invoked in the discourse of transplantation, at once among professionals and in the population at large. For present purposes, I ignore its currency elsewhere (in philosophy, psychology and the like) and avoid using it as analytic (I am not concerned with what is or is not altruistic behaviour).

Technical transplant terminology has long applied the idea of altruism to living donations. 'Altruistic' is an epithet for donations to a common pool, the donor thus being in no relation with any potential recipient. A distinction has recently crept in between 'non-directed altruistic donation', where the recipient remains anonymous, and 'directed altruistic donation', where donation is made to a known person. The latter simply underlines what altruism conveys in these circumstances, for the relationship between donor and recipient is not in any meaningful sense prior to the donation itself, which is the only cause of the relation between them. In this usage, then, altruism means that there is no pre-existing relation that is being served by the act. If the consequence of donation is that another's interests are met through sacrifice of one's own, the two sets of interests should not be joined together. The motivations or intentions on each side are irrelevant to the act. In its advice to non-directed altruistic donors to think carefully about their decision, NHSBT states: 'you need to think about the fact that you have no relationship or emotional link with any of the recipients or donors involved in the chain of transplants that may follow your donation. This means that you do not experience the pleasure of seeing a loved one benefit [from your donation]'.[10] Otherwise put, this is a mandated case of collaboration between strangers; indeed, the alternative rubric to 'altruistic' is 'stranger' donation.

But how strange is the stranger? Ordinarily the very term donation points to a nexus of concerns where considerations of motivation or intention are intrinsic. As articulated in medical ethics at large, altruism here acquires a whole second set of connotations, applicable whether organs come from living or from deceased bodies. This kind of altruism is imagined as an internal disposition expressed in people's thoughts or feelings, which will affect their behaviour. At its largest, an other-orientation embraces society, as in the celebrated words of one of the first in the UK to donate a kidney to a stranger because 'she wanted to give something back to society' (BMA 2012: 84). Insofar as such a society is imagined in terms of a flat (non-heterogeneous, non-stratified) sharing of interests, commonality is implied. Commonality aside, there is also a specific sense in which the interests of donor and recipient may in fact be imagined as joined, in which the pleasure of seeing a loved one benefit seemingly becomes a template for anonymous interchange as well (e.g. Healy 2006: 116).

The gift-of-life language that saturates transplant talk summons up the very opposite of technical altruism, namely a concrete image of interpersonal relations, 'obligations' even, both colouring the voluntary nature of the act implied in securing consent and personalizing the outcome of the benefits. A beneficiary, a recipient, can be visualized. The gift supposedly matches a mental orientation on the part of the donor, who demonstrates he or she is unselfishly thinking of others as other persons.[11] To a voluntary act is added selflessness, then, people's *willingness* to incur a cost to themselves with others' interests in mind. Altruism, in the view of those who endorse it in this second sense, is not at all to be taken for granted, but should be cherished as a moral disposition, a positive virtue to the extent that an ethical principle is made of it. The very existence of such a principle implies a community of interests between those who share it. Already in one direction donor and recipient are joined in the knowledge each has of the nature of medical need (ultimately, they have the same kind of physical body),[12] although there is a difference of opinion as to whether recipients should be 'deserving' or not, that is, share a like impulse to think of others. Now, in this other direction, insofar as altruism is taken as a personal virtue with public consequences, its enactment may well summon the imagined presence of a likely type of recipient. This is so even when it is given an unambiguous civic cast. Where a general disposition to help others is interpreted as an orientation towards the good of society at large, and thus as bestowing public benefit, particular acts can entail the visualization of particular categories of beneficiary. Indeed, while such thinking in the abstract encourages impersonal charitable outreach to anonymous recipients, present-day publicists often try to re-personalize that outreach as an imagined donor–recipient relation. Although discouraged by procurement specialists in the early years of deceased donation, professionals today admit the extent to which their patients/clients engage in such personalization. A visualization of persons may thus lead to a visualization of relations; donor kin and recipients (as reported from the US) adopt all kinds of 'creative strategies for defining their relationships' (Sharp 2006: 171). A joining of interests.

Under this second connotation, altruism may itself be treated as though it were a common good. It has a resource-like aspect, in as much as the discourse around organ shortage also entails a sense that altruism might be in short supply. That it *has* to be nurtured or protected is one reading of the Human Tissue Act's (2004)[13] prohibition on commercial dealings in human material for transplantation, the stance also taken in soft law regulation by the 1997 Council of Europe's Oviedo Convention, the 2008 Declaration of Istanbul and the EU Organ Directive, among others. World Health Organization (WHO) guiding principles make explicit reference to 'the societal recognition of the altruistic nature of cell, tissue and organ donation' (NCOB 2011: 69). With no expectation of material return, the gift of an organ must come from altruistic motives. But how could such a generous disposition or other-directedness ever be in short supply? Surely it has no limits?

The answer is already anticipated in these prohibitions. Because of the oft-voiced antithesis between self-interest and other-interest, altruism is regarded as an impulse (to behave in a particular way) in competition with diverse other impulses that flourish to quite opposite ends, those that feed selfishness. In this nexus of concerns around organ donation, self-interest carries a negative value, one invariably expressed through the concrete image of commerce. Money stalks the very definition of the gift. Public consultations on donation practices meet vexing and unresolved questions about the cost of making a donation (paying expenses), or the kind of debt that recipients of cadaver organs feel (a need to make some kind of return). Such transactions may be interpreted as the thin end of a sinister wedge that would erode the virtually ubiquitous international prohibition on organ purchase. Gift-giving lives under the constant shadow of a market alternative, so much so that the slightest suggestion of monetary recompense for donors can lead to expressions of moral outrage. Here the virtues of other-interest may be closely allied with disinterest. In the discursive arena of transplant practices, altruism (a personally disinterested interest in others) and money (a means of self-interest) are in open conflict.

By no means the only way of assembling the various elements involved in organ donation, this antithesis dominates as a model of its transactional aspects.[14] The background assumption is that money invariably has the trumping hand, while altruism invariably needs propping up. Self-interest requires no champions; it is often invoked as a default position of 'being human'. At the same time, altruism is prone to perpetual shrinkage. The evidence lies in the very extent to which people have to cherish it, by voicing its value, encasing it in regulation, in short, working on its behalf. Observing such exertions, someone from outside the model might say that the more altruism is explicitly talked about, the more it is implicitly presented as under threat. It is in this respect, it seems to me, that altruism is treated as though it were a non-excludable resource but for the exclusions created by contrary impulses. Unlike organs, it could not be said to exist in the wild: it has to be intensively cultivated, flourishing only if everyone contributes to it. The capacity for altruism, in this view, might be exercised for the common good in that any person might benefit from other people's altruistic impulses, but these expectations are liable to disappear unless safeguarded. Inroads come not from those who use the resource in such a way that the cost is concealed in being borne by numerous others; they come rather from people's failure to articulate its value or live up to its moral imperative and *thus make it into* something all have in common.

Inroads also come from that other quarter, from the language of money, assumed these days to be ever-expanding, from the financialization of all kinds of decision-making to the ability to put a figure on anything. An explicit argument heard over and again against money or other forms of material recompense (which can always be given a monetary value) being used to increase the supply of organs is that anything like remuneration would undermine or crowd out the altruistic impulse.[15] In a model where money is an index of self-interest, remuneration would turn a selfless commitment to society at large into a routine reward for services. Hence, some fear, were legislation to make it possible for someone or their relatives to be remunerated for donating, each remuneration would in effect decrease ('crowd out', 'weaken') a principle based on other-interest; the idea of being alike in basic need, 'everyone in it together' in an oft-quoted phrase, would be eroded. Other-interest is axiomatically most evident when it is held in common. This contributes to the sense in which altruism is itself a common resource on which anyone might one day find themselves depending.

It is intriguing, then, that exactly these criticisms about crowding have been made in relation to schemes for opt-out, that is, where consent is presumed unless the contrary is stipulated. In 2008, the Department of Health's Organ Donation Taskforce was asked if it would recommend an opt-out system for the use of deceased donor organs across the UK. It rejected the idea, concluding that such a system would undermine the concept of donation as a gift, erode trust in practitioners and actually reduce rather than increase donor numbers (NCOB 2011: 103). Now, with legislation (the Human Transplantation [Wales]

Act 2013) coming into effect in 2015, the Welsh Assembly is in the process of implementing an opt-out scheme for Welsh hospitals. It formulates a 'soft' procedure, in which the presumption of consent ('deemed consent') is backed by consultation with the deceased's family. This is to confirm what is known about the donor-to-be's wishes.[16] Consent is thus retrieved as a paramount consideration. At a minimum, it is arguable that information about such wishes helps conserve the justification of using the word donation: organs are deemed given, not taken.

The Organ Donation Taskforce was earlier fearful of an encroachment on altruism. Yet what we have here seems an interesting limitation to the very model of an antithesis between self- and other-interest. Insofar as everyone is given the opportunity to opt-out of automatic donation, everyone is also given the opportunity to stay in. There is no need to appeal to a heightened sense of other-interest as an incentive (and money drops outs of the picture).[17] Individual and thus heroic acts of altruism are no longer visible, and by the same token we might question whether the opting-out population is embodying self-interest (in any strong sense) any more than the UK majority who decline to join or ignore the Organ Donor Register. Indeed, opt-out suggests itself as an example of what, in quite other situations, Amin's *Land of Strangers* (e.g. 2012: 50) envisions as the sociality underpinning a politics of care, where he talks of strangers becoming collaborators. Perhaps operationalizing presumed consent, as the opt-out logic has it, simply takes to an extreme a practical or organizational possibility for shaping care for others, a collective labour of sorts, of the kind that surfaces from time to time in organ donation procedures generally. The role being ascribed to families, however, introduces a further turn in the topic, and an altogether different limitation to the antithesis.

Enter Kinship

In what sense is altruism a limited resource? It may appear so in the (antithesis-driven) model of values erosion described here, and more generally perhaps in debates based on the premise that ethical values must be made visible or else they will (of course) disappear. Altruism seems always in danger of disappearing. Yet if we look at people's actions over the last few years in the UK, there has been a steady if small rise both in those joining the ODR and in those who, whether as living or deceased donors, have contributed to a rising number of transplant operations.[18] Now something approaching half of all donors are living (donating mainly kidneys, but also liver and, rarely, lung). While a tiny but annually increasing number come forward for 'non-directed' transplants, that is to strangers, the majority involve donations to people who are known to the donor, in short, relatives or friends. No shrinking of a commons, no shortage of altruism here! Nonetheless, the involvement of kin relations gives one pause.

An observer might argue that when it comes to relatives, it is actually nonsense to disentangle self-interest from other-interest. Between kinspersons, reciprocities that might look for all the world like tit-for-tat transactions are intrinsic to the ongoing nature of relationships, the heterogeneous temporalities of give and take. Insofar as thinking of others and thinking of oneself run together, organ donations among relatives confound the other-interest versus self-interest model that dominates so much of the discussion. Kinship, the observer might remark in parenthesis, also cuts across any simple division of public and private interests. And as to what is 'self' or 'other',[19] if the observer is an anthropologist he or she might quote Aristotle's dictum of kinship as 'the same entity in discrete subjects' (Sahlins 2013: 20),[20] or in defining personhood find in kinship 'the relations that are perceived as being intrinsic to the person' (Carsten 2004: 107). Such mutuality may be to expansive or to coercive effect. Kaufman at al. (2009: 33) voice the reasoning of a reluctant organ recipient: 'my family needs and wants me to live . . . Therefore I need to live, so they . . . will offer to donate a kidney for me, and (though it may not seem right) I must accept it'.

Money ceases to have quite its demonic signature. Ties of kinship are by and large not appropriately expressed in market terms, yet finance plays a huge role (McKinnon and Cannell 2013; Zelizer 2005). One only has to think of household provisioning, inheritance, present-giving. Spending on others (who are close to one) is in a sense spending on oneself (who belongs to others).[21] To the extent that a relative is already part of the donor, then donation between relatives is for the donor as well as for the recipient, as the awkward reluctance of some recipients, and shared joy of others, attests. So if, in the context of living organ donation, payment within families is inappropriate, it is hardly because altruism needs to be protected. Rather, the contrast between altruistic reasons and selfish reasons is thoroughly ambiguated. I do not mean to imply that individuals cannot act in all kinds of positive and negative ways towards their relatives, including with lesser and greater degrees of selfishness, but when they act *as relatives* their actions raise very specific expectations. Doing everything for one's child or nothing for it translates neither into simple other-interest nor into self-interest. It is thus uncertain where the self-interest of a selfish mother (that is, in relation to her children) is to be located. Of course, to continue with this example, not all self-interest is in the ordinary sense 'selfish'. Is a concept nearer to enlightened self-interest the answer? This would imply a fusion of selflessness and selfishness, echoing the particular kind of market logic that sees private benefit as also being for public benefit, first voiced – with enduring consequences – at the time of the Scottish Enlightenment (Adam Smith's 'invisible hand' by which self-interest promotes others' interests). For Hardin (1968), of course, assuming that the best decision for the individual, locked as he or she is into a specific situation, will be best for all was the fatal flaw in thinking about limited resources. We return to Enlightenment arguments, but for the moment note that kinship affairs are far from the operations of an invisible hand. On the contrary, the relations that families and relatives maintain are highly personalized, one guarantee of continuing relations among kin being that reciprocities over time are open-ended and visible. Much that is bundled up in the self-interest/other-interest antithesis simply seems not to apply.

The same is also true of another category of interpersonal relations: friendship. And here too relations are visible. As with kin, and by contrast with acquaintances, friends not only enjoy one another's goodwill but crucially know of the basis for their interaction and each 'knows that the other knows it' (Beer and Gardner 2015: 426). Indeed, in some respects there appears no difference between relatives and friends, as the facilitators of organ transplants acknowledge. The NHSBT website (https://www.nhsbt.nhs.uk, 27 March 2015) describes living donors as likely to be close relatives or 'individuals who are not related but may have an established emotional relationship with the recipient such as a partner or close friend'. The list of persons able to give consent in organ donation because of their relationship with the deceased similarly pairs relatives and friends, a bracketing endorsed by the wording of the Welsh legislation. Thus, instead of consent being deemed, someone may prefer to voice 'express consent' by appointing a 'relative or friend of long standing' as a representative who will know the deceased's view. Concomitantly, a 'relative or friend' with such knowledge may object to consent – not just anyone who knows the wishes of the deceased, but if not a relative then specifically 'a friend' whose relationship implies long-term familiarity.[22]

Now the antithesis between self-interest and other-interest has been the focus of an argument from sociology about the very category of friend in the political and philosophical work of early modern writers, insofar as they contrasted a new commercial society with pre-commercial societies that could offer no possibility of disinterested relations. Speaking of scholars of the Scottish Enlightenment, Silver (1990: 1491) posits that their 'theoretical project requires an enlarged domain of indifferent persons available for market exchanges and contractual engagements'. It was 'authentically indifferent co-citizens' who, in this imagining, peopled the then new 'strangership' of commercial society (1482–83). Encouraging the exercise of anonymous self-interest, this (commercial) sphere was thus identified with the development of instrumental relations between notional strangers, explicitly removed from the restrictions of pre-existing bonds – and from the mutual interests that strengthened them – once held to engage kin and friends alike. At the same time, he famously argues (1990: 1486, 1492), these writers imagined commerce as precipitating a second, distinct sphere of 'personal and civic friendship', 'a new concept of non-instrumental personal relations' based on common sympathies. Applied alike to intimate sociability and to generalized benevolence towards others, it fostered the development of friendship for its own sake.[23] In the early formation of this antithesis to self-interest, the language was as much of disinterest as of other-interest.

The anthropologist might add that this Enlightenment vision required the conceptual detachment of persons, as individual selves, from relations. Thus, the interests of established relationships had no part to play in the indifferent ('disinterested') marketplace precisely because 'self-interest' did, while conversely the individual friend was selfless ('disinterested') only to the extent of downplaying self-interest, for he or she would be investing in the interests of the very relationship itself.[24] In hindsight, arguably, some of the ambiguities of self-interest and dis- or other-interest turned on whether interest was attached to the person or the relation.

Kinds of Commoning

This brings the narrative to an interesting conjunction.[25] One might argue that an emphasis on altruism belongs precisely to the sphere of rhetorical solidarities upheld in the image of interpersonal obligation and civic orientation that Amin sees as a distraction to contemplating already-present and future modes of sociality. The alternative is to identify the functionality of social formations through their infrastructures, through collective labour in the contingencies of situated practices. Organ transplantation discourse affords an example of rhetorical solidarity, and of the problem it creates. If altruism's constant battle against self-interestedness and commerce is a sort of experiment in strangerhood, it is one that constantly trips itself up, precisely because the battle is all-consuming. However, the same discourse has also led to developments along the lines of new functionalities: the Welsh opt-out scheme as an infrastructure of (not quite automatic) enablement. The scheme makes more clear, not less, where common interests lie – and it side-steps the antithesis altogether. In fact, I hazard, there might be kinds of commoning defined through their very suspension of that antithesis.

This chapter has toyed with the idea of (embodied) organs and (impersoned) altruism being commons-like resources, insofar as they are at once available to anyone and, although treated as always in short supply, not otherwise discrete as goods or commodities. However, this is not the burden of my conclusion. Rather, it points to the implications of the brief foray into another arena where the self-/other-interest antithesis hardly applies.

The technical phrase 'altruistic' or 'stranger' donation for living organ donation to a common pool denotes a kind of collaboration between strangers, an impersonal one by contrast with collaborations between those who, already known to one another, enact out their personal relations at the same time. The logic of the situation allows the observer to reflect back on what is happening when the latter are donors and recipients, as kin and friends may become. Insofar as the paradigmatic organ transplant has been (deceased) transfer between strangers, as blood donation was originally conceived between strangers (Whitfield 2013), perhaps we can also imagine them (friends, kin) acting as 'strangers' would act. This would be to see them as though they were a kind of non-anonymous counterpart to today's 'intimate publics', which Amin (2012:

30–31) discerns in the society of strangers. For we are not obliged to think of friends and kin only in terms of the compulsions of community, of the solidarities and group allegiances that get in the way of imagining new forms of social living. But there is a question about where to put relationships.

I deliberately did not refer to the enabling infrastructures of opt-out organ donation as 'impersonal', for the personal/impersonal axis simply reinvents the old antithesis.[26] A severe problem generated by these antitheses is the imagination of social relations,[27] the kind of sociality they project. Here is a piece of Enlightenment legacy that English-speakers might wish to reconsider. It concerns not the well-known detachment of person (as conscious self) from body, and we have seen how today that is taken care of in transplant protocols, but the detachment of person (as individual) from relations. Such detachment was openly promoted to the invisible benefit of all, so that 'relations' – family, friends – must flourish only for themselves; these days, the technical usage of 'altruism' explicitly brackets off pre-existing relations. As organ donation has developed into its present lived state of affairs, however, perhaps we have chanced on ways of acting, and a capacity for action, that require perceptions of relationships – not just of the 'other' person – that take kinship and friendship in new directions.[28] Intimate strangers, collaborators in one another's projects, living one another's lives?

We can imagine, with Amin (2012: 49–50), present-day epistemic communities coordinated by interactive technologies, where 'coalitions are short-lived, the individuals self-centred, the work divided, the identities formed elsewhere [where] ... strangers become collaborators but not friends, co-generators of often quite extraordinary innovations, but without interpersonal ties'. What this chapter might have interpolated is a question about where to put those excluded capacities for friendship and interpersonal ties, extending as they do over time. Kinship and friendship do not of themselves need to entertain appeals to common humanity or to the politics of community solidarities. At least, this is arguably the case insofar as kin and friends alike are indifferent to the antithesis of self-interest and other-interest. Rather, an infrastructure of enablement, to good or ill, and whether or not to anyone else's benefit, lies in their very relation to one another. They do not have to find any other reason to act. Such a 'coming together as one', as Amin and Howell (2016: 10) phrase it, has always been the case. If what is held in common is produced through the relationship as such, conceivably we have chanced on an(other) resource for thinking about future commons more generally.

Acknowledgements

My warm thanks to Hugh Whittall and Katherine Wright of the Nuffield Council on Bioethics for encouraging me to write on this topic. In 2010–11 I chaired the Council's Working Party on organ and tissue donation (NCOB

2011). The chapter draws on no information that is not in the public domain; the conclusions are entirely mine and not attributable in any way to the Council or its directorate.

Marilyn Strathern is Emeritus Professor of Social Anthropology at Cambridge University (ms10026@cam.ac.uk). She is now retired from the Department of Social Anthropology and from being head of Girton College, both at Cambridge University. She is (hon.) Life President of the Association of Social Anthropologists of the UK and Commonwealth. Her ethnographic forays are divided between Papua New Guinea and Britain. Over the last twenty years she has written on reproductive technologies, on audit and accountability, and on intellectual and cultural property. She chaired a working party for the Nuffield Council on Bioethics on 'Human Bodies: Donation for Medicine and Research'.

Notes

This chapter was originally published in A. Amin and P. Howell, (eds), *Releasing the Commons: Rethinking the Futures of the Commons* (Routledge 2016), 161–76. Reproduced with permission of The Licensor through PLSclear.

1. Many transplant professionals see this as the most succinct way to talk about waiting lists, but it is generally widespread in public discussions about health funding allocations.
2. There is no match between individual donors and transplants: in deceased donations, more than one organ may be taken from a body. Over the same period, the number of people signed up to the ODR increased from 18 million (about 30% of the UK population over 18 years of age) to 20.2 million; by April 2014 it was 21 million. (The NHSBT was actively campaigning over this period.) This information comes from NHSBT annual reports as summarized on the NHSBT website (https://www.nhsbt.nhs.uk). (2009–10 figures are reproduced in NCOB 2011: 87; 2013–14 activity report accessed 27 March 2015.)
3. The allusion here is to 'naturalism', in Descola's ([2005] 2013) fourfold scheme of world cosmologies, or to Viveiros de Castro's ([2009] 2014) mononaturalism as opposed to the multinaturalism of Amerindian perspectivist thinking.
4. Drawn from a work of Yonemoto Shōhei published in 1985. Lock is well known for demonstrating the local nature of physiologies created by specific conditions, as opposed to notions that ascribe universality to the body's workings. This is akin to Tsing's advocacy of the 'non-scaleable', indicating entities with relations attached. To opposite effect, planters were experimenting with types of cane and soil in order to facilitate the interchangeability of forms; the varieties so propagated were genetic isolates without interspecies ties. 'One must create *terra nullius*, nature without entangling claims' (Tsing 2012: 513, original italics).
5. The contrast is specifically with Americans but would include the British too. On French exceptionalism when it comes to notions of body and person, see, for example, Dickenson 2007.

6. The UK Human Tissue Act 2004 sets out a list of such qualifying relationships, first relatives in terms of distance from the deceased, then 'friend of long standing' (see NCOB 2011: 59).
7. When time is at a premium. As we shall see, the Welsh scheme is a 'soft' version, which does re-establish the issue of consent insofar as families are routinely consulted.
8. This is separate from the fact that organs fit for transplant only exist through immense investment in (the research, productive, financial activity of) transplant services (Waldby and Mitchell 2006).
9. And in the UK legally speaking the property of no-one, including the person to whom the body 'belongs', despite widespread notions of ownership to the contrary. It is in the context of ideas about property that questions explicitly address the language of the commons; see, for example, Dickenson's (2007) discussion, which takes into account diverse arguments over applying concepts such as *terra nullius* or the 'new enclosures' to bodily materials. However, property is a dimension that must be left to one side here. With reference to body parts, it is taken up by Fannin (2016); both she and Gibson-Graham, Cameron and Healy (2016) would challenge the scope of the scarcity model that is my ethnographic starting point insofar as it underpins current approaches to organ procurement.
10. NHSBT website (https://www.nhsbt.nhs.uk), 'Organ donation: non-directed altruistic donation' (accessed 27 March 2015).
11. The gift is here understood with its vernacular connotations of something freely given and with no expectation of return (the last being contentious, but ideally summoned when the obligation to return is taken as extrinsic rather than intrinsic to the gifting). The gift is thus detached from the person; elsewhere (e.g. Strathern 2012) I have pointed to the severance work that this kind of detachment does in rendering organs ethically fit for transplanting, the medical need for the differentiation of the organ from the individual person who supplies it being discussed by, among others, Healy 2006; Lock 2002; Waldby and Mitchell 2006.
12. They are joined *by* that medical knowledge. Apropos 'deserving', people may equivocate about the ethics of donating to those who have brought their medical condition on themselves through indulgence/abuse or 'selfishness'.
13. Applicable to England, Wales and Northern Ireland, Scotland being covered by the Human Tissue (Scotland) Act 2006.
14. There is a wide range of positions voiced in the UK on the issues described here, and many potential models. But whether they subscribe to it (aligning the actions of themselves or others by it), or vehemently deny it (the antithesis need not or does not exist), at present the antithesis itself seems a foundational axis to many people's mobilization of the diverse values they bring to the subject.
15. Here, and in other references to public or professional opinion, I draw on the information and contributing literatures summarized in NCOB 2011. (The remit of that report included an enquiry into the role of material and immaterial incentives in promoting bodily donation.) It would be an interesting but separate enterprise to triage these discussions in the public domain, so-called, with respect to the diverse circumstances of the UK's many populations.
16. The procedure adapts the already existing convention of qualifying relationships (see note 6 above) in order to ascertain if there is any objection to consent being deemed in place.
17. The antithesis is equally rendered irrelevant at the opposite extreme, the all-money market model for increasing organ donation (e.g. Erin and Harris 2003; Harris 2003).

18. Much of this can be put down to the concerted campaign by NHSBT (see note 2 above). Living donor numbers in the UK increased from 858 (2007–8) to 1045 in 2010–11 to 1136 in 2013–14 (in 2013–14 deceased donors numbered 1320). The increase in numbers of living donations is facilitated by medical developments reducing the trauma of the operation for the donor.
19. It is no surprise that the antithesis is elaborated in contexts where the individual (as a psychological or legal entity, say) is a significant descriptive of the person.
20. Sahlins (2013: 21) continues: 'kinsmen are persons who belong to one another, who are parts of one another, . . . whose lives are joined and interdependent'. Needless to say, the realities play out in myriad ways, and the extent to which the ideas sketched here inform specific situations must be, as Edwards (2009: 5) would remark, ethnographic questions.
21. 'Close' should be divested of its affective connotations, for this will otherwise be read as a sentimental view of kin relations. Disruption and avoidance between kin may be as much a mark of 'close' kinship as the opposite. In this cosmology, kin become disengaged from one another as kin to the extent that they bring to the fore other aspects of their social being, e.g. the capacity to act as independent individual persons.
22. The potential proximity of kin and friends (family as 'friends', friends as 'family') is relevant. Kaufman et al.'s (2009) study of living donation in the US reports the sentiment of a woman who donated a kidney to a friend: there was no question because he was 'like family'.
23. 'Only with impersonal markets in products and services does a parallel system of personal relations emerge' (Silver 1990: 1494). He observes that, by contrast with later developments, these Enlightenment thinkers saw 'commercial society' as positively releasing personal relations from their former instrumentalism; antithetical in character, the two spheres nonetheless supported each other. Those later developments gave social science, among other things, both an enduring, albeit contested, analytical contrast between 'the public domain of economics and politics' and 'the private domain of kinship', as Bodenhorn (2013: 131) summarizes it, and 'the personal and non-institutional character of kindness' as a philosophical entry into the concept of cosmopolitanism (Josephides 2014: 1).
24. Silver's (1989: 277) own exegesis (albeit of modern friendship) ignores the relationship as an object of interest.
25. In the theoretical understanding of the sociality at stake, not in any policy-informed sense. The tension is to be lived with, for, as to the latter, this is not the time to jettison the public discourse of 'altruism', any more than that of 'human rights', or any more than feminist activism could ever dispense with the often analytically dubious concept of 'women'.
26. The personal/impersonal antithesis fuels the conventional late twentieth-century/ early twenty-first-century audit-driven 'distrust' of people's commitment to institutional projects, and the motivation to put 'impersonal' measures in their place. The issue is simply noted; in the present political climate, it would be as hazardous to do away with the 'impersonal' as a public virtue as it would be to do away with 'altruism' (see note 25).
27. I use this old-fashioned phrase, as throughout this chapter, to suggest an emphasis on relations between persons, since of course relationality as such is a pervasive and ubiquitous property of systems of all kinds.
28. Whether to lament or celebrate, a radical example of innovation in relations lies to hand. Over the English-speaking seventeenth and eighteenth centuries, 'friend'

changed from connoting a closely related supporter, including the most loyal of one's kin, to being the archetype of the disinterested (non-kin) relation perpetuated for own sake. (There were concomitant changes in conceptions of kinsfolk.)

References

Amin, A. 2012. *Land of Strangers*. Cambridge: Polity Press.
Amin, A., and P. Howell. 2016. 'Thinking the Commons', in A. Amin and P. Howell (eds), *Releasing the Commons: Rethinking the Futures of the Commons*. Routledge, pp. 1–17.
Beer, B., and D. Gardner. 2015. 'Friendship, Anthropology of', in *International Encyclopedia of the Social and Behavioral Sciences*, vol. 9, 2nd ed. Elsevier, pp. 425–31.
BMA [British Medical Association]. 2012. *Medical Ethics Today: The BMA's Handbook of Ethics and Law*, 3rd ed. Chichester: Wiley-Blackwell for BMA Medical Ethics Department.
Bodenhorn, B. 2013. 'On the Road Again: Movement, Marriage, Mestizaje, and the Race of Kinship', in S. McKinnon and F. Cannell (eds), *Vital Relations: Modernity and the Persistent Life of Kinship*. Santa Fe: School for Advanced Research Press, pp. 131–54.
Carsten, J. 2004. *After Kinship*. Cambridge: Cambridge University Press.
Demian, M. 2004. 'Seeing, Knowing, Owning: Property Claims as Revelatory Acts', in E. Hirsch and M. Strathern (eds), *Transactions and Creations: Property Debates and the Stimulus of Melanesia*. Oxford: Berghahn Books, pp. 60–82.
Descola, P. [2005] 2013. *Beyond Nature and Culture*, trans. J. Lloyd. Chicago: University of Chicago Press.
Dickenson, D. 2007. *Property in the Body: Feminist Perspectives*. Cambridge: Cambridge University Press.
Edwards, J. 2009. 'The Matter in Kinship', Introduction to J. Edwards and C. Salazar (eds), *European Kinship in the Age of Biotechnology*. Oxford: Berghahn Books, pp. 1–18.
Erin, C., and J. Harris 2003. 'An Ethical Market in Human Organs', *Journal of Medical Ethics* 29: 137–38.
Fannin, M. 2016. 'Revisiting a Bodily Commons: Enclosures and Openings in the Bioeconomy', in A. Amin and P. Howell (eds), *Releasing the Commons: Rethinking the Futures of the Commons*. Routledge, pp. 177–92.
Gibson-Graham, A.F., J. Cameron and S. Healy 2016. 'Commoning as a Postcapitalist Politics', in A. Amin and P. Howell (eds), *Releasing the Commons: Rethinking the Futures of the Commons*. Routledge, pp. 192–212.
Hardin, G. 1968. 'The Tragedy of the Commons', *Science* 162(3859): 1243–48.
Harris, J. 2003. 'Organ Procurement: Dead Interests, Living Needs', *Journal of Medical Ethics* 29: 130–34.
Healy, K. 2006. *Last Best Gifts: Altruism and the Market for Human Blood and Organs*. Chicago: University of Chicago Press.
Josephides, L. 2014. 'We the Cosmopolitans: Framing the Debate', Introduction to L. Josephides and A. Hall (eds), *We the Cosmopolitans: Moral and Existential Conditions of Being Human.* Oxford: Berghahn Books, pp. 1–28.
Kaufman, S., et al. 2009. 'Aged Bodies and Kinship Matters: The Ethical Field of Kidney Transplant', in H. Lambert and M. McDonald (eds), *Social Bodies*. New York: Berghahn Books, pp. 17–46.

Lock, M. 2002. *Twice Dead: Organ Transplants and the Reinvention of Death*. Berkeley: University of California Press.
McKinnon, S., and F. Cannell. 2013. *Vital Relations: Modernity and the Persistent Life of Kinship*. Santa Fe: School for Advanced Research Press.
NCOB [Nuffield Council on Bioethics]. 2011. *Human Bodies: Donation for Medicine and Research*. London: NCOB.
Sahlins, M. 2013. *What Kinship Is – And Is Not*. Chicago: University of Chicago Press.
Sharp, L. 2006. *Strange Harvest: Organ Transplants, Denatured Bodies and the Transformed Self*. Berkeley: University of California Press.
———. 2014. *The Transplant Imaginary: Mechanical Hearts, Animal Parts, and Moral Thinking in Highly Experimental Science*. Berkeley: University of California Press.
Silver, A. 1989. 'Friendship and Trust as Moral Ideals: An Historical Approach', *European Journal of Sociology* 30: 274–97.
———. 1990. 'Friendship in Commercial Society: Eighteenth Century Social Theory and Modern Sociology', *American Journal of Sociology* 95(6): 1474–504.
Strathern, M. 2012. 'Gifts Money Cannot Buy', in H. High (ed.), 'The Debt Issue', *Social Anthropology special issue* 20(4): 397–410.
Tsing, A. 2012. 'On Nonscalability: The Living World Is Not Amenable to Precision-Nested Scales', *Common Knowledge* 18(3): 505–24.
Viveiros de Castro, E. [2009] 2014. *Cannibal Metaphysics*, trans. and ed. P Skafish. Minneapolis: Univocal.
Waldby, C., and R. Mitchell. 2006. *Tissue Economies: Blood, Organs, and Cell Lines in Late Capitalism*. Durham, NC: Duke University Press.
Whitfield, N. 2013. 'Who Is My Stranger? Origins of the Gift in Wartime London, 1939–45', in J. Carsten (ed.), 'Blood Will Out: Essays on Liquid Transfers and Flows', *JRAI special issue*: S95–S117.
Zelizer, V. 2005. *The Purchase of Intimacy*. Princeton, NJ: Princeton University Press.

8

On Being Selfish – Or Not
Explorations of an Idea from the Mountains of Oaxaca and the Alaskan Tundra

Barbara Bodenhorn

Tutqiksi: that feeling of contentment you get when you come back from hunting with lots of food to share. . . .
—Raymond Neakok, Sr., personal communication

The whale gives itself to all of the community; and it expects to be shared by all of the community. That's what holds us together.
—Patrick Attungana, to the Alaska Eskimo Whaling Commission, translated by James Nageak

Somos un equipo (we are a team).
—Three Ixtlán teachers when offered the price of a single ticket to participate in a teacher workshop in Cambridge

Introduction

For centuries one prominent mode of thinking about how the world 'works' within the Western intellectual tradition has been some form of what is today called 'rational choice theory': individuals are assumed to allocate scarce resources rationally to infinite needs. From Thomas Hobbes to Herbert Spencer, Margaret Thatcher and beyond, it is assumed that individuals must compete to protect their own self-interest, and out of competition comes creativity, innovation and – with social evolutionist thinking – progress. The naturalization of this model of individualistic competition often calls on versions of 'selfish gene theory' to give 'neoliberalism' a determinist edge.[1] The quotes with which I opened this chapter suggest alternative points of view.[2]

Many chapters in this volume interrogate the concept of selfishness through the lens of selflessness as its moral opposite, whether the selfless love of a parent for a child, the altruism of the antislavery movement, or a zen-like ethics that strives to get beyond self altogether. Drawing on comparative material from Barrow, Alaska (USA) and Ixtlán de Juárez, Oaxaca (Mexico), what I explore in this chapter are some of the ways in which being not selfish does not correspond to any sense of selflessness, but rather enables one to be part of and contribute to a sense of 'us'. In Barrow, to be 'selfish' implies a lack of generosity – which may discourage animals from returning. In Ixtlán, *egoísmo* implies an unwillingness to pull one's weight in public life. In both contexts, the moral threat is to a collective; in both cases, to be 'selfish' does not suggest an excess of self, but rather implies an incomplete one. Its opposite is not an erasure of self, but rather an expansion of it.

This notion – that proper selves are expanded ones – brings up two further issues which I explore in the pages to come.

First, if we are speaking of expansion, we have to ask about limits: where does 'us' stop? In both Barrow and Ixtlán, we hear non-anthropocentric views of the world. In the mega-biodiverse mountains of the Sierra Norte of Mexico, the communally organized forest-based community of Ixtlán manages its care of pine forests around the notion of 'father trees' and the same competitive model mentioned above; individual pines compete with each other for light, water and nutrients. Human agency, however, is articulated through the idioms of 'care' and 'respect' for the mountains and forests of the area. Despite the fact that Ixtlán's inhabitants are profoundly Christian, I have never heard that God gave the earth (or the forests) to humans for their use. Instead, as a delegation of Ixtlán primary school teachers emphasized in 2017, 'we are all part of the same world; we are not above it; this is the most important thing we need to teach to our young people'.[3]

In Barrow, as well as Ixtlán, the universe of social membership and social responsibility is explicitly understood to extend beyond the realm of the human. Iñupiaq whalers living in the minimal Arctic ecosystem of the Alaskan North Slope maintain a strong social relation with all of the animals on which they depend, but most explicitly with whales who are said to give themselves to 'all of the community'. People's willingness to share is what brings the animals back. Thus, the theme of interspecies cooperation (humans and forests in Ixtlán; humans and animals in the Arctic) invites us to ask what sorts of selves are involved.[4]

Secondly, if I am asserting that the high value of 'the collective' does not imply an erasure of the individual self, we have to ask who individuals are in these contexts. In Ixtlán, as well as in Barrow, individual autonomy is highly prized, in practice as well as in theory, even while collectives are organized along the principles of common property and require a willingness to contribute to the common good to be able to claim membership. In Ixtlán the epithet of *egoísta* (translated into English as 'selfish'), and in Barrow the charge of 'being greedy', are very strong, negative judgements. My weak argument, then, is to emphasize the importance of recognizing these distinct components of 'selfishness' as a category that people draw on discursively to make moral judgements about social action. In neither case, however, can we assume that a commitment to a collective must necessarily stand *as opposed to* individual self-interest. Here I come to my stronger argument as suggested above: proper self is an expanded one.

Far from being examples of 'exotic' and slightly contradictory behaviour, I further suggest that this capacity for realizing a strong sense of self through collective as well as autonomous action – for selves to be expansive as well as concentrated – can be found in the small towns of upper New York State as well as Oaxaca. The final question of the chapter, then, is to ask how people learn the value of expanded selves. My answer is practice – on multiple levels and across many media.

This material invites us to ask what it takes to open out models such as rational choice theory rather than deny and substitute them. Individuals in many contexts (including the ones described here) *do* compete within a logic of self-interest – for economic resources, political influence, air time, admiration, voice, and fifteen minutes of fame. Sometimes the results are breathtakingly creative; at other times they are appallingly self-destructive. But we also cooperate, share, help each other, laugh together and pool resources.

Given the relentless pressure to naturalize the selfish individual as the main driver of social life, it is urgent that we keep not just the idea, but the existence, of these alternatives in view.[5]

An Ethnographic Beginning

Several years ago, I was invited to my first *quinceañera* – the major party thrown by many Mexican families for a daughter when she turns fifteen. In Ixtlán de Juárez, Oaxaca, a village of some four thousand, mostly Catholic inhabitants, the *quinceañera* proceeded to her family home on foot from the church where she had attended Mass, accompanied by family, friends, the man responsible for marking the procession with firecrackers, and a local band. The street in front of her house had been 'domesticated', so to speak – blocked off and set up with tables for guests, a dais for music and speeches, and a stage area in front for celebratory ritual dances as well as general merriment. It was both private, in that it was clearly a family affair and guests were invited, and public, in that not only did it take place on a public street, but it was also in plain view, in stark contrast to daily domestic life which is usually conducted within enclosed spaces.

The ceremonial core of the evening was, as always, a moment in which the *quinceañera* danced on her own with a doll – the quintessential girl's plaything – then handed it over to her grandmother, who danced with her granddaughter murmuring advice in her ear and then left the floor carrying the doll. The young woman then turned to her *galanes* (suitors) for a final, transformational spin around the floor, dancing with each suitor in turn. The entire event – from the dress to the highly choreographed dance, to the multi-tiered cake that must be cut by the *quinceañera* – announced that this was a young woman ready for marriage. How striking, then, that on this evening, the speech by the *padrino* (godfather) was an exhortation both to the young woman and to the assembled guests. Here is a young woman on the verge of adulthood, he said. It is up to all of us, if we see her 'losing her way' in public – acting irresponsibly – to help her understand what it means to be, not a 'good wife' or 'good mother' or 'good woman', but a 'good citizen'. That is what adulthood is.[6]

Not present in this rhetoric, but directly part of my fieldwork experience, is the figure of *'la mujer abnegada'*, the woman who puts herself last through the erasure of personal desire – selflessness that is particularly gendered. This latter form of being is about being a 'good woman', not necessarily about doing 'good works', and thus provides provocative contrast to notions of altruism – something discussed elsewhere in this volume. Thus, in the social geography of this one community – and staying for the moment with the spaces open to women – we already have two possible alternatives to the *egoísta*, the selfish self: the good citizen, whose selfhood is defined through active membership in a moral (and relatively non-gendered) community, and another heavily gendered self whose virtue is judged by a denial of sensory individual desire ('I'm not hungry; I don't like meat; I don't need to sit down'). Although in terms of agentive behaviours they seem quintessentially distinct, they are not opposed to each other as social categories.

I begin with this extended bit of ethnography because it seems to me that to understand what being a 'good citizen' implies in Ixtlán helps us to understand the entirely judgemental epithet of *egoísta* – a person who puts ego first – translated into English as 'selfish'. By contrast, what it means to call someone 'selfish' in Barrow, an Iñupiaq community of equal size to Ixtlán and with a similar organizational role in the region, suggests a moral failure of quite a different character – a lack of readiness to share, a tendency to hoard. Just how these seem to point to quite different qualities will be a central focus of this chapter. What we are not confronted with is an easily bifurcated notion of self that in Lévi Straussian terms has either too much or too little of 'it'; rather, we are looking at quite a complex moral geography in which 'the (moral) self' appears in a myriad of ways.

A Bit More Context

Ixtlán is a sustainable forest community located in the Sierra Norte approximately an hour and a half northwest of Oaxaca City. It is organized along two forms of collective entity. The first is the commune (literally, the *Bienes Comunales* – the common wealth), a landholding collective of 384 families who hold rights in nineteen thousand hectares of inalienable terrain (primarily pine/oak boreal forest) and rights in governance through a general assembly of *comuneros*, predominantly men, each of whom represents one of the *comunera* families. The second, the 'free and sovereign municipality', is more inclusive and is governed through a general assembly of all citizens – men and women over the age of eighteen. Throughout Ixtlán, spatial division is Catholic (regardless of the religious affiliation of the residents): every *barrio* (neighbourhood) is defined by its patron saint, each of whom requires an annual three-day celebration that is the responsibility of neighbourhood families to organize. 'Good standing' in each of these is dependent upon individual contributions of time, and often of material goods, realized in the formal institutions of *cargo* and/or *tequio*, which support the proper continuity of the collective.[7] The community of Ixtlán itself is prosperous in regional terms: few houses remain with an earthen floor; most have access to electricity and potable water. Although being thought to be *egoísta* may allude to many aspects of bad character, it is the refusal to place the collective first that generates the strongest approbation. In 2005, when I asked the then president of the Bienes Comunales how he had developed his sense of community belonging, he responded as if he had just finished reading Durkheim: 'fighting forest fires and taking part in fiestas'.[8] By contrast, during my 2016 stay in Ixtlán, I was struck by how frequently *egoísmo* (and less frequently *individualismo*) was produced (entirely unsolicited, I hasten to add) to explain a number of challenges currently confronting the collective – from falling attendance at General Assemblies to arguments regarding proper management strategies, to territorial disputes between family members, or indeed between communities. It was usually accompanied by laments that (some) people seem to be losing the sense of *comunalidad*.[9]

Like Ixtlán, Barrow has around four thousand inhabitants; it too has a complex of politico/economic organizations which divides along local/regional and 'tribal'/state lines.[10] The Utqiagvik Iñupiaq Corporation (UIC) administers inalienable territory held in common for corporation members, all of whom are Iñupiaq and born in the Barrow region; the Arctic Slope Regional Corporation (ASRC) is a regional Iñupiaq corporation whose oil-related financial success has gained them entry into the Fortune 500. In addition, we find a regional tribal governing authority (the Iñupiaq Community of the Arctic Slope) and the Native Village of Barrow; in these latter institutions, elected representatives are charged with responsibilities over specifically Iñupiaq resources as stipulated by federal law. Finally, the City of Barrow is the municipality that governs the local community according to Alaska State law, and the North Slope Borough is a Home Rule Borough, also a state entity. Whaling continues to be the activity that is profoundly felt to 'hold the community together', and it is whaling that requires the greatest collective effort. Like in Ixtlán, social life is punctuated by regular events that celebrate the collective through ceremonialized commensality and dance.

Cargo and *Tequio:* Working for the Public Good in Ixtlán

Municipal, communal and church organizations in Ixtlán are dependent on members being willing to contribute to the common good. Members of the commune benefit from access to the forest, which is the communal patrimony, utilities, and financial support for business or educational projects. But eligibility is predicated on taking part in the community. *Tequio* is generalized labour, from keeping ditches clear of underbrush to fighting forest fires. If a fire is reported, the public announcement system will call for help, and within minutes the central square is filled with men wielding machetes ready to be transported wherever they are needed. When it is over, a list of names is publicly announced. These are people who did not show up and are being summoned to the central office to account for their absence. *Cargo* is a system of specific jobs with increasing levels of responsibility, from public safety through to the organizing of *barrio* and community fiestas, to the highest authorities in the political structure: president, secretary, treasurer and the like. Only these final positions are paid. These jobs are nominated by the General Assemblies and require the nominees to give up their day jobs, so to speak, for about eighteen months. In some communities, in fact, people are summoned from wherever they may have landed (Oaxaca, Mexico City or the US) to return to fulfil their *cargo* responsibilities so that they can ensure that they and their families can continue to enjoy membership. For those who are not incorporated into the commune (and there are many reasons this might be so), there are other civic organizations that people actively seek out in order to participate. The results of these forms of public participation are performed throughout the year. Most of these are religious events, such as the Day of the Dead, Christmas and Easter. But the event I propose to discuss here, for its counter-intuitive civic character, is Mothers' Day. In the United States and Great Britain, Mothering Sunday is primarily a domestic affair whereby individual mums are acknowledged with cards, gifts and perhaps a special meal on the part of immediate family. In Ixtlán, the event is organized through the municipality and is public, gendered more than kinshipped, and inclusive. In 2006 (the last year that I was in Ixtlán for the event), the day began when all women (who stand for mothers whether they have children or not) were invited for hot chocolate and sweet rolls in the one corn mill that is still in operation in the town. By late morning, most of the community was assembled in the primary schoolyard, which had been transformed into a bower by the teachers but which was also flanked by the symbols of state: flags, a dais for speakers, and an honour guard. Every woman was given a raffle ticket for gifts that had been supplied by local businesses – gifts that clearly reflected motherly responsibilities: kitchen goods, children's clothes, cleaning supplies. As with the *quinceañera* example I gave earlier, the surprise came with the speeches, when the discursive emphasis was not on how important mothers were to the health of families, but on the central role they played in the health of the community. We then all trooped over to another public space, the civic auditorium, where women only were served a celebratory meal (*mole; mezcal*) and given a parting gift that, as before, spoke of domestic responsibility. Thus, once again we have a public event where the domestic is folded into the civic, where both organizational effort and public and private financial resources are brought into play in order to make the civic nature of this moral relationship visible both materially and rhetorically.

Such all-enveloping sociality may appear coercive (and in a number of communities around Oaxaca many young people certainly feel that way), but I have also had many conversations with young Ixtlecos who are on the cusp of deciding whether they will apply to join the commune or not. As with many young Iñupiaq whalers, one of the major draws for these young men and women is a profound and spiritual relationship with *el monte* – the mountain terrain that supports Ixtlán's forest, a primary source of village identity. Ixtlán takes pride in its status as a sustainable community, and the major responsibility of the Communal Assembly in this general effort is the management of its forest resources in a way that provides economic resources for its members and protects the forest ecology.

Working for the Public Good as a Function of Inter-species Cooperation in the Arctic

To elaborate the notion of inter-species cooperation introduced earlier, I want to tell a story – one that continues to play an important role in Barrow public life today. It is the story of how the Messenger Feast – an event that celebrates inter-village sociality as well as inter-species responsibility – got started:[11]

> Toolik told his wives, 'In the morning early I will go to the mountains to hunt'. . . . Toolik started up a steep trail . . . All of a sudden . . . he saw a giant bird dropping down towards him. . . . Toolik took out his bow fast, put in an arrow and aimed it at the giant bird. . . . The giant bird wobbled and . . . slowly sailed down into the valley below. When Toolik got close, he saw that the bird was truly a tingmiakpak (giant eagle).
>
> He started to walk away from the dead bird when he heard a voice: 'Toolik! turn around!' . . . There was a man standing there. Toolik knew that it was a spirit even if it looked like a man.[12] 'You have been hearing a drumming sound', [the spirit said]. 'It is the heartbeat of the tingmiakpak's mother. She was so shocked and sad when she saw you had killed her son that her heart began to pound. There is only one way to make the mother's heart feel better. You must return the tingmiakpak's spirit to his mother'.
>
> 'Now, you must do certain things in order to return the spirit to the mother. You will see other spirit persons like me. Listen carefully to what they say. Look at everything they show you. You will be able to remember everything. We will help you to learn what you must do. You must go back to your village and . . . teach them to do the things we show you how to do'.

[Gloss] That first spirit showed Toolik how to construct a *kalukauk* (a wood and water drum that is customarily only used to celebrate this story). 'This is the first thing to remember', he said, and disappeared. Then two spirit people showed up.

> 'You are a human. You cannot return the tingmiakpak's spirit to his mother yourself. Watch us and tell the Kawerak people to do just as we do. . . . When you do everything, we spirits are teaching you, we can take the bird's spirit to his mother. Send two men to all the villages near and far around Kawerak . . . Your men will be messengers. They should invite the other village to take part in a great dance. At the same time, they must ask four strong hunters at each village to bring things to give. . . . All these men will exchange things at the Feast. When they do this, they will be helping to return the tingmiakpak's spirit to his mother'.
> [Then Toolik saw] a circle of spirit dancers [who] danced a lively dance . . . Spirit people were practising songs. Toolik listened for a long time. They were all new to him. Then a spirit man said, 'Do not worry . . . You will remember the songs so that you can teach the people at Kawerak. We will help you'. They finish with a great feast and Toolik is instructed to return home and prepare the village for the event which will restore the mother eagle's spirit.

In many ways, this story echoes other tales of originary teaching and learning. The protagonist is taken out of time and instructed how to do things properly; he is exhorted to practise so he can share what he has learned and others may learn how to act properly. But it is also quite an extraordinary story – this story of learning how to be social through learning how to share beyond the individual household.

We are, I assume, all familiar with stories in which humans are turned into animals for a time in order to understand nonhuman social worlds.[13] The mark of an Iñupiaq shaman is the capacity to shape shift in this way. But in this case, animals not only take on human form in order to teach, they provide a social context in which company, food, dancing and song are shared.

If Hobbes' 'state of nature' assumes a world of isolated individuals whose lack of communication leads to fear and the presumed need for pre-emptive strikes, this story – of the necessity of human sociality for proper human/nonhuman relations – is the opposite: an original sin (the improper killing of the mother eagle's son) is met, not with wrath, but with teaching. The moral goal is to restore proper inter-species relations with the Mother Eagle. It is thus about restitution rather than atonement; the importance of social interaction between human and nonhuman persons through cross-species communication is presented repeatedly in this story as the way to restore the *tingmiakpak*'s spirit to his mother. You restore her spirit not by taking gifts to her, but by sharing with each other.

From Narrative to Practice

The Messenger Feast plays a visible role in Iñupiaq public life in the early twenty-first century, both as story and event. Discursively, it is acted out in dance form every New Year's Eve, drawing in young people as well as elders. As an event, the Messenger Feast was revived in the 1980s by then-mayor George Ahamagoak and continues to bring circumpolar peoples together in Barrow every few years.[14] The drama never fails to impress the audience – whether this is largely made up of Iñupiaq Barrow residents (as with Kalukaq), or includes the international crowd attracted by Kivgiq. Other ceremonial distributions of whale and other hunted meat also mark the annual cycle: Nalukataq (to celebrate a successful spring hunt), Thanksgiving and Christmas, in which shared food is an explicit expression of thanks to the animals who have given of themselves.

The morality of sharing is, however, not just about ceremonial events; it is about daily practice that is understood to emerge from and depend on cross-species communication and understanding. This is the subject of powerful story-telling as well as reflected in daily conversation – both, in my experience, most frequently elaborated in terms of whaling. In his address to the Alaska Eskimo Whaling Commission in 1986, Patrick Attungana (Episcopal minister and Eskimo whaling captain from Point Hope) told how whales decide every year 'where to go camping' – that is, to which whaling crew camped out on the ice they will give themselves up. That decision is based on the whales' perception of respectful human/whale interaction as well as of harmonious and generous behaviour between humans themselves. To 'feel welcome', whales must know that people are working 'in harmony', that their (whale) bodies will be treated 'tenderly', that they will have a clean place to be stored, and that their meat will be shared 'with everyone'. If treated properly, the whale spirit will tell other whales that the whaling captain couple have acted as 'good hosts' and that it will return to give itself to them another year. The sense of this narrative assumes both communication and reciprocity between whales, between whales and humans, and among humans themselves. 'This', in Attungana's words, 'is what holds us together'.

But we need to pay attention to what people do and how they do it, as well as what they say. Most pertinent to the argument at hand is a distinction I wish to propose between individualistic social organization and individualism. As seems to be the case in many hunting societies, individual autonomy on the North Slope is highly valued; as I mentioned above, no one really has the right to tell anyone else what to do.[15] At the organizational level, it is important to recognize that it is individual labour that gains one the right to earn a share in the outcome of collective hunting (see Burch 1988; Bodenhorn 2004). But this does not imply that the needs of individual humans have priority in a world that is marked by the boundary-crossing social relations celebrated in the stories like the one about the origin of the Messenger Feast.

This leads me to a first elaboration of what I mean when I say that proper Iñupiaq selves are expanded selves. Over the years, the most frequent assertion of Iñupiaq identity that I have heard is some version of: 'I am Iñupiaq; I eat Iñupiaq food'; Iñupiaq food is social food. If individuals can organize their own labour to gain shares so as to avoid dependency on particular others for survival, it is the sociality of sharing that is underpinned by and depends on an expanded sense of personhood that extends beyond the individual – indeed, the human species – level.

The logic of Iñupiaq social organization enshrines the responsibility of adults to care for young, without rigidly defining the universe of who should care for whom. As I have discussed elsewhere (1990, 2000a, 2004), proper Iñupiaq houses have adults and children in them. There is no felt need that those children 'should' be a physical extension of parental selves; adoption is the norm in that most households have adopted in, or out, or both (Bodenhorn 1988, 1990, 2000a).[16]

If adoption expands the universe of who counts as 'your' child in the present, the power of Iñupiaq names marks this as an intergenerational process. The fact that many, if not most, of the Iñupiat I know on the North Slope are devoutly Christian does not eclipse the feeling that Iñupiaq persons are at least in part a reflection of the principle of return – of a kind of reincarnation. Many years ago, I asked Raymond Neakok, Sr. whether the Iñupiaq name he was best known by – Natchigun (which literally means a device for catching seals) – was a name he had earned by virtue of being the excellent hunter he was. 'No!' he exclaimed. 'I wish it was, but it is the person – the person of the name.'[17] Throughout the circumpolar North, there is the strongly held belief that when a person dies, s/he will return, taking up residence in the body of a newborn. Thus, a baby who seems to recognize a camping site associated with the deceased, or who smiles when a relative of the deceased comes into the room, is providing evidence of the who of its person. But names and persons are not singular identities – people may accrue them as life goes on, each one potentially underpinning a different set of social relations. Raymond – who had several names – explained, 'I can't be everyone at once, but whoever you call me, I will be that person – to you'. Thus, if the right to a share is earned as a person-as-individual (it makes no difference who your name is, who you are married to, or who your uncle is), then the principles of adoption and naming expand that personhood.[18]

Iñupiaq oral historian Rachel Edwardson (2016) has made this point. Also drawing on Patrick Attungana, she noted that if whale iñua/spirits constantly return as long as they are properly treated and human person/names also continuously circulate, then the whale eaten by her grandfather might well be the same spiritual substance shared by her grandchildren. Cross-generational continuity is made possible through these renewing forms of sociality.

'Being selfish', then, is about being greedy – hoarding – more or less saying you don't need the sociality that is made possible by and maintained through sharing food, names, children. Being not selfish is about a form of sociality realized through generosity – a collective self that crosses species both in the present and over time. Individual autonomy does not lead, inevitably, to a worldview that puts individual (human) needs first. In fact, I suggest, it is the combination of the possibility of expanded personhood with this very sensibility to the agency of many sorts of persons – human and nonhuman – that invites the development of a non-self-centred sense of self.

Discussion

What does this comparison offer? By starting with two contexts that seem, on the surface, quite similar by virtue of a shared recognition of the importance of property held in common and maintained through collective labour, comparison brings out the distinct visions of what selfishness implies. In Ixtlán, both citizenship and *comunero* status are forms of proper personhood that entail working for the common good of a known collective, whether the municipality or the commonwealth. Iñupiaq moralities expand that universe in terms of the need to share all sorts of resources with all sorts of persons, human and nonhuman. Selfishness as a form of isolationist non-citizenship and selfishness as a form of anti-social greed point out different aspects of how the term is deployed in English. But these are both forms of self-centredness and, in both cases, are felt to be antithetical to properly social persons who take part in an 'us'. Proper Iñupiaq and Ixtleco persons should be not-selfish, but this does not imply – in either case – that they should be selfless.

I cautioned early on that we should not slide into an easy assumption that the ethnography I have just presented is exotic, or exceptional. These communities are organized around principles of common property and collective membership. But sociality in the Hudson River Valley of rural New York also depends on initiatives which depend on a sense of collective responsibility. Here I mention only one: the town of Montgomery (Orange County, NY) had a population of over twenty-two thousand in 2010, approximately four times as large as either of the communities in which I have been working. Its entirely volunteer fire department, which responds to urgent calls from Montgomery residents, as well as from neighbouring fire departments if necessary, clearly does not restrict its contribution to the common good to a collective of known persons. But neither is its universe as expansive as that described by Patrick Attungana. It seems to me that one take-home message from this collection of examples is that the impulse to realize a sense of collective self – whether through social activism or feasting a whale – is moral, political and multiple. And not the exception.

The social sciences in general, and social anthropology in particular, have sought to explore the nature of social cohesion as well as the roots of social division. From Malinowski, through Firth's 'transactionalism', to late-twentieth-century 'rational choice theory' and 'neoliberalism', one trajectory of this inquiry has been to assume that individuals following their own best self-interest may find it in their interest to cooperate but cannot be assumed to do so – at least at certain levels.

In the face of challenges thrown up by increasingly complex global systems, there has been considerable recent work exploring the roots of collective (human) behaviour. Meeker-Lowery (1983) and Elinor Ostrom ([1990] 2015) both take a case study approach to critique models that assume the ultimate failure of collective endeavours that are not centrally organized to prevent 'cheating' ('free riders', in Ostrom's words). Ostrom uses her case material systematically to deconstruct the modelling process, and to delineate the conditions in which processes seem to unfold in one direction rather than another. She reviews three influential models of (failed) collective action: Hardin's 'Tragedy of the Commons' (1968), which is a theory of responsibility (if a good belongs to everyone, no one will take care of it); emerging from this, the 'Prisoner's Dilemma' (see Dawes 1975), which revolves around questions of trust (if everyone acts in good faith, everyone wins, but if anyone acts in bad faith, they win and everyone else loses); and Olson's (1965) 'Logic of Collective Action', whose very specific critique focused on the assumptions of 'Rational Choice Theory' that common interests will result in rational cooperation – which seems manifestly not true empirically. 'What makes these models so interesting and so powerful', Ostrom suggests ([1990] 2015: 6–7),

> is that they capture important aspects of many different problems that occur in diverse settings in all parts of the world. What makes [them] so dangerous – when they are used metaphorically as the foundations for policy – is that the constraints that are assumed to be fixed for the purpose of analysis are taken on faith as being fixed in empirical settings . . . I would rather address the question of how to enhance the capabilities of those involved to change the constraining rules of the game.

To do this, Ostrom insists, you need to move away from the models and consider different initiatives as they are actually taking place, being willing to take the time to discover the complexities of context. She concludes that the challenges of trust presented in prisoners' dilemma-like contexts seem least likely to form a lose-lose trap (a) when information is freely available; (b) when the constraints on decision-making are not externally imposed; and (c) when actors show the capacity to change. 'Learning', she asserts ([1990] 2015: 190), 'is an incremental, self-transforming process'. Institutional change, she continues, needs to take incremental transformation into account.

In the final chapter of an updated version of *The Selfish Gene* ([1976] 2006), entitled 'Nice Guys Finish First', Dawkins comes to a similar conclusion. Reiterating a point he makes more than once over the course of the book, he recognizes that humans are not simply mechanical housings for genes. We can learn.

Joel Robbins (2018) asks an important question: if we recognize the weaknesses of a model of 'culture' that assumes an internally coherent system of shared values and customs that get handed down over time, how do social worlds develop in which values nonetheless come to be shared? Why are we not running around with individually generated ideas of the good, the true and the beautiful? For this, he suggests, 'we need a theory of exemplars' and, drawing on C. Humphrey's (1997) work on exemplars and his own material in Papua New Guinea, he puts forward his understanding of the close relationship between exemplars and values. Instead of asserting, as Dawkins does, *that* we can learn, Robbins sees the power of the exemplary in extraordinary persons and rituals as a way of understanding *how* we learn.

How, then, do we learn not-selfishness (in whatever form that takes in particular settings) as a value? This chapter offers one account of modes through which (at least some) people come to think of themselves as social in ways that take an 'us' as the norm. Robbins' (and Humphrey's) argument certainly invites us to consider the story of the Messenger Feast as an exemplar; it offers a complete – and dramatic – story of the need for responsibility and reciprocity that underpin human/animal relations. It is institutionalized as a dance marked by headdresses signifying the animals who helped with the first feast. But, unlike the stories discussed by Keith Basso (1996), working with Western Apache, or Julie Cruikshank (1998), working in Western Canada, the story itself does not seem to serve as a template for teaching young people (or, indeed, wayward adults) the proper way to behave. The notion that animals respond to human behaviour and that this is a moral relationship can be heard in casual conversation – deployed to explain either specific human or animal action, or both. But I have never heard these conversations refer to the story as the basis for teaching the value of sharing. And here I would like to turn to two conversations I had during a recent stay in Ixtlán that illustrate the different modes through which a commitment to some form of common sociality seems to come into being. In both cases, we are looking at the sort of incremental learning process suggested by Ostrom, above, that comes to shape people's environmental understanding. During early August, I spent the day with Rosalinda Hernández, a native of the *serrana* community of Natividad and one of the primary school teachers with whom I have worked for the past three years. She was talking with her daughter, explaining Patrick Attungana's account of how whales decide to give themselves up to whalers who will treat them tenderly and with respect. 'The really beautiful thing', she said, 'is that this is all mixed up with practice. It's not just talking about talking about (*hablar de hablar*)'. A few days later I was talking with Montserrat Gorgonio, a young Ixtleca woman who has just finished her master's in genetics, but who also has a passion for local cultural traditions. As she has been up to Barrow twice and has had long conversations with Iñupiaq elders as well as whale biologists, I wanted to know if there was anything corresponding to these stories that so explicitly extol the value of sharing when it comes to being 'not *egoísta*' in Ixtlán. 'Not really', she replied, 'you get stories about respect' (*respeto*) for the forest and for the animals but really nothing about 'community'. 'Then how do people come to learn "it"?', I asked. 'Practice' (*la práctica*), was her response. And here her answer was probably more Ingoldian (in terms of embodied discipline) and less Durkheimian (in terms of intense collective action) than the answer given to me by Edilberto Pérez when I first asked the question ten years ago.[19] Because for her, 'practice' meant exactly that: playing a musical instrument for one of the many local bands that provide music for fiestas, weddings, funerals, *quinceañeras* and the like – music that requires practising together in order to be able to perform together;[20] practising traditional dances for hours in order to perform for local events; practising the art of *el convivir* (literally, living with – as a noun), which means (for a woman) learning how to make *mole*, *pozole*, *tamales* – the painstaking, time-consuming and complex dishes without which a proper coming together, a *convivio*, would not take place. And here is the interesting part. During my visit with *la maestra* Rosalinda, we went to Xiaqui, a neighbouring village finishing the fiesta for its patron saint. We were sitting in the plaza waiting for a contest of *jarabes* (a traditional dance common in the Sierra) to begin. Rosalinda commented that the festivities the day before seemed not to have attracted young people. This afternoon, however, most of the musicians were young, and people coming out to show off their *jarabe* skills ranged from their early teens to their eighties. One young woman mentioned that her (eight-year-old) son preferred traditional dancing to watching television. In a similar way, young Iñupiaq men and women are eager to join dance groups as well as whaling crews – collectives that require dedicated practice before recognition as a group is forthcoming. Clearly there is something about these forms of practice that is not only rule-governed, but compellingly attractive for young people.

I am not suggesting that any of the communities that I have talked about are seamlessly unified in terms of belief or behaviour concerning unselfishness. In recent years, trusted members of Ixtleco organizations have made off with significant funds; Barrow is riven with arguments about the relative merits of protecting marine habitat or enabling further oil development, about deciding who has the right, as well as the responsibility, to decide the future. What is striking, however, in local responses to these challenges is the extent to which the starting point as well as the end goal continues, for the moment anyway, to be 'us', not I.

Barbara Bodenhorn is a Senior Research Associate in the Department of Social Anthropology, University of Cambridge (bb106@cam.ac.uk). She has worked as a social anthropologist in Arctic Alaska since 1980 and in Oaxaca, Mexico since 2004. She is currently Fellow Emerita at Pembroke College and faculty member in the Department of Social Anthropology, University of Cambridge. Her focus on kinship, gender, economics and cosmology has often led her to questions about self, personhood and agency. Her most recent work has had a focus on learning and young people's environmental knowledge practices.

Notes

1. I am not proposing to represent Dawkins' own views, but rather how the image of 'selfish genes' gets invoked. (See Layne, Chapter 1, this volume).
2. Hobbes perhaps continues to exert the strongest legacy, with his assumption that the pre-emptive strike underpins the 'state of nature'. Polar bear behaviour is exemplary of his argument: a mama bear will not wait around to find out what human intentions may be in the presence of her cubs. She will try to eliminate what she sees to be a potential threat. This does not hold for caribou, though, who are good examples of a species that generally opts for 'flight' over 'fight'. For relatively current ethnographic critical analysis, see Howell and Willis (1989). In his most recent version of *The Selfish Gene*, Dawkins ([1976] 2006) (re)considers his choice of 'selfish' to modify 'gene'; I return to this at the end of the chapter.
3. This was a workshop held in Cambridge, UK, March 2016. It involved teachers from participant schools as part of our Arts and Humanities Research Council (AHRC)-sponsored project 'Pathways to Environmental Understanding', which included schools from East Anglia, Mongolia, Mexico, Alaska, Italy and Nepal. When I went to the primary school in Ixtlán to say we had found the money to bring one teacher from each school to England, the response was, 'We are a team. If the project is willing for us to share the money, we will come up with the rest'. And they did.
4. I have been working on the North Slope of Alaska since 1980 and in Ixtlán since 2004, in both cases on projects developed collaboratively with local institutions and with the financial support of PAPIIT (National University of Mexico); the National Science Foundation (grant 0813635) and AHRC (AH/K006282/1). Selfishness was not the subject of any of that funding, but the information would not have been gathered without it. As a linguistic note, Iñupiaq (literally, real person) is the singular and adjectival form referring to the original inhabitants of the Alaskan Arctic; Iñupiat refers to the collective. In Alaska, inuit simply means people and carries no ethnic content. In Spanish, serrano/a refers to anyone or anything coming from the Sierra – in this case, the Sierra Norte de Juárez.
5. Ostrom (1990) and Meeker-Lowry (1983), among others, examine these forms of collective organization institutionally; I return to them in the discussion.
6. The language of citizenship as part of daily discourse is much more marked in (especially rural) Mexico than anywhere else I have worked.
7. As noted by Wolf (1966), Nader (1991), Gross (2001), Ramos Morales (2006) and others, this pattern holds for a significant part of rural Oaxaca; the political implications of this are too complex to be explored adequately here.
8. Edilberto López Pérez was president of the Bienes Comunales when I first arrived in Ixtlán in 2004. For readers for whom Durkheim is but a dusty memory, he suggested in the *Division of Labour* ([1933] 1913) that a sense of 'collective effervescence' would develop when otherwise self-sufficient individuals had to band together in the face of an extreme threat.
9. See Ramos Morales (2006) for a discussion of *comunalidad* in the Sierra Iuárez. Although I had been asking people directly how they define *egoísmo*, the conversations reported here were, I thought, about other things. My interlocutors also reflect disparate subject positions – from people firmly embedded in authority structures to those quite marginal to them. For the moment, I read this as a trope expressing disquiet rather than as a description of radical change.
10. 'Tribal' is not a term I would use to describe the political organization of any of the people I work with. It does, however, have particular meanings within US federal

Indian law with reference to the right to govern autonomously as a people who were exercising sovereignty over their territories before the arrival of Europeans and/or EuroAmericans (see Deloria and Wilkens 2011).
11. I am here drawing on a textual version contained in William Oquilluk's collection of oral narratives (1973: 150–60). Iñupiaq oral accounts contain many origin stories – I am not implying that this one is the only one.
12. The generic word for the spirit embodied by every animal is iñua, literally 'its person'.
13. I am thinking of Merlin's childhood experiences in T.H. White's ([1939] 1958) *The Once and Future King* for an Anglo-based example, as well as Ann Fienup-Riordan's (1994) discussion of 'The Boy Who Became a Seal', for a Yup'ik case.
14. Bill Hess (1994) has a splendid photo essay of this event.
15. Perhaps the most famous instance of this is the response Richard Lee received when he asked a !Kung hunter about hierarchy. 'Of course, we have headman', he was told, 'each one is headman for himself' (1982: 50).
16. See also Rivière (1974) for his assertion that Inuit adoption in general creates 'real', not 'fictive' kinship.
17. For the full text of this interview, see Bodenhorn 1988; for a full discussion of the power of names drawing on this and other North Slope material, see Bodenhorn 2006.
18. This resonates strongly with M. Strathern's offering of 'dividuals' – dispersed personhood – as a way of thinking about Mt. Hagen sociality (see, e.g., Strathern 1988). There is not enough space here to explore the similarities and the distinctions between the notions of dispersed and expanded persons.
19. Ingold, for some time now, has been arguing that an anthropological focus on 'representation' weakens our understanding of the importance of embodied practices experienced as lines (walking; weaving; story-telling; reading music) in the development of our being in the world (see, e.g., Ingold 2000, [2007] 2016).
20. In December of my first year in Ixtlán, I was walking up the hill from the local preparatory school with a student. Since the school had just closed its doors for the Christmas holidays, I asked this young man if he had lots of fun things planned with his friends. He gave me a very odd look. 'I play the trumpet', he said. 'It's a lot of work; you're playing all the time.' I have since learned how very literal he was being. There is very little down time for community musicians during religious holidays.

References

Attungana, P. 1986. 'Address to the Alaska Eskimo Whaling Commission', in *Uiñiq: The Open Lead*, trans. James Nageak. North Slope Borough, Alaska, p. 16.

Basso, K. 1996. *Wisdom Sits in Places: Landscape and Language among the Western Apache*. Albuquerque: University of New Mexico Press.

Bodenhorn, B. 1988. 'Names, Souls, Children and Other Things That Are Good to Share: Core Metaphors in a Contemporary Hunting Society', *Cambridge Anthropology* 13(1): 1–19.

———. 1990. '"I'm Not the Great Hunter; My Wife Is": Iñupiat and Anthropological Models of Gender', *Etudes/Inuit/Studies* 14(1/2): 55–74.

———. 2000a. '"He Used to Be My Relative": Exploring the Bases of Relatedness on Alaska's North Slope', in J. Carsten (ed.), *Cultures of Relatedness: New Approaches to the Study of Kinship*. Cambridge: Cambridge University Press, pp. 128–48.

------. 2000b. '"It's Traditional to Change": A Case Study of Strategic Decision-Making', *Cambridge Anthropology* 22(1): 24–51.

------. 2004. '"It's Good To Know Who Your Relatives Are, But We Were Taught to Share with Everyone": Shares and Sharing on Alaska's North Slope', in G. Wenzel et al. (eds), *The Social Economy of Sharing, Resource Allocation and Modern Hunter-Gatherers*. Osaka: SENRI Ethnological Series, 53: 13–41.

------. 2006. 'Calling into Being: Names and Being Named on Alaska's North Slope', in G. Vom Bruck and B. Bodenhorn (eds), *The Anthropology of Names and Naming*. Cambridge: Cambridge University Press, pp. 139–56.

Brower, H. Sr. 2004. *The Whales They Come to Me: Conversations with Harry Brower, Sr.* (with Karen Brewster). Fairbanks: University of Alaska Press.

Burch, Ernest S. Jr. 1988. 'Modes of Exchange in North-west Alaska', in Tim Ingold, David Riches and James Woodburn (eds), *Hunters and Gatherers: Property, Power, and Ideology*, vol 2. Oxford: Berg.

Callison, C. 2014. *How Climate Comes to Matter*. Durham, NC: Duke University Press.

Cruikshank, J. 1998 *The Social Life of Stories: Narrative and Knowledge in the Yukon Territory*. Vancouver: University of British Columbia Press.

Dawes, M. 1975. 'Formal Models of Dilemmas in Social Decision-Making', in M.F. Kaplan and S. Schwartz (eds), *Human Judgment and Decision Processes: Formal and Mathematical Approaches*. New York: Academic Press, pp. 87–108.

Dawkins, R. [1976] 2006. *The Selfish Gene*, with new introduction for the 30th anniversary edition. Oxford: Oxford University Press.

Deloria, V., and D.E. Wilkens. 2011. *The Legal Universe: Observations of the Foundations of American Law*. Fulcrum Publishers.

Durkheim, E. [1893] 2013. *The Division of Labour in Society*, ed. S. Lukes, trans. W.D. Halls. Basingstoke: Palgrave Macmillan.

Edwardson, R. 2016. 'Looking Back to Move Forward'. Virtual paper delivered to the Arctic Futures panel, moderated by B. Bodenhorn and O. Ulturgasheva, at the Anthropology, Weather and Climate Change Conference, British Museum, 27–29 May.

Fienup-Riordan, A. 1994. *Boundaries and Passages: Rule and Ritual in Yup'ik Oral Tradition*. Norman: University of Oklahoma Press.

Gross, T. 2001. 'Community and Dissent: A Study of the Implications of Religious Fragmentation in the Sierra Juarez', unpublished PhD thesis, Cambridge University.

Hardin, G. 1968. 'The Tragedy of the Commons', *Science* 162: 1243–48.

Hess, W. 1994. *A Photographic Celebration of Kivgiq: The Messenger Feast*. Barrow, AK: North Slope Borough.

Howell, S.E., and R.E Willis (eds). 1989. *Societies at Peace*. London: Routledge.

Humphrey, C. 1997. 'Exemplars and Rules: Aspects of the Discourse of Morality in Mongolia', in S. Howell (ed.), *The Ethnography of Moralities*. London: Routledge, pp. 25–47.

Ingold, T. 1987 'The Principle of Individual Autonomy and the Collective Appropriation of Nature', in *The Appropriation of Nature: Essays on Human Ecology and Social Relations*. Manchester: Manchester University Press, pp. 222–42.

------. 2000. *The Perception of the Environment: Essays on Livelihood, Dwelling, and Skill*. London: Routledge.

------. [2007] 2016. *Lines: A Brief History*. London: Routledge (Classics edition).

Lee, R. 1982. 'Politics, Sexual and Non Sexual in an Egalitarian Society', in E. Leacock and R. Lee (eds), *Politics and History in Band Society*. Cambridge: Cambridge University Press, pp. 37–59.

Meeker-Lowry, S. 1983. *Invested in the Common Good*. Philadelphia: New Society Publishers.
Nader, L. 1991. *Harmony Ideology: Justice and Control in a Zapotec Mountain Village*. Palo Alto, CA: Stanford University Press.
Olson, M. 1965. *The Logic of Collective Action: Public Goods and the Theory of Groups*. Cambridge, MA: Harvard University Press.
Oquilluk, W. (with L. Bland). 1973. *The People of Kawerak*. Anchorage: Alaska Pacific University Press.
Ostrom, E. [1990] 2015. *Governing the Commons: The Evolution of Institutions for Collective Action*. Cambridge: Cambridge University Press.
Ramos Morales, M.F. 2006. 'Cultura y Desarrollo en Sta Maria Yavesia, Oaxaca, México', Masters in Rural Development, Universidad Autónoma Metropolitana – Xochimilco.
Rivière, P. 1974. 'The Kith and the Kin', in J. Goody (ed.), *The Character of Kinship*. Cambridge: Cambridge University Press.
Robbins, J. 2018. 'Where in the World Are Values? Exemplarity, Morality and Social Process', in B. Bodenhorn, M. Holbraad and J. Laidlaw (eds), *Recovering the Human Subject*. Cambridge: Cambridge University Press, pp. 174–92.
Strathern, M. 1988. *Gender of the Gift*. Cambridge: Cambridge University Press.
White, T.H. [1939] 1958. *The Once and Future King*. London: Penguin.
Wolf, E. 1966. *Peasants*. Prentice Hall.

Conclusion

Starting Points

Modest Contributions to the History and Anthropology of Moralities and Ethics

Linda L. Layne

The anthropology of morality/ethics (AM/E) is flourishing. It now includes numerous theoretical manifestos, edited collections and ethnographic monographs.[1] Our volume offers a new, and we trust complementary, approach. The sources of our innovations may be traced to our starting points in terms of topic selection, research questions, collaborators and purpose. This 'conclusion' is offered as a springboard towards more interdisciplinary explorations of moral matters.[2]

Our first point of departure is in our object of study. Rather than the abstract, high-level notions of 'morality' and 'ethics',[3] we chose mid-level concepts, the moral categories of 'selfish' and 'selfless'. Importantly, these are what Geertz would call 'experience-near' concepts. Eighteenth-century British slave traders and abolitionists, twentieth-century British breastfeeders and anti-sexist men, American or British single mothers by choice and their critics, and both critics and marketers of sperm donors, all use the labels 'selfish' and 'selfless' 'spontaneously, unselfconsciously, as it were colloquially . . .; they do not, except fleetingly and on occasion, recognize that there are any "concepts" involved at all' (Geertz 1983: 58). The contributors to this volume, in contrast, do. It is precisely by considering selfishness and selflessness as 'concepts', as 'objects of thought', that we achieve critical distance, make the familiar if not strange, at least remarkable enough to deserve systematic, sustained consideration. One might say we are working in a theoretical sweet spot between 'experience-distant' and 'experience-near' concepts (Geertz 1983: 57). Our aim has been to 'critically . . . assess the value of the values we think of as morality' (quoted by Laidlaw 2002: 316), and our over-arching research question, 'What work do these moral judgements do and for whom?', is both empirical and theoretical.

Our joint efforts provide the beginnings of a social history of 'selfishness' and 'selflessness'. We trace when the words and their cousins entered the English language and then see that interest in these categories appears to increase during periods of dramatic change, including the present. We then follow the social lives of these categories in a variety of times and places. We found that 'selfish' and 'selfless' do not always have a negative or positive moral charge, and that while they are often deployed in gendered ways, they are not consistently associated with gender categories, even though they are often used as if they do. We found that those who are vulnerable to accusations of selfishness often defend themselves by turning the tables and arguing that it is others who are in fact selfish, for instance the British women contemplating becoming single mothers by choice who explained to Graham that they weren't selfish, that it was their former boyfriends, who would not agree to or kept postponing having children, who were.

We discovered that these concepts played a mobilizing role in two quite distinct social movements (eighteenth-century antislavery and twentieth-century anti-sexism) aimed at achieving more inclusive, liberal, egalitarian goals. For example, Delap documents how post-1960s, British anti-sexist, profeminist men and feminist women developed a critique of 'selfish masculinity', which they saw as an important component of male hegemonic power over women and led to the attempt on the part of profeminist men to develop 'a selfless form of politics – a giving up of male power and privilege in favour of women's empowerment'.

We also found that even given the diversity of instantiations, the concepts can be limiting, for the people we study, for our understanding of what matters to them. For example, Mohr shows how the discourse that frames commercial sperm donation is dominated by the opposing dichotomies of selfish indulgence and altruistic giving. Neither of these capture the diverse, profound, surprising experiences of the Danish sperm donors Mohr studied. Instead of the misleading and essentializing either/or of selfish/selfless, Mohr reveals 'the intricate interplay between biomedical regulation and the affective spaces of masturbation in which men performatively remake themselves as specific moral and gendered individuals'. (This is comparable to the 'self work' that the long-term breastfeeders described by Faircloth are engaging in, making themselves again and again into 'specific moral and gendered' beings.) Scholars and social critics who question the motivations of sperm donors, or surrogates, or just as often simply assert that they are either venal or altruistic, have already so narrowed the parameters of what matters that they shutter out other aspects of moral judgement and enactment.

The selfish/selfless dichotomy was also shown to be a hindrance in terms of imagining alternative futures. Strathern marvels at the seemingly 'irrepressible momentum to the type of thinking that opposes self-interest to other-interest' despite the fact that, just as Mohr demonstrated, this type of thinking does such 'a poor job of helping us interpret "the lived state of affairs"'. Strathern proposes instead a radical departure, the notion of 'the commons', which steps outside the supply-demand model that presumes scarcity. Rather than presuming that our body parts remain ours after death, and that it is up to us to decide whether or not to share them with others, Strathern engages in the thought experiment – bodies are something to which we have usufruct rights during our lifetimes; at death they return to the commons.

A version of the commons also informs Bodenhorn's alternative to the selfish/selfless dichotomy drawn from long-term field research among Iñupiaq in Barrow, Alaska and Ixtlecos in Mexico, who have communal rights to and responsibilities for the care of natural resources. In both cases, 'interspecies cooperation (humans and forests in Ixtlán; humans and animals in the Arctic) and a high value of "the collective" does not imply an erasure of the individual self'. On the contrary, in both settings, 'individual autonomy is highly prized . . . even while collectives are organized along the principles of common property and require a willingness to contribute to the common good to be able to claim membership. Thus, commitment to a collective does not stand as opposed to individual self-interest'. In both cases, 'to be "selfish" does not suggest an excess of self, but rather implies an incomplete one. Its opposite is not an erasure of self, but rather an expansion of it, one that includes not only other humans, but also nature'. Theoretically, her aim is to 'open out models such as rational choice theory rather than deny and substitute them'.

Bodenhorn's goal, and that of the volume more generally, differs from those of many AM/Es to the extent to which the latter view their work as a 'discipline-building project' (Lempert 2014: 465). One of the leading practitioners, James Laidlaw (2014: 1–2), endeavours to transform 'modern social theory' and offers a prospectus for doing so. Faubion seeks to create 'generative programmatics' and claims that AM/E is, if not 'the marker of an epochal shift', at least 'a bit of game changer' (2014: 439).[4]

Given these ambitions, perhaps it makes sense to look to another discipline for inspiration. A striking feature of current anthropological approaches to ethics and morality is their deep engagement with philosophy. Indeed, one appellation for this approach is 'philosophical anthropology' (Mattingly 2014, Mattingly and Jensen 2015). This orientation towards philosophy follows in some ways from the selection of topic. *Collins Dictionary* defines 'ethics' as 'moral philosophy, the philosophical study of the moral value of human conduct and of the rules and principles that ought to govern it'.

The primacy of philosophy in shaping the approach of many AM/Es (see also Yan 2011) can be seen in the chief questions posed:

> Do humans act morally because they obey socially defined rules and norms, as the result of a routine of inculcated behaviors, or an embodied fear of sanction or perhaps both? Do they act morally because they decide to do so as a consequence of rational evaluation? In other words, do they follow a Kantian ethics of duty or an Aristotelian ethics of virtue? (Fassin 2014: 429)

Not surprisingly, most AM/Es find these either/or options unsatisfactory. The straw men of Kant versus Aristotle and Durkheim versus Foucault do not hold up in the face of ethnographic complexity. Robbins concludes that 'both approaches capture aspects of the social experience of morality' (2007: 311), and Fassin notes that 'empirical research shows that most of the time subjects simultaneously take into account moral norms, practice ethical reflection and consider the consequences of their acts' (2014: 433).[5]

AM/Es have found a large range of philosophers useful (see Fassin 2014a: 430), but one striking feature is the importance of the ancient Greeks (e.g. Mattingly 2014; Zigon 2008).[6] Laidlaw's book, *The Subject of Virtue* (2014), is in large part a detailed critique of Aristotelian virtue ethics, especially as developed by Alasdair MacIntyre, a philosopher who has been particularly influential among anthropologists. Laidlaw makes the case for an alternative approach, one informed by the philosopher Bernard Williams' account of archaic Greece and also drawing on Foucault's interest in the same. In a section titled 'Why Athens?', Laidlaw explains that in his pursuit of a 'genealogy of ethics', Foucault was 'surprised by how far back [he] had to go before [finding] the resources to "think differently"' (Laidlaw 2014: 99). Mattingly explains her turn to the ancient philosophers because they provide a different perspective to the 'Enlightenment universalist ideals, . . . objectivity, truth, and rationality' (Good 1994, cited in Mattingly 2014: 34). Holbraad describes this 'shifting the standpoint' to that of the ancient Greeks as one of three 'strategies of analytical displacement' that anthropologists are adopting in their attempts to 'step away' from 'moralism' (2018: 32). Of course, cross-cultural comparison continues to be available to anthropologists for just such a purpose (see Strathern 1980 and Bodenhorn, this volume).

Rather than turning to philosophers for inspiration, our project builds on the affinity between social anthropology and the 'companionate field' of social history. In her chapter on 'Anthropology and History' in a new book produced by Cambridge anthropologists, Susan Bayly characterizes the two fields as 'troubled allies', but asserts that the tension has been productive. She credits anthropology's engagement with history as having 'far-reaching theoretical innovations' (Bayly 2018: 108). Bayly believes that there is now wide acceptance of the view 'that anthropology cannot develop conceptually without making history a key concern', notably in the 'burgeoning area of the anthropology of morality and ethics' (2018: 116).

I am not certain I agree with either the 'wide acceptance' claim or the assurance of 'far-reaching theoretical innovations', but our modest collaboration with historians is one of the things that distinguishes our effort. In addition to the two historians included in this volume, the project was enriched by those who participated in our workshops. Siân Pooley examined 'the uses to which the rhetoric of selfishness and selflessness were put by those seeking to explain the complex collection of changes in cultures of reproduction that took place in England between 1850 and 1914 as the two-child family, childless relationships and delayed or rejected marriage became increasingly common' (Pooley 2012). Leah Astbury explored the way selfishness and selflessness were deployed in 'discourses of judgement' regarding infant feeding in Early Modern England (Astbury 2012), and Eve Colpus presented work on British women's philanthropy c.1918–1939 which traced the apparent contradictions in the ways in which philanthropy is conceived – both as transcendence of the self (putting oneself in the shoes of another) and as a process of self-affirmation (Colpus 2012).

Our project provides a glimpse of what social historians can offer in terms of deepening our understandings of moralities, particularly those that have European Enlightenment roots. These studies suggest the value of attentiveness to temporalities and change over time in relation to 'moral economies' and other formulations of morality. Many claims about selfish and selfless behaviour are couched in terms of contrasts between before and after, old and new, tradition and modern. They are also distinctively oriented to the immediate context. Understanding this can allow for more informed comparative understandings of moral rhetorics and judgements that have very diverse historical/cultural trajectories.

Historians also recognize the potential benefits of cross-pollination. In Keith Thomas's seminal essay on 'History and Anthropology' (1963) in Britain's leading social history journal, aptly named *Past & Present*, he began by noting, 'there is nothing new or eccentric about the suggestion that historians might profit from an acquaintance with anthropology'. He pointed to Tawney's 1933 inaugural lecture at the London School of Economics, but noted that this recommendation was one of the few Tawney made that was not embraced by the field (1963: 3). Thomas's own interest was sparked by a lecture given in 1961 on 'Anthropology and History' by E.E. Evans-Pritchard (1963: 3), in which he asserted that 'the differences between the two subjects were those of technique rather than of aim'. Thomas believes that 'anthropologists are engaged in a roughly similar activity' to that of historians and that there are many things historians might learn from them. In the intervening years, with the ascent of 'oral history' (Delap, this volume) and of 'life histories' (e.g. Watson and Watson-Franke 1985) and 'narrative analysis' in anthropology (e.g. Layne 2003, 2013), the differences have become even less apparent.

Like anthropologists, historians could also be said to have always studied morality.[7] They have studied many of the same subjects as anthropologists: not just 'socially approved habits 'including religious practice, ritual, reciprocity, and kin relations' (Zignon 2008: 1) but also, importantly, conflicts in these domains including changing gender relations, the reformation of manners, religion and magic. Two classic examples were published in 1971: Keith Thomas's *Religion and the Decline of Magic* and E.P. Thompson's article on the challenges to the 'moral economy of provision' that the emergence of the new political economy of the free market of eighteenth-century Britain posed.

But there has been no comparable 'ethical turn' in history, no edited volumes analogous to *The Ethnography of Moralities* (Howell 1997), *The Anthropology of Moralities* (Heintz 2009), *The Ethnographies of Moral Reasoning* (Sykes

2009), *Ordinary Ethics: Anthropology, Language, and Action* (Lambek 2010), *A Companion to Moral Anthropology* (Fassin 2012) or *Moral Anthropology: A Critical Reader* (Fassin and Leze 2014), nor monographs by historians akin to Zigon's (2008) *Morality: An Anthropological Perspective*, Faubion's (2011) *An Anthropology of Ethics*, or Laidlaw's (2014) *The Subject of Virtue: An Anthropology of Ethics and Freedom*. Perhaps this is because social historians are not dealing with the same postcolonial disciplinary troubles and have reflected less on the moralities of their own methods. It may be that the recent 'turns' in historiography (spatial, cultural, material, emotional and so on) have not lent themselves to the elucidation of how moral judgements change over time, or have been rooted in a postmodern celebration of difference and diversity that has eschewed questions of values.[8]

Nevertheless, they continue to contribute compelling accounts of the complexities of moral struggles during periods of change. For example, like E.P. Thompson, Roodhouse (2006, 2013) has examined 'the multiple moralities' evident in the provision of food during times of shortage in Britain. In his study of the black market in Britain from 1935 to 1955, Roodhouse counters the portrayal of black-market consumers, dealers and producers of illicit goods as selfish, unpatriotic and immoral. He shows that they understood themselves to be behaving ethically. They felt 'entitled to obtain "a little bit extra" or make "a decent living" as reward or compensation for the many personal sacrifices they made at central government's behest' (2006: 254). Furthermore, he found that illegal markets did not pose a serious threat because of Britons' sense of fairness. Would-be evaders had to justify their offences both to themselves and others, and they did so 'by invoking popular notions of a fair price, a fair profit, and a fair share' (2006: 254).

Another example is the work of historian Matthew Grimley, which highlights the paradoxes of the Church of England's role in the 'permissive' legal reforms of the 1960s concerning homosexuality, the abolition of the death penalty and the rights of immigrants (2009: 726). 'In advocating the separation of crime and sin, senior Anglicans were promoting the secularisation of the criminal law' (725). Grimley (2012) has also probed the paradoxes of Thatcher's moralism, paradoxes that were not evident at the time. She wished to renew Britain as a Christian nation, and for the church and religious organizations to take charge of the needed 'remoralisation of society' (78). Nevertheless, she 'presided over and celebrated a culture of rampant materialism' (93). Rather than cast this discrepancy as evidence of hypocrisy, Grimley uses her to represent a 'link between two utterly opposed moral systems which ... [were] the story of Britain in the twentieth century' (93). These works have begun to offer a broad sense of the different traditions and registers of thinking about morals in a specific context, and suggest the need to span histories of culture, religion, politics and economics in this pursuit.

Historians and anthropologists have collaborated to good effect in the interdisciplinary area of gender studies. See, for instance, the chapters by historians of eighteenth- and nineteenth-century thought in France and Britain, in the volume *Nature, Culture and Gender* edited by anthropologists Carol MacCormack and Marilyn Strathern (1980). Laidlaw pictures ethics and morality to be comparable to gender, in their pervasive influence visible in every topic. If this is the model, and it seems a good one to me, an interdisciplinary approach like that pursued to such good effect in gender studies is likely to prove most fruitful.

Keith Thomas ends his essay on history and anthropology by asserting that 'the justification of all historical study must ultimately be that it enhances our self-consciousness, enables us to see ourselves in perspective and helps us towards that greater freedom which comes from self-knowledge' (1963: 23). It is my hope that together anthropological and historical perspectives might lead to greater understanding, and perhaps even strategies for us as citizens and scholars, to help us navigate and contribute to this moment of moral challenge and change.

Acknowledgements

I am very grateful to James Laidlaw, Lucy Delap, Barbara Bodenhorn and G.J. Barker-Benfield for reading and commenting on a draft of this conclusion, especially given the time pressure. Your suggestions were well taken.

Linda L. Layne is a Bye-Fellow and Director of Studies for Social Anthropology, Girton College, and a Visiting Professorin the Reproductive Sociology group at the University of Cambridge (LL427@cam.ac.uk). She has written books on collective identity in Jordan and pregnancy loss in the US and is currently working on *All the Credit, All the Blame: An Intimate History of One American Single Mother by Choice* and on *Uncanny Kinship: Absent Presences in Contemporary EuroAmerican Families*, a comparative study of SMC families, two-mom families, two-dad families, and families that have suffered a pregnancy loss.

Notes

1. These include Bornstein 2012; Daswani 2015; Dow 2016; Hellweg 2011; Kuan 2015; Lester 2005; Londoño-Sulkin 2012; Muehlebach 2012; Oxfeld 2010; Pandian 2009; Parish 1994; Paxson 2004; Prasad 2007; Roberts 2016; Rogers 2009; Simon 2014; Singh 2015. Thanks to James Laidlaw for drawing my attention to these works.
2. One subject ripe for historical/sociological/anthropological inquiry might be the sin of avarice and the Church of England's use of its power to extend the moral prohibition of usury onto secular laws (Tawney [1926] 1962: 36–55), and current political struggles in the US over predatory lending practices, payday lenders, credit card pushing to college students, student loans and the .01%.

3. Although the terms 'ethics' and 'morality' are commonly used (according to *Collins Dictionary* each of them is among the four thousand most commonly used words), they are not treated as colloquial terms, but as experience-distant ones, by AM/Es. The history of their usage differs. Use of the religiously inflected term 'morality' peaked in the later part of the eighteenth century; the more secular or ecumenical term, 'ethics', did not come into popular use until the 1980s. Faubion (2011: 13) and Fassin and Leze (2014: 1) remark on a notable increase in 'talk of ethics', not just within anthropology but also outside it. Certainly, one area of growth has been bioethics (Dow 2016: 16).
4. Given the disciplinary ambitions of AM/E, it is no wonder that some of the primary questions that practitioners are asking concern the nature of their enterprise, such as: is it possible to 'delineate something called "morality" from within the whole gamut of human endeavor?' (Howell 1997: 2); 'what are the parameters of the ethical domain?' (Faubion 2011: 13); 'can there be an anthropology of morality?' (Howell 1997: 2); or 'why there should be an Anthropology of Moralities' (Heintz 2009: 1).
5. The theoretical dispute between normative social constraint and individual freedom that informs so much of AM/E is eerily like the dispute in a Spanish village that Jane Collier writes about in *From Duty to Desire* (1997). Villagers, and those who had moved to the cities, told the 'standard modernization story of progress from constraint to freedom' to account for changes that had occurred between the 1960s and 1980s. Some celebrated progress from repression to freedom, others lamented a moral decline, evidenced by people now being 'free to act out their selfish and base desires' (1997: 5), but according to Collier, neither the 'before people thought for us' or the 'now we think for ourselves' account accurately described reality.
6. Mattingly (2014: 34) looked 'backward' conceptually, to 'Western antiquity', in her quest to 'problematize modernity's primary moral stances'. Although Zigon's *Morality: An Anthropological Perspective* is very different from Mattingly's, he too chooses the ancient Greek philosophers as his starting point. Zigon's (2008: 1) first sentence is, 'Morality ... has been of philosophical interest for over 2,000 years', and his Part I, 'Philosophical and Theoretical Foundations', begins with Plato and Aristotle. *Moral Anthropology: A Critical Reader*, edited by Fassin and Leze (2014), also starts with the legacies of moral philosophies but they begin with the French Renaissance.
7. A striking number of AM/Es begin their inquiries by asking, 'Haven't anthropologists been studying morality all along?' Writing in 1997, Howell notes, 'It might be argued that anthropologists have, ultimately, always been studying the variety of social constructions of morality' (1997: 6). A decade later Zigon begins his book by presenting 'the contested claim' that anthropologists have 'been studying morality all along', and Fassin revisits this question in 2014 (2014a: 430, 2014b: 2).
8. Thanks to Lucy Delap for these insights.

References

Astbury, L. 2012. 'Discourses of Judgment: Infant Feeding in Early Modern England', paper presented at the Interdisciplinary Workshop on the Rhetoric of Selfishness/Selflessness, CRASSH, University of Cambridge, 21 June.

Bayly, S. 2018. 'Anthropology and History', in M. Candea (ed.), *Schools and Styles of Anthropological Theory*. London: Routledge, pp. 108–20.

Bornstein, E. 2012. *Disquieting Gifts: Humanitarianism in New Delhi*. Stanford, CA: Stanford University Press.
Collier, J.F. 1997. *From Duty to Desire: Remaking Families in a Spanish Village*. Princeton, NJ: Princeton University Press.
Colpus, E. 2012. 'Gaining Pleasure and Reward through Transcending the Self: British Women's Philanthropy c.1918–1939', paper presented at the Interdisciplinary Workshop on the Rhetoric of Selfishness/Selflessness, CRASSH, University of Cambridge, 21 June.
Daswani, G. 2015. *Looking Forward, Moving Backward: Transformation and Ethical Practice in the Ghanaian Church of Pentecost*. Toronto: University of Toronto Press.
Dow, K. 2016. *Making a Good Life: An Ethnography of Nature, Ethics, and Reproduction*. Princeton, NJ: Princeton University Press.
Fassin, D. (ed.). 2012. *A Companion to Moral Anthropology*. Malden, MA: Wiley-Blackwell.
———. 2014a. 'The Ethical Turn in Anthropology: Promises and Uncertainties: Comment on Laidlaw, James. 2014. *The Subject of Virtue: An Anthropology of Ethics and Freedom*'. *Hau* 4(1): 429–35.
———. 2014b. 'Introduction: The Moral Question in Anthropology' in D. Fassin and S. Leze (eds), *Moral Anthropology: A Critical Reader*. London: Routledge, pp. 1–11.
Fassin, D., and S. Leze (eds). 2014. *Moral Anthropology: A Critical Reader*. London: Routledge.
Faubion, J. 2011. *An Anthropology of Ethics*. Cambridge: Cambridge University Press.
———. 2014. 'Anthropologies of Ethics: Where We've Been, Where We Are, Where We Might Go'. Comment on Laidlaw, James. 2014. *The Subject of Virtue: An Anthropology of Ethics and Freedom*', *HAU: Journal of Ethnographic Theory* 4(1): 437–442. doi:10.14318/hau4.1.026.
Geertz, C. 1983. '"From the Native's Point of View": On the Nature of Anthropological Understanding', in *Local Knowledge: Further Essays in Interpretive Anthropology*. New York: Basic Books.
Grimley, M. 2009. 'Law, Morality and Secularisation: The Church of England and the Wolfenden Report, 1954–1967', *The Journal of Ecclesiastical History* 60: 725–41. doi:10.1017/S0022046908005952.
———. 2012. 'Thatcherism, Morality and Religion', in B. Jackson and R. Saunders (eds), *Making Thatcher's Britain*. Cambridge: Cambridge University Press, pp. 78–110.
Heintz, M. (ed.). 2009. *The Anthropology of Moralities*. New York: Berghahn Books.
Hellweg, J. 2011. *Hunting the Ethical State: The Benkadi Movement of Côte d'Ivoire*. Chicago: University of Chicago Press.
Holbraad, M. 2018. 'Steps Away from Moralism', in B. Kapferer and M. Gold (eds), *Moral Anthropology: A Critique*. Oxford: Berghahn Books, pp. 27–48.
Howell, S. (ed.). 1997. *The Ethnography of Moralities*. London: Routledge.
Kapferer, B., and M. Gold (eds). 2018. 'Introduction: Reconceptualizing the Discipline', in B. Kapferer and M. Gold (eds), *Moral Anthropology: A Critique*. Oxford. Berghahn Books, pp. 1–26.
Kuan, T. 2015. *Love's Uncertainty: The Politics and Ethics of Child Rearing in Contemporary China*. Berkeley: University of California Press.
Laidlaw, J. 2002. 'For an Anthropology of Ethics and Freedom', *Journal of the Royal Anthropological Institute* 8(2): 311–32.
———. 2014. *The Subject of Virtue: An Anthropology of Ethics and Freedom*. Cambridge: Cambridge University Press.

Lambek, M. (ed.). 2010. *Ordinary Ethics: Anthropology, Language, and Action*. New York: Fordham University Press.
Lambek, M., V. Das, D. Fassin and W. Keane. 2015. *Four Lectures on Ethics: Anthropological Perspectives*. Chicago: Hau Books.
Layne, L. 2003. *Motherhood Lost: A Feminist Account of Pregnancy Loss in America*. New York: Routledge.
———. 2013. '"Creepy," "Freaky," and "Strange": How the "Uncanny" Can Illuminate the Experience of Single Mothers by Choice and Lesbian Couples Who "Buy Dad"', *Journal of Consumer Culture* 14(2):140–59.
Lempert, M. 2014. 'Uneventful Ethics'. Comment on Laidlaw, James. 2014. *The Subject of Virtue: An Anthropology of Ethics and Freedom' HAU* 4(1): 465–472.
Lester, R.J. 2005. *Jesus in Our Wombs: Embodying Modernity in a Mexican Convent*. Berkeley: University of California Press.
Londoño-Sulkin, C.D. 2012. *People of Substance: An Ethnography of Morality in the Colombian Amazon*. Toronto: University of Toronto Press.
MacCormack, C., and M. Strathern (eds). 1980. *Nature, Culture and Gender*. Cambridge: Cambridge University Press.
Mattingly, C. 2014. *Moral Laboratories: Family Peril and the Struggle for a Good Life*. Berkley: University of California Press.
Mattingly, C., and U.J. Jensen. 2015. 'What Can We Hope for? an Exploration in Cosmopolitan Philosophical Anthropology', in S. Liisberg, E.O. Pedersen, and A. L. Dalsgård (eds), *Anthropology and Philosophy: Dialogues on Trust and Hope*. Oxford: Berghahn Books, pp. 24–56.
Muehlebach, A. 2012. *The Moral Neoliberal: Welfare and Citizenship in Italy*. Chicago: University of Chicago Press.
Oxfeld, E. 2010. *Drink Water, But Remember the Source: Moral Discourse in a Chinese Village*. Berkeley: University of California Press.
Pandian, A. 2009. *Crooked Stalks: Cultivating Virtue in South India*. Durham, NC: Duke University Press.
Parish, S.M. 1994. *Moral Knowing in a Hindu Sacred City: An Exploration of Mind, Emotion, and Self*. New York: Columbia University Press.
Paxson, H. 2004. *Making Modern Mothers: Ethics and Family Planning in Urban Greece*. Berkeley: University of California Press.
Pooley, S. 2012. '"They Must Both Be Very Chilly Hearted": Parenthood, Child-Rearing and the Limits of Choice in England, c.1850–1914', paper presented at the Interdisciplinary Workshop on the Rhetoric of Selfishness/Selflessness, CRASSH, University of Cambridge, 21 June.
Prasad, L. 2007. *Poetics of Conduct: Oral Narrative and Moral Being in a South Indian Town*. New York: Columbia University Press.
Robbins, J. 2007. 'Between Reproduction and Freedom: Morality, Value, and Radical Cultural Change', *Ethnos* 72(3): 293–314.
Roberts, N. 2016. *To Be Cared For: The Power of Conversion and the Foreignness of Belonging in an Indian Slum*. Princeton, NJ: Princeton University Press.
Rogers, D. 2009. *The Old Faith and the Russian Land: A Historical Ethnography of Ethics in the Urals*. Ithaca, NY: Cornell University Press.
Roodhouse, M. 2006. 'Popular Morality and the Black Market in Britain 1939–1955', in F. Trentmann and F. Just (eds), *Food and Conflict in Europe in the Age of the Two Wars*. London: Palgrave, pp. 243–65.
———. 2013. *Black Market Britain: 1939–1955*. Oxford: Oxford University Press.

Simon, G.M. 2014. *Caged in on the Outside: Moral Subjectivity, Selfhood, and Islam in Minangkabau, Indonesia*. Honolulu: University of Hawai'i Press.
Singh, B. 2015. *Poverty and the Quest for Life: Spiritual and Material Striving in Rural India*. Chicago: University of Chicago Press.
Strathern, M. 1980. 'No Nature, No Culture: The Hagen Case', in C. MacCormack and M. Strathern (eds), *Nature, Culture and Gender*. Cambridge: Cambridge University Press, pp. 174–222.
Sykes, K. (ed.). 2009. *The Ethnographies of Moral Reasoning: Living Paradoxes of a Global Age*. New York: Palgrave.
Tawney, R.H. [1926] 1962. *Religion and the Rise of Capitalism: A Historical Study*. Gloucester, MA: Peter Smith.
Thomas, K. 1963. 'History and Anthropology', *Past & Present* 24: 3–24.
———. 1971. *Religion and the Decline of Magic*. New York: Scribner's.
Thompson, E.P. 1971. 'The Moral Economy of the English Crowd in the Eighteenth Century', *Past & Present* 50: 76–136.
Tomasello, M. 2011. *A Natural History of Human Morality*. Cambridge, MA: Harvard University Press.
Watson, L.C., and M. Watson-Franke. 1985. *Interpreting Life Histories: An Anthropological Inquiry*. New Brunswick, NJ: Rutgers University Press.
Yan, Y. 2011. 'How Far Away Can We Move from Durkheim? Reflections on the New Anthropology of Morality', *Anthropology of This Century* (2). http://aotcpress.com/articles/move-durkheim-reflections-anthropology-morality/. Accessed 6 December 2019.
Zigon, J. 2008. *Morality: An Anthropological Perspective*. Oxford: Berg.

Index

abnegation, self, 11–12, 28, 62n13, 76.
accusations: counter-accusations, 14, 84, 128, 137, 141, 218; gendered, 86–87, 113, 156; of self-indulgence, 56, 84; of selfishness, 6, 14–15, 25, 34, 56, 63n25, 97, 123, 144–149; of sexual self-assertion, 86; of witchcraft, 6
abstinence ('abstention'), 3, 13; ejaculatory, 16, 170, 172, 174, 176–177. *See also* self-denial
ascetism, 4, 81, 94. *See also* abstinence, self-denial
altruism: 2, 17, 38, 108, 117, 200, 202, Chapter 7; alternatives to, 57; in biology, 52–53, 63n20; as a brand, 63n18; critique of, 27; 'effective' 43; and liberalism, 44; ontological status of, 27–29; as opposite of narcissism, 27, 38–44; 'pathological', 42; the science of, 43
Aristotle, 190; and ethics, 219, 220, 224n6
Astbury, Leah, 220
atonement, 206
avarice, 91, 223n2
Axelrod, Robert, 43

Banner, Michael, 3, 13
Bayly, Susan, 220
Beck, Ulrich and Beck-Gernsheim, Elizabeth, 15, 125–126
benevolence, 80, 81, 96–97, 191; God's, 91; 'universal', 85

biology, 46, 100, 121, 130; evolutionary, 33, 48, 99; neuro-, 41, 46, 53; philosophers of, 100; and altruism, 100. *See also* brain, Darwin, Dawkins
Black Lives Matter, 60
black: market, 222; moral symbolism of, 27; and sex, 54
bluestockings, 160, 144, 151
Bornstein, Erica, 43, 54, 223n1
brain, 49, 74; female and male, 41, 147; reptilian and mammalian, 48; *The Selfish Brain*, 53
brother: brotherly love, 94; brotherhood (brethren), 82, 83, 93–94; symbol of empathy, 83–96
Buddhism: and selflessness, 31, 46, 62n9

Campbell, Colin, 81, 86
Cannell, Fenella, 3

caregivers, 55, 57, 114, 124–137, 144, 200, 208, 219
charity, 7, 44, 64n36, 85. *See also* altruism, philanthropy, virtue
Christ (Jesus): as challenge to bounded, individual selfhood, 12, 31, 47, 60; as exemplar of selflessness, 12, 18n6, 32–37, 44, 62n12, 63n21, 63n23. *See also* sacrifice
Christianity: Anglicanism, 4, 80, 96, 148, 222; Baptists, 48; in Britain, 106, 222; Calvinism, 39, 81, 94; Catholicism, 8, 107, 201, 203; Episcopalianism, 207;

Christianity: Anglicanism (*cont.*)
evangelical, 4, 9, 32, 88, 89–90, 97; Methodism, 13; ministers, 38, 81, 84, 96, 207; Mormonism, 44, 48, 58; Presbyterianism, 9; Quakerism, 13, 94; in the US v UK, 24, 37. *See also* Protestantism
collective, a: action, 17, 201; action, theories of, 209–11; in Alaska, 203, 219; 'collective effervescence', 213; 'collective narcissism', 40; goals, 60; in Ixtlán, 200–203; labour, 189, 192, 209; self, 209; 'The Achilles Heel' collective, 112–118; will, 13
common good, the, 10, 65n4, 91, 187–188, 200, 204, 209, 219
Commonwealth, 202, 209
'commons, the', 16, 51, 189, 195n9, 218–219; commoning, 182, kinds of, 192–194
Commons (the House of), 90
common property, 5, 200, 209, 219
cooperation, the study of, 42–43, 210; inter-species, 200, 205–209, 219
Collier, Jane F., 18n4, 22–23, 39, 60, 224n5
Collier, James Lincoln, 106
Colpus, Eve, 43, 221
Coleridge, Samuel Taylor, 12
Communism: ideological association with selflessness (China, Cuba, Russia), 48, 63n25

Darwin, Charles, 43
Daly, Irenne, 31
Daum, Meghan, 18n9, 31, 40
Dawkins, Richard, 40, 43, 53, 108, 120n2, 210–211, 213n1
Denmark, 109, 143, Chapter 6, 166–181
Dombek, Kristin, 40, 42, 54, 62n16
Douglas, Mary, 3
Douglas, Ann, 39, 58
Dow, Katie, 159n26, 159n27, 223n1, 223n3
Durkheim, Émile, 18n3, 203, 213n8, 219

ego, 64n36, 125; male, 112, 114, 118
egoism, 2, 7, 27, 38; *egoisma*, 200–203
Evans-Pritchard, E.E., 22

fair, share, 2, 32, 35, 37, 222; price, 222; profit, 222
fairness, 142, 222
Fassin, Didier, 5, 23, 29, 43–44, 56, 219–220, 222, 224n3, 224n6, 224n7
Faubion, James, 46, 47, 222, 224n3, 224n4
Figert, Anne, 39
Fishwick, Carmen, 39, 49, 64n28
food: breast feeding, 123–140; hogging of (gluttony), 32–34; sharing of (commensality), 32, 34, 35, 199, 54, 64n33, 199, 203, 206, 207 208, 222; and sex, 64
Foucault, Michel, 1, 8, 46, 174, 219–220
France, 3, 30, 137, 223
freedom (individual, personal), 16, 28, 95, 223; freedoms, 60; and liberalism, 10; and modernity, 224n5; sacrifice of, 14, 16; sexual, 98, 158n16, 171, 177; topic of anthropology of morality, 5, 224n5; for women and slaves, 13
Freud, 39, 42, 54, 133

Geertz, Clifford, 12, 217
Gerhardt, Sue, 48–49, 53, 108
Giddens, Anthony, 14, 91, 106, 125
gifts, in anthropological theory, 3; gendered, 47; for mothers, 30–31, 204–205, 206; of organs, 187; of self, 142; self-gifting, 47, 65n40; and sex, 47, 142; the 'gift of life', 16, 168, 186; versus the market, 167–170, 87, 188–190. *See also* charity, philanthropy
Goffman, Irving, 125
'Good Samaritan, The', 4, 62n6, 85
greed, 2, 7, 24, 32, 34, 48, 54, 91, 108, 200, 208; anti-social, 209; corporate, 35; cult of, 64n27. *See also* avarice
Greenblatt, Stephen, 8, 12, 44
Grimley, Mathew, 222

Heintz, Monica, 222, 224n4
heroes, 8, 28, 29, 57, 63n22, 189; Christian, 44; heroines, 87; military, 12
Hobbes, Thomas, 9, 86, 91, 199, 206, 213n2; opposition to, 80, 82–83, 94, 100
homosexuality, 18n10, 99, 222
heterosexuality, 15, 42, 141–146, 148, 152, 156, 159n26
Howell, Signe, 2, 23, 213n2, 221, 224n4, 224n7
Huber, Mary, 3
humility, 7, 37, 44, 60, 65n37
Humphry, Caroline, 44, 221
humanity, 6, 8, 14, 80–81, 84, 86, 89, 91
humane, 84, 90–91; inhumane, 40, 92
humanitarianism, 29, 43–44, 56, 81. *See also* altruism
humanitarian aid workers, 24, 29
human: nature, 25, 52–53, 80, 82–84, 94, 97, 107, 131–132, 150, 193; non-human, 199–216; rights, 146, 196n26;

individualism, 2, 9–10, 48–49, 64n27, 83, 105–108, 118–119, 199, 207; individuality, 9, 130–137

Jacob, Margaret, 86
James, Oliver, 38–39, 48, 49

Kant, Emmanuel, 56, 219
Kardashian, Kim, 40

Laidlaw, James, 2–4, 43–44, 217, 219, 220, 222–223
Lambek, Michael, 23, 24, 222
Larkin, Philip, 49
Levecq, Christine, 10
Locke, John, 10

MacFarquhar, Larrissa, 39, 42–43, 45
MacPherson, C.B., 80. *See also* possessive individualism
MacCormack, Carol, 25, 46, 51; and Strathern, 3, 32, 223

MacIntyre, Alasdair, 44, 220
masturbation, 218; Christian attitudes towards, 16, 18n10; and narcissism, 39; and pollution, 15; regulation of, 166–181; single mothers by choice, 148; women's, 86. *See also* self-pleasuring, sperm donors
Mattingly, Cheryl, 62n8, 219–220, 224n6
Mauss, Marcel, 2–3, 18n3, 58–59
McKearney, Patrick, 43, 57
Me-Too Movement, 60
Mexico, 17, 22, 200–205, 209–212, 213n3, 213n4, 213n6, 219
Montaigne, Michel de, 8
Moore, Henrietta, 8
morality: categories, 105, 217; challenges to, 2, 222; debate about, 61, 167; decline of, 48–51, 61 224n5; discourse of, 5, 15, 23, 119; duty, 55, 107; failings, 38, 52, 156, 202; geography, 36, 202; goals, 37, 206; judgements, 1, 2, 4, 7, 15, 24, 37, 38, 39, 50, 60, 105, 141, 201, 217, 222; landscape, 36, 42, 59, 60, 166; moral economy/ies, 44, 108, 221; moral exemplars, 44–46, 211, 221; obligations, 4–5, 9, 15; outrage, 22, 166, 187; panic, 40; peril, 38; philosophy of, 3, 219, 224n6; reasoning, 221; standards, 28, 45, 48, 178; of the story, 35, 85; struggles, 13, 24, 222; superiority, 31, 43, 168; system, 32, 60, 222; threat to, 200; universe, 26, 37; values, 4, 52, 79, 106–7
morality plays, 8
'moral sense, the', 82–101
Mother Teresa, 62n7, 63n21

narcissism: 2, 24, 34, 39–42, 48, 112; v altruism, 38; epidemic, 39–40; Freud, 42, 133; and gender, 40–42, 141; Greek myth, 39; insult, 40; promotion of, 54, 63n24; psychiatric disorder, 39; sexy, 54; and social media, 49, 64n28; types of, 39–40

Needham, Rodney, 25, 32, 62n2
Nietzsche, Friedrich, 2–5, 62n13. *See also* asceticism, obligations, slave morality
norms, 5, 211, 219–220; breach of, 32, 128, 174; diminishing consensus about, 6, 106; gendered, 134, 156; numerical, 37; 106, 220, taken-for granted, 16

permissiveness, 105, 106, 222
philanthropy, 85, 97–98; and gender, 43, 221; as measure of societal health, 49. *See also* charity, humanitarianism
Pooley, Sian, 220
Protestantism: mainline, 3; and moral reform, 12, 18n6; liberal, 38; 'The Protestant Ethic' 81, 94; the Reformation, 59, 81
Putnam, Robert, 49, 65n41

Rand, Ayn, 27, 52, 63n25, 64n35, 108
Rational choice theory, 17, 199, 201, 209–210, 219
Reagan, Ronald, 48
reciprocity: absence of, 57; inter-generational, 106, inter-species, 207, 211; among kin, 190–191; subject for anthropologists and historians of morality, 221
Redfield, Peter, 43, 229
resources: allocation of, 199; common, 185, 190, 192, 199; competition for, 201; financial, 43, 114, 149, 205; natural, 16, 17, 203, 205, 219; scarce, 185; shared, 209
restitution, 206
Robbins, Joel, 3, 5, 6, 26, 44–46, 51, 61, 62n11, 210–211, 220
Roodhouse, Mark, 222
Rose, Nicolas, 125

Sacks, Oliver, 50
sacrifice, self- 11–15, 20, 28, 30, 43, 44, 106, 151, 186; Christ's, 18n6, 63n21, 63n23; disavowal of, 133, 137; gender, 107, 135–137, 171–177; and group cohesion, 135; military, 28–29; one's pleasures, 93, 171–177, 222; 'the ultimate', 29; suspicion of, 55. *See also* exemplars, heroes, saints
saints, 43–44, 203, 212
secular, the: secularization, 106, 222, 223n2; and the self, 59; as a theoretical concept, 3, 12, 224n3;
selfhood, 2 8, 202; subject position, 59–60
self-absorption, 2, 7, 18n9, 24, 40, 46; and sex, 54, 147. *See also* self-centeredness
self-centeredness, 2, 7, 24, 37, 41, 47, 63n23, 146, 193, 209
self-portraiture, 8
self-assertion: of men, 86; of women, 86, 90, 95
self-denial, 4, 11, 24; among abolitionists, 12; among aid workers, 29; among anti-sexist men; among breast-feeders, 14; and Christianity, 12, 62n13; gendered, 84; rejection of, 14; among sperm donors, 29; Victorian, 9. *See also* ascetism, sacrifice
self-fashioning, 11, 87
self-help, 26,
selfies, 37, 40, 45, 49, 64n28, 65n39
self-indulgence, 2, 9, 11, 93, 97, 100, 120n1; accusations of, 56, 81, 84, 86, 107, 116; gendered, 55, 88; and late twentieth-century youth culture, 106; and sex, 54, 87, 166; and shopping, 127
self-interest, 2, 14, 16, 29, 56–57, 63n26, 81–82, 88–96 passim, 100, 108, 116, 201, 210; Ayn Rand on, 27, 53; 'enlightened' 190; other-interest, 182, 187, 190–192, 218–219
service, Christian, 28, 44, 60; ethic of, 106; military, 12, 28–29, 58; National Health, 75, 166, 183–196; public, 185; selfless service, 29–30, 44, 58, 63n25
Shakespeare, William, 8
Schapiro, James, 8

sins, 7, 18n10; 40; vs crime, 222, 223n2; original, 206; seven deadly, 7. *See also* vices, virtues
Skinner, Quentin, 80
Smith, Adam, 5, 38, 82–86, 190; on families, 92, 94; on women and men, 83–84, 86, 88–89, 99. *See also* moral sentiments and sympathy
Spencer, Herbert, 199
Strathern, Marilyn, 3, 25, 27, 32, 46, 51, 124–126, 131, 136, 137, 214n18, 220, 223. *See also* MacCormack, Strathern
Steinberg, Avi, 40–41, 49
Sterne, Lawrence, 84–89, 93–94, 101n2
Sykes, Karen, 18n3, 221

Tawney, R.H., 81, 221, 223n2
Tempany, Adrian, 39, 41
Tennyson, Alfred, 12
Thatcher, Margaret, 48, 105, 108, 222; post-Thatcher Britain, 64n27; Thatcherism, 117, 108, 199; 'Selfish society', 48, 106, 117, 119
Thomas, Keith, 221, 223
Thompson, E.P., 221, 222
Thompson, Charis, 167

Trump, Donald, 30, 40, 42, 62n16, 63n17, 158n16; era, 65n41. *See also* narcissism
Tocqueville, Alexis de, 10, 49
Turkle, Sherry, 49

usury, 123n2

vices, 7–9
virtues, 7–10, 50, 62n8, 182, 186–187; gendered, 62n8, 84, 88–89, 99, 202; personal, 187; public, 196n26; social, 80, 92; virtue ethics, 18n11, 44, 46, 219–220; *The Subject of Virtue*, 222; *The Virtue of Selfishness*, 52, 64n35

Wales, 109, 157n6, 188–192, 195n7
Weber, Max, 81, 94
Wilde, Oscar, 35
Williams, Bernard, 3–5, 220
Williams, Raymond, 62n1
Wollstonecraft, Mary, 88–89, 99, 159n20
Woolf, Virginia, 40, 56, 107

Zigon, 220, 222, 224n6, 224n7

www.ingramcontent.com/pod-product-compliance
Lightning Source LLC
Chambersburg PA
CBHW051538020426
42333CB00016B/1983